Praise for the poetry of LUCILE ADLER . . .

"Lucile Adler gives us poems as hermetic and open as Georgia O'Keeffe's landscapes that haunt for the same reason, plain and mysterious, rich in their austerities. . . . [She] is a poet on her way, to be met and recognized again with joy as she travels out, this time further into the lives of women."

—May Sarton

"[Lucile Adler] is a mature and accomplished poet who has found an extraordinarily poignant way of accounting for the wisdom and dedication of a lifetime. . . . The range of her poems is at once touching, expansive, humorous, and resilient."

—Ben Belitt

"Great poetry draws attention to that which is greater than itself, testifying on behalf of our propensity for love, justice or their opposites. Adler offers such a testimony."

—Demetria Martinez

"Lucile Adler's region is not so much the Southwest as the heartland common to us all. Her sane, vivid poems are among its natural wonders."

—James Merrill

"[Lucile Adler is] one of the really interesting poets in America. The combination of substance and the grace of language makes it a poetry of remarkable beauty."

—Winfield Townley Scott

"Lucile Adler has long been one of my favorite poets. . . . [She] writes of flowers . . . and trees, stones, and canyons. But these objects of the quotidian world are at once themselves and yet not quite themselves. Her landscapes are often those of that unquiet borderland between the waking consciousness and dream. . . . Here the familiar is rendered strange and strangely familiar."

—Frederick Turner

ALSO BY LUCILE ADLER:

The Traveling Out
The Society of Anna
The Ripening Light: Selected Poems 1977–1987

The
PINK MADONNA

The
PINK MADONNA

Selected Poems

LUCILE ADLER

Juniper Press

Santa Fe, New Mexico

Published by: Juniper Press
            Route 4 Box 59
            Santa Fe, NM 87501

Edited by Christopher Merrill and Ellen Kleiner
Book design by Richard Harris and Kathleen Adler Harms
Cover production by Janice St. Marie
Cover design by Janice St. Marie and Kathleen Adler Harms

Cover photograph by Ellen Auerbach; color print by Eliot Porter
Interior art copyright © 1998 by Kathleen Adler Harms

Printed in the United States of America on acid-free recycled paper

Publisher's Cataloging-in-Publication Data

Adler, Lucile.
        The pink madonna: selected poems / Lucile Adler. — 1st ed.
        p. cm.
        Preassigned LCCN: 97-73958
        ISBN 0-9659508-0-8

        1. Aging—Poetry. 2. War—Poetry. I. Title.

    PS3551.D6L48 1998   811'.54
                                   QBI97-41053

10 9 8 7 6 5 4 3 2 1

With Love

for

K. and J.

I wish to thank Kathleen Adler Harms, Christopher Merrill, Elise Turner, and Mary Van Ness, who helped bring this book to life.

CONTENTS

I

II

*There is no insurmountable solitude. All paths lead to the same goal:
to convey to others what we are. And we must pass through solitude
and difficulty, isolation and silence, in order to reach forth to the
enchanted place where we can dance our clumsy dance and sing our
sorrowful song—but in this dance or in this song, there are fulfilled
the most ancient rites of our conscience in the awareness of being
human and of believing in a common destiny.*

— Pablo Neruda
Nobel Peace Prize speech

I

Halfway round the world to find an orchard, a thrashing among fruit tree branches, a heavy black bird lunging down — halfway round to watch the shining raven dive through half-forgotten summer, a yellow cherry in its beak . . .

AT THE CAVE MOUTH

Fires
Amber as eyes watching
Pine boughs burn
Lie down on the cave floor

A woman with oiled hair
A gentlewoman wrapped
In bloody hides and red fox fur
Stirs embers with a bone

Then opens her cloak to share
Nakedness
In the stone-cold dark
The first civility

Overhead
Painted gods
Hidden by night-smoke
Chase a red antelope

The woman blouses a child
At her bare breast
And enfolds a worn hunter
Glistening
Dreams
Oxblood polish on earth
Floors, flourish of horns
Through arches of rare wood
Where dyed flowers on wool

17

Hang at cold openings
Inventions   Civilities
Even love
Later

The fire lies down
And dies in the dark

Overhead
Warrior gods
Loose red spears and sleep
Unseen
Man and child
Swathed in silence
Sleep

From the cave mouth
The sparks of her eyes
Look out

Then wakeful
Soul leaping white dawns
The woman chases
Tomorrow   Alone

GERANIUM FLAME

Anna runs home under a dark beam of air coming near.

We go home, too, along the ashen road to meet
Closed fists or open arms; fearful or unafraid,
Go to prepare red wine, bread on a red cloth,

Ample portions of heartbreak or honey
Under eaves waiting to bear the weight coming near.
What oppresses, oppresses us all.

Faces linen with fear, we light brass lamps
Or marigolds in a jar, or like the child, light love;
Bravura alone could never tend house here.

All we own — yellow kerchiefs of light — we give
At doors compassion opens on charred night.
All we are, meager or brave, we kindle and prepare

As thunder crashes on lamplight. Child, stranger,
Dear friend, defiant gifts gather and rise, sparks
Tremble into bloom on the hearth that shares us.

What oppresses, oppresses us all —
Each rare geranium of flame rising alone
To light the way past fear or follow

Though the dangerous dark has fallen and is here.

PAPYRUS

Little One
small bright parcel of sun
           in the dark

parchment-bound
ancient infant tight-wound
           by light
like papyrus strips torn
open and ready to rise now

from the rushes to requite loss
among hard waves of days
           carved out
around your bloodied cradle
it is early yet   time still

to unwind what binds you
in Time to grow tall   free
           as a stylo
inscribing on dry linen pages
a liquid babble of syllables

that song risen inside you
from an amber-dark past
           lacquered with sun

Little One small parcel of light
small naked gift emerging   live
from broken waters and torn
tissue   History too   breaks
           open to ink Dark

over sun over Dark   little scribe
waiting like Day itself waiting

to issue forth in Time again
a warm live child ready to be
               unwrapped and poured over —
tomorrow's message   shared
before we risk daring you to live

        daring to let you go

"ARDUOUS TIMES"

Long ago, Child, a wolf-pack sky loped in
Over black apple trees, barnyards,
And the frozen courtyards of Provence —

Over small timber houses, small torn
Hearts and bones crumbled by fear.

Wiser now, we know wolves mean no harm;
Unlike us, they "attack only when starving."

Still we stand too much at bay, too gnawed
By uncertainty not to turn on them when sky howls

Winter, gray snow covers naked apple trees
In rutted farmyards and grows menacing,

And a furred head appears at the window
Outlined in ice; then the family cringes

Famished and fearful, raw fear sucking
Its marrow. As the old wolf-pack sky lopes

Near again, we fumble for lights and knives,
Shouting alarm; and our old seigneur, old
Broken man, cries over the frozen courtyard here,

"I tell you, these, too, are arduous times . . ."

L'ÉCOLE DES RÊVES JOYEUX

I

Little One, as soon as your blue uniform
Is buttoned and the Light, le Soleil, Sun
Adjusts itself over elm allée and macadam

Where dun-faced chores and children
In stained pinafores stand waiting,
It will be time to start your day's Devoirs . . .

II

In that one day, Little One, you will
Grow, matriculate, wed, give birth,
Bake bread and hold a funeral urn — You!

An explorer advancing, at first alone,
On your long journey from Convent dreams
Into the Light, le Soleil, Sun perhaps . . .

III

Later you will assure your rosy daughter
You made the journey for her sake alone;
True or not, will claim you straddled

Two fierce blue continents to discover
The one habitable one inside, concealing
Only how you filled old frozen diaries

Of your pride with tales of rotted
Sealskins and torn hide tents —
Your lofty inexperience racing forward

IV

To cross the last crevasse — where
You no longer ache to be known,
But exhausted, yearn finally to Know —

Sprawled in a dream tent, so blind
You mistook its chapel dark for Clarity —
The radiant continent you could map

And guide her to, somehow surviving
On bloody seal meat and bird bones
Chewed to feed the marrow of the common
                    name you shared . . .

V

Little One, as soon as your blue uniform
Is buttoned, the Light, le Soleil, Sun
Will ease what you most feared, racing

From safe sumac Autumns to alcohol-blue fires
On the long-ago of that wintry expedition
Over tracks black as flayed bark scarring

Hard snow, whose arêtes pierced both you
And your child-to-be — and fear, that melanoma
Of the spirit, rose through lesions in the ice . . .

VI

Before the end, Little One, issue to your snowy child
A warning, a tiny red "blessure" that yields a sample
Of raw tissue to a glass slide of ice beginning, to melt . . .

Dire directions toward what may become
For her a sturdy transience — your courage,
Her safe passage under the flag of a benign
                        and arduous joy . . .

VII

Aware that later, from her own dream
Of elm allée or macadam, her own École
Des Rêves Joyeux, freezing but nourished

Past failure, by altitudes you sought
(And never reached), buttoned in Light,
Le Soleil, Sun, your darling child may yet

Smile back on you, having drawn from
The heart of the day's Devoirs her own
                        Cold nerve and poetry . . .

FROM THE I CHING

"The lean pig has it in him to rage around."

The lean pig does not rest in this orchard.
Oh no! He roots through soaked sunflower stalks
And chewed ribs of anger in the poorest yard.

Or crazed as that famous boar stalked by beaters,
Waits red-eyed in thickets the gods attack,
It being his dream and fate, in backyard or violet

Pleasure-forest, always to be ready to tusk
Any threat, any exposed heart down here.
At home in us, he waits to charge against shovel

Or javelin — it being his mean fate,
So far past succulence, to die as he lives —
Fabled, ugly and bare of garlands; not so much as

One rosy apple, sweet or basted with anger,
To pass from his mouth to ours. Oh yes, oh yes
The lean pig has it in him to rage around
                    in us forever . . .

ON THE DAY AFTER
(in memory of E. M. S.)

A dark amethyst light
A dark twilight in the morning
Falls on red clay and granite —

On petunia-white soft faces
Amethyst-hard shadows grow.

A storm is coming, one daughter says.
And one: My toothache aches all over me.

Death, a sunburst on the road,
Came yesterday. Now, twilight
At dawn and death at home,
The storm draws near. One daughter
Says of the night between, It's over.
And one says, No.

Soon trees knee-deep in snow
Will shadow amethyst bird tracks
And then your tracks

As they go, daughters not my daughters —
"Where will you go?" —

"Out to assess the damage."

THE LEVEL EYE

When I say willows are dying
by the dry streambeds
and people are moving away
I mean trees are dying
everywhere and day by day
water is sinking back
to strata in the rock
no one can reach

and the people
(they are what matter)
the people like willow leaves
coated with silver on one side
lie too tarnished and dry
for love, or to reach
water drawing away
out of reach everywhere

what I mean falls
like a stone in the sand
where people and water
(they are what matter)
go on moving and drawing away
from each other farther
and deeper each day

and who will dive down
to find their sunken
silver ghosts together at last?
I mean who will be left
to drink a lonely toast
to all that mattered
around the glittering table in the dark?

THE RED PEAR TREE

Beside the red pear tree
And the ice-crusted pond, ready
To push off in broken shoes,
Antonio stands with his back to school.
He would not care if they told him
About genius, or how a barefoot
Freezing boy once pushed Samuel Johnson
In his chair across the London ice.
Which would he admire? The genius or
The skater raw and panting under
An ordinary mind and extraordinary burden?
It is enough for him to skim a moment,
A rose-red-shirted boy springing
Away from the dark schoolroom and
Darker more forbidding home — to fly,
To be his own flame budding,
Skating in cracked black shoes
Beyond cold History and the red pear tree,

                                Free . . .

HERE LIES

here lies the good child
who early on understood
what scholars said, and wild
to wear their laurels, fled
from home through weltering words
in the dark to find instead
of a lost child's frail song

weedy waves over deep woods
of green words risen in flood
where the orphan child stood
ankle- then knee-deep in blood
of knowledge drained and swilled

down by scholars drunk in the dark,
all dazed and reeling, their guild
undone by words netted then nailed
wrong into the dank wood of their world
and in the aged and oaken dark swirled
through what no good child could
honor at the end by calling "good" —

those poor greedy souls who should
at least have sewn a sail or emerald song
for the one who went wrong with words
having drunk from their tankard of dark,
Darkness, and too late understood
why it was, though they had sadly failed,

it was the child who bled

TWO VIEWS FROM THE
SANGRE DE CRISTOS

I

through the gap where the light
falls
in the V of the mountain's throat
the view   stand just here the view
opens out a fine raw silk fan
a moth wing dusted with light
or a piece of bright lint
brushed up from a sunny condo rug
in the town   all dusty glitter
and tiny seen from here
as an infant's bead bracelet
or the ankle band of an eagle
overhead   holding all houses
all fans and fine feathers
together
and you too looking back
up   and   out   mute
a flake of light watching
egos rise in eyes large
each one as the entire town
seen from up here   always
with room for one more light-dazed
iris to seize baubles of ice
or jabots of light
from the long throats of women
swollen with mea culpas and cries
for wood fires near smoky births
among those moth wings
                    rising there to here —

II

stand back please   tell me   help me
seize for my own mind's eyes
this space fanned open   tell me
here or there in the dim far sparkling
which view is grander   before distance
closes and the light   the Light
            dries away our last hosannas

TRAMPAS — 37 MILES

Who are you? Mind closed like a fist,
Fist closed on the wheel, driving away
Or driving home between mountains that leap
Sudden as children from scrub oak
Out of hiding on the plain — who are you?

What lies ahead? Is there nothing beyond
Driving? No destination, no familiar
Brown house seen through a shivering
               flame
Of Autumn trees, no simmer of white water
By the bruised knees of the simple giants
You pass, going where? Home? Away from there?

It is all guessing, of course.

Can you slow down? Have you time to touch
Unsmiling children, lives and houses
              waiting?
Or time, as you go on driving, to lift
An open hand from the wheel and salute
The silver skirmish of wings by patches
Of willow beginning to burn?

Are they the same wings, willows, mountains
Over and over again? Will you forget, or come
To hold them all later, at home, after driving
Through turbulent days past the slow giants

Thrown like children out across the plains?
          Who are you,

Driving? What place can you hold in your mind?

Where is Here? Where Away? *Drive Slow.*

There was a time when the world kissed you
Into place for a second as you passed.

Beyond that it is all guessing, of course:

Perhaps a house lies ahead for you,
A home, a destination that will know who you are
When your clenched fist finally opens
                    on the wheel
And your open hand throws its shadow across plains
Your closed mind drove through, plains that lie
Out there, immense
                    but too impersonal for games.

YOU WILL GO FAR

Children,
There are roads to be gathered,
Possibilities lashed with willow
Leading out everywhere:

You will go far.

The roads wait
Like bare stalks shaken
From silver lakes of the North —
Clusters of roads,
Armloads
Petaled with blood
Or bronze light
For you to share later.

But your start will be abstract
As air on the face saying: you may go
(Dangerously blessed) . . . anywhere.
And so you will,
Lean as streaks of grass
Along the sky
Racing

Past ancient viaducts
Or brown canals
To taste caresses,
The play and stab of places
Where derelicts prowl
And statues rooted in amber pools
Hold out stained hands
Forever to the rain —

You will go far.

Storms even of joy
Will weather you
Till your own daughters,
Like rain blown backward
From dark stems of roads,
Pour through antique leafy dreams
To slake your longing
With their own lilt of vision
Opening everywhere
       On an air full of pardons:

You will go far to gather in.

ONLY GOD KNOWS

God knows if it was the right thing to do.
Only God knows if what the seed foretold
Of this one flowering, this dark-veined
                    opening, was true:

If it was wise for the man in pin- or prison-stripes
To go on climbing the stone stairs to Justice.

Only God knows or can imagine the skull
In the desert drying, or a rosy brain alive
In a stone cell praying for rain of a kind,
Something fluid with which to rinse away pain
Though suffering on, while the Just and the Unjust
Both try to decide if "it was the right thing to do."

Imagine the seed of the act before its bold
Blossoming — alone but fresh, rare, a-blush
With enterprise — No? Then climbing marble
Stairs, trying to hold erect and proud as though
Hearing inside that "it was indeed the only, the
                    right thing to do."
Dreadful to be aware how worn-out by Justice
He is, how dire for us His weariness — dreadful
To wonder where truth lies when it grows free
Of the seed God knows, when only God knows
                    If He is truly there . . .

WHAT MATTERS AND
WHAT DOES NOT MATTER

What matters and what does not matter
Ride in the brain like hawk and dove,

One pale as rain obscured by rain
Above a beacon-bead of grain,

One dark as storm and diving down
On prey that rises to its eye —

What does it matter what they mean,
The winged names that cross the brain

Confused by weather, space, and choice?
The hawk attacks, the dove flies low,

A sprig of laurel in its beak. No voice
Will blend them, flight on flight,

But in the space we each contain,
Hawk and dove are what we are,

Scarred by rain and plumed with light,
Vague airborne patterns carving air

Above immensities we bear —
Where one force wings both war and love

And forces us to trace on sky
The meaning of the hawk, the dove . . .

ESSENCE

what you are

wild currant leaves in a white china pitcher
in the wide light moment before twilight

what you are
when saffron scarves at the throats
of hills fall away and white bones wait
where they say lions mate in the desert
                              by moonlight
what we see you are
(in blue-striped white rough cotton and silver beads
from deserts far away   fades in a twilight once
clear as the foreheads of hills or beautiful women
near naked sands where moonlit lions play)

comes slowly forward   all the rest falls away

till what you are shines clear in our lamplight
as scent of wild currants in a white pitcher
or highlights   on the curved china like daylight
on the cheeks of unformed   promising girls

your gift   what you are
the pungent rough bouquet

Now in our slow age, we recognize what must be held or woven by two or one alone, clean as a new wicker basket meant to carry fresh melons or ripe berries from a garden not yet planted, for a picnic not yet shared, near the blue humble feet of mountains or right here. Now is the time to learn to pack meanings, like fresh produce. Will the basket be heavy or light? Does it matter? What we are approaching must be born. Come on, time to begin . . . push down . . . harder . . . yes?

II

Old friend, tell me when it's time for reaching out, time for folding in —
if it's wrong to go slow down the long field to tag the rushing young,
or wrong to close the door and gaze at a calm pear ripening in its
bowl. Tell me, is it well, at leisure and alone, to eye perfection — to
taste the golden pear and stare along the field where the young loves
run, as age begins its song? Old friend, tell me when it's time for
reaching out, time for folding in.

ADVICE FROM A SPINSTER

"Let us love better. "
—Emily Dickinson

An old box-elder bug thinned down by cold
Crawls in red-blazoned shield close to the fire
And the dim red mate sprawled out to greet him.

We are at home tonight, generations
Grown coppery-red as the fox in the field
By firelight, but tired; trying so tired
To say what must be hotly said
In answer to the cold rage coming;

We watch the slow red insects flush
And fatten by our fire, exchanging shields.

Dear ones, guarded or not,
There's nothing left to do but love;
No way to prepare (as we brush ardent bugs away),
But face to blazing face across red fields of fire,
To swear we will obey our spinster friend
        by loving better, if we can in time.

MARRY TONIGHT

Now a sunflower sun opens over bare trees,
Over snow fields and a black-shawled old woman
Who casts blessings like dark seeds
From woolly hands. It is a wedding day
Today, naked, and crowned with petals of light.

Two ravens swerve then settle on branches
                    that reach out to them.
The old woman plods her way slowly,
                    work done, looking for night.

Time grows virginal as she passes.

Like the marriage, it too waits for nightfall;
Like the lovers, its impatient eyes scan
                    low black wings and branches;
And like the old woman among clouds of snow
That veil omens — but of what? — Time waits,

Eager for consummation, then grows bored.
The ravens rise again, the old woman pauses.
Clenching brown hands that are empty now,
She stares about her with the cold patience of one
To whom time is a seed of Time merely;

Knowing that what is bedded in body or snow
Will be born through the weather of omens,
Enfolding a chance to become conflict and storm,
Or a fertile burst of sunflower sun —
A chance, either way, merely one. Yes.

Marry tonight, tomorrow who knows . . .

NETTLES

here in the bare field you own
there are nettles under your hand
there is water somewhere below

it is hard work standing alone
not knowing how to begin
there are nettles under your hand

old weeds to clear away first
dry rage at growing alone
here in the field you must work

you are crying dying of thirst
determined to harvest alone
there is danger under your hand

it is hard work beginning again
though water lies somewhere below
to feed the green field you will win

never say never to love

NO OTHER "I"
TO CALL YOU "THOU"
(for W. T. S.)

no other "I" to call you "Thou"
no answer when you plead with night
this is the Arctic of the soul
the white storm at the northern pole
where "I"s like snowbirds flying low
are ripped by lightning and by ice
no bright red swill of blood to light
the frozen darkness of the snow
nor smoke from wreckage of a soul
to guide and warm your nakedness
till love can reach the deadly place
and wings caress your "I" with "Thou"
      in broken feather of a voice

OUTCOME

all Emily loves tonight is weather
and all that she trusts is stone

if Time were to bind old ways together
and mild days gently flesh out bone

might the lithe rose tree of her mind
slowly expose its radiant grain

to Creation's brown and calloused hand
that lays down love on rock through rain

might a light-veiled Emily then discover
on the bare moor of her naked soul

wild scents of hope like heather over
what it means to ripen and grow whole

knee-deep in promises sweet to gather
from rain-fathered gardens sweet to own

though now she loves only forbidding weather
and all she dares trust tonight is stone . . .

MATEO I

Mateo
wait

dreaming   slow
days like kind mothers
who gather
to splash water
over children in white porcelain tubs

when twilight
pale as olive leaves
leans
over a glitter of seeds

dream

you are fed once again
in a cool kitchen
ice from the old icebox
melting
bath water rushing
into the white tub   upstairs

dream you wait

for someone simple
and eloquent
as a kind mother
wearing amber beads

to lean down at twilight
      and gather you in

MATEO II

When they come running
    What will you do?

    Will you join them
        and run, too,
    Waving your fear, that poor flag?

Will you whine
    "I am orphaned.
    I have slept with nine thin girls.
    But I still don't know what love is"?
    (Confession is good for the cadres.)

Or will you, crying and afraid,
    Orphan that you are,
    Say,
    "I will stay till I find her.
    I will stay,"
    Then stay
Till you can tell a mere flag from a banner?

MATEO III

Mateo, learn
to love the bare bone
on the plate in the sun

then love
the naked plate alone
a garland of fruit painted on

make of fasting a joy

till you burn with love
for sun on the bare plate's
blue plums sugared with light

and make of waiting a feast

as you dream
juicy flesh on the bone
sweet past imagining, then savor

love again   the rare taste
of a ripe plum on a real plate in the sun

AT THE GREEN BAIZE BLACK MESA

A man shuffles cards over and over again
on the green mesa top at dawn, on the table land
bare but for faces of players shadowed by hawk wings —

always the same face, the game always the same,
his hands always fast, flicking the deck, arcing
cards slick as ice over the tufa stone — an expert,

the man in a beaded vest leaning across to spread
his prayers — What kind of game is this? Who
is the man? A maimed escapee from God-only-knows

what cells of night? (Only God knows the expertise
those cells may breed.) — What faces of betrayal and love
lean over the green baize Black Mesa's tufa top

see how keen and sharp the man is, with what keen
eyes he stares down at ankle-belled feet that ring
on rock — no dance or game — only day, win or

lose, early under stark wings and card-shark eyes
a run of aces fountaining down from open hands
spread wide over another reckless dawn — see

how the man at the Black Mesa plays always against
the wind and the scared faces of players shadowed
by hawk wings, always, God only knows why, daring
        weather or men like us to raise the ante

SAN ACACIO MORNING

I

Now we stand with the old men of San Acacio
Beside the lilacs, listening.

All the talk of this and that confuses us;
Birds and airwaves collide over our bent heads,
Feeding us torn shreds of answers, like white scraps

Of paper to be sorted as we sort the dried-out
From ripe piñon nuts in the shade, to find the ones
With ivory kernels. We wait beside the lilac bushes,

Helpless as all disregarded old men tangled
In sentiment, stained with tobacco juice and
Plain ways, waiting to go home to a bare room.

II

Who still wades the brown mountain stream or rests
In available shade? For whom do acacias glitter,
And glaciers scoop out bright basins of knowledge?

We are waiting. Somewhere patient minds scrabble
For grains of meaning ripe to feed us all, all
The starving from Somalia and Sudan on . . .

The airwaves chatter over secrets, over dry
Anguish feeding a chaff of undernourished lives.
If you hold a mirror in your transparent hand

You will see us on the road that is pocked here and there
By a child like a drop of rain. That child,
Shining, may be an answer, unspoken yet.

III

All the talk. We are scared but holding, holding on,
Leaning against standards of lilac that sprout dust,
Waiting. Old men wrap us in chains that will flake,

Not rust, but rain. Who will stand with feet
In the shade and hand in ours? With the slow force
Of glaciers, who will bring visions blue as Madonnas,

Or silver as trout rising? What, who will it be?
Who will assert the past, yet pour signs clear
As water into cupped souls or cells that will come?

IV

We are the old men of San Acacio, stained
By mirages and harsh wine. Strangers' talk
Confuses us; we are silent as the dust on our boots —

Or the dusty road that promised all possible journeys,
Though we sway here, fearful of blowing faceless and away.
We once waved to children under banners of lilacs —

We knew firm and valorous men. Listen. A brave
Fist of cloud salutes our veined hands praying.
It is not enough, of course, but from our wilderness
Contours emerge over heads bent in silence,
Over eloquent hearts clenched in silence,
As, on this San Acacio morning, the wet young answers form.

THE DAMAGED CHILDREN

The damaged children run
Past the white plum tree
In a moment sprung so calm
So fresh and firm and calm
From the bud of time
It seems perfection
Never could succumb
To ragged nights of storm
Or children torn as these
Crying as they run;
But damaged children strike
Dreams of perfection down —
Till twilight cups its hand
And time buds hope again
To kiss the wrongs that ache
Like broken fingers when
Our tears fall through

FOR THE INTRUDERS

I

Newcomers
You arrive too late.

Your weavers of willow baskets
Weave out from the core with hot hands.

In your language there are no words
                for black lightnings
Woven into baskets of black sage and prayer
You now hold dear as our old silver channeled in sand.

There is no word for the thunder of prayer.
The pungent   slow   strong dance
                to the thunder of prayer is gone.

Too late your shamans try to piece magic together,
Trying to shape the unyielding heart of the clay
Or mend shards of a clay pot painted with sunrise.

Your shamans handle lives with hot minds.

Your lives burn our mornings. Charred feathers,
Shell, coral, isinglass, and grains
Of blackened sand clack into place — too late.

The black crow over the hogan we all revere
Decorates your empty air — too late.
The deer others prayed to before the kill
Bloodies your hunt — till dark red, the thunder
Of the prayer of hooves in the dance pounds
                                unheard.

II

The eagle whose feathers you watched at dawn
Dies of our thirst on the mountain top. Though
Lightning strikes, the rains fall elsewhere.

It is too late to climb the broken rainbow arc
And pin Spider Woman's torn web in place again.

Poor devils listening for thunders
                                    you have no word for,
Your prayers are shards. Your baskets hang empty.
Though you try to barter your hunger for our pride,
Your longing for our proud faith, you are too late.
                  Too late .   .

                  Our chants died yesterday.

"JE RÉPONDERAI"
—Isak Dinesen

Je Réponderai:

With a shotgun from the far green hills — that is one way,
Or when a prisoner or desert rat runs from the gun —
That's another. In a garden of tin cans shining, where
Espaliered trees and men with outstretched arms plead
Then begin to mutiny and someone screams, another . . .

   Of course, the ways are numerous as storms, stunted minds
   Or torn tents on desert sands where young men drill,
   And a young woman sees the gun and the truth clearly,
   Then cries out as though giving birth to the old child
                      already dead beside her —

                      II

An answer, of course, the way she held that child, or the way
We hold the chewed-on core of an apple, the way we observe
Lost gardens, bleached cities, sandstorms, wars and starvation,
The way we see what we call Truth; tells not only who we are
And what stands we have taken here on the true desert's edge,

(Where it all began, lizards slid away and drums began to beat
As they will till the end, when we stop seeing or trying to see)
But yields other stark answers, like empty open arms raised
To surrender all but victory, when weapons are thrown away
And a lifetime, unaware it is ending once and for all of us,

   Cries out in yet another way   again
   "Je Réponderai" . . .

"THE HEART DETERMINES"
—Martin Buber

Five white stones in an earthen bowl
Or five men in a stone valley
Between mountains, or any number.

Who will examine them?
Who will study the water,
The women, the hands
That make them shine sleekly?

Who will prove the men are not stones,
Streaked by darkness as men are?

Who will prove the stones are not men
With dark eyes, lolling in streams
Where live women wade?

Who will determine,
Who will explore and determine
What is worth stroking and loving,

What sums we must guess to make one?

The mountains don't care.
No valley or clay bowl holding men
Or stones loosely, cares or will care.

One man willing to take stones
Or lives in his hand, five or one,
Bends over water, kneels
To drink meaning

That tastes like a woman wading a stream.
Will he marry? Let him prove love.

In the end his whole heart will determine.

Always we move through twilight with the stories of others like frozen apples in our gloved hands, our faces becoming the faces of neighbors, old-timers, oldsters who fumble their feet into thick boots slowly, frowning over memories like ours . . . Is it possible? See, beyond the crevasse . . .

III

The pink Madonna in Nicaragua or further away tilts her head in its straw hat with ribbons; her palms are cupped open to hold gold-foil roses before an old altar crowned with fire and floored with death. Where her hands end, fear begins. Her face, painted ochre and rose, gleams through the dust over broken stones, and over fear's afterbirth, the live bloody flower in bloom. From far away we stare at her, at Sorrow itself wearing a torn pink-ribboned straw hat like a halo; we touch her wooden hand, still open to strangers, though against the dark that prevails there and everywhere the question is not of our trust in her, but who the pink Madonna, created by and for Trust, can offer herself to in a world so foreign and depleted beyond her crumbling altar these sad days.

HISTORY LESSON

a man
in a long black coat
and a broad black hat
emerges
through falling snow

behind him a road
a charcoal fence
a village lost in snow
stretch back and back

no morning bark or bell
only the man
a bar of narrow black
walking slow
through snow and silence
nears

snow fell all night
snow blurs the past we wake to
are you awake?

tell me, will a face
bright as snow in sun
when day comes clear
appear at last
below the low hat brim
to illumine us?

we must go back
and back
to welcome him

remember
how once the Hasidim prized joy
dressed all in black
and opposed themselves to suffering . . .

AFTER THE SIEGE
OF LENINGRAD

Akhmatova

wrote of a willow tree
in the snow
that was all

a young tree
alive still
among the ruins

so simple, so frail
grand, gay, and free
she wept

longing to lead
the way beyond despair
at last

through silvery green
unimprisoned light
that could bend

like her heroic line
and rise, a small willow
in the snow or heroine

an Akhmatova, free
to heal silence

her profile a coastline
eroded but strong beside a distant sea

ARSON

were you there at the time?
did you see it happen?
who told you?

you think I'm out of touch
cut off like a cottonwood stump
no leaves to hear with

stuck in a grove without
god or assassins
where were you at the time?

did you see the blood bubble and burn?
who told you?
you think I didn't know?

I may be leafless
too bare to catch and hold the rain
but I hear echoes

before they're rung

before morning bells
enter the burning building
the crash site
the evening jazz festival

I hear the suspect
moan for Satan or salvation
on a snow-peaked mountain
beyond the cottonwoods

it was cold at the time
before fire broke out
and the heart struck arson

did I see it happen?
who told you?
who told you

I was there   I was the one

A MURMUR IN THE FLAME
(for Tanya — Vietnam, 1972)

Tanya
The bright wings of your name
Cross our hearts with fire

We cannot sleep or sing
Or love green leaves in Spring

Remembering your face, the spring
Beside your house — a murmur

In the flame — we cannot sing
Your name or rock you tenderly

Who rocked you with their arms
And tucked your flesh on air

We take your bowl and go
Begging through the Spring

Forgiveness in your name
While planes through nightmare air

With dark consuming song
Wrap you again in flame

Till love and promise lie
Forever lulled by fire

Defiled, the childlike spring
Scalds our bowls with shame

No leaves are left to sing
Our hearts choke on the fire

We cannot breathe your name

O Tanya   Tanya

THE SHIITE WOMEN
(Zikar, Iraq — 1992)

three women
pole
weathered rowboat prows
through low marsh grasses
that grow
in shallow water

motionless
among broken reeds
spreading
around and behind them
to the grainy gray horizon
they stare out
at the camera

one woman in a bleached robe
thrusts an ancient oar
in a crude gesture
of defiance
through air not water

another woman
wrapped in black
with bare forearm and wrist
stabs
a broken stick
into the dark smear
of muddy water

from the lower
left-hand corner
of the photo
the wrinkled face

of an older
black-shawled woman
confronts us

a woman we see at once
knows everything
about the economy
of Zikar
and why its women
(wives of soldiers
away at war perhaps)
farm

the gray marshes
for their thin harvest
of soaked reeds

she is the one
staring out
who offers in return
for our goodwill
and unforgivable ignorance

a toothless grim sympathy
the mean splinter of her smile

IN SOMALIA

the women
crouch
or lie on what appears to be
a flat dry sandy road
by a dry gully
the saffron stripes
of their robes
erased   by sun

enormous eyes
grown expressionless
with pain
giving birth again
to unbearable human pain
they stare
away from what once
were their live children

sprawled   fleshless now
in harsh cradles of bone —
in arms that rocked them
tenderly   on laps
of bright-colored stripes
as they were breasted and fed

by those Somali mothers   resting
long ago   near a live well
or stream   where they stopped
to drink water

and all the women sang to their children

PROFILE

Across the gully is an old woman with white crimped hair
like a soiled wig framing a Grecian profile and an olive-pit
eye. A stooped old woman wrapped in dun-colored wool,
her feet in thick leather-laced old boots, props herself to
rest by a fence post, then, slipping in mud, struggles slowly
down to join those on the other side of the gully who wait
for the day's passing event — a cart stacked with gray-faced
bodies, or a carload of crushed bread loaves perhaps.
Where is the old woman? Of what nationality is she?
Whose dire war does she share? What will happen next?

REMEMBERING SREBRENICA

If you cry, it is because you still hear
Isaiah's beloved lie, "All shall be well
and all shall be well and all manner of thing
shall be well"   in snow passes
    where ice crystals were then
    and are still the only food . . .

And if you cry with pain over the terrible
faces of children and their grandmas dying,
let me say again: As you wait
in mountain snows of a long-ago war
for relief or death, for prisons to open
and broken flyers or farmers to mend
    and walk out carrying children
    who revived once too often
    and so became you, haunted still, wounded
still by rage over suffering seen again
through frozen spicules and red nets of tears
knowing it is time for tears to burn
    both far away and here
    though no longer with faith that
    "all shall be well and
    all manner of thing shall be well" . . .

LIKE TUZLA

once
in the wide light
over our old house
at the far end of the field

we watched
two young foxes
burnished flanks and bushy tails
at play
in high-tossing grasses
near the red haw tree and the lilacs

today
beyond the same field we see
a house like our house
on a hill like ours
            but far away

broken open by mortar fire
all its lives, lilacs, and berries
spilled, scattered, or crushed —
all its people (who look like us),
those still alive, gone away

lost in a tarnished smoky light
no two red foxes here or there
            would deign to dance through
            this cruel day

YOU ARE A WEAPON TOO

Little One

blood   bone   raw silk   and hope
alone in the burning park
where love once went to school
beside a frozen arc
       of apple boughs, you face
the bloodied fruit and fire
       of exploding genes —

a target who resists
by guarding what Love means —

till all you were meant to be,
grown potent, will advance

where love once went to school
to outface Fate and prove
what your young heart in action knows —

Little One, for our sakes
alone
in the burning park

blood   bone   torn silk   and Light

INVINCIBLE
       you are a weapon too

CROSSING INTO ZAIRE

far away a ragged clay-colored soldier
hands the last one   a child   her mother's wide
broken straw hat and aims the child   alone   west
from the bridge toward a locust-brown countryside
where we watch her run   hobble rather   the last
creature   this poor scared one   to go from
the bridge into Zaire dead ahead lying bare
on and on   there nameless and roadless   to find
dazed by sun glare   somehow   the place her mother
among others struggling and falling   fell   herself
hatless down through sun   offscreen hard by
the bridge soldiers still shove others with bundles
back using rifle butts as the child   the last one
                to be released   a small agony
                lurches slowly forward
                directionless
far   far beyond us now   toward no known
                horizon   no horizon known to us

Child, I beg you to remember bells, the sound of bells over hoar frost, war, and brown morning fields. It will be a long time ago. You will be saying, "Goodnight, how early it grows late," and tears will toll in you for children crying in a steamy room where someone, a man, cried earlier. It is necessary not to forget ordinary bells— marriage bells, funeral bells, and solace, warnings, and tremors of joy over black ice (or over the child who ran sparkling across the frosty fields). I beg you, give to the perilous air that was already coming, clamorous and silvery, the sound of armor breaking into bells. Give to the child in you and to that child's sterling child the brown field you saved and held to hold out later— over the sound of crying, the sound of bells.

IV

"Dear One," the dark woman whispers, waiting alone — "My falcon, storm, and song, you escorted me. What I thought your heart spoke never seemed a lie. One last time, tell me the truth as though we lay at home together still in a dawn where wings, rising clouds, and bells ring us close as they once did to wake us — tell me, so I may go on unescorted as I must now be, so far from our great fête in the snow, tell me — Where do the old loves go?"

BLACK IN THE SNOW AS A DANCING SLIPPER

we know

after years of matching
thread to hem and blood to sunset,
letting out and letting down
muslin gardens for wayward daughters
to wander their burned-toast Autumns in —

after grief
black in the snow as a dancing slipper,
losses reeking of crêpe and cedar,
and passion hiding its tiny feathers
under Auntie's embroidery flame
while the Sunday joint cried out and bled —

after choices of mates and carving platters,
so many births in so many beds,
and spilled milk days by nursery fires,

we know
why genius through the green baize door
and intellect in the passage fled
from thorny gardens and long-stemmed chores —

free now of course, but too engaged
to sort old lavish trash of flowers
                    for remnants of gold, a burning red

BE VALIANT

Who says, "Be Valiant"?

Enough that we lean down to touch cold toes at dawn
Then rise to face one slow thing at a time —
A praying mantis gawky on a grape leaf
Or love's face dented dark by time, facing
The last star in the night window:

"Be sparing with your tears," they mean,
Officious with fear and unaware that
Souls like ours refuse even *kind* generals
For guides.   Thank you. We'll find the way,

Stumbling on our own through arbors
Lavish with laughter or forbidden tears,
Where transparent wings of pain hide
On a grape of shade. We'll harvest

And preserve ripe fruit, sealed
With hungry care in clean Mason jars
Forever, and on our own, alone, wait

As the last star marches into pallor
And the beloved face fades — to try
And touch our toes again at dawn.
Who dares command us to be valiant?
Stumbling, stubborn, and afraid,
          we already are.

BARLEY'S MAP

Her mission: to meet herself walking,
To welcome herself in that hunched
　　　　　　　figure in the snow

Near a row of wild ducks on a floe
In the storm, motionless below the pines.

Her eyes blurred by snow crystals
Burning to behold what she will never be.

She walks far but cannot find one soul
　　　　　　　running wild —
Only a huddled woman scarved in air

Voluminous and dark. Snow falls
On wild ducks frozen there; snow falls

On water and on snow and her.

THERE COMES A TIME

Barley knows
there comes a time
      when it is time to go
when we no longer know
how to read the tides
flowing through our blood

don't know for sure
if we are bad or good
oldness is so new
there is no certitude
though we bring ferny herbs

to ease the mutinous tides
of pain that sunder us,
or drape our floundering wills
past sorrows of old age
in folds of lustrous silk

and dreams of being "good"
warm-wrapped in ancient grace
of milk and flame and blood
as we begin to move
fearless or not through night

now that it's time to go
past outstretched cradling arms
toward a final resting place —
that wrist of a minor star
you guide us to at last —

you small bright button on Time's sleeve . . .

84

ENDURANCE

this year . . .

on his birthday
not the date of his death
you understand
but the day of his birth

the air was happy
in the apple tree
leaves moved
over young apples

and when she looked up at the sky
she saw two birds together
very close
wheel and dive as one
down toward the blooming tree
you understand

on a June day when air is happy
over birds and apples
you may well wonder
how long a love like theirs can endure

IN UNRIPE AGE, COURAGE

Time and indigence dress her so
in scraps of raw experience
too scant to cover flesh that shrank
from Venus myth and Venus lie
on bones that creak humility

outside a raven and a crow
wing sharply black
through freezing air

while higher still
myths bloom again
a goddess grows
diaphanous
and rose paint flakes
the raddled skin
of old cheeks rouged
against despair

dressed in her lack of History
she ventures gravely out to greet
night of the raven and the crow

where a wounded goddess bleeds
warning words to make her wise
and guide her through her Present Tense
then help her go, wrapped
in a past of tattered lace —
is there a way to make her glow
and glitter through forbidding night?
a rhinestone diadem to place
over the small orb of her mind?
is there a way

for meager grace
cloaked in sheer scraps of stubbornness
to sally forth victorious?

JUNIPER REACHES OUT

Old Juniper Woman
reaches out to us, smiling.

She knows us as she knows young rivers,
deserts afire, hens cackling anger,
birth in the sand, prayers for rain,
the rank stain of yarrow, and arms
                kinder than stone.

Benign and smiling, she offers us
clouds, dried apples and cornmeal,
her silence in our language promising:

In time
you will be brave enough
to cross the panicky waves
of the dangerous river that now
                divides
desert from Desert, lover from Love . . .

YOU NO ONE

Juniper Woman,
You splendid No One, you Elect,
Waving from mesa sunset
To the savage crowd of one below . . .
Some day souls meaner than your own
Will dream green sprigs of pine
That coronet your hair, and rise
Ennobled, to outwit despair once more —

You queenly No One, you Elect,
Waving Peace to the crowd of One
       tumultuous with banners
          far below

THE MESA WE CLIMBED

The mesa we climbed has no twin

Just as no light on pine tree or snow,
No face lit by love has a twin.

Together we discovered
Landscapes and seasons to live in
And part of us knows now
Not how foreign they were,
But how it is to be foreign
Anywhere,

An alien stifled by silence,
Who must break out again
Into light unlike the sovereign
Light we climbed, must
Set out to find, neither
Escape route nor neighborhood —
But a calm level space,
A terrain like a green mesa top

Where a new language might arise
With or without pine tree or
Snowlight or house, saying

Now you are gone, how it is
To be alien anywhere —
Saying, love,

The mesa we climbed has no twin.

SMIKE

"You were my home."
— Nicholas Nickleby

you were my home
I live there still

the heart you gave
tells me to go
where live things grow
tells me to range
out far and change
and so I will
my guide your love
where life is strange
your love my hearth
on star or earth
your will my fire
and passionate
already late

dear blazing heart
it's time to start
to change and grow

though I must go
you are my home
I live there still
and always will
and always will

RILKE'S ANGELS

You asked for red rocks and wild red flowers once.

Instead
I would have tall Angels descend the air
Over your bowed head, their massive wings
                                rustling light,
Light scooping sockets from which flight springs
And stiff feathers gleam when they fold down.
Motionless, eyes even with yours, I would have them offer
Gifts measureless as those you possess already.

And I would have you unbend in their presence
                                remembering
What the master of their silence spoke
When you first bowed your head to mysteries
You felt approaching — poet and Angel —
                                the flawed man
With his creation . . . before they turned
To spread their sculpted wings, and ascend the air
                                                again.

I would have you recognize those angels bronzed by light
                                where you stand
Awed, applauding in the throb of heights, his words:
"I don't know whether I am a falcon or a storm or a song."

                    *   *   *   *

More:
I wish for you what you desire most, with supple fortitude
                                and power
In the shadow of wings where even genius falters —
Your own plain song, plain rocks, red rustling
                                                flowers.

REMEMBERING N.
IN THE FIELD

We can't see him for the clarity
of the morning where he bends
in a blue work-shirt to mend
the wire fence — the clarity

of an immense field framed by white
midges, white butterflies, sun
and Time, as one sturdy man
blurred by tears and whorls of light

leans to his chore without a shadow —
fine bowed head and hand and mind
set in the shimmering heat to tend
a smudge of bright cornflower blue

all erased by noon, a splendor caught
between wire fence and the white sky — a
blaze too dazzling and intense
to focus on and follow into the white-hot
                    heart of Light

PLAISIR

old love, wake up, it's time
to strip the house we filled
for over thirty years

wake up, I hear the bells
foreign fresh and clear
chiming *l'avenir*
across alfalfa fields

I hear a crazy bird
in the olive tree
singing
cross but pure
by the blue window blind

wake up and listen too!
we haven't time to save
less than all we love
before we face Goodwill

I promise if we learn
what that wild music means
wings green songs and bells
will fill the house again
and so prolong our stay

wake up and translate please
plaisir   dear love   *plaisir*

PRETEND YOU GIVE ME YOUR HAND

pretend you give me your hand
pretend we go out

early
to hear the mourning doves
in the field

pretend you trust me
so much you believe

their clear voices
rinsing the bare field
in the early morning

cry
as I promise they will

Rejoice   Rejoice

old friend dear one
thin pancakes wait
in the copper pan
inside

PROTECTRESS

Here she is, aglow,
The left side of serenity
Torn from the *Times* one Sunday long ago,
A yellowed grainy photo of a saint alive in stone
Brought from her parapet to grace
The empty wall space of an infidel.

Young, curly-haired and calm she leans,
Most tender stone profiled by light.
Bare-toed below the slow folds of her gown,
Grave as a child, she poses, at home
And easy on her pedestal of space,
Holding more than mere mortal could —
A House! An eaved small home of gingerbread
Or wood, a toy of cozy stone nestled
In the bare crook of one sturdy arm
(Her left) against her flat stone
Gentle breast — farm girl, nursemaid
And protectress, sturdy shoulder bent
And bent head (fillet bound) bowed,
As though a child slept in her arms —
A weighty precious treasure she must guard
Against the wolves of night that prowl,
                   ferocious still . . .

ON THE NIGHT OF THE DAY
THE WORLD ENDS

If we must die
Let us lie one last time
Like a coastline
   glimmering
And the sea
Joined in silvery debris
   and litter of light
All the long way to the world's end.

Let us lie past Time
As shining waves die
   sighing out our banns,
And our names die,
Drams of joy lost
   in dried-out fields
With all that will be lost.

If we must die
Let us lie past separateness
Where lineage of the light we bore
   will seed all vanishing
And requite our end
   with stars

Like children safe in space,
Whose parents loved
   and at the last,
Most brilliantly, were wed.

GOODBYE

the black pine
alone in the field
    before dawn
fathers
cone-shaped small
dark-shawled bodies
broken from night boughs

carved rosettes of dream
scurrying
home
over the cold field

before snow
fills the high nest
or day
soaks through dark wool

at dawn when
father rests

and all birds call as one

Sometimes in the rowboat moored to a stone below a willow tree, sometimes in bed, hands on oarlock hipbones, a final journey is planned for our very dangerous expedition, this cold and radiant marvel that lasts a lifetime.

ABOUT THE AUTHOR

Lucile Adler was born in Kansas City, Missouri, and educated at Bennington College. She lived in Cambridge, Massachusetts, before settling with her family in Santa Fe, New Mexico. She is the author of three previous books of poetry: *The Traveling Out* (Macmillan, 1960), *The Society of Anna* (Lightning Tree Press, 1974), and *The Ripening Light: Selected Poems 1977–1987* (Peregrine Smith Books, 1989).

Her poems have appeared in *The New Yorker, The New Boston Review, Century, El Palacio, The Raddle Moon, Puerta del Sol, The Massachusetts Review, The Bennington Review, In Context, Inscape, La Confluencia, Poetry, Poets West, The Nation, Poetry Northwest, The San Marcos Review, Southwest Review,* and *The Sunstone Review,* as well as other periodicals. Her poetry has also been published in anthologies, such as *The New Yorker Book of Poems, The New York Times Book of Verse, The Desert Review Anthology, I Hear My Sisters Saying, The Forgotten Language,* and *New Mexico Poetry Renaissance.* A prose piece is included in the anthology *I've Always Meant to Tell You . . . Letters to Our Mothers* (Pocket Books, 1997).

A selection of Ms. Adler's poems was tape-recorded at the Lamont Library Poetry Room at Harvard. She has given readings at St. John's College in Santa Fe, New Mexico State University, and the Santa Fe Writer's Conference, and was guest speaker at the Breadloaf Conference at St. John's College. Three of her poems have been set to music by John Kander for soprano Carol Van Ness to perform in concert.

Molecular and Translational Medicine

Series Editors
William B. Coleman
Gregory J. Tsongalis

For further volumes:
http://www.springer.com/series/8176

Linda S. Pescatello • Stephen M. Roth
Editors

Exercise Genomics

Foreword by Claude Bouchard

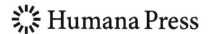 Humana Press

Editors
Linda S. Pescatello
Human Performance Laboratory
Department of Kinesiology
Neag School of Education
University of Connecticut
Storrs, CT 06269-1110, USA
Linda.Pescatello@uconn.edu

Stephen M. Roth
Department of Kinesiology
School of Public Health
University of Maryland
College Park, MD 20742-2611, USA
sroth1@umd.edu

ISBN 978-1-61779-730-9   ISBN 978-1-60761-355-8 (eBook)
DOI 10.1007/978-1-60761-355-8
Springer New York Dordrecht Heidelberg London

Linda's dedication: I will conclude my comments by acknowledging my colleagues from the Department of Kinesiology at the University of Connecticut and Department of Cardiology at Hartford Hospital, and my past and current students who continue to inspire me with the enthusiasm for the work they do. Most importantly, I acknowledge my husband Dave, daughter Shannon, and son Conor, my parents and other family members, and my good friends who have provided me with the love, support, and balance that has enabled me to pursue a career that continues to excite me.

Steve's dedication: I am indebted to my many colleagues in the field of exercise genomics for their collaboration and encouragement, and am particularly grateful to my wife and three children for their unconditional love and support.

Foreword

We have seen in recent years a major increase in the number of scientific, peer-reviewed papers dealing with the genetic and molecular basis of physical activity level and indicators of health-related fitness and physical performance. This information explosion has been complemented by a number of initiatives that sought to integrate data and trends across technologies and areas of exercise science and sports medicine. The first example of the latter was the 1997 book on *Genetics of Fitness and Physical Performance* [1]. Subsequently, beginning in 2000, a series of reviews focusing on the evolution of the fitness and performance gene map were published in *Medicine and Science in Sports and Exercise* [2, 3]. This annual encyclopedic summary of the published research has now morphed into a new annual review emphasizing the strongest publications with discussions on their implications [4]. A third major undertaking took the form of a volume published in the *Encyclopaedia of Sports Medicine* series of the *International Olympic Committee* dealing exclusively with the genetics and molecular basis of fitness and performance [5]. Authors from 48 laboratories in 13 countries contributed the 33 chapters of this large effort. The most recent addition to these initiatives is this volume *Exercise Genomics* in a series on *Molecular and Translational Medicine* whose aim is to provide integrated, horizontal views of where the field stands and how to apprehend the future [6].

The editors, Drs. Pescatello and Roth, have asked me to write an introductory comment on their volume with an emphasis on key findings from the *HE*ealth, *RI*sk factors, exercise *TrA*ining and *GE*netics, or HERITAGE Family Study. The primary purpose of the HERITAGE, Family Study was to examine the health fitness-related responses to 20 weeks of aerobic training in 742 sedentary, healthy subjects without chronic disease from approximately 200 families [7].

It is well recognized by now that genetic variation plays a significant role in the global human heterogeneity in exercise-related traits. This advancement has been documented for many health-related fitness and performance endophenotypes and phenotypes in several ethnic groups but perhaps more strikingly in the HERITAGE Family Study. HERITAGE provided strong evidence that maximal oxygen uptake (VO_2 max) is characterized by a substantial genetic component among sedentary adults, with an estimated heritability of at least 50% [8]. One of the underlying assumptions of HERITAGE was that it would be easier to identify and dissect the genetic component of the response to a standardized training program than to undertake the same effort with traits measured in a cross-sectional cohort. In retrospect, this assumption appears to be correct.

In HERITAGE, after 20 weeks of exercise training, in 473 adults from 100 families of Caucasians the mean increase in VO_2 max was about 400 mL $O_2 \cdot min^{-1}$ but the standard deviation of the gain reached 200 mL $O_2 \cdot min^{-1}$. There were individuals who did not gain at all, and a large fraction who qualified as low responders. On the other hand, a fraction registered a gain of at least 600 mL $O_2 \cdot min^{-1}$, and some improved by as much as 1,000 mL $O_2 \cdot min^{-1}$. These individual differences in trainability were not randomly distributed as evidenced by the fact there was 2.5 times more variance in the VO_2 max gains between families compared to the variance in response observed among family members. The heritability coefficients of the VO_2 max gains adjusted for age, sex, baseline body mass, and baseline VO_2 max attained 47% [9]. The same trends were observed for training induced changes in fasting insulin, insulin sensitivity, high-density lipoprotein cholesterol (HDL-C), exercise blood pressure and heart rate, exercise stroke volume and cardiac output, indicators of adiposity, and other phenotypes [10–20]. There is evidence from other studies that similar patterns of human variation and familial aggregation are found for the trainability of muscular strength and power as well as short-term predominantly anaerobic performance [21, 22, 23].

For much of the last two decades, the focus of exercise genomics has been on testing a single or a small number of markers in candidate genes. Such studies were typically conducted on small number of subjects, often less than 100, and were based on one-time, cross-sectional observations. Not only were these reports grossly underpowered, but they were also potentially contaminated by the effects of uncontrolled confounders [4]. More recently we have seen a trend towards the use of larger sample sizes but they still remain small compared to recommendations for contemporary human genomics research [24, 25]. Progress in exercise genomics will require more prospective study designs but especially experimental studies with large sample sizes and well-defined interventions.

Over the last 15 years, we have seen a shift in the way candidate genes were identified or prioritized. An early approach was based on genome-wide scans using panels of highly polymorphic microsatellite markers examined in family members. This method yielded positional candidates, but few of them were confirmed in studies that subjected them to direct testing. It turned out that this technology is not very powerful when it comes to genes with small effect sizes. We are now beginning to see genome-wide association studies (GWAS) with large panels of single nucleotide polymorphisms (SNPs) focused on exercise-related traits [26]. This development should provide a flurry of new candidate genes for further in-depth investigation. Another important recent development is the use of gene expression profiling as a tool to identify key genes that can subsequently be subjected to genetic exploration [27, 28]. All these methodological advances will be helpful in the effort to identify SNPs and genes associated with exercise endophenotypes and traits.

Over the last few years, we have realized that the effect sizes of the genes typically identified through GWAS were quite small [29]. GWAS small effect sizes have been repeatedly found with disease endpoints such as type 2 diabetes [30, 31], obesity [32, 33], hypertension [34], ischemic heart disease [35, 36], and for physical traits such as body height [37]. However, there is some indication it may be easier to find genes and variants associated with exercise-related traits as the effect size is larger for some of them [28]. This is not a trivial issue. There are a few reasons why this may be so. For instance, in the case of GWAS focused on disease gene discovery, the ability to identify a significant SNP is strongly influenced by the fact that an unknown fraction of the subjects in the control group is not affected yet by the disease but has the genetic predisposition. In exercise genomics, this weakness can be almost completely eliminated if a well-defined and accurately measured phenotype such as VO_2 max or maximal isometric strength is used. Exercise-oriented studies would offer even cleaner phenotypes in situations where the changes in muscular strength or cardiorespiratory fitness were investigated after exposure to an appropriately standardized and fully controlled training program. In such an experimental setting, the variance in response to training is unlikely to be influenced in a major way by confounders, thus enhancing the ability to identify markers and genes with relatively small effects in comparison to cross-sectional studies.

To expand on the previous paragraph, a whole body of twin and family research indicates individuals with the same genotype respond more similarly to training than those with different genotypes [38, 39]. In this regard, the variance in training response together with its strong genetic determinant represents one of the most striking examples of a genotype-environmental effect, in this case a genotype-training interaction effect. The search for genetic markers of trainability is an area of research that is likely to pay enormous dividend as the training gain constitutes a powerful trait measured very reliably.

In a recent report, we demonstrated it was possible to identify DNA markers of the VO_2 max response to standardized exercise training programs [28]. We first used skeletal muscle RNA expression profiling to produce a panel of 29 genes whose baseline expression levels (i.e., in the sedentary state) predicted the VO_2 max training response. We combined these 29 targets with other candidates identified in the HERITAGE Family Study and hypothesized DNA variants in 35 genes would explain the heterogeneous responses to exercise training in humans. We genotyped SNPs in these genes in the 473 white subjects of HERITAGE. In the end, we were able to show that a panel of 11 SNPs could explain 23% of the variance in gains in VO_2 max, which corresponds to about ~50% of the estimated genetic variance for VO_2 max response in HERITAGE. Bioinformatic in silico studies suggested several of the genes associated with these 11 SNPs were involved in developmental biology pathways including angiogenesis.

Another example can be highlighted from the metabolic changes observed in response to exercise training. Global gene expression profiling was used in the HERITAGE Family Study to identify genes associated with insulin sensitivity training response based on the minimal model computer-based method (MINMOD) of determining insulin sensitivity derived traits [27]. Total RNA was extracted from vastus lateralis muscle biopsies from 16 subjects: eight of them were high responders improving insulin sensitivity by 100%, while the remaining eight were age-, sex-, and BMI-matched nonresponders (i.e., zero gain). RNA samples were pooled within each responder group, labeled with fluorescent dyes, and hybridized onto in situ-generated microarrays containing 18,861 genes. Using a cut-off value of 40%, we found there were 42 transcripts that were overexpressed at baseline and 240 posttraining in the high responders compared to the nonresponders. In contrast, five transcripts were downregulated at baseline and 121 posttraining in the high responders vs. the nonresponders. A total of 47 and 361 transcripts were differentially expressed between high and nonresponders before and after the training program, respectively. Five genes (C-terminal binding protein 1 [*CTBP1*], four and a half LIM domains 1 [*FHL1*], pyruvate dehydrogenase kinase [*PDK4*], v-ski sarcoma viral oncogene homolog [*SKI*], and titin [*TTN*]) exhibiting at least 50% difference in expression between high and nonresponders either at baseline or posttraining were selected for validation experiments.

The *FHL1* gene was of particular interest as it is encoded on the X chromosome which allows for a clean test of the effect of each allele in males. SNPs were typed at the *FHL1* locus and tested for associations with exercise training-induced changes in insulin metabolism phenotypes (Xq26) [40]. SNP rs2180062 was associated with fasting insulin ($p=0.012$), insulin sensitivity ($p=0.046$), disposition index ($p=0.006$), and glucose disappearance index ($p=0.03$) training responses in white males. In white women, SNP rs9018 was associated with disposition index ($p=0.016$) and glucose disappearance index ($p=0.008$) changes; in the white males, the same SNP showed suggestive association with fasting insulin training response ($p=0.04$).

It is obvious from these two examples that the combination of transcriptomics and genomics is a powerful one which is likely to shed light on the molecular and genetic architecture of exercise biology and exercise behavior traits. Exercise genomics is a field that can take advantage of advances in epigenomics, proteomics, and metabolomics in combination with transcriptomics and genomics to develop a comprehensive and integrated picture of all biological mechanisms participating in the regulation of human variation in exercise-related traits. In this regard, making use of animal models to inform human exercise biology particularly for tissues that cannot be accessed for molecular studies is likely to be a productive path. For exercise biologists to acquire a sophisticated understanding of individual differences in cardiorespiratory fitness, muscular strength and power, propensity to exercise, health-related fitness and performance response to regular exercise, and other relevant traits will require information from the genome, epigenome, transcriptome, proteome, and metabolome to be incorporated in research paradigms ever growing in complexity but becoming also more and more powerful.

The anticipated development of individualized genomic medicine will impact the exact position exercise will have in the future of public health, primary and secondary prevention, treatment, and rehabilitation. In this regard, exercise genomic and other omic research is timely and of the greatest importance. In the field of athletic performance, exercise genomics is poised to generate scientific advances that will revolutionize our understanding of the mechanisms driving the potential of tissues and organs to be trained and the nature of the limiting factors in sports performance relying heavily on endurance, strength, or power.

The present volume covers some of the most important topics of the exercise genomics agenda. It includes an exposé of the basic concepts and methods of genetics and genomics as well as statistical genetics. A detailed overview of the data pertaining to the role of genetic determinants on physical activity and inactivity levels follows, in addition to the role of genetic variation in the association among exercise and glucose, insulin, and type 2 diabetes mellitus; body composition and obesity; and blood pressure and lipoprotein-lipids. Additional chapters are devoted to muscular strength and size, aerobic capacity, and endurance performance. The book ends with a discussion of the challenges facing exercise genomics and the translation of our growing understanding of the role of genetic differences for scientists and practitioners. The editors have done a great job in being able to secure the contributions of leaders in the field of exercise genomics. The result is a readable, compact book that I am pleased to recommend to exercise science and public health communities.

Baton Rouge, LA, USA   Claude Bouchard

References

1. Bouchard C, Malina RM, Perusse L. Genetics of fitness and physical performance. Champaign: Human Kinetics; 1997.
2. Bray MS, Hagberg JM, Perusse L, Rankinen T, Roth SM, Wolfarth B, Bouchard C. The human gene map for performance and health-related fitness phenotypes: The 2006–2007 update. Med Sci Sports Exerc. 2009;41(1):35–73.
3. Rankinen T, Perusse L, Rauramaa R, Rivera MA, Wolfarth B, Bouchard C. The human gene map for performance and health-related fitness phenotypes. Med Sci Sports Exerc. 2001;33(6):855–67.
4. Rankinen T, Roth SM, Bray MS, Loos R, Perusse L, Wolfarth B, et al. Advances in exercise, fitness, and performance genomics. Med Sci Sports Exerc. 2010;42(5):835–46.
5. Bouchard C and Hoffman EP, editors. Genetic and Molecular Aspects of Sport Performance, Vol. XVIII of the IOC Encycopeadia of Sports Medicine, an IOC Medical Commission Publication. West Sussex: Wiley-Blackwell; 2011.
6. Exercise genomics. Humana Press/Springer; in press.
7. Bouchard C, Leon AS, Rao DC, Skinner JS, Wilmore JH, Gagnon J. The HERITAGE family study. Aims, design, and measurement protocol. Med Sci Sports Exerc. 1995;27(5):721–9.
8. Bouchard C, Daw EW, Rice T, Perusse L, Gagnon J, Province MA, et al. Familial resemblance for VO2max in the sedentary state: The HERITAGE family study. Med Sci Sports Exerc. 1998;30(2):252–8.
9. Bouchard C, An P, Rice T, Skinner JS, Wilmore JH, Gagnon J, et al. Familial aggregation of VO2 max response to exercise training: Results from the HERITAGE family study. J Appl Physiol. 1999;87(3):1003–8.
10. An P, Perusse L, Rankinen T, Borecki IB, Gagnon J, Leon AS, et al. Familial aggregation of exercise heart rate and blood pressure in response to 20 weeks of endurance training: The HERITAGE family study. Int J Sports Med. 2003;24(1):57–62.

11. An P, Rice T, Gagnon J, Borecki IB, Bergeron J, Despres JP, et al. Segregation analysis of apolipoproteins A-1 and B-100 measured before and after an exercise training program: The HERITAGE family study. Arterioscler Thromb Vasc Biol. 2000;20(3):807–14.
12. An P, Rice T, Gagnon J, Leon AS, Skinner JS, Bouchard C, et al. Familial aggregation of stroke volume and cardiac output during submaximal exercise: The HERITAGE family study. Int J Sports Med. 2000;21(8):566–72.
13. Gaskill SE, Rice T, Bouchard C, Gagnon J, Rao DC, Skinner JS, et al. Familial resemblance in ventilatory threshold: The HERITAGE family study. Med Sci Sports Exerc. 2001; 33(11):1832–40.
14. Hong Y, Rice T, Gagnon J, Perusse L, Province M, Bouchard C, et al. Familiality of triglyceride and LPL response to exercise training: The HERITAGE study. Med Sci Sports Exerc. 2000;32(8):1438–44.
15. Hong Y, Weisnagel SJ, Rice T, Sun G, Mandel SA, Gu C, et al. Familial resemblance for glucose and insulin metabolism indices derived from an intravenous glucose tolerance test in blacks and whites of the HERITAGE family study. Clin Genet. 2001;60(1):22–30.
16. Leon AS, Gaskill SE, Rice T, Bergeron J, Gagnon J, Rao DC, et al. Variability in the response of HDL cholesterol to exercise training in the HERITAGE family study. Int J Sports Med. 2002;23(1):1–9.
17. Perusse L, Gagnon J, Province MA, Rao DC, Wilmore JH, Leon AS, et al. Familial aggregation of submaximal aerobic performance in the HERITAGE family study. Med Sci Sports Exerc. 2001;33(4):597–604.
18. Perusse L, Rice T, Province MA, Gagnon J, Leon AS, Skinner JS, et al. Familial aggregation of amount and distribution of subcutaneous fat and their responses to exercise training in the HERITAGE family study. Obes Res. 2000;8(2):140–50.
19. Rice T, An P, Gagnon J, Leon AS, Skinner JS, Wilmore JH, et al. Heritability of HR and BP response to exercise training in the HERITAGE family study. Med Sci Sports Exerc. 2002;34(6):972–9.
20. Rice T, Despres JP, Perusse L, Hong Y, Province MA, Bergeron J, et al. Familial aggregation of blood lipid response to exercise training in the health, risk factors, exercise training, and genetics (HERITAGE) family study. Circulation. 2002;105(16):1904–8.
21. Hubal MJ, Gordish-Dressman H, Thompson PD, Price TB, Hoffman EP, Angelopoulos TJ, et al. Variability in muscle size and strength gain after unilateral resistance training. Med Sci Sports Exerc. 2005;37(6):964–72.
22. Simoneau JA, Lortie G, Boulay MR, Marcotte M, Thibault MC, Bouchard C. Inheritance of human skeletal muscle and anaerobic capacity adaptation to high-intensity intermittent training. Int J Sports Med. 1986;7(3):167–71.
23. Thomis MA, Beunen GP, Maes HH, Blimkie CJ, Van Leemputte M, Claessens AL, et al. Strength training: Importance of genetic factors. Med Sci Sports Exerc. 1998; 30(5):724–31.
24. Sale MM, Mychaleckyj JC, Chen WM. Planning and executing a genome wide association study (GWAS). Methods Mol Biol. 2009;590:403–18.
25. Wu Z, Zhao H. Statistical power of model selection strategies for genome-wide association studies. PLoS Genet. 2009;5(7):e1000582.
26. DE Moor MH, Liu YJ, Boomsma DI, Li J, Hamilton JJ, Hottenga JJ, et al. Genome-wide association study of exercise behavior in dutch and american adults. Med Sci Sports Exerc. 2009.
27. Teran-Garcia M, Rankinen T, Koza RA, Rao DC, Bouchard C. Endurance training-induced changes in insulin sensitivity and gene expression. Am J Physiol Endocrinol Metab. 2005; 288(6):E1168–78.
28. Timmons JA, Knudsen S, Rankinen T, Koch LG, Sarzynski M, Jensen T, et al. Using molecular classification to predict gains in maximal aerobic capacity following endurance exercise training in humans. J Appl Physiol. 2010;108(6):1487–96.
29. Manolio TA, Collins FS, Cox NJ, Goldstein DB, Hindorff LA, Hunter DJ, et al. Finding the missing heritability of complex diseases. Nature. 2009;461(7265):747–53.

30. Dupuis J, Langenberg C, Prokopenko I, Saxena R, Soranzo N, Jackson AU, et al. New genetic loci implicated in fasting glucose homeostasis and their impact on type 2 diabetes risk. Nat Genet. 2010;42(2):105–16.
31. Sladek R, Rocheleau G, Rung J, Dina C, Shen L, Serre D, et al. A genome-wide association study identifies novel risk loci for type 2 diabetes. Nature. 2007;445(7130):1–5.
32. Hofker M, Wijmenga C. A supersized list of obesity genes. Nat Genet. 2009;41(2):139–40.
33. Li S, Zhao JH, Luan J, Luben RN, Rodwell SA, Khaw KT, et al. Cumulative effects and predictive value of common obesity-susceptibility variants identified by genome-wide association studies. Am J Clin Nutr. 2010;91(1):184–90.
34. Sober S, Org E, Kepp K, Juhanson P, Eyheramendy S, Gieger C, et al. Targeting 160 candidate genes for blood pressure regulation with a genome-wide genotyping array. PLoS One. 2009;4(6):e6034.
35. Arnett DK, Li N, Tang W, Rao DC, Devereux RB, Claas SA, et al. Genome-wide association study identifies single-nucleotide polymorphism in KCNB1 associated with left ventricular mass in humans: the HyperGEN study. BMC Med Genet. 2009;10:43.
36. Vasan RS, Larson MG, Aragam J, Wang TJ, Mitchell GF, Kathiresan S, et al. Genome-wide association of echocardiographic dimensions, brachial artery endothelial function and treadmill exercise responses in the framingham heart study. BMC Med Genet. 2007;8 Suppl 1:S2.
37. McEvoy BP, Visscher PM. Genetics of human height. Econ Hum Biol. 2009;7(3):294–306.
38. Bouchard C, Dionne FT, Simoneau JA, Boulay MR. Genetics of aerobic and anaerobic performances. Exerc Sport Sci Rev. 1992;20:27–58.
39. Prud'homme D, Bouchard C, Leblanc C, Landry F, Fontaine E. Sensitivity of maximal aerobic power to training is genotype-dependent. Med Sci Sports Exerc. 1984;16(5):489–93.
40. Teran-Garcia M, Rankinen T, Rice T, Leon AS, Rao DC, Skinner JS, Bouchard C. Variations in the four and a half LIM domains 1 gene (FHL1) are associated with fasting insulin and insulin sensitivity responses to regular exercise. Diabetologia. 2007;50(9):58–66.

Preface

Linda S. Pescatello, Ph.D.: I embarked on this facet of my career in 1998 when Dr. Paul D. Thompson, Director of Cardiology, Hartford Hospital, CT, invited me to join the Exercise and Genetics Collaborative Research Group. Dr. Thompson formed this multicenter, collaborative research group with the intent of conducting large exercise genomics studies that would position exercise as important lifestyle therapy in the field of personalized medicine. Investigations undertaken by this Group have included, *Does Apo E Affect the Lipid Response to Exercise?* funded by the Donaghue Medical Research Foundation; *Functional Single Nucleotide Polymorphisms Associated with Human Muscle Size and Strength* or FAMuSS funded by the National Institutes of Health and National Institute of Neurological Disorders; *The Effect of Statins on Skeletal Muscle Function* or STOMP funded by the National Institutes of Health, and the National Heart, Lung and Blood Institute; and *Establishing an Exercise Dose Response for Postexercise Hypotension* funded by the American Heart Association.

My involvement with the Exercise and Genetics Collaborative Research Group provided me with the good fortune of working with leading scientists in the young field of exercise genomics. These scientists include Dr. Eric Hoffman, Director of the Research Center for Genetic Medicine, Children's National Medical Center, Washington, DC, and other members of his research team, Dr. Joseph D. Devaney, Assistant Professor, and Dr. Heather Gordish-Dressman, Biostatistician. Drs. Devaney and Gordish-Dressman are coauthors of Chap. 2, Statistical and Methodological Considerations in Exercise Genomics. Others esteemed scientists from this Group include Dr. Priscilla Clarkson, Distinguished Professor, Kinesiology Department, and Dean, Commonwealth College, University of Massachusetts, Amherst, MA, who is a coauthor of Chap. 5, Genetic Aspects of Muscular Strength and Size; Dr. Gregory Tsongalis, Director of Molecular Pathology, Dartmouth Medical School, Dartmouth Hitchcock Medical Center, Lebanon, NH; and Dr. Paul Thompson.

Stephen M. Roth, Ph.D.: I am fortunate to have training in both exercise science and human genetics and have maintained a personal and professional interest in this area for nearly 15 years. Dr. Jim Hagberg of the University of Maryland first opened my eyes to this field while I was a Ph.D. student, and he secured my transition into genetics research by introducing me to Dr. Robert Ferrell at the University of Pittsburgh, with whom I completed postdoctoral training in human genetics and began to develop a research specialization in the genomic aspects of exercise and health. At the University of Maryland, I'm honored to direct the Functional Genomics Laboratory, a 1,000 sq ft wet lab dedicated to exercise genomics research. I work closely with several investigators there, most notably Dr. Hagberg with whom I have coauthored several exercise genomics articles, as well as numerous colleagues from around the world. I have been fortunate to be funded by the National Institutes of Health for a variety of exercise genomics studies resulting in over 65 peer-reviewed articles, book chapters, etc., including a sole-author textbook published by Human Kinetics entitled, "Genetics Primer for Exercise Science and Health."

We would like to thank Dr. Tsongalis who presented us with the opportunity to edit, *Exercise Genomics* of the *Molecular and Translational Medicine Series*. It was because of his enthusiasm and belief in the clinical importance of the work in this field that encouraged us to undertake this project. In this book, we have invited leading international scientists in key content areas of exercise genomics to provide up-to-date findings and a vision for their translation into clinical practice. As the reader will see, the outstanding caliber of their contributions has made this project a pleasure to be a part of. We also thank Garrett Ash, M.S., Michael Bruneau, Jr., BS, and Margaux Guidry, Ph.D., graduate students in the Department of Kinesiology at the University of Connecticut for their editorial assistance. Finally, we are indebted to the leadership of Richard Hruska at Springer/Humana in shepherding this book into print, as well as the many dedicated staff who had a hand in making this book an important contribution to the growing field of exercise genomics.

Storrs, CT   Linda S. Pescatello
College Park, MD   Stephen M. Roth

Contents

Contributors

Claude Bouchard
Pennington Biomedical Research Center, 6400 Perkins Road, Baton Rouge,
LA 70808, USA

Molly S. Bray
Department of Epidemiology, University of Alabama at Birmingham,
1530 3rd Avenue S, Birmingham, AL 35294, USA

Ema C. Brito
Genetic Epidemiology and Clinical Research Group, Department of Public
Health and Clinical Medicine, Division of Medicine, Umeå University Hospital,
Umeå 90 187, Sweden

Priscilla M. Clarkson
Department of Kinesiology, University of Massachusetts, Amherst,
MA 01003, USA

Joseph M. Devaney
Children's National Medical Center, Research Center for Genetic Medicine,
111 Michigan Avenue, N.W., Washington, DC 20010, USA

Paul W. Franks
Genetic Epidemiology and Clinical Research Group, Department of Public
Health and Clinical Medicine, Division of Medicine, Umeå University Hospital,
Umeå 90 187, Sweden

Heather Gordish-Dressman
Children's National Medical Center, Research Center for Genetic Medicine,
111 Michigan Avenue, N.W., Washington, DC 20010, USA

James M. Hagberg
Department of Kinesiology, School of Public Health, University of Maryland,
College Park, MD 20742-2611, USA

Monica J. Hubal
Department of Integrative Systems Biology, George Washington University
School of Medicine, Research Center for Genetic Medicine,
Children's National Medical Center, Washington, DC 20010, USA

J. Timothy Lightfoot
Department of Health and Kinesiology, Sydney and JL Huffines Institute
for Sports Medicine and Human Performance, Texas A&M University,
159 Read Building, TAMU 4243, College Station, TX 77845-4243, USA

Linda S. Pescatello
Human Performance Laboratory, Department of Kinesiology,
Neag School of Education, University of Connecticut, Gampel Pavilion
Room 206, 2095 Hillside Road, U-1110, Storrs, CT 06269-1110, USA

Yannis Pitsiladis
College of Medicine, Veterinary and Life Sciences, Institute of Cardiovascular
and Medical Sciences, University of Glasgow, Glasgow, Scotland, UK

Stephen M. Roth
Department of Kinesiology, School of Public Health, University of Maryland,
College Park, MD 20742, USA

Mary H. Sailors
Department of Epidemiology, University of Alabama at Birmingham,
1530 3rd Avenue S, Birmingham, AL 35294, USA

Martine A. Thomis
Research Centre for Exercise and Health, Department of Biomedical Kinesiology,
Faculty of Kinesiology and Rehabilitation Sciences, Katholieke Universiteit
Leuven, Tervuursevest 101, B-3001 Leuven, Belgium

Maria L. Urso
U.S. Army Research Institute of Environmental Medicine (USARIEM),
Military Performance Division, Natick, MA 01760, USA

Guan Wang
College of Medicine, Veterinary and Life Sciences, Institute of Cardiovascular
and Medical Sciences, University of Glasgow, Glasgow, Scotland, UK

Bernd Wolfarth
Department of Preventive and Rehabilitative Sports Medicine, Technical
University Munich, 80809 Munich, Germany

Chapter 1
Fundamental Concepts in Exercise Genomics

Stephen M. Roth and Martine A. Thomis

Keywords Angiotensin converting enzyme • Alpha-actinin-3 • Beta-2-adrenergic receptor • Allele • Apolipoprotein E • Candidate gene • Chromosome • Complex trait • Copy number variation • Dizygotic twins • DNA • DNA biology • DNA methylation • Dominant • Epigenomics • Familial aggregation • Functional genomics • Gene (or genotype)×environment interaction • Genes • Genetic association study • Genetics • Genome sequencing • Genome-wide association study • Genotype • Haplotype • Heritability • Heterozygote • Homozygote • Human genome • Insertion/deletion polymorphism • Linkage analysis • Linkage disequilibrium • Logarithm of the odds score • Measured genotype approach • Mendelian trait • miRNA • Monozygotic twins • mRNA • Mutation • Nucleosome • Nucleotide • Polymorphism • Proteomics • Quantitative trait loci • Recessive • RNA • Single nucleotide polymorphism • siRNA • Systems biology • Trait variability • Transcription • Transcriptomics • Translation • Unmeasured genotype approach • Variable number tandem repeat

Introduction

The role of genetics in athletic performance has long been recognized. The actual study of genetic aspects of exercise adaptation and performance (i.e., "exercise genomics"), however, has a more limited history and has only recently gained attention as a major area of research in the exercise sciences. As such, few students and professionals in kinesiology and sports medicine are introduced to the core concepts of genetics in exercise science, let alone undergo formal training. The goal of this chapter is to provide readers with an overview of the basic elements of genetics in exercise science by providing an introduction to the basic aspects of DNA biology and the study of genetics. Information on the present state of the science and speculation

S.M. Roth (✉)
Department of Kinesiology, School of Public Health, University of Maryland,
College Park, MD 20742, USA
e-mail: sroth1@umd.edu

L.S. Pescatello and S.M. Roth (eds.), *Exercise Genomics*,
Molecular and Translational Medicine, DOI 10.1007/978-1-60761-355-8_1,
© Springer Science+Business Media, LLC 2011

about future techniques and approaches that are anticipated to represent the typical approaches in the near future are included. References are provided for readers to gain additional depth into various topics. Readers will also want to consider the information in Chap. 2 of this volume by Drs. Gordish-Dressman and Devaney, which addresses details of methodological techniques and statistical analysis that will add depth to much of the material presented here. A brief list of key terms and definitions is included in Table 1.1 that readers will see not only in this volume but also throughout the exercise genomics literature. Additionally, the Appendix in this book provides readers with a list of various web-based resources relevant to the study of genomics.

Table 1.1 Key terms and definitions commonly found in the exercise genomics literature

Allele	Genes or nucleotides that are located at the same position on two corresponding or homologous chromosomes
Complex trait	A phenotype that is influenced by both genetic and environmental factors, and likely the interaction of genetic and environmental factors
Epistasis	The interaction among multiple genes, in which one or more modifying genes influence the action of another gene
Exon	Region of DNA sequence within a gene that encodes for amino acids
Genotype	The combination of two alleles present within a single individual, corresponding to the two alleles present on the paired chromosomes
Haplotype	A specific combination of neighboring alleles from different polymorphisms that tends to be inherited together
Heterozygote	The term used to describe the presence of two different alleles present at a particular polymorphism in both gene copies
Homozygote	The term used to describe the presence of two identical alleles at a particular polymorphism in both gene copies
Intermediary trait	A trait influenced by fewer genetic and environmental factors that contributes to a more complex trait; also known as a sub-phenotype or endophenotype
Intron	Region of DNA sequence that separates two exons within a protein-coding gene
Linkage disequilibrium (LD)	The nonrandom association of distinct alleles at two or more polymorphisms
Mendelian trait	A phenotype that is determined by a single gene, especially as it relates to disease gene mutations; also known as a *single-gene disease or trait*
Mutation	Refers to a genetic sequence variation with two or more alleles present at a particular DNA sequence position in different individuals. A mutation differs from a *polymorphism* in that the rare allele is observed in less than 1% of the population
Phenotype	Any observable or measurable trait, often determined by the combination of genetic and environmental factors; also known as a *trait*

Table 1.1 (continued)

Polymorphism	A genetic sequence variation with two or more alleles present at a particular DNA sequence position in different individuals. A polymorphism differs from a *mutation* in that the rare allele is observed in more than 1% of the population
Quantitative trait loci (QTLs)	A specific chromosomal location in linkage (cotransmitted) with a gene associated with the phenotype under study
Single nucleotide polymorphism (SNP)	A DNA sequence variation that consists of two different alleles, each of which is only one nucleotide in length

Adapted from Roth [1]

Basics of the Human Genome and DNA Biology

Our genetic material, or genome, is comprised of DNA located in both the nucleus of the cell and the mitochondria [1, 2]. The nuclear genome consists of the bulk of our DNA, including the 22 numbered chromosomes known as autosomes and the sex chromosomes. Each mitochondrion contains a separate smaller DNA component with a small number of genes dedicated to mitochondrial biogenesis and metabolism. Though all of this DNA material is considered the "human genome," the bulk of research interests is focused on the nuclear material and that will be the focus of this chapter.

Within the nucleus are 23 pairs of DNA strands known as chromosomes: 44 autosomes (two copies of each) and 2 sex chromosomes, X and Y. DNA is inherited in a systematic manner with one of each autosome and one sex chromosome being passed down from each parent via sperm or egg (gametes). During the formation of the gametes (gametogenesis), genetic variation is induced; when during meiotic division, chromosomal regions of homologue chromosomes are exchanged (chromosomal crossovers). The egg or sperm therefore contains new combinations of genetic material from the grandparents of the child to be born in a haploid form (23 chromosomes). At conception, egg and sperm fuse and the offspring then acquires the complete DNA complement (2×23 chromosomes). Each chromosome contains a specific complement of genes, and other information that is nearly identical across all individuals with some exceptions is discussed below. Because two copies of each chromosome are present within each nucleus (with the exception of the sex chromosomes in men), each person has two copies of every gene (important exceptions noted below). The consequence is that genetic variation has to be considered for each copy of every gene and the individual in total.

The DNA is housed within the nucleus of the cell where it is accessed by an incredible array of regulatory and transcription-related molecules [3]. The DNA strands total nearly 2 m in length in each nucleus meaning highly efficient packaging is needed. That packaging is in the form of nucleosomes around which DNA is wrapped in a complex three-dimensional arrangement. Regions of DNA that require frequent access by regulatory components are less tightly wrapped than those that are not needed by the cell. Nucleosomes are made up in part by histone proteins that can be chemically modified to alter the ability of DNA to bind, and thus wrap around the nucleosomes. The histone modifications are important for determining the accessibility of DNA to regulatory and transcriptional machinery.

The genetic material provides the information our cells use to build proteins and other cellular components. The DNA contains approximately 23,000 known protein-coding genes along with sequences that encode various RNA-only products. In fact, only a small fraction of DNA is dedicated to protein-coding sequence, so vast stretches of DNA are dedicated to production of regulatory RNAs and other functions. DNA is comprised of two complementary strands of just four nucleotide bases: adenine (A), guanine (G), cytosine (C), and thymine (T). Specific sequences of these four letters provide the information for DNA regulation and RNA/protein production among other functions. Within protein-coding genes, three-letter combinations of these nucleotides in the protein-coding exon sequences (Fig. 1.1) are read at the ribosome in order to assemble the amino acid chain. Sixty-four three-letter codons are possible and their assignment to specific amino acids or stop codons is based on a near-universal genetic code. The genetic code is structured on the RNA sequence, which is complementary to the original DNA sequence with the exception that all thymine nucleotides are replaced with uracil (U).

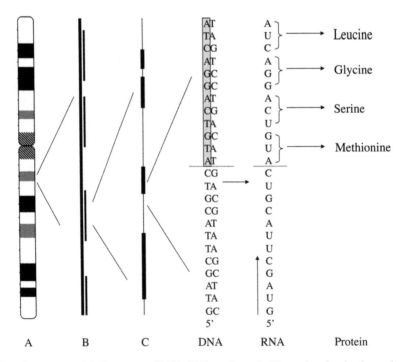

Fig. 1.1 The hierarchical structure of DNA, RNA, and protein. The various levels of organization of DNA regions are shown, as are the processes of transcription (DNA to RNA) and translation (RNA to protein). Adapted, with permission, from Roth [1]

For protein-coding genes, the first stage of the process of building a protein is transcription during which the DNA sequence is copied into a complementary RNA sequence. That initial RNA sequence, which encompasses the entire gene region and includes all introns and exons, then undergoes posttranscriptional modification including the splicing of exons and removal of introns. The mature messenger RNA (mRNA) then moves to the cell cytoplasm where it binds with a ribosome and is subject to translation, a process by which the three-letter codons are translated into an amino acid sequence. The assembled protein often undergoes posttranslational modification as well. The examination of the RNA molecules present in a cell or tissue is known as transcriptomics while the study of proteins present in a cell or tissue is known as proteomics.

The last decade has revealed a considerable role for nonprotein-coding genes, specifically those genes that produce regulatory RNA sequences that are never translated into protein. Many regulatory RNAs are known including micro-RNA (miRNA), small interfering RNA (siRNA), and others. These regulatory RNAs have significant roles in the regulation of gene expression, posttranscriptional modification, and protein interactions [4]. The genes of these regulatory RNAs are also transcribed using the typical transcription machinery, but are often retained in the nucleus to perform their regulatory roles. The importance of regulatory RNAs in exercise-related adaptations has started to emerge recently [5], but little work has been done in this area.

Gene Sequence Variation

Though the "macro" scale of DNA is considered identical across all healthy humans, minor variations in the "micro" scale of our DNA sequence contribute to each individual's unique anatomy, physiology, and disease predisposition. These sequence variations can take many forms (Table 1.2), the most common of which is the single nucleotide polymorphism or SNP. The human genome contains several million SNPs found around the world in which two different nucleotide bases are commonly found at a particular location in the DNA sequence rather than one. Thus, the specific sequence of a particular region of DNA (micro scale) can differ between two individuals while the overall structure of the gene region (macro scale) remains similar.

An example of a SNP frequently studied in the exercise sciences is in the beta-2-adrenergic receptor (*ADRB2*) gene. In the 27th codon of the gene, individuals in a population will carry either a cytosine (C) or guanine (G) nucleotide [6, 7]. Thus, because the gene has two copies in the genome, individuals can carry a genotype of C/C, C/G, or G/G, representing the two alleles present between the two gene copies.

While SNPs are the most common type of genetic variation, several other types of variation are also important. For example, variable number tandem repeat sequences (VNTRs) are short, repetitive sequences of DNA in which the number of repeats is variable among individuals (Table 1.2). For example, the androgen receptor

Table 1.2 Common types of DNA sequence variation

Type of variation	Example DNA sequences – chromosome copy 1 and copy 2[a]	Alleles	Possible genotypes
Single nucleotide polymorphism (SNP)	ACT GGT CAT GCA ATT CCT GAT ACT GGT CAT GAA ATT CCT GAT	C and A	C/C; C/A; A/A
Insertion/deletion polymorphism	ACT GGT CAT GCA ATT CCT GAT ACT GGT CAT G - - ATT CCT GAT	Insertion (I) and deletion (D)	I/I; I/D; D/D
Variable nucleotide tandem repeat (VNTR)	ACT GGT CAT GCA **CAG CAG** ATT CCT GAT ACT GGT CAT GCA **CAG CAG CAG CAG CAG CAG** ATT CCT GAT	Number of CAG sequences (2 and 5 shown); variable number across many individuals	Many possible, reflecting the many possible numbers of repeats
Copy number variation (CNV)	ACT GGT CAT **(GCA … AAA) (GCA … AAA)** ATT CCT GAT ACT GGT CAT **(GCA … AAA)** - - - … - - - ATT CCT GAT	Large sequences (1,000 bp up to 5 Mb) can occur in multiple copies, or be deleted	Multiple possible, reflecting the number of duplicates or loss (deletion)

[a] Only one strand of DNA double helix is shown

(*AR*) gene contains a VNTR in its first exon in which the sequence CAG is repeated several times. On average, individuals carry about 20 CAG repeats in series in this region of the gene, though the range is from 15 to 30 in healthy individuals (repeat numbers higher than 40 often result in disease) [8]. In addition to VNTRs, entire fragments of DNA sequence can be present or absent from a gene region. These variants are known as insertion-deletion polymorphisms in which some members of a population will have a specific sequence fragment present while others will not (Table 1.2). A common example in exercise science is an insertion/deletion poly-morphism in the angiotensin converting enzyme (*ACE*) gene that has been related to endurance performance phenotypes [9].

Another type of variation that has recently gained attention is known as a copy number variation (CNV). In this case, entire genes are found duplicated (or more) or deleted on one or both chromosome copies with the result being the total number of genes present in an individual can be different from two (Table 1.2). While CNVs have been previously associated with Mendelian-type diseases, more recent investigations have identified CNVs that are quite common in healthy individuals and may make substantial contributions to common disease risk [10, 11]. For example, a higher copy number of the chemokine gene *CCL3L1* has recently been associated with elevated risk for rheumatoid arthritis [12].

As described above, DNA is accessed primarily as an information source for the transcription of RNA sequences that are then often translated into proteins. The genetic variants present throughout the genome have the capacity to disrupt regula-tion of these transcription processes by altering transcription factor binding sites or other regions important to posttranscription processing. When variants are present within the coding region of a protein-coding gene, the consequences may include a change in the amino acid sequence of the final protein (i.e., a missense variant) or even the introduction of a novel stop codon (i.e., a nonsense variant). For example, the alpha-actinin-3 (*ACTN3*) gene harbors a nonsense polymorphism in which indi-viduals either carry a C-allele in exon 16 that encodes the amino acid arginine (codon: CGA) or carry a T-allele that results in a premature stop codon (codon: UGA) [13]. Thus, individuals with two copies of the T-allele would have two gene copies with premature stop codons resulting in no functional copies of the gene and deficiency of the alpha-actinin-3 protein. Having two copies of the premature stop codon has been associated with lower skeletal muscle performance, elite-level sprint performance in particular [14]. This polymorphism is also known as R577X, which denotes the different consequences of the two DNA alleles at the protein with either arginine (R-allele) or no amino acid (X-allele) encoded at the ribosome. Similarly, the C/G polymorphism in *ADRB2* described above is a missense poly-morphism resulting in either a glutamine or glutamic acid being encoded in the protein; the polymorphism is often labeled as Gln27Glu.

Importantly, gene variants do not act in an isolated manner. Rather, each gene region is likely to contain many gene variants that will often act in concert (i.e., as a haplotype) with their overall impact on that gene region. For example, the *ADRB2* gene harbors not only the Gln27Glu missense polymorphism but also the nearby Arg16Gly missense polymorphism in codon 16. Accounting for multiple genetic variants (both within and across genes) is a major challenge in studying the genetic contributions to a particular trait. One typical approach to examining a larger fraction of genetic variation within a gene region is by studying haplotypes rather than individual genotypes. Haplotypes represent specific combinations of alleles at nearby polymorphisms in a gene region that tend to travel together during chromosome recombination events associated with sex cell development [15]. Alleles that are linked in this manner are said to be in linkage disequilibrium (LD). Specific haplotypes can then be studied in relation to disease, allowing a broader analysis of the genetic variation within a gene region. A common example of a haplotype is found in the *APOE* gene in which two nearby missense polymorphisms, Arg112Cys and Arg158Cys, are in LD. Specific combinations of the alleles in these polymorphisms are commonly found in a population. The combination of Cys112 and Cys158 together on the same strand of DNA is a haplotype that is known as ε2, while the combination of Arg112 and Arg158 on the same strand of DNA is known as haplotype ε4. The ε4 haplotype has been significantly associated with Alzheimer's disease risk [16], though interactions with physical activity appear to reduce that risk [17, 18].

A brief note about gene nomenclature is useful here. For humans, gene labels (as determined by gene databases; see Appendix) are written using all capital letters in italics, such as *ACTN3* and *APOE*. The proteins encoded by those genes are generally written with capital letters without italics or using other standard conventions in the literature. For example, the gene for insulin-like growth factor 1 would be written as *IGF1* while the protein would be abbreviated as IGF-I. For mice, the other common species for studying genetic influences on exercise- and health-related traits, gene labels are written in italics using only the first letter capitalized, such as *Actn3* or *Apoe*, with proteins following the same approach as with humans. Readers are referred to various web-based resources listed in Appendix for specific gene labels and other information for specific genes of interest.

With regard to gene polymorphism nomenclature, SNP labels generally include the two alleles present at the site along with a number indicating the specific nucleotide position (e.g., A57T). Additional details, generally present in the initial report of the SNP, are needed to confirm the specific location (e.g., within exon 2, etc.). Insertion/deletion polymorphisms follow a similar convention, with the labels I and D used to indicate the alleles. When these SNPs are missense or nonsense, then the two possible amino acids are abbreviated (one- or three-letter abbreviations) with the label's number indicating the specific amino acid position (e.g., Arg158Cys or R577X). Most polymorphisms are now cataloged in gene variation databases (e.g., Entrez SNP or dbSNP; see Appendix) and are registered with specific "reference SNP" or "rs" numbers that allow researchers to get additional detailed information about the DNA sequence surrounding the polymorphism, the nucleotide position, alleles present, and additional details regarding studies associated with the particular variant. For example, the R577X nonsense polymorphism is registered as rs1815739.

Contributions to Trait Variability

As described above, genetic sequence variation can contribute to phenotypic variation, but several questions are raised: what is the evidence genetic factors contribute to interindividual variation in exercise responses and adaptations? in what ways do genetic factors contribute to these traits? and how do we study these genetic contributions? The reader is referred to the specific chapters in this book for details about specific exercise-related phenotypes; in the remainder of this chapter, a general overview of some of the primary approaches to answering these important questions is provided.

With an eye to the historical aspects of exercise genomics, the profound variability in various exercise performance-related phenotypes should be noted. Interindividual variability in anthropomorphic characteristics is easily visible in even homogeneous populations. These first observations led to the initiation of family-based investigations seeking to determine rough estimates of genetic vs. environmental contributions to this variability. More quantitative studies of the variability of exercise adaptation phenotypes have made their way into the literature more recently [19, 20], including extensive reporting of variability in a number of traits related to aerobic exercise training documented as part of the *HE*ealth, *RI*sk factors, exercise *TrA*ining and *Ge*netics (HERITAGE) Family Study [21–23]. These investigations have provided a foundation from which specific studies of genetic contribution can be performed.

In general, complex traits are governed by both genetic and environmental factors, but determining the fraction of variability attributed to each is very challenging [24]. Both genetic and environmental factors can contribute to complex traits in various ways, making such distinctions challenging. For example, a genetic influence can be either dominant or recessive, meaning for a dominant influence only one allele copy is necessary, while a recessive allele must be present on both gene copies to have an effect on the trait. When both alleles contribute equally, they are considered additive. Beyond dominant and recessive influences, genetic factors may only influence a phenotype when in interaction with another gene or environmental factor. Such gene×gene interactions, known as epistasis, are remarkably challenging to identify because of the many combinations of different genes and gene variants that might be interacting. With regard to environment, unique vs. common environmental factors can be distinguished, i.e., common environmental factors impact all individuals within a sample or family, while unique factors are specific to a particular individual.

In general, two major approaches are recognized to study the importance of genetic factors in complex traits: (1) the unmeasured genotype or top-down approach and (2) the measured genotype or bottom-up approach [25]. Below, the methodologies applied in the study of human variation in exercise performance and health-related phenotypes based on both approaches are presented with the older unmeasured approach discussed first.

Familial Aggregation and Heritability

When the measured genotype is not available (historically the measured approach was not feasible up to a few decades ago), inferences about genetic influences on a phenotype are based on statistical analyses of the similarities in performance or health-related measures in genetically related individuals and families based on the theoretical framework of biometrical genetics, i.e., top-down approach (Chap. 3 in Neale et al. [26]). In this approach, two major study designs are used to quantify genetic and environmental contributions to the observed variation in multifactorial phenotypes: twin studies and family studies. In twin studies, monozygotic (MZ) and dizygotic (DZ) twins are studied. Since MZ or identical twins have an identical genetic background, they will be more similar (higher intrapair correlation) in a trait that is under genetic control than DZ twins who share on average half of their genetic variation. When using twin data, genetic as well as environmental factors unique to the individual and shared within families can be identified. Under certain assumptions, dominant genetic effects also can be identified.

In family studies, the similarities among parents and offspring and between sisters and brothers are studied. This approach allows the identification of genetic plus cultural transmission of traits and estimates of maximum transmissibility. If disease status is studied, familial aggregation examines the risk ratio of an individual having the disease given his/her relative has the disease compared to the overall population risk of having the disease. Multiple designs can be used to quantify this risk; however, it is never an exact estimate of the true genetic risk [27]. If data from more extended or combined pedigrees (e.g., twins and their parents) are included, more sophisticated models can be tested. Analyses of different familial or twin covariances can be done using path analysis, in which several of the contributing sources of variation mentioned above can be quantified by testing a hypothetical model to the observed familial (or twin) variation/covariation matrices [26].

Heritability is the quantitative estimate of the importance of genetic factors to a trait. Assessment of heritability is based on the basic genetic model that the total variation (V_{tot}) in traits is partitioned into genetic (V_G), common environmental (V_C), and individual-specific or unique environmental (V_E) variance components ($V_{tot} = V_G + V_C + V_E$) [1, 2]. Heritability ($h^2$) refers to the proportion of the total variation that can be attributed to genetic effects (V_G/V_{tot}). In most studies, it is assumed that the effects of different genes are additive (a^2), meaning the genotypic effect of the heterozygote genotype on the phenotype falls between the genotypic effects of both homozygote genotypes. Dominance genetic effects refer to the interaction between alleles at the same locus (heterozygote effect is not intermediate between the two homozygote genotype effects), and epistasis describes the interaction between alleles at different loci. The contribution of environmental factors shared by family members (common environmental factors, $c^2 = V_C/V_{tot}$) and the proportion of environmental factors that act on an individual level can also be estimated ($e^2 = V_E/V_{tot}$) [1, 2].

When using this additive genetic model of sources of variation, several assumptions should be met: no interaction between gene action and environment (different genotypes all react equally to similar environmental factors); no gene×environment correlation (similar exposure of environments for different genotypes); no gene × gene interaction; and no assortative mating for the trait (one assumes people mate randomly for the phenotype in question). In all likelihood, most influences on exercise performance- or health-related measurements do not follow all of these assumptions. The heritability coefficient is specific for the studied population, and can be estimated using analysis of variance (ANOVA) or genetic modeling techniques. All of these methods provide only a measure of the importance of genetic factors for a particular trait, whereas more sophisticated genetic models (e.g., complex segregation analysis) can provide indications of the actions of major genes and modes of inheritance among others.

Special attention is given to the analysis of genotype × environment interaction in the unmeasured genotype approach. As intervention studies (e.g., endurance or resistance training, diet interventions) are of major focus in exercise science, the underlying sources of interindividual variation in responses to those interventions can also be studied. Bouchard et al. [28] applied the MZ twin design in several intervention studies [29] (i.e., overfeeding, energy restriction, endurance training, intermittent training). Individual differences in the responses to the intervention are decomposed in within-pairs (same genotype) and between-pairs (different genotypes) variances based on measurements before and after the intervention. A larger variance between MZ pairs compared to the within-pair variance suggests the response to the experimental treatment is more heterogeneous in subjects who are genetically different. Also, intraclass correlations for the absolute or relative responses in the MZ twins are informative for the similarity in response and the importance of genotype × environment interaction. For example, seven MZ twin pairs in the long-term negative energy balance protocol study by Bouchard and Tremblay [29] showed a high similarity in the change in visceral fat (cm²; intrapair correlation of $r=0.84$), and the genotype × treatment F-value was 11.7, meaning there was about 12 times larger variation in treatment response between MZ pairs compared to the within pair variance in response. Thus, the unmeasured genotype approach provides an estimate of the importance of genetic factors to a trait of interest, providing an important foundation for measured genotype approaches that seek to identify specific gene regions and genetic factors that contribute to the trait.

Measured Genotype Approaches

Linkage Analysis

The measured genotype methods (bottom-up approach) are used to identify specific genes that contribute to a multifactorial phenotype. Complementary strategies are available in humans to identify genes that explain variability in complex traits as studied in the wide field of exercise sciences (Fig. 1.2). First, attempts to localize and identify individual gene regions (i.e., loci) that make up the genetic component of performance phenotypes by quantitative trait loci (QTLs) linkage analysis are briefly discussed.

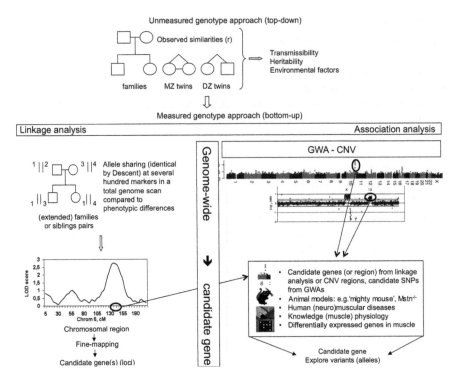

Fig. 1.2 Schematic representation of unmeasured and measured genotype methods in the search for genetic influences on performance and exercise adaptation (adapted from Beunen and Thomis [63]). The *upper part* of the panel (unmeasured genotype approach) shows schematically the study of phenotypes in family and twin studies in which similarities yield information on the heritability of a trait (□ male; ○ female; □–○ mating parents). The *lower part* shows a continuum of methods in the measured genotype approach. In linkage analysis (*left*), a nuclear family is shown with marker allele information (e.g., 1‖2, represents allele 1 at one of the chromosomes and allele 2 at the other chromosome in the father), which forms the basis to estimate the amount of alleles (by descent) related individuals share at the marker locus. This information is then linked with the phenotypic differences (e.g., in strength) between those related individuals. Linkage analysis will provide information of chromosomal locations, harboring quantitative trait loci. The figure on the *left* shows the hypothetical results from a linkage analysis study of several microsatellite loci on chromosome 6. The *right* part of the figure represents genome-wide and candidate gene strategies in genetic association studies. On *top*, a "Manhattan plot" and "genome-wide copy number plot" is represented. Significant findings in these genome-wide analyses form the basis for follow-up studies at the candidate gene level. Additional strategies to select candidate genes are included in the text box

Second, methodology for allelic association studies is described. Within the scope of this chapter, only general descriptions of both approaches are presented.

Linkage analysis is an important initial tool for mapping genetic loci. One of the advantages is that it requires no a priori knowledge of physiological mechanisms. A total genome linkage study uses several hundreds of highly variant DNA markers regularly spaced (e.g., each 5–10 cM) throughout the human genome (e.g., Marshfield map 7 [30]) or large sets of SNP panels (e.g., Illumina SNP-based linkage panel IV – 5,861 SNPs). Both parametric and nonparametric methods are now available to test whether a marker at a specific location is in linkage (cotransmitted) with a gene causing the phenotype under study. In a quantitative trait such as muscular strength, the gene or locus is called a QTL. In the parametric method, the recombination fraction between a marker and a causal gene is tested with the logarithm of the odds (LOD) score, with a value of 3 (1,000-to-1 odds in favor of linkage) indicating significant linkage between a marker locus and a locus causing the phenotype ($\theta < 0.5$).

Among other parameters like penetrance and (disease) allele frequencies, the mode of inheritance is needed to perform this type of model-based analysis on family data. Since health-related and exercise performance characteristics are determined by environmental factors and a large set of genes of which the mode of inheritance is unknown, several model free (or nonparametric) methods have been developed [31, 32], mostly applied in sibling pair or nuclear family datasets. All available methods link a measure of "genetic relatedness" at the genetic marker, with "phenotypic (dis)similarity." This genetic relatedness is based on the determination of the number of alleles that two relatives "share" when it is known they are inherited from the same ancestral chromosome. For example, two siblings both have the genotypes "4/2" at a marker locus. From parental and grandparental genotypes, one can derive that both sibs share allele #4 from their father's father, whereas one of them received allele #2 from his mother's mother, and the other from his mother's father. Their identical by descent (IBD) status at this locus is then 1, although they have both alleles identical by state (IBS). Several methods have been proposed to determine the expected proportion of alleles IBD from marker genotype data of which the Lander-Green algorithm is often applied [31, 32]. In 1972, Haseman and Elston developed a regression method (reviewed in Ferreira [31] and Sham [32]) for the analysis of sibling pair data. Evidence for linkage is provided when the squared sibling pair trait differences decrease with an increase in the proportion of alleles shared IBD at the marker locus. This method has been updated [33], and variance component methods have been developed [31, 32].

Multipoint linkage mapping refers to the fact that genotypic data of nearby flanking markers is used together with the marker of interest to better estimate the number of alleles shared by individuals at the marker of interest. Linkage analysis will only result in the identification of chromosomal regions that can contain several tens to hundreds of genes. Also QTLs that contribute to less than 10% of the overall phenotypic variation need very large samples to be detected with sufficient power. Fine mapping strategies are then needed to follow up the search for specific genes and gene variants. Several approaches are used often in different stages or steps to narrow down this large region [34]. Such approaches are described in several chapters of this book for various traits.

Genetic Association Studies

A second set of strategies concerns allelic association studies. This approach examines the effect of a specific (polymorphic) marker allele, until now mostly within a candidate gene on the mean exercise- or health-related trait value in groups of different genotypes for this polymorphism. Significant differences in allele frequencies in a case control design can also be tested, meaning the occurrence of one specific allele is counted in a group such as elite athletes and compared to the frequency of this allele in a control group. SNPs, insertion/deletion polymorphisms, or VNTRs (Table 1.2) can be used in allelic association studies. When a positive association is found, the "increasing" allele under study might be the true functional variant or might be in tight linkage (i.e., LD) with the true functional allele. Often, multiple polymorphisms within one or more genes are studied. Instead of testing for association with each polymorphism separately, haplotypes can be analyzed and then tested to determine whether a specific haplotype is associated with increased or decreased phenotype. Statistical considerations are described in greater detail in Chap. 2.

Association studies do not need genetically related subjects; however, family data can be included in the analyses to overcome problems of hidden population stratification, an effect that could induce false positive association findings [32]. The success of association analysis depends largely on the choice of the candidate gene(s) under study. Figure 1.2 presents several possible "guiding" sources of information to select good candidate genes. These sources could be (1) the QTL, or genes under the highest linkage peaks from genome-wide association studies (GWAS) or designed-linkage analysis; CNV regions or SNPs from GWAS (discussed below); (2) animal models (e.g., $Mstn^{-/-}$ or "mighty" mouse [35]) related to the specific characteristics of the phenotype; (3) knowledge of genes involved in the pathophysiology of diseases related to the phenotype under study; (4) knowledge of genes involved in typical physiology (e.g., muscle physiology); and (5) differences in gene expression (mRNA) levels based on gene expression microarray scans between, e.g., high or low responders to an exercise regimen. Presently a shift is seen from "single candidate gene studies" to multiple gene studies, or studies exploring gene variants within certain (signaling) pathways. Gene × gene interactions (combined action of polymorphisms in genes A and B, known as epistasis) are also studied; however, large sample sizes are needed to have sufficient power to test interaction effects.

Gene × environment interaction studies focus on the mediating effect of the environment given a specific genotype (see also Chap. 4 by Franks and Brito). Although focus is presently on the discovery of causal sequence variation in explaining phenotypic variation, both cohort or population studies with measured environmental factors could provide insight into the mediating effects of environmental factors [36, 37]. However, true cause-effect might be best studied in smaller intervention studies in which the environmental factors are strongly standardized and the responses to these environments very well characterized. Such approaches are well suited to exercise genomics (also referred to as kinesiogenomics [1] or genetophysiology [38]), which emphasizes the role of exercise training as an interacting influence on the relationship between gene variants and health-related traits.

Genome-Wide Association Studies

Given the reduction in genotyping cost and the development of high-throughput SNP array techniques, it has become possible to genotype 500,000–1,000,000 SNPs per individual and associate these genotypes with the phenotype of interest. This approach, known as GWAS, has been successfully applied to the search for genes in complex diseases or traits like type 2 diabetes [39], body composition [40], Crohn's disease [41] and a first GWAS has been published on physical activity behavior [42]. Like linkage analysis, no a priori knowledge about candidate genes is needed as this technique is seen as a hypothesis free or hypothesis-generating approach. Furthermore, the outcome of GWAS is the identification/detection of specific variants (SNPs) that are either the functional SNPs themselves or are in close LD with the functional variants. However, the significance threshold for 500,000 ANOVA tests is very stringent ($p < 0.00000001$), and large numbers of subjects (thousands) need to be genotyped, both in the discovery phase and in replication and follow up phases. As a consequence, GWAS are performed on a "consortium" basis and are able to discover genetic variants with small effect sizes (e.g., the fat mass and obesity associated (*FTO*) gene variants increase body mass index (BMI) by 0.4–0.66 units per risk allele [43]). As GWAS are also informative for the study of CNVs [11, 44], the efforts taken for GWAS will be extended by the study of CNVs, and the association tests for copy number polymorphisms [45] are now available to be applied to complex disease and exercise-related phenotypes [46]. Additional details on GWAS can be found in Chap. 2.

Whole Genome Sequencing

The introduction of GWAS has proved fruitful for a number of fields and may shed light on the gene variants important to exercise-related adaptations. Yet, GWAS have significant limitations especially when contributing variants have rare alleles. Growing literature is indicating that at least a fraction of the genetic contribution in complex common disease traits is determined by relatively rare alleles [47]. Combinations of these rare alleles would then contribute, perhaps in concert with more common alleles, to the phenotypic outcome.

Despite the progress made by GWAS, a surprising finding is how little GWAS have contributed to the identification of genetic factors for some traits, providing support for the rare allele hypothesis [47]. These findings are pointing more and more to a future of whole genome sequencing that would allow identification and analysis of all gene variants in an individual. While the technology does exist, at present the costs are too high to allow for meaningful analysis of population scale risk. Moreover, the analysis techniques needed to fully exploit a full genome sequence in relation to disease risk are only beginning to be developed. But recognition is growing that future clinical usefulness of genetic information will ultimately hinge not only on population attributable risk but also on individual disease prediction and treatment outcomes that will be derived from an individual's DNA sequence. As costs drop over the next decade to an anticipated $1,000 per genome, larger scale studies will be designed that will exploit both common and rare alleles (and their combinations, i.e., deep sequencing) to more accurately determine genetic contributions for complex disease traits.

Functional Genomics

Functional genomics is the phrase often used to describe the process of identifying the functional effects of particular gene variants, confirming the causality of an association. Because of the issue of LD described previously in this chapter and in Chap. 2, a gene variant associated with a trait of interest may not necessarily be causally linked with that trait. In many cases, common alleles are in LD with a number of nearby alleles, so the specific functional effect of a specific gene variant needs to be verified. For example, an intronic polymorphism may have an impact on a regulatory region within a gene, it might also contribute variation to a miRNA that works through a completely different regulatory pathway, or it may instead not have any direct relevance at all to a trait, the association representing only LD with the true functional polymorphism in another area of the genome. While a gene association by itself can have clinical importance even if the causality of the association is unknown, functional genomics studies seek to fully understand the biology underlying a specific gene association. Such an understanding will allow for eventual exploitation of the gene variant for prevention or treatment approaches.

An example of the functional genomics approach in the exercise sciences has recently emerged around the *ACTN3* gene. As described above, this gene harbors a nonsense polymorphism known as R577X, in which individuals either carry an R allele that encodes the amino acid arginine in the protein sequence or carry a premature stop codon (X allele) that renders the protein inactive. Individuals carrying two copies of the X allele (i.e., X/X genotype) are deficient in alpha-actinin-3 protein owing to stop codon generating alleles in both *ACTN3* gene copies. Several associations with the X/X genotype have been found for athletic performance [48–50] and while the lack of a protein clearly establishes the X allele as a causal gene variant, how the lack of the protein results in associations with performance is currently unknown. Recent studies have thus sought to identify the underlying biology (e.g., functional genomics) of this association by examining more specific phenotypes that underlie performance (e.g., muscle strength, muscle fiber type proportion, muscle gene expression) [51, 52], and also through the development of a knockout mouse model, in which both copies of the Actn3 gene have been rendered nonfunctional (*Actn3$^{-/-}$*) that might shed further light on underlying mechanisms [53, 54].

Epigenomics

While the bulk of this book will be focused on the role of DNA sequence variation in interindividual variation in exercise responses and adaptations, another level of genetic contribution is being recognized as likely contributing to complex disease traits. Epigenomics refers to chemical modifications of the genome that can alter the regulation of the DNA sequence without altering the sequence itself. Epigenomics encompasses several chemical modifications including DNA methylation as well as various chemical modifications of histones such as methylation or acetylation. These chemical modifications affect DNA nucleotides either directly (e.g., cytosine methylation in the DNA sequence) or indirectly (e.g., density of DNA packaging around the histone proteins). Epigenomic modifications of DNA sequence and histone proteins have been shown to affect gene transcription. For example, increased levels of methylation in the promoter of a gene region can reduce transcription of that gene.

While the contributions of epigenomic mechanisms to disease biology are only beginning to be known, the emerging information points to a source of genetic contribution that might be quite substantial [55, 56]. Epigenomic factors have been studied for many years in cancer, and there is clear recognition that epigenomic modifications play an important role in tumorigenesis. In animal models, dietary factors have been shown to alter methylation of various genes in multiple tissues across multiple generations [57, 58]. In humans, epigenomic factors are known to result in some Mendelian diseases [59], and both alcohol and tobacco consumption have been shown to alter methylation of gene promoters [60]. While minimal work has been done in the area of exercise, there is little doubt chemical modifications of DNA that alter gene transcription will necessarily alter an individual's response to an exercise stimulus. Thus, epigenomic regulation becomes another layer of genetic contribution to complex traits.

Systems Biology

The complexity of genetic variation and epigenomic contributions to complex disease traits is made more complex by the interaction of these components with various environmental factors. In effect, acute exercise and exercise training are environmental stimuli that influence gene transcription across multiple tissues, thus interacting with specific genes and gene variants with implications for numerous phenotypes. While reductionist methods have yielded important information about the specific genes and pathways that underlie the anatomical and physiological adaptations to exercise, optimizing the use of exercise for disease prevention and treatment will necessarily mean understanding the more complex picture of interaction among various genetic/epigenomic and environmental factors. The field of systems biology has that large scale understanding of multiple biological mechanisms underlie a trait as its goal.

In particular, systems biology seeks to understand biological networks that inform disease-related traits, in effect linking the molecular pathways back to the anatomical and physiological systems [61, 62]. Various environmental factors will disrupt the homeostasis of these networks in different (presumably predictable) ways, and genetic variation will result in interindividual differences in network responses, and thus phenotypic outcomes. Advances in technology will allow greater understanding of these networks and how their various components interact to yield a particular trait outcome. While such work is only now emerging in the exercise sciences, we have no doubt that such approaches will quickly become mainstream.

The Future?

As described in some of the sections above, genetic technologies are advancing rapidly. GWAS are quickly becoming the standard approach in genetic association analysis, and advances in systems biology and functional genomics are making detailed functional analysis of candidate genes and polymorphisms easier to tackle. Large scale consortia have been organized for a number of health-related traits to better perform well-powered GWAS and genetic epidemiology investigations. Such consortia will be equally important in exercise genomics studies where the high costs and complex logistics of exercise training make execution of such studies very challenging. More and more investigations will be able to address multiple levels of analysis within a single study, such as genetic association, epigenomics, and functional genomics. Such studies will help solidify those candidate genes and polymorphisms emerging from the GWAS findings and help establish the clinical and translational relevance of those loci for public health. Analytical approaches that rely on whole genome sequences will first emerge in areas of unique genomic diseases, especially cancer, but will then quickly spread to other disciplines. No doubt there will be rare alleles hidden from GWAS that will emerge as important regulators of exercise-related traits using such whole genome deep sequencing approaches. And as we learn more about the genes and polymorphisms that conclusively contribute to exercise- and health-related traits, we will have learned more about the significant interindividual variability that has plagued our interpretation of exercise and other interventions for many years. Thus, professionals in kinesiology, public health, and sports medicine will be able to return to those intervention studies with the knowledge gained from years of reductionist methods and better understand the physiological variability that underlies individual responses and move toward the personalized medicine that has been the very promise of genomics and genomic medicine for many years.

Practical Implications

The components of this chapter provide the reader with an overview of DNA biology and its relevance to the study of interindividual differences in exercise-related responses and adaptations and other health-related traits. Various references are included, most of which provide points of entry for further in-depth reading and understanding of the various topics covered. In addition to this broad framework, this chapter also introduced readers to some emerging areas of science that we see as informing future research in exercise genomics. The last decade has brought enormous and in some ways unpredictable changes to the pace and direction of research to date, so continued uncertainty must be expected. At minimum, readers can take the information presented here and comfortably access much of the genomics-related literature in the exercise science field and have a reasonable grasp of the issues that will inform research into the near future. Readers are encouraged to read Chap. 2 for additional practical information for moving forward with research in exercise genomics.

References

1. Roth SM. Genetics primer for exercise science and health. Champaign: Human Kinetics; 2007.
2. Bouchard C, Malina RM, Perusse L. Genetics of fitness and physical performance. Champaign: Human Kinetics; 1997.
3. Attia J, Ioannidis JP, Thakkinstian A, McEvoy M, Scott RJ, Minelli C, et al. How to use an article about genetic association: A: background concepts. JAMA. 2009;301(1):74–81.
4. Carninci P, Hayashizaki Y. Noncoding RNA transcription beyond annotated genes. Curr Opin Genet Dev. 2007;17(2):139–44.
5. Safdar A, Abadi A, Akhtar M, Hettinga BP, Tarnopolsky MA. miRNA in the regulation of skeletal muscle adaptation to acute endurance exercise in C57Bl/6J male mice. PLoS One. 2009;4(5):e5610.
6. Large V, Hellstrom L, Reynisdottir S, Lonnqvist F, Eriksson P, Lannfelt L, et al. Human beta-2 adrenoceptor gene polymorphisms are highly frequent in obesity and associate with altered adipocyte beta-2 adrenoceptor function. J Clin Invest. 1997;100(12):3005–13.
7. Bray MS, Hagberg JM, Perusse L, Rankinen T, Roth SM, Wolfarth B, et al. The human gene map for performance and health-related fitness phenotypes: the 2006–2007 update. Med Sci Sports Exerc. 2009;41(1):35–73.
8. Nelson KA, Witte JS. Androgen receptor CAG repeats and prostate cancer. Am J Epidemiol. 2002;155(10):883–90.
9. Woods D. Angiotensin-converting enzyme, renin-angiotensin system and human performance. Med Sport Sci. 2009;54:72–87.
10. Ionita-Laza I, Rogers AJ, Lange C, Raby BA, Lee C. Genetic association analysis of copy-number variation (CNV) in human disease pathogenesis. Genomics. 2009;93(1):22–6.
11. Conrad DF, Pinto D, Redon R, Feuk L, Gokcumen O, Zhang Y, et al. Origins and functional impact of copy number variation in the human genome. Nature. 2010;464(7289):704–12.
12. McKinney C, Merriman ME, Chapman PT, Gow PJ, Harrison AA, Highton J, et al. Evidence for an influence of chemokine ligand 3-like 1 (CCL3L1) gene copy number on susceptibility to rheumatoid arthritis. Ann Rheum Dis. 2008;67(3):409–13.
13. North KN, Yang N, Wattanasirichaigoon D, Mills M, Easteal S, Beggs AH. A common non-sense mutation results in alpha-actinin-3 deficiency in the general population. Nat Genet. 1999;21(4):353–4.
14. Yang N, Garton F, North K. Alpha-actinin-3 and performance. Med Sport Sci. 2009;54:88–101.
15. Crawford DC, Nickerson DA. Definition and clinical importance of haplotypes. Annu Rev Med. 2005;56:303–20.
16. Green RC, Roberts JS, Cupples LA, Relkin NR, Whitehouse PJ, Brown T, et al. Disclosure of APOE genotype for risk of Alzheimer's disease. N Engl J Med. 2009;361(3):245–54.

17. Rovio S, Kareholt I, Helkala E-L, Viitanen M, Winblad B, Tuomilehto J, et al. Leisure-time physical activity at midlife and the risk of dementia and Alzheimer's disease. Lancet Neurol. 2005;4(11):705–11.
18. Schuit AJ, Feskens EJ, Launer LJ, Kromhout D. Physical activity and cognitive decline, the role of the apolipoprotein e4 allele. Med Sci Sports Exerc. 2001;33(5):772–7.
19. Bouchard C, Rankinen T. Individual differences in response to regular physical activity. Med Sci Sports Exerc. 2001;33(6 Suppl):S446–51. discussion S452–3.
20. Hubal MJ, Gordish-Dressman H, Thompson PD, Price TB, Hoffman EP, Angelopoulos TJ, et al. Variability in muscle size and strength gain after unilateral resistance training. Med Sci Sports Exerc. 2005;37(6):964–72.
21. Bouchard C, An P, Rice T, Skinner JS, Wilmore JH, Gagnon J, et al. Familial aggregation of VO2 max response to exercise training: results from the HERITAGE family study. J Appl Physiol. 1999;87(3):1003–8.
22. Leon AS, Gaskill SE, Rice T, Bergeron J, Gagnon J, Rao DC, et al. Variability in the response of HDL cholesterol to exercise training in the HERITAGE family study. Int J Sports Med. 2002;23(1):1–9.
23. Boule NG, Weisnagel SJ, Lakka TA, Tremblay A, Bergman RN, Rankinen T, et al. Effects of exercise training on glucose homeostasis: the HERITAGE family study. Diabetes Care. 2005;28(1):108–14.
24. Hemminki K, Lorenzo Bermejo J, Forsti A. The balance between heritable and environmental aetiology of human disease. Nat Rev Genet. 2006;7(12):958–65.
25. Sing CF, Boerwinkle EA. Genetic architecture of inter-individual variability in apolipoprotein, lipoprotein and lipid phenotypes. Ciba Found Symp. 1987;130:99–127.
26. Neale MC, Cardon LR, North Atlantic Treaty Organization, Scientific Affairs Division. Methodology for genetic studies of twins and families. Boston: Kluwer Academic Publishers; 1992.
27. Zimmerman R, Pal DK, Tin A, Ahsan H, Greenberg DA. Methods for assessing familial aggregation: family history measures and confounding in the standard cohort, reconstructed cohort and case-control designs. Hum Hered. 2009;68(3):201–8.
28. Bouchard C, Perusse L, Leblanc C. Using MZ twins in experimental research to test for the presence of a genotype-environment interaction effect. Acta Genet Med Gemellol (Roma). 1990;39(1):85–9.
29. Bouchard C, Tremblay A. Genetic influences on the response of body fat and fat distribution to positive and negative energy balances in human identical twins. J Nutr. 1997;127(5 Suppl):943S–7.
30. Broman KW, Murray JC, Sheffield VC, White RL, Weber JL. Comprehensive human genetic maps: individual and sex-specific variation in recombination. Am J Hum Genet. 1998;63(3):861–9.
31. Ferreira MA. Linkage analysis: principles and methods for the analysis of human quantitative traits. Twin Res. 2004;7(5):513–30.
32. Sham P. Statistics in human genetics. London: Wiley; 1997.
33. Sham PC, Purcell S, Cherny SS, Abecasis GR. Powerful regression-based quantitative-trait linkage analysis of general pedigrees. Am J Hum Genet. 2002;71(2):238–53.
34. Windelinckx A, Vlietinck R, Aerssens J, Beunen G, Thomis MA. Selection of genes and single nucleotide polymorphisms for fine mapping starting from a broad linkage region. Twin Res Hum Genet. 2007;10(6):871–85.
35. McPherron AC, Lawler AM, Lee SJ. Regulation of skeletal muscle mass in mice by a new TGF-beta superfamily member. Nature. 1997;387(6628):83–90.
36. Bouchard C. Gene-environment interactions in the etiology of obesity: defining the fundamentals. Obesity (Silver Spring). 2008;16 Suppl 3:S5–10.
37. Vimaleswaran KS, Li S, Zhao JH, Luan J, Bingham SA, Khaw KT, et al. Physical activity attenuates the body mass index-increasing influence of genetic variation in the FTO gene. Am J Clin Nutr. 2009;90(2):425–8.
38. Grocott M, Montgomery H. Genetophysiology: using genetic strategies to explore hypoxic adaptation. High Alt Med Biol. 2008;9(2):123–9.

39. Frayling TM. Genome-wide association studies provide new insights into type 2 diabetes aetiology. Nat Rev Genet. 2007;8(9):657–62.
40. Loos RJ, Lindgren CM, Li S, Wheeler E, Zhao JH, Prokopenko I, et al. Common variants near MC4R are associated with fat mass, weight and risk of obesity. Nat Genet. 2008;40(6):768–75.
41. Barrett JC, Hansoul S, Nicolae DL, Cho JH, Duerr RH, Rioux JD, et al. Genome-wide association defines more than 30 distinct susceptibility loci for Crohn's disease. Nat Genet. 2008;40(8):955–62.
42. De Moor MHM, Liu YJ, Boomsma DI, Li J, Hamilton JJ, Hottenga JJ, et al. Genome-wide association study of exercise behavior in Dutch and American adults. Med Sci Sports Exerc. 2009;41:1887–95.
43. Loos RJ, Bouchard C. FTO: the first gene contributing to common forms of human obesity. Obes Rev. 2008;9(3):246–50.
44. McCarroll SA. Extending genome-wide association studies to copy-number variation. Hum Mol Genet. 2008;17(R2):R135–42.
45. Plagnol V. Association tests and software for copy number variant data. Hum Genomics. 2009;3(2):191–4.
46. Sha BY, Yang TL, Zhao LJ, Chen XD, Guo Y, Chen Y, et al. Genome-wide association study suggested copy number variation may be associated with body mass index in the Chinese population. J Hum Genet. 2009;54(4):199–202.
47. Bodmer W, Bonilla C. Common and rare variants in multifactorial susceptibility to common diseases. Nat Genet. 2008;40(6):695–701.
48. Yang N, MacArthur DG, Gulbin JP, Hahn AG, Beggs AH, Easteal S, et al. ACTN3 genotype is associated with human elite athletic performance. Am J Hum Genet. 2003; 73(3):627–31.
49. Niemi AK, Majamaa K. Mitochondrial DNA and ACTN3 genotypes in finnish elite endurance and sprint athletes. Eur J Hum Genet. 2005;13(8):965–9.
50. Roth SM, Walsh S, Liu D, Metter EJ, Ferrucci L, Hurley BF. The ACTN3 R577X nonsense allele is under-represented in elite-level strength athletes. Eur J Hum Genet. 2008;16(3):391–4.
51. Vincent B, De Bock K, Ramaekers M, Van den Eede E, Van Leemputte M, Hespel P, et al. ACTN3 (R577X) genotype is associated with fiber type distribution. Physiol Genomics. 2007;32(1):58–63.
52. Norman B, Esbjornsson M, Rundqvist H, Osterlund T, von Walden F, Tesch PA. Strength, power, fiber types, and mRNA expression in trained men and women with different ACTN3 R577X genotypes. J Appl Physiol. 2009;106(3):959–65.
53. MacArthur DG, Seto JT, Raftery JM, Quinlan KG, Huttley GA, Hook JW, et al. Loss of ACTN3 gene function alters mouse muscle metabolism and shows evidence of positive selection in humans. Nat Genet. 2007;39(10):1261–5.
54. MacArthur DG, Seto JT, Chan S, Quinlan KG, Raftery JM, Turner N, et al. An Actn3 knockout mouse provides mechanistic insights into the association between alpha-actinin-3 deficiency and human athletic performance. Hum Mol Genet. 2008;17(8):1076–86.
55. Feinberg AP. Epigenetics at the epicenter of modern medicine. JAMA. 2008;299(11): 1345–50.
56. Gluckman PD, Hanson MA, Buklijas T, Low FM, Beedle AS. Epigenetic mechanisms that underpin metabolic and cardiovascular diseases. Nat Rev Endocrinol. 2009;5(7):401–8.
57. Burdge GC, Slater-Jefferies J, Torrens C, Phillips ES, Hanson MA, Lillycrop KA. Dietary protein restriction of pregnant rats in the F0 generation induces altered methylation of hepatic gene promoters in the adult male offspring in the F1 and F2 generations. Br J Nutr. 2007;97(3):435–9.
58. Lillycrop KA, Phillips ES, Jackson AA, Hanson MA, Burdge GC. Dietary protein restriction of pregnant rats induces and folic acid supplementation prevents epigenetic modification of hepatic gene expression in the offspring. J Nutr. 2005;135(6):1382–6.

59. Rodenhiser D, Mann M. Epigenetics and human disease: translating basic biology into clinical applications. CMAJ. 2006;174(3):341–8.
60. Foley DL, Craig JM, Morley R, Olsson CJ, Dwyer T, Smith K, et al. Prospects for epigenetic epidemiology. Am J Epidemiol. 2009;169(4):389–400.
61. Schadt EE. Molecular networks as sensors and drivers of common human diseases. Nature. 2009;461(7261):218–23.
62. Auffray C, Chen Z, Hood L. Systems medicine: the future of medical genomics and healthcare. Genome Med. 2009;1(1):2.
63. Beunen G, Thomis M. Gene powered? where to go from heritability (h2) in muscle strength and power? Exerc Sport Sci Rev. 2004;32(4):148–54.

Chapter 2
Statistical and Methodological Considerations in Exercise Genomics

Heather Gordish-Dressman and Joseph M. Devaney

Keywords Additive model • Analysis of covariance • Analysis of variance • Base pair • Candidate single nucleotide polymorphism • Chi square • Codominant model • Confounding • Dominant model • Epistasis • Expression quantitative loci • Genome-wide association studies • Genomic control • Genetic risk score • Hardy–Weinberg equilibrium • Lewontin's D' • Linkage disequilibrium • Logistic regression • Multiple testing • Odds ratio • Population stratification • Power calculations • Correlation coefficient (r^2) • Recessive model • Sample size calculations • Single nucleotide polymorphism • Structured association • Transcription factor 7-like 2 • Thyrotropin-releasing hormone receptor • Tag SNP • X chromosome • Y chromosome

Introduction

This chapter discusses the basic statistical concepts necessary for the analysis of genetic data. It focuses on single nucleotide polymorphism (SNP) data, a very active research area, and describes the methods used for data analysis and some important issues that arise specifically with genetic data. Information is given for studies using single SNPs, i.e., candidate gene studies, and for studies using multiple SNPs, such as genome-wide association studies (GWAS). Further information on GWAS describes how they can be a useful tool for academicians, clinicians, health/fitness professionals, and exercise scientists by detailing both what has been done and what is expected for the future. This chapter will provide the reader with an outline of things to consider when planning a study using genetic data and things to consider when reading a published report using genetic data.

H. Gordish-Dressman (✉)
Children's National Medical Center, Research Center for Genetic Medicine,
111 Michigan Avenue, N.W., Washington, DC 20010, USA
e-mail: hgordish@cnmcresearch.org

L.S. Pescatello and S.M. Roth (eds.), *Exercise Genomics*,
Molecular and Translational Medicine, DOI 10.1007/978-1-60761-355-8_2,
© Springer Science+Business Media, LLC 2011

Statistical Considerations in Exercise Genomics

The statistical analysis of genetic data requires special considerations and encounters challenges not usually seen with other data types. These considerations include: calculation of Hardy–Weinberg equilibrium (HWE) and linkage disequilibrium (LD), additional requirements when performing power and/or sample size calculations, choosing the correct genetic model to analyze data, issues with nonautosomal loci (i.e., those on the X and Y chromosomes), and issues of confounding in the sample due to genetic factors. The statistical considerations in exercise genomics section of this chapter will focus on statistical techniques used to study genetic information in nonfamilial populations, specifically the analysis of single nucleotide polymorphism (SNP) data. Other methods to examine genetics in family groups (i.e., familial aggregation, segregation, and linkage analysis) will not be covered here, but are discussed in Chap. 1 of this book.

Analysis of nonfamilial populations falls into two major types, candidate gene association studies and their extension to GWAS. The candidate gene approach examines a limited number of associations with gene loci with known related functions that could be relevant to the phenotype of interest. GWAS, on the other hand, explore nearly all loci known to have a polymorphism to determine if any are associated with the phenotype of interest. The candidate gene approach is useful if there is prior knowledge of a gene, its function, and relationship to your phenotype. In contrast, GWAS are used when there is no or minimal prior knowledge and there is general interest in testing up to one million loci to see if any are associated with the phenotype. Both types of approaches use similar statistical methods, but GWAS in particular require additional considerations.

Hardy–Weinberg Equilibrium

The HWE principle states allele and genotype frequencies are in equilibrium (i.e., they remain constant from generation to generation unless other processes act to change them). The HWE formula predicts the expected genotype frequencies given their allele frequencies and statistically tests them against those observed in the sample. HWE assumes a large population size, random mating, and an absence of mutation, migration, or natural selection. In most populations HWE is assumed, as there is often no information on migration, mutation, or selection, and mating is random is an inherent assumption. When a biallelic locus shows deviation from HWE, it can mean that one or more of the HWE assumptions have been violated, but it more commonly suggests genotyping errors [1]. It is for this reason that each genetic locus is tested for HWE. The genotyping for any loci not in HWE should be verified. In addition, association tests using loci not in HWE can lead to biased estimates of the association's magnitude [2], yet another reason for testing each SNP for HWE.

The HWE formula ($1 = p^2 + 2pq + q^2$) is used to calculate expected genotype frequencies and a one degree of freedom Chi square (χ^2) test compares them to the observed frequencies [3]. For a biallelic locus with alleles A and B, p^2 corresponds to the frequency of the homozygous AA genotype, q^2 to the BB genotype, and $2pq$ to the heterozygous AB genotype. Allele frequencies are calculated from these genotype frequencies, and finally the expected genotype frequencies are determined. A one degree of freedom χ^2 test compares the expected to observed genotype frequencies. The χ^2 tests the null hypothesis of no statistically significant difference in the distribution of genotype frequencies between the observed and expected. Therefore, a nonsignificant p value indicates HWE. A significant p value indicates a deviation from HWE, and the genotypes should be verified. HWE is one of the few statistical procedures where a nonsignificant p value is desirable.

Calculation and testing of HWE requires several steps. Given a SNP with the following genotype frequencies TT=418, TG=253, GG=33, and total sample size=704, the first step is to calculate allele frequencies from the observed genotype frequencies.

$$\text{Allele frequency of T}: p(T) = ((TT * 2) + TG) / (\text{Total} * 2)$$
$$= ((418 * 2) + 253) / (704 * 2)$$
$$= 0.773,$$

$$\text{Allele frequency of G}: p(G) = ((GG * 2) + TG) / (\text{Total} * 2)$$
$$= ((33 * 2) + 253) / (704 * 2)$$
$$= 0.227.$$

Second, the allele frequencies are used to calculate the expected genotype frequencies.

$$\text{Genotype frequency of TT} = p(T)^2 * \text{Total} = (0.773)^2 * 704 = 421,$$

$$\text{Genotype frequency of GT} = 2 * p(T) * p(G) * \text{Total}$$
$$= 2 * 0.773 * 0.227 * 704 = 247,$$

$$\text{Genotype frequency of GG} = p(G)^2 * \text{Total} = (0.227)^2 * 704 = 36.$$

Finally, the observed genotype frequencies (418, 253, and 33) are compared to the expected frequencies (421, 247, and 36) using a 1 degree of freedom χ^2 test to yield $\chi^2=0.455$; $p=0.4999$. Thus, in this case, the $p>0.05$ indicates the SNP is in HWE, the desirable outcome.

Linkage Disequilibrium

LD is defined as the nonrandom association of SNPs located near each other in the genome [4] arising because certain sections of the genome tend to be inherited together more often than expected by chance. The closer together two SNPs are, the less likely that a recombination event occurs between them. Therefore, the more likely they are inherited together. SNPs in high LD are almost always inherited together and can serve as proxies for one another [5, 6].

There are two major reasons why LD is important in any analysis of genetic data. The first relates to inference of causation. A strong association between a SNP and phenotype may indicate that particular SNP is the causal locus; alternatively, the true causal locus may be another SNP in high LD with the one tested. Two SNPs in high LD would be expected to show similar associations with a phenotype. Consequently, a SNP at one locus may appear to be associated with a phenotype, but only because it is in high LD with the true causal locus [7].

The second reason is that LD relates to the error rates of statistical tests, particularly their effect on the simultaneous analysis of many SNPs as in GWAS. All statistical tests have an error rate α, which is the rate at which the true null hypothesis of no difference is incorrectly rejected. In other words, the results of the test indicate there is a statistically significant difference when there is not. This alpha level (α) is conventionally set to 0.05, corresponding to a 5% chance of incorrectly rejecting the null hypothesis and stating a significant difference. For a single statistical test or even a handful of tests, this is a reasonable level of error most scientists and clinicians are comfortable with reporting. But when multiple statistical tests are performed on the same data (i.e., when testing associations among many SNPs and a phenotype), this error rate is no longer acceptable. For example, when performing 100 statistical tests with the same $\alpha = 0.05$, five rejections of the null hypothesis are expected to be solely due to chance. This becomes an even greater problem with GWAS, which attempt to test a phenotype against all known SNPs in the genome. Technology now allows us to simultaneously test one million SNPs (and that number will increase as technology moves forward). With the same $\alpha = 0.05$, 50,000 significant results due to chance alone would be expected. So from the resulting list of significant p values, 50,000 are false positives and are due to chance rather than a true association between the SNP and phenotype. Of course which 50,000 associations are false positives and which are true associations are not known, making interpretation of our results extremely difficult if not impossible. One solution to the problem of multiple SNP and phenotype testing is to perform fewer statistical tests (i.e., relying on LD).

Two SNPs in high LD are essentially giving the same information and are expected to show the same associations with the phenotype. There is no reason to test both SNPs against the phenotype. The total number of SNPs tested can be decreased by excluding redundant SNPs that are in high LD with each other. Most products available to perform GWAS have already taken LD between SNPs into consideration and have removed many redundant SNPs [8]. When performing multiple statistical tests on many SNPs from a candidate gene, the overall number of test being performed can be decreased by measuring LD between the SNPs beforehand. Testing for LD leads to a decrease in the overall error rate and an increased confidence in drawing the correct conclusions from the data.

There are several different measures of LD, each having its own characteristics. Those most commonly encountered are the r^2 (correlation coefficient) and D' (Lewontin's D'). For an excellent definition and comparison of LD measurements, see Devlin and Risch [9]. The calculations of both r^2 and D' use only allele frequencies of the two SNPs and are related. If the frequencies of the alleles at two loci are defined as p_A, p_a, p_B, p_b, then, $D = p_{AB} - p_A p_B$. Because the sign of D depends on the arbitrary assignment of which allele is A and which is B, D' is more commonly used. $D' = |D/D_{max}|$ where D_{max} is the lesser of $p_A p_b$ or $p_a p_B$ if D is positive and the lesser of $p_A p_B$ or $p_a p_b$ if D is negative. A further common LD measure, r^2, is defined as $r^2 = D^2 / p_A (1 - p_A) p_B (1 - p_B)$ [7]. There are several resources available to calculate LD and a helpful list is given at http://www.genes.org.uk/software/LD-software. shtml (see Appendix).

D' has been deemed the most appropriate for fine mapping [9] because it is directly related to recombination rate, and it is the only LD measure not sensitive to allele frequencies. However, D' can be upwardly biased in small samples, especially those with rare alleles, since its magnitude is highly dependent on sample size. The term D' is also difficult to interpret when its values deviate from the extremes of 0 and 1 [10]. A value of $D'=1$ indicates complete LD and a $D'=0$ indicates no LD, but interpretation of intermediate values is difficult. Therefore, r^2 has been shown to have several properties making it more useful than D' [7]. The measure r^2 has more reliable sample properties at low allele frequencies (a common occurrence with SNPs), has the strongest relationship with population genetic theory, and has a simple linear relationship with sample size [7, 11]. r^2 is one of the most common LD measures reported, but exhibits sensitivity to the variation in allele frequencies across loci making the comparison of r^2 values between different locations (and different studies) problematic. As with D', an $r^2=1$ indicates perfect LD where the observations at one locus provide complete information about the other locus and $r^2=0$ indicates no LD. However, intermediate values are more intuitive since the value of r^2 is related to the amount of information provided by one locus about the other [10], just as the r^2 value from a linear regression provides the amount of variability of one variable described by the other. For example, if two SNPs have an LD of $r^2=0.43$, by knowing an individual's genotype for one of the SNPs, we then can confidently predict the genotype of the other SNP for only 43 out of the 100 individuals. Higher LD, and thus higher r^2 values, allows us to accurately predict the second SNP for more individuals.

The magnitude of LD measurements considered strong and weak has evolved largely by convention. Many define strong LD as an r^2 value larger than or equal to 0.80 [12]. Others define strong LD with confidence intervals where the one-sided upper 95% confidence interval bound on D' is greater than or equal to 0.98 [3].

Power and Sample Size Considerations with Genetic Data

Making estimates of sample sizes and/or power is an important part of any proposed experiment. Not only are they usually required by funding agencies as part of grant application, they are also important for the researcher to ensure adequate testing of the hypothesis of the sample of interest. The methods used to calculate sample size and power estimates are the same with genetic data as with other traditional data types, but allele frequencies need to be taken into consideration when using genetic data. Typical sample size calculations yield a number of subjects, usually per group, that are necessary to detect a significant difference between those groups. If a calculation indicates a sample size of 50 per genotype group is required, the allele frequency of the minor allele then needs to be considered to calculate how many total subjects you need to get 50 heterozygous mutants (the rarest genotype). For example, a sample size calculation might determine that you need 50 homozygous wild-type individuals (AA) and 50 homozygous mutant individuals (BB) to adequately test a hypothesis. If the SNP has a major allele frequency of 0.85 [$p(A)$] and a minor allele frequency of 0.15 [$p(B)$], it would require a total sample size of 2,500 to ensure there are 50 homozygous mutants in the sample. One can determine the number of individuals of each genotype directly from the allele frequencies according to HWE, just as one does for HWE calculations. Given 100 individuals, the number of those of each genotype is given by:

$$\#AA = p(A)^2 * total = 0.85^2 * 100 = 72.25 = 72,$$

$$\#AB = 2 * p(A) * p(B) * total = 2 * 0.85 * 0.15 * 100$$
$$= 25.5 = 26,$$

$$\#BB = p(B)^2 * 100 = 0.15^2 * 100 = 2.25 = 2.$$

So with a minor allele frequency of 0.15, only two individuals out of every 100 would have a homozygous mutant genotype. Therefore, 2,500 subjects are needed to ensure that there are 50 homozygous mutants in the sample. The allele frequency of the minor allele greatly increases the total number of subjects needed for the study and is an additional important consideration.

Choosing the Most Appropriate Genetic Model

For any biallelic locus (with alleles A and B), there are three possible genotypes (AA, AB, and BB), and each allele can differentially influence the phenotype. In other words, the A allele can dominate the B or vice versa. This penetrance of each allele leads to different genetic models. The first model is the codominant model where all three genotypes have a different effect on the phenotype, and if those correspond to a dose–response with the effect of the phenotype increasing (or decreasing) with the number of mutant alleles, it is considered an additive model. Sometimes the heterozygote genotype's effect on the phenotype is more similar to either the homozygous wild-type or the homozygous mutant genotypes. In this case if the heterozygotes and homozygous wild-type individuals show similar outcomes, a recessive model can be used where the homozygous mutants (BB) are tested against the combination of the heterozygotes and homozygous wild types (AA+AB). If the heterozygotes are similar to the homozygous mutants, a dominant model can be used (AA vs. AB+BB).

Examples of three SNPs, each tested against a phenotype where each SNP demonstrates a different genetic model, are now described. In the first instance, the mean relative difference in one repetition maximum (1RM) dynamic muscle strength was compared to a genetic variant in the Resistin gene (i.e., *RETN* −420 C>G) where C is the major allele and G is the minor allele. The relative differences in 1RM means±SEM for each genotype were CC=37.2±3.0%, CG=31.7±2.7%, and GG=21.3±5.3% [12]. Each of the means appears to be independent, and there seems to be a dose–response with a decreased mean difference with the G allele. In this case, the data show a codominant (additive) model and are best analyzed as three genotypes. A comparison of subcutaneous fat volume with the insulin-induced gene 2 (i.e., *INSIG2* − 101,025 G>C) (G=major allele, C=minor allele) showed the following mean±SEM: GG=243,473±5,713mm³, GC=269,331±5,645mm³, and CC=263,941±10,940 mm³ [13]. In this case, the means for the GC and CC genotypes are much more alike than the homozygous wild-type GG genotype, indicating that this locus may follow a dominant model. Combining the AC and CC genotype together and comparing the AA genotype, a dominant model would be a good choice for analysis. Lastly, a comparison of isometric strength with rs3739287 (A=major allele, G=minor allele) showed the following: AA=63.6±1.2 kg, AG=62.7±2.8 kg, and GG=103.7±5.5 kg (unpublished data). Here the AA and AG genotypes are very similar and both very different from the GG genotype, indicating that this locus may follow a recessive model. Analyzing as a recessive model, combining the AA and AG and comparing to GG would be the best choice here.

Recessive models are the most difficult to test from a sample size perspective, i.e., if the SNP has a low minor allele frequency, the total number of homozygous mutants (BB) may be too low to effectively test. The codominant and/or additive models have the additional need to adjust resulting p value for multiple comparisons because we are comparing three genotype groups.

X and Y Chromosome SNPs

Most genetic variations for association studies are located on one of the 22 autosomal chromosomes, but those on the X and Y chromosomes have special considerations [14]. For SNPs on autosomal chromosomes, each individual has two copies of the allele, one inherited from each parent. Therefore, genotypes report two alleles for each subject (AA, AB, or BB). SNPs located on the X chromosome are similar in females having two X chromosomes, i.e., each female has two alleles for each X chromosome loci. Males, on the other hand, are termed hemizygous, having only one X chromosome and only one allele. Depending on the platform performing the genotyping, X chromosome loci in males are often represented in a similar fashion to autosomal loci and show two alleles, while in reality, they only have one. So a male with an A allele at a X chromosome locus will be represented by a genotype of AA, and a B allele represented as BB even though there is truly only one allele. Normal males cannot be heterozygous for an X chromosome locus. Therefore, a heterozygote genotype usually indicates a genotyping error, or more rarely, a misclassification of gender or a genetic condition such as Kleinfelter's syndrome where the man has more than one X chromosome. Similarly, females cannot have genotypes for Y chromosome loci. Calculation of HWE for a nonautosomal chromosome locus is usually done in females only for an X chromosome locus and in males only for those on the Y chromosome locus.

Analysis of Multiple SNPs – Epistasis

Often, especially when studying complex traits or diseases, we have several SNPs that together may affect our phenotype. One SNP may mask or alter the effect of another. Epistasis refers to the phenomenon where the effects of one gene are modified by one or several other genes [15]. The classic example of epistasis comes from Bateson in 1909 [15]. In the following table, we see the phenotype (hair color) in mice with known genotypes at two loci, 1 and 2.

	Genotype at locus 2		
Genotype at locus 1	g/g	g/G	G/G
b/b	White	Gray	Gray
b/B	Black	Gray	Gray
B/B	Black	Gray	Gray

We see that at the 1 locus, the B allele is dominant, i.e., any mouse that has at least one B allele has black hair, but that effect is overridden by the 2 locus. Every mouse having the G allele has gray hair, regardless of which B allele they have. The effect of locus 1 is not observable unless the genotype at locus 2 is g/g. This is an example of epistasis where the effect of one locus is modified by the presence or absence of an allele at another locus. One can easily see how with phenotypes expected to be affected by several loci, epistasis can occur.

There are several methods to deal with testing for epistasis. The most common way uses standard methods to incorporate several SNPs into the same statistical model, often with terms defining the interactions between loci. The success of this method depends heavily on the number of loci being tested and the size of the sample. Putting too many terms into a single model runs the risk of overfitting the model, where the model describes random error instead of the underlying relationship between variables and usually arises when the model is excessively complex in relation to the amount of data available. The larger the sample size, the more complex a model it can support. It is easy to imagine the problem where you have a continuous phenotype and only two SNPs. When investigating a single SNP, the phenotype mean for individuals of each genotype is calculated and the three groups are compared. With two SNPs, if the means for each combination of genotypes are compared, there are now nine groups to compare. The sample size needed to adequately compare nine means is much larger than that needed to compare three means. Additionally, if the minor allele frequencies are low, a much larger sample size is needed to see any subject's homozygous mutant for both SNPs.

A more recent method of combining SNPs into a single model is called the genetic risk score [16], which combines data from several SNPs into a composite value.

There are a few ways to derive this genetic risk score. One can test each phenotype/single SNP association and use the regression coefficients from those models to weight a final derived composite score for each individual. This score is then used as the independent variable in a model with the phenotype of interest. Horne et al. [16] describe this method in detail. Another method simply looks at each phenotype/SNP association and determines which allele is the "risk" allele. The number of risk alleles for all SNPs is then counted for each individual and phenotype of interest is tested against this genotype score [16, 17]. For example, when testing four SNPs against body mass index (BMI), each SNP has a risk allele; therefore, each individual can have 0, 1, 2, 3, or 4 total risk alleles. Mean BMI is compared between these five groups to determine if there is a trend with BMI increasing and an increasing number of risk alleles.

Sample Selection Considerations

Any sample population can be affected by confounding measured or unmeasured factors. When testing hypotheses using genetic data, another form of confounding by ethnicity or population stratification can occur [18]. Population stratification arises when there is a systematic difference in allele frequencies between subpopulations within the large sample due to differing ancestry [19, 20]. Allele frequencies can vary widely between ethnic groups that can be problematic in association studies. If an allele is more frequent in one ethnic group and the sample has many individuals of that group, the strength of the association could be positively biased. Alternatively, if a true relationship between an allele and an outcome exists only in one ethnic group, but the sample has few individuals of that group, the association, if present, may not be detected.

There are several methods to deal with population stratification in a sample population of unrelated individuals; the two most common being genomic control and structured association. Genomic control uses a nonparametric method to control for any influence of shared genetic background by adjusting the underlying distribution used for determining statistical significance and is described in detail in Devlin and Roeder [21]. Structured association uses unlinked genetic markers to infer details of the population structure and to estimate the ancestry of individuals in the sample [15]. This information, described in Pritchard and Rosenberg [20], is then controlled for in the analysis to remove any possible effects of population stratification.

Candidate SNP Association Studies

One of the most important steps when analyzing SNP data is adequately defining the phenotype or outcome of interest whose form determines the statistical methods that will be used (Table 2.1). The website titled a New View of Statistics (http://www.sportsci.org/resource/stats/) [22] developed by Hopkins details all of the

Table 2.1 Typical statistical methods for the analysis of SNP data

Dependent variable (outcome/phenotype) data type	Independent variable (SNP) data type	Statistical test/model	Information gained
Categorical	Categorical	χ (chi) square test	Detects significant association between outcome and SNP
Categorical with two levels (dichotomous)	Categorical	Logistic regression	Detects significant association between outcome and each level of SNP; provides OR and 95% CI to assess the strength and direction for association
Categorical with three or more ordered levels	Categorical	Ordinal regression	Same as logistic regression
Categorical with three or more unordered levels	Categorical	Nominal regression	Same as logistic regression
Continuous	Categorical with two levels	Independent t-test	Detects a significant difference in means between levels of the categorical variable
Continuous	Categorical with three or more levels	ANOVA	Detects a significant difference in means between levels of the categorical variable
Continuous	Categorical with three or more levels	ANCOVA	Detects a significant difference in means between levels of the categorical variable; allows the addition of covariates
Continuous with repeated measures	Categorical with two levels	Paired t-test	Detects a significant difference in means between levels of the categorical variable; allows the use of phenotypes measured at multiple times
Continuous with repeated measures	Categorical with three or more levels	Repeated measures ANOVA/ANCOVA	Detects a significant difference in means between levels of the categorical variable; allows the use of phenotypes measured at multiple times
Continuous	Categorical	MANOVA	Detects significant differences in means between levels of the categorical variable; additionally allows testing of interaction between multiple dependent variables
Continuous but nonnormally distributed	Categorical with two levels	Wilcoxon sign rank (Mann–Whitney U test)	Detects a significant difference in medians between levels of the categorical variable
Continuous but nonnormally distributed	Categorical with three or more levels	Kruskal–Wallis test	Detects a significant difference in medians between levels of the categorical variable

methods discussed here with examples taken from exercise and sports science and is a valuable resource for analysis (see Appendix).

The two major types of phenotypes are those which are categorical and those which are continuous. Further, continuous data can be categorized into groups to be analyzed as categorical data, but this practice should be discouraged. Categorizing continuous data can cause problems beyond the obvious loss of information, such as a decrease in statistical power, differing conclusions depending on the categorization scheme, and the introduction of an erroneous association [23]. Therefore, it is best to treat continuous data as a continuous trait rather than categorizing it even though categorized data are sometimes more easily interpreted and better understood clinically.

The method commonly used to analyze a categorical outcome is the Chi square (χ^2) test [22]. This test indicates if there is a statistically significant association between the categorical outcome and the SNP of interest by comparing the distribution of genotype frequencies between those in different groups of the category. While this test is simple to perform, it gives only a minimum amount of information, namely whether an association exists or not. It does not give detailed information on the strength of the association, or if one particular genotype shows a stronger association with the outcome than the others. In order to determine that information, the analysis must move to a regression model; logistic regression if the categorical outcome is dichotomous or takes on only two possible values, ordinal logistic regression if the outcome takes on three or more ordered levels, and nominal logistic regression if the outcome takes on three or more unordered levels. These regression models allow measurement not only of the strength of the association, but also to specifically test each of the genotypes or alleles against one another. Each logistic regression model reports an odds ratio (OR) for each level of the factor (normally a genotype or an allele) in reference to the baseline level (usually the homozygous wild-type subjects or those with the most common genotype), which quantifies the risk (and the direction) associated with the outcome given each level of the factor. Each OR has a p value and a 95% confidence interval, allowing one to determine the strength of the association. An OR of 1.00 denotes no excess risk associated with that factor, an OR > 1.00 an excess risk, and an OR < 1.00 a decreased risk. If comparing genotypes, each can be tested against the other to determine if an excess risk is associated with any genotype. For example, a logistic regression model comparing a SNP in the *FTO* gene (rs3751812) with type 2 diabetes mellitus (T2D) showed an OR = 1.16 with a $p = 0.008$ and a 95% confidence interval of 1.04–1.30 [24]. In this instance, the number of individuals with and without the mutant allele was compared to the number of individuals with and without T2D. The OR = 1.16 showed the odds of having T2D with the mutant allele was 1.16 times greater than the odds of having T2D with the common allele. The 95% confidence interval shows the amount of uncertainty in the calculation and that the true OR is between 1.04 and 1.30.

The analysis of continuous outcomes must first start with a determination of normality. The normality of each outcome, or quantitative trait as continuous outcomes are often referred to, must be tested to determine whether parametric or nonparametric tests are appropriate. Although parametric statistical tests (e.g., t-tests and analysis of variance [ANOVA]) are better known than their nonparametric counterpart tests (e.g., Wilcoxon and Kruskal–Wallis), using a parametric test on data that violates the assumptions of normality (and variance homogeneity) can lead to biased error rates severe enough to incorrectly reject the null hypothesis [25, 26]. Therefore, assessing normality, graphically using a histogram, and/or using a normality test such as the Anderson-Darling or the Shapiro–Wilk test is one of the most important initial steps in the analysis of data. If the phenotype is not normally distributed, a variety of data transformations such as log, square root, and inverse are available, but the normality of the transformed data should be assessed to determine if the transformation provided a normally distributed phenotype.

The simplest analysis of normally distributed continuous data is done using a t-test for comparing a phenotype between two genotypes and ANOVA for comparing three genotypes. These statistical tests will determine if there is a statistically significant difference in means between genotypes. If a significant difference is found with an ANOVA, an additional step of testing multiple comparisons is necessary. ANOVA models yield an F statistic denoting at least two of the means being compared are significantly different, but it does not define which of the means are different. To determine which means are different, post hoc pair-wise statistical tests are performed between each genotype, and the resulting p values are adjusted for multiple comparisons using one of the several methods available (i.e., Bonferroni, Tukey, LSD, or Sidak).

If there are other measurements, typically demographic characteristics such as age and gender, that can affect the phenotype or the relationship between the phenotype and the SNP, they can be incorporated into the analysis as covariates. Analysis of covariance (ANCOVA) is used to test differences between means, while simultaneously adjusting for or removing the variance attributable to the covariates.

If the outcome or phenotype includes repeated measurements made over time, a paired t-test (if comparing only two groups) or a repeated measures ANOVA or ANCOVA (if comparing three or more groups) is used to test for differences between groups. These methods allow partitioning and accounting for between-subjects and within-subjects variance and to test for significance of those effects. They also allow a test for interactions between groups (usually genotype) and the repeated measurement to see if the change in measurement is different between groups.

Lastly, nonnormally distributed continuous data must be analyzed using nonparametric tests. There are several nonparametric tests available including the Wilcoxon rank-sum (also known as the Mann–Whitney U test), which is analogous to an independent t-test used to compare a continuous outcome between two independent groups. The Wilcoxon sign rank test is used in place of a paired t-test for comparing a continuous outcome between two paired groups. When comparing three independent groups, the Kruskal–Wallis test is used in place of ANOVA. More complicated analyses with repeated measures data in more than three groups or with the inclusion of covariates can be done by taking the continuous data, ranking the values, and using parametric tests on the ranks rather than the raw data values.

Genome-Wide Association Studies (GWAS)

GWAS are defined by the National Institutes of Health as a study of common genetic variation across the entire genome designed to identify genetic associations with observable traits [5] and have become more and more common as the technology to perform them has evolved and improved. Over 100 loci for more than 40 common diseases have been identified though GWAS in just the last few years and that number is growing [5]. The National Human Genome Research Institute (NHGRI) produces a searchable catalog of all published GWAS freely available for download from http://www.genome.gov/gwastudies/ (see Appendix).

GWAS can be described as unbiased but comprehensive association studies investigating most of the genome for causal variants [19]. An outcome, either categorical or continuous, is tested for association with an enormous number (currently one million) of SNPs located throughout the genome. GWAS is an especially important development in the study of complex diseases, which most likely involve many loci, each of which contributes minimally to the effect size [27]. Traditional family-based linkage studies have been successful in identifying genes with large effect sizes, but not multiple genes with small effects. GWAS offer an unprecedented opportunity to study the genetic unpinning of common and complex diseases by interrogating the entire genome in unrelated individuals without the need for prior hypotheses, but this revolutionary technology has some limitations that must be understood and addressed.

The greatest benefit of a GWAS is that no prior assumption of the location of a causal variant is needed. Therefore, GWAS can be performed without having any idea of where a causal variant may be located or even what the function of the causal variant may be [19, 27]. This approach differs greatly from candidate gene association studies where the loci investigated are chosen based on prior knowledge of biological meaning and/or location. When the biological underpinnings of a disease are completely unknown or when the location of the possible gene involved is unknown, candidate gene association studies are not very efficient [27] because a prior knowledge of the loci being studied is needed. GWAS, on the other hand, can scan the entire genome to find loci that are possibly associated with the outcome. There is no prior guessing as to what genes are involved in the outcome or where they are located in GWAS.

There are several things to be considered when performing a GWAS and when interpreting the results of a published GWAS report. These considerations include, among other things, the study design, selection of study subjects, sample size, quality control, analysis of the data, and replication. An excellent review published by the NCI-NHGRI Working Group on Replication in Association Studies in 2007 describes in detail those factors to consider when reading or performing a GWAS [28].

One of the first considerations in a GWAS is the study design and what type of subjects will be used. There are a few study designs that can be used for GWAS, the most common of which is the case/control design where the outcome is a dichotomous yes or no answer, but cohort designs where the outcome is a quantitative trait are beginning to be published. Both designs have advantages and disadvantages. Case control samples are usually drawn from the same population, decreasing the chance of bias or differences between the groups unrelated to the factor(s) defining cases, but the classification of cases must be very rigorous. Misclassification of cases, and less importantly controls, can markedly reduce the power to detect associations [5]. Appropriate control of possible confounders must be done to avoid the risk of identifying associations not with the outcome of interest, but with the confounding factor instead [5]. Cohort samples have a better chance of homogeneity of participants, decreasing the chance of bias, but usually require a larger sample size, especially if the expected effect size is small [5]. Both types of samples are vulnerable to population stratification, and it is recommended GWAS assess it. A more recent development is the multistage design where a smaller number of individuals are subjected to genotyping the entire genome; only those SNPs found to be significant or promising are then genotyped in successively larger samples.

The NCI-NHGRI Working Group on Replication in Association Studies recommends the sample size for a GWAS should be sufficient to detect a modest effect size and be "suitably large," but does not specifically define the term [28]. Simulation studies [29] have shown the power to detect a moderate effect size of 1.3 is nearly zero with a sample size of 1,000 cases and 1,000 controls and only increases to ~50% with a sample three times larger. A list of GWAS (http://www.genome.gov/gwastudies/) (see Appendix) published from November 2008 to November 2009 shows sample sizes ranging from the smallest at 60 to the largest at 81,000 with a wide range of effect sizes. To help with designing a GWAS and estimate the power of a proposed study given a particular sample size and budget, a module for the R package (a free software environment for statistical computing and graphics – http://www.r-project.org/) is available from http://www.stats.ox.ac.uk/~marchini/#software (see Appendix).

Quality control of genotyping is essential to any association study, including GWAS. Genotyping errors can cause spurious results, especially if the errors occur differentially between the cases and controls in a case control study [5]. Therefore, several quality control features should be present including the SNP genotyping call rate, the SNP minor allele frequencies, the results of HWE, and concordance rates in duplicate samples. NCI-NHGRI also recommends those SNPs shown to have significant associations be genotyped on a different platform to confirm results and known associations be verified in the sample under study [28].

Many of the issues arising from GWAS stem from the data analysis. The problem of multiple testing described in an earlier section becomes a critical issue when testing upwards of one million SNPs in a single experiment [30]. There are methods to adjust the resulting p values to deal with the issue of multiple testing and reduce the false positive rate. The most commonly applied is the Bonferroni approach where the critical p value to determine significance is divided by the number of tests done (i.e., if the nominal critical p value is 0.05, the new critical value for significance with 1,000,000 SNPs is 5×10^{-8}). This adjustment has been criticized for being overly conservative because it assumes each statistical test on each SNP is independent which is not true due to extensive LD between SNPs within the genome [5].

Other methods are available, but are not as widely used and require more computation beyond the amount necessary to calculate the *p* values themselves.

The last consideration for GWAS is replication. Any SNP association initially found to be significant should ideally be replicated in another independent sample [20]. This replication can be built in to the initial study through a multistage design or can be made in an entirely different sample with similar characteristics. However, if the finding from the initial GWAS is a false positive, it will not be detected in a follow-up replication study.

The analysis of data from a GWAS is computationally intensive and requires a computer program designed specifically for its analysis. There are several commercially available programs including Partek Genomic Suite (http://www.partek.com/) and Golden Helix (http://www.goldenhelix.com/). There are also several freely downloadable programs available. The most commonly used is PLINK (available at http://pngu.mgh.harvard.edu/~purcell/plink/) and a list of other programs is given at http://www.stats.ox.ac.uk/~marchini/software/gwas/gwas.html (see Appendix).

Using GWAS as a Tool for Exercise Science

GWAS are valuable tools for the exercise scientist and clinician. A GWAS is an unbiased method to ascertain genetic variation (in the form of SNPs) in the human genome, and the tools to analyze these scans are available (discussed previously). Never before has one been able to scan the genomic landscape with the precision of a GWAS. This development has resulted in the identification of new genes or regions of the genome that may have some biological significance for a particular phenotype such as skeletal muscle mass.

The statistical challenges of a GWAS are many, but it will be an important method that will be used for the foreseeable future in the study of exercise genomics. For example, many scientists feel GWAS results are genetic variants with weak effect sizes and a small fraction of heritability is explained by these variants. Heritability is the amount of phenotypic variation in a population that is explained by genetic variation among individuals. However, with the identification of new regions of the genome obtained by GWAS, new biological insights are obtained that will lead to clinical advances. This will lead to the development of new biomarkers of exercise performance and health fitness-related phenotypes which can be used to track the positive effects of exercise. For example, there are increases in the phosphorylation of p70-S6 kinase (S6K1) after resistance exercise [31]. GWAS might identify new biomarkers that have pathways that have never been implicated using in vivo models of resistance training. Understanding how these technologies will be used is a question that remains unanswered and will require thought and deliberation from exercise scientists choosing to undertake this work. This next section of the chapter will focus on the use of GWAS as a tool in exercise science including what has been done in the field thus far. Finally, the next steps for GWAS will be discussed.

With the publication of the draft sequences of the human genome project in 2001 [32, 33], the field of genomics exploded. Now, almost the entire sequence of the human genome is completed [34] and is in searchable online databases (http://www.ncbi.nlm.nih.gov/ or http://genome.ucsc.edu/) (see Appendix). Even with the completed human genome sequence, the number of genes remains a mystery. An analysis by scientists at Ohio State University suggested the number of genes was between 65,000 and 75,000 [35], while another study published in *Cell* in 2001 predicted a total of 42,000 genes [36]. However, a recent paper found there to be only 20,500 genes [37]. The number of genes was lowered based on a rejection of open reading frames that are not conserved between species. The final number of human genes will not be known for many years and will differ based on different definitions of a gene.

Why is the number of genes important for GWAS? GWAS is designed as a method to survey the entire genome using SNPs distributed at certain intervals of base pair (bp) length in an attempt to capture the genetic diversity of the individual [19]. Therefore, understanding the coding and noncoding regions of the genome is important. The goal of the Human Genome Project was to provide scientists with powerful new tools to help them clear the research hurdles that now keep them from understanding the molecular essence of other tragic and devastating illnesses, such as schizophrenia, alcoholism, Alzheimer's disease, and manic depression.

There is predicted to be ten million sites (SNPs) that are variable (at least 1%) in human populations (about 1 SNP per 300 bp) [38]. With this information, identifying SNPs associated with a phenotype such as skeletal muscle strength should be straightforward and involve genotyping the ten million sites to discover frequency differences for the SNPs between the individuals who are stronger vs. those who are not as strong. However, there are cost issues and structural polymorphism variants that would not be identified (i.e., insertions, deletions, and inversions) using GWAS which only examines SNPs. Therefore, methods to complete a GWAS remain to be developed.

There have been numerous studies showing that individuals who carry a particular SNP allele at one site often predictably carry specific alleles at other nearby variant sites. This correlation is known as LD; a particular combination of alleles along a chromosome is termed a haplotype. LD exists because of the shared ancestry of contemporary chromosomes [38]. The International HapMap project (http://hapmap.ncbi.nlm.nih.gov) (see Appendix) was developed to find these genome-wide database of patterns of human genetic variation [38]. The HapMap project was a logical next step in defining the human genome and was started in 2003 [38].

Four different populations with African, Asian, and European ancestry were used in the completion of the HapMap (http://hapmap.ncbi.nlm.nih.gov) project that sought to determine the frequencies and patterns of association among roughly three million common SNPs for use in GWAS. The website can be used with genomic positions or gene names and will show the SNPs that are in LD (or linked). This website can be used to reduce the number of SNPs used for a GWAS study because redundancy is eliminated.

The HapMap project ushered in new technological advances that made GWAS a possibility with cost-efficient methods to genotype up to one million SNPs.

In addition, new insights into the evolutionary pressures on the human genome began to be understood. For example, functional portions of the genome (those that code for proteins) are under selective pressure to contain less polymorphisms [39]. Changes in the amino acid sequence of a protein by a SNP may render the protein useless, and thus there would be selective pressure by evolution to remove that SNP from the gene pool. Finally, understanding the function of genetic variation (which will be discussed later in this chapter) has become a priority.

GWAS is a fantastic tool that has been used to find strong associations between a specific chromosomal locus and complex human diseases such as T2D (please see Chap. 4 for additional information on T2D). The single largest effect size for T2D identified to date resides within the transcription factor 7-like 2 (*TCF7L2*) gene [40]. This gene has been replicated in numerous GWAS [41–43]. In addition, there have been numerous loci identified that are associated with lipids such as variants within or in close proximity to the Sortilin 1 (*SORT1*) and Cadherin, EGF LAG seven-pass G-type receptor 2 (*CELSR2*) genes [17, 44, 45].

GWAS is in its infancy for understanding exercise genomics. Only one such study has been published on a skeletal muscle phenotype, lean body mass (LBM). Liu et al. [46] found two SNPs, rs16892496 ($p=7.55\times10^{-8}$) and rs7832552 ($p=7.58\times10^{-8}$), within the thyrotropin-releasing hormone receptor (*TRHR*) gene were significantly associated with LBM after testing 379,319 eligible SNPs in 1,000 unrelated US Whites. Subjects carrying unfavorable genotypes at rs16892496 and rs7832552 had, on average, 2.70 and 2.55 kg lower LBM, respectively, compared to those with alternative genotypes. As is important for a GWAS, the results were replicated in three independent samples: (1) 1,488 unrelated US Whites, (2) 2,955 Chinese unrelated subjects, and (3) 593 nuclear families comprising 1,972 US Whites [46]. The meta-analyses of the GWA scan and the replication studies yielded *p* values $=5.53\times10^{-9}$ for rs16892496 and 3.88×10^{-10} for rs7832552. This functional data point to the *TRHR* gene as a component of the mechanism for LBM.

The *TRHR* gene encodes the TRHR, which belongs to the G protein-coupled receptor 1 family. Thyrotropic-releasing hormone (TRH) is a tripeptide (Glu-His-Pro) hormone secreted by the hypothalamus. TRH binds to TRHR on the surface of pituitary thyrotrophs. The primary consequence of the TRH:TRHR binding is activation of the inositol phospholipid-calcium-protein kinase C transduction pathway that stimulates secretion of thyroid-stimulating hormone (TSH) and prolactin. The TSH response to TRHR is the first step in the hormonal cascade of hypothalamic-pituitary-thyroid axis (HPTA) that eventually leads to the release of thyroxin, which is important in the development of vertebrate skeletal muscle [47]. Additionally, thyroxin is required for the full anabolic action of the growth hormone-insulin-like growth factor-I (GH-IGF1) axis that is central in its role in muscle protein balance and adaptive changes to resistance training [46]. Results of this study, together with the functional relevance of TRHR in muscle metabolism, support the *TRHR* gene as an important gene for LBM variation. This type of work is an excellent model for the type of work that needs to be performed to examine the influence of genetic variation on health fitness and exercise performance phenotypes in exercise science.

GWAS as a Tool to Uncover Functional Gene Variants

One of the most exciting areas of study within the realm of GWAS is the uncovering of functional genetic variants that may control gene expression. Gene expression or a change in the level of mRNA is the underlying force for cellular phenotypes including muscle growth [48, 49]. For example, when a skeletal muscle undergoes contraction, IGF1 is secreted [49]. Gene expression has been used to understand the pathways that underlie the response of skeletal muscle to resistance training [50]. The understanding of how gene expression regulates key biological functions is not well understood and is just beginning to be explored. The technical development of microarrays as a biological tool has allowed the measure of gene expression on a global scale, which has changed the face of molecular biology [51]. Gene expression is used to discover pathways that drive diseases such as muscular dystrophy [52] and/or the response of skeletal muscle to resistance training [50]. This development is now coupled to GWAS to identify individual differences in the quantitative levels of gene expression (i.e., expression quantitative loci [eQTLs]). In exercise science, this will be a key to the development of new pathways that affect skeletal muscle response or aerobic response to training.

Gene changes that are identified using gene expression profiling can be used in conjunction with GWAS data to map genetic variants that have an effect on gene expression. This will be valuable for the discovery of new genes and the genetic variants that influence gene expression involved in the response of the skeletal muscle to resistance training. But this can be used with any type of exercise in any type of tissue. For example, the brain of a mouse undergoing aerobic training could be expression profiled and these data analyzed with genetic variants to find SNPs that control brain response to aerobic training. In addition, the discovery of new genetic variants and the genes that they exert control over may solidify the current pathways present in the literature. If a genetic variant that elevates the expression of *IGF1* is identified using GWAS and whole genome expression profiling, it is possible that individuals with that variant may have an improved response to some types of resistance training. These new tools will lead to the development of an arsenal of new genes for further study by matching gene expression data with GWAS data. In addition, these new pathways maybe specific to skeletal muscle and will need to be explored in the other tissues in the human body.

The Future?

Throughout this chapter, we have included comment on our vision for the future regarding statistical and methodological considerations. In summary, as technology advances, the data management and statistical tools to effectively analyze the resulting data will evolve. Platforms to genotype larger sets of SNPs are being developed, and the methods to deal massive amounts of data will be needed. Along with SNP data, data from other sources such as gene expression and proteomics will have to be integrated in order to get a more complete picture of biological processes. The development of next-generation sequencing will require statistical methods to deal with the data it produces. All of these are areas of active research that are driven by the increasing technical ability to produce more detailed biological information. The exercise scientist doing genomics research will need to become an expert in understanding complicated genetics and the statistical methods to process the data.

Practical Applications

We have commented on practical applications throughout this chapter. Briefly, all of the statistic methods discussed in this chapter can and are being used by exercise scientists. The advent of new genotyping methods involving larger data sets and methods to interrogate more genetic variation will require new methods of data handling. In addition, the methods in this chapter will be used to examine minor statistical effects from genetic variation.

References

1. Hosking L, Lumsden S, Lewis K, Yeo A, McCarthy L, Bansal A, et al. Detection of genotyping errors by Hardy–Weinberg equilibrium testing. Eur J Hum Genet. 2004;12(5):395–9.
2. Trikalinos TA, Salanti G, Khoury MJ, Ioannidis JP. Impact of violations and deviations in Hardy–Weinberg equilibrium on postulated gene-disease associations. Am J Epidemiol. 2006;163(4):300–9.
3. Stern C. The Hardy–Weinberg law. Science. 1943;97(2510):137–8.
4. Gabriel SB, Schaffner SF, Nguyen H, Moore JM, Roy J, Blumenstiel B, et al. The structure of haplotype blocks in the human genome. Science. 2002;296(5576):2225–9.
5. Pearson TA, Manolio TA. How to interpret a genome-wide association study. JAMA. 2008;299(11):1335–44.
6. Pritchard JK, Przeworski M. Linkage disequilibrium in humans: models and data. Am J Hum Genet. 2001;69(1):1–14.
7. Weiss KM, Clark AG. Linkage disequilibrium and the mapping of complex human traits. Trends Genet. 2002;18(1):19–24.
8. Wallace C, Dobson RJ, Munroe PB, Caulfield MJ. Information capture using SNPs from HapMap and whole-genome chips differs in a sample of inflammatory and cardiovascular gene-centric regions from genome-wide estimates. Genome Res. 2007;17(11):1596–602.
9. Devlin B, Risch N. A comparison of linkage disequilibrium measures for fine-scale mapping. Genomics. 1995;29(2):311–22.
10. Qin S. Linkage disequilibrium: Biostat830: advanced topics in biostatistics lecture notes. http://www.sph.umich.edu/~qin/biostat830/LDnote.doc. Accessed 9 Nov 2009.
11. Wall JD, Pritchard JK. Haplotype blocks and linkage disequilibrium in the human genome. Nat Rev Genet. 2003;4(8):587–97.
12. Pistilli EE, Gordish-Dressman H, Seip RL, Devaney JM, Thompson PD, Price TB, et al. Resistin polymorphisms are associated with muscle, bone, and fat phenotypes in white men and women. Obesity (Silver Spring). 2007;15(2):392–402.
13. Orkunoglu-Suer FE, Gordish-Dressman H, Clarkson PM, Thompson PD, Angelopoulos TJ, Gordon PM, et al. INSIG2 gene polymorphism is associated with increased subcutaneous fat in women and poor response to resistance training in men. BMC Med Genet. 2008;9:117.

14. Zheng G, Joo J, Zhang C, Geller NL. Testing association for markers on the X chromosome. Genet Epidemiol. 2007;31(8):834–43.
15. Cordell HJ. Epistasis: what it means, what it doesn't mean, and statistical methods to detect it in humans. Hum Mol Genet. 2002;11(20):2463–8.
16. Horne BD, Anderson JL, Carlquist JF, Muhlestein JB, Renlund DG, Bair TL, et al. Generating genetic risk scores from intermediate phenotypes for use in association studies of clinically significant endpoints. Ann Hum Genet. 2005;69(Pt 2):176–86.
17. Kathiresan S, Melander O, Anevski D, Guiducci C, Burtt NP, Roos C, et al. Polymorphisms associated with cholesterol and risk of cardiovascular events. N Engl J Med. 2008; 358(12):1240–9.
18. Thomas DC. Statistical methods in genetic epidemiology. Oxford: Oxford University Press; 2004.
19. Wang WY, Barratt BJ, Clayton DG, Todd JA. Genome-wide association studies: theoretical and practical concerns. Nat Rev Genet. 2005;6(2):109–18.
20. Pritchard JK, Rosenberg NA. Use of unlinked genetic markers to detect population stratification in association studies. Am J Hum Genet. 1999;65(1):220–8.
21. Devlin B, Roeder K. Genomic control for association studies. Biometrics. 1999;55(4): 997–1004.
22. Hopkins WG. A new view of statistics. http://www.sportsci.org/resource/stats/index.html2010. Accessed 4 November 2009.
23. van Walraven C, Hart RG. Leave 'em alone – why continuous variables should be analyzed as such. Neuroepidemiology. 2008;30(3):138–9.
24. Ng MC, Tam CH, So WY, Ho JSK, Chan AW, Lee HM, et al. Implication of genetic variants near NEGR1, SEC16B, TMEM18, ETV5/DGKG, GNPDA2, LIN7C/BDNF, MTCH2, BCDIN3D/FAIM2, SH2B1, FTO, MC4R, and KCTD15 with obesity and type 2 diabetes in 7705 Chinese. J Clin Endocrinol Metab. 2010;95(5):2418–25.
25. Cribbie RA, Keselman HJ. The effects of nonnormality on parametric, nonparametric, and model comparison approaches to pairwise comparisons. Educ Psychol Meas. 2003;63(4):615–35.
26. Pappas PA, DePuy V. An overview of non-parametric tests in SAS®: when, why, and how. http://analytics.ncsu.edu/sesug/2004/TU04-Pappas.pdf2010. Accessed 6 November 2009.
27. Hirschhorn JN, Daly MJ. Genome-wide association studies for common diseases and complex traits. Nat Rev Genet. 2005;6(2):95–108.
28. NCI-NHGRI Working Group on Replication in Association Studies, Chanock SJ, Manolio T, et al. Replicating genotype-phenotype associations. Nature. 2007;447(7145):655–60.
29. Spencer CC, Su Z, Donnelly P, Marchini J. Designing genome-wide association studies: sample size, power, imputation, and the choice of genotyping chip. PLoS Genet. 2009;5(5):e1000477.
30. Hunter DJ, Kraft P. Drinking from the fire hose – statistical issues in genomewide association studies. N Engl J Med. 2007;357(5):436–9.
31. Nader GA, Esser KA. Intracellular signaling specificity in skeletal muscle in response to different modes of exercise. J Appl Physiol. 2001;90(5):1936–42.
32. Lander ES, Linton LM, Birren B, Nusbaum C, Zody MC, Baldwin J, et al. Initial sequencing and analysis of the human genome. Nature. 2001;409(6822):860–921.
33. Venter JC, Adams MD, Myers EW, Li PW, Mural RJ, Sutton GG, et al. The sequence of the human genome. Science. 2001;291(5507):1304–51.
34. International Human Genome Sequencing Consortium. Finishing the euchromatic sequence of the human genome. Nature. 2004;431(7011):931–45.
35. Wright FA, Lemon WJ, Zhao WD, Sears R, Zhuo D, Wang J, et al. A draft annotation and overview of the human genome. Genome Biol. 2001;2(7):1–18.
36. Hogenesch JB, Ching KA, Batalov S, Su AI, Walker JR, Zhou Y, et al. A comparison of the celera and ensembl predicted gene sets reveals little overlap in novel genes. Cell. 2001;106(4):413–5.

37. Clamp M, Fry B, Kamal M, Xie X, Cuff J, Lin MF, et al. Distinguishing protein-coding and noncoding genes in the human genome. Proc Natl Acad Sci U S A. 2007; 104(49):19428–33.
38. International HapMap Consortium. The international HapMap project. Nature. 2003; 426(6968):789–96.
39. Davidson S, Starkey A, MacKenzie A. Evidence of uneven selective pressure on different subsets of the conserved human genome; implications for the significance of intronic and intergenic DNA. BMC Genomics. 2009;10:614.
40. Sladek R, Rocheleau G, Rung J, Dina C, Shen L, Serre D, et al. A genome-wide association study identifies novel risk loci for type 2 diabetes. Nature. 2007;445(7130):881–5.
41. Diabetes Genetics Initiative of Broad Institute of Harvard and MIT, Lund University, and Novartis Institutes of BioMedical Research, Saxena R, Voight BF, Lyssenko V, Burtt NP, de Bakker PW, et al. Genome-wide association analysis identifies loci for type 2 diabetes and triglyceride levels. Science. 2007;316(5829):1331–6.
42. Zeggini E, Scott LJ, Saxena R, Voight BF, Marchini JL, Hu T, et al. Meta-analysis of genome-wide association data and large-scale replication identifies additional susceptibility loci for type 2 diabetes. Nat Genet. 2008;40(5):638–45.
43. Zeggini E, Weedon MN, Lindgren CM, Frayling TM, Elliott KS, Lango H, et al. Replication of genome-wide association signals in UK samples reveals risk loci for type 2 diabetes. Science. 2007;316(5829):1336–41.
44. Kathiresan S, Melander O, Guiducci C, Surti A, Burtt NP, Rieder MJ, et al. Six new loci associated with blood low-density lipoprotein cholesterol, high-density lipoprotein cholesterol or triglycerides in humans. Nat Genet. 2008;40(2):189–97.
45. Willer CJ, Sanna S, Jackson AU, Scuteri A, Bonnycastle LL, Clarke R, et al. Newly identified loci that influence lipid concentrations and risk of coronary artery disease. Nat Genet. 2008;40(2):161–9.
46. Liu XG, Tan LJ, Lei SF, Liu YJ, Shen H, Wang L, et al. Genome-wide association and replication studies identified TRHR as an important gene for lean body mass. Am J Hum Genet. 2009;84(3):418–23.
47. Larsson L, Li X, Teresi A, Salviati G. Effects of thyroid hormone on fast- and slow-twitch skeletal muscles in young and old rats. J Physiol. 1994;481(Pt 1):149–61.
48. Coffey VG, Hawley JA. The molecular bases of training adaptation. Sports Med. 2007;37(9):737–63.
49. Glass DJ. Molecular mechanisms modulating muscle mass. Trends Mol Med. 2003;9(8): 344–50.
50. Chen YW, Nader GA, Baar KR, Fedele MJ, Hoffman EP, Esser KA. Response of rat muscle to acute resistance exercise defined by transcriptional and translational profiling. J Physiol. 2002;545(Pt 1):27–41.
51. Mahoney DJ, Tarnopolsky MA. Understanding skeletal muscle adaptation to exercise training in humans: contributions from microarray studies. Phys Med Rehabil Clin N Am. 2005;16(4):859–73, vii.
52. Hoffman EP, DuBois DC, Hoffman RI, Almon RR. Expression profiling and pharmacogenomics of muscle and muscle disease. Curr Opin Pharmacol. 2003;3(3):309–16.

Chapter 3
Can You Be Born a Couch Potato?
The Genomic Regulation of Physical Activity

J. Timothy Lightfoot

Keywords Physical activity • Exercise • Genetics • Candidate genes • Quantitative trait loci • Positional cloning • Heritability of activity • Human heritability of activity • Mouse heritability of activity

Introduction

There is a plethora of evidence that physical inactivity is the root cause of a large variety of chronic health conditions [1–6]. Physical inactivity is ranked as the second leading actual cause of death in the United States with approximately 250,000–400,000 deaths per year directly attributed to physical inactivity. This total is larger than the next seven actual causes of death *combined* [7, 8]. Additionally, increasing physical activity level is a well-known treatment that prevents and ameliorates the effects of a host of diseases including cardiovascular disease [9], some forms of diabetes [10], some forms of cancer [11], and several musculoskeletal diseases (e.g., sarcopenia [12]). Sadly, a recent study [13] that directly measured physical activity in a large cohort ($n = 6,329$) showed less than 3.5% of adults completed at least 30 min of total activity per day. The evidence is unquestionable that even moderate levels of physical activity have significant impact on quantity and quality of life. Yet, the rates of physical activity in children and adults continue to decrease at a precipitous rate. This factor, probably more than any other, is the one contributing to the exponential increase in several different disease entities including obesity [14].

J.T. Lightfoot (✉)
Department of Health and Kinesiology, Sydney and JL Huffines Institute
for Sports Medicine and Human Performance, Texas A&M University,
159 Read Building, TAMU 4243, College Station, TX 77845-4243, USA
e-mail: TLightfoot@hlkn.tamu.edu

L.S. Pescatello and S.M. Roth (eds.), *Exercise Genomics*,
Molecular and Translational Medicine, DOI 10.1007/978-1-60761-355-8_3,
© Springer Science+Business Media, LLC 2011

Physical Activity and Genetics

It is generally accepted that an individual's behavior arises from three factors: biological/genetic influences, environmental influences, and/or the interaction among biological and environmental factors. The primary influence on physical activity status has commonly been considered to be environmental. The sheer weight of literature focused on and investigating a variety of environmental influences on physical activity tends to sway discussion regarding physical activity/inactivity toward a consideration of common environmental influences as if they were the sole factors (e.g., Dunton et al. [15]). However, the preponderance of research investigating environmental influences has not and does not eliminate the possibility of genetic/biological influences on physical activity. In fact, in an elegant summary of the sparse literature at that time, Rowland [16] suggested quite strongly that there were significant biological/genetic influences that drove physical activity and inactivity. For example, while there are likely some environmental influences, it is well known that physical activity differs significantly by sex (Fig. 3.1). In lower mammals, females are generally more active than males with distinct physiological pathways suggested that drive this difference [17]. However, in higher mammals, both in westernized populations and hunter/gatherer populations, females are generally less active than males (Fig. 3.1). It is not clear why the sexes differ in physical activity depending on where they fall on the evolutionary tree,

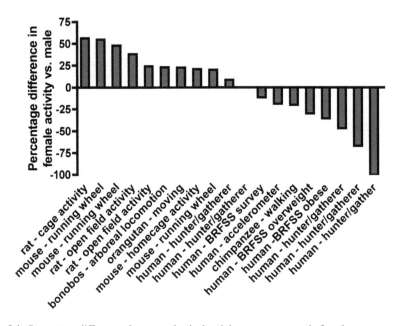

Fig. 3.1 Percentage differences between physical activity measurements in females versus males. Positive percentage difference indicates higher activity in females. *BRFSS* Behavioral Risk Factor Surveillance Survey (data for graph derived from [13, 34, 38, 41, 105–115])

and whether these sex differences arise because of some genetic mechanism inherent in one of the sexes or is the downstream result of biological differences. However, it is clear that there are biological/genetic sex differences in physical activity distinct from environmental influences on activity.

Since Rowland's original hypothesis, progress has occurred rapidly in the area of "physical activity genetics" especially with the adoption and use of molecular, cellular, and genetic techniques in the area. Thus, the purpose of this chapter is to describe the current "state of the art" regarding physical activity genetics: what we know and what we do not know; and where we have been and where we are going. This chapter is focused on the discovery and elucidation of the genetic mechanisms that influence and regulate physical activity levels – whether they are high or low activity levels. In this context, activity level is always the dependent variable being acted upon by genetic/biological factors as opposed to the common use of physical activity as the independent variable used to affect other systems.

The Heritability of Activity: Are Couch Potatoes Born or Made?

Physical activity is usually considered the total amount of activity a person accomplishes in the course of a day and includes not only formal exercise, but movement that is part of everyday living (e.g., walking up stairs, yard work, etc.). Thus, the term *physical activity* actually represents a continuum of activity from very low, sedentary behaviors to more active lifestyles that include regular exercise. Individuals can present with varying levels of physical activity. Interestingly, the actual within-individual variance in physical activity appears constant across animals (coefficient of variation 23% [18]) and humans (coefficient of variation of 20–23%) regardless of age, sex, and/or nationality [18–22]. The consistency of activity in spite of varying species, environments, and other external factors suggests there is biological/genetic control of physical activity and that physical activity levels may be heritable.

Heritability is generally considered the influence of heredity on a specific characteristic or phenotype; [23] in our case, the phenotype of interest would be the physical activity level of the individual. On a quantitative basis, heritability is often estimated using either "broad-sense" or "narrow-sense" approaches and represented as either a percentage value (e.g., 60%) or a decimal value (e.g., 0.60). Broad-sense heritability is usually defined as the influence of all genetic effects on a phenotype [24] and is a liberal estimation of heritability. In most cases, either intraclass correlation or coefficient of genetic determination used primarily for inbred mouse strains results in estimates of broad-sense heritability denoted as either h^2 or g^2, respectively [25, 26]. Conversely, narrow-sense heritability theoretically represents how much children represent their parents without representation of other genetic effects [24]. Thus, narrow-sense heritability estimates are more conservative and usually give estimates of heritability that are lower than those that arise from broad-sense heritability estimations. Narrow-sense heritabilities are usually derived using offspring–parent regression and sibling analysis methods [23].

Human Studies of Physical Activity Heritability

The number of studies investigating heritable influences on activity has been slowly growing with the majority consisting primarily of large-scale epidemiological studies. There are now at least six studies that have used a human-twin design and one that used a family design (Table 3.1). The use of twin and family research designs allows investigators to ascribe the amount of influence on physical activity which arises from genetic factors, common environmental factors, and unique environmental factors. Common environmental factors are those influences experienced and shared by both members of a twin set or by all members of a family such as the home environment, parental influence, and to some extent, common external influences such as educational experiences. Conversely, unique environmental factors are those experienced solely by each individual participant, regardless of their membership in either a twin set or a family, and may consist of unique peer interactions or individual exposure to differing life experiences.

One of the earliest estimations of the heritability of physical activity level came from Kaprio et al. [27] who surveyed the daily activity levels of 1,537 monozygous (MZ) male twins and 3,057 dizygous (DZ) male twins. After adjusting for age and using interpair correlations, Kaprio et al. [27] estimated that the heritability of physical activity was 62%, the common environmental effects were zero (0%), and the unique environmental effects were 38%.

Similar to Kaprio et al.'s results [27], Lauderdale et al. [28] surveyed physical activity level in 3,344 twin pairs that were part of the Vietnam Era Twin Registry. Lauderdale et al. [28] used questionnaires and estimated the broad-sense heritability of intense activity varied from 39 to 58%, with one specific measure, running at least 10 miles/week, having a heritability of 53%. The heritability estimates for the moderate exercises were generally lower, but were significant averaging 38%. Lauderdale et al. [28] were careful to point out that the results from the MZ twins might have been inflated due to similar lifestyles, even though their analysis revealed no common environmental effects. Similarly, Carlsson et al. [29] measured 13,362 twin pairs (5,334 MZ and 8,028 DZ) and showed the variance in self-reported daily activity due to heritage was 57% in males and 50% in females. Environmental influences common to both individuals in a twin pair accounted for only 3–6% of the total variance [29].

In the largest study to date on this topic, Stubbe et al. [30] used self-reported leisure time behavior data from 37,051 twin pairs from 7 countries. They observed in all countries with the exception of Norwegian males that environmental factors common to both twins exerted no effect on activity. Rather, in all cases, genetics and unique environmental factors played the major roles in determining exercise participation levels with the median genetic effect averaging 62% (range 26.5–70.5%).

Table 3.1 Estimates of the heritability of physical activity

Study author	Number of subjects	Design	Index of activity	Genetic influence	Common EI	Unique EI
Kaprio et al. [27]	5,044 Twin pairs	Human twin	Survey of leisure activity	0.624	NR	NR
Lauderdale et al. [28]	3,344 Twin pairs	Human twin	Survey; various moderate and vigorous exercise scales	0.38 (Moderate activity scale)	0.00	0.62
Perusse et al. [31]	1,610 from 375 Families	Human family	Survey of level of habitual physical activity	0.29	0.71 (Not partitioned into common and unique)	–
Stubbe et al. [32]	2,628 Twin pairs	Human twin	Survey of sports participation	0.85 (19–20-year-old twins)[a]	0.00	0.15
Carlsson et al. [29]	13,362 Twin pairs	Human twin	Survey; leisure time activity	Males – 0.57, females – 0.50	Males=0.03, females=0.06	Males=0.40, females=0.44
Stubbe et al. [30]	85,198 (37,051 Complete twin pairs)	Human twin	Survey; exercise participation	Average=0.63 (range=0.265 –0.705)	Average=0.00 (0.368 reported for nor. males)	Average=0.457 (range=0.295 –0.519)
Joosen et al. [33]	20 Twin pairs	Human twin	Accelerometer measure	0.78	0.00	0.22
Festing [40]	26 Inbred strains (total n=217)	Inbred mouse strain screen	Wheel-running (revolutions/day)	0.26–0.29	NR	NR
Lerman et al. [42]	7 Inbred strains (total n=28–42)[b]	Inbred mouse strain screen	Wheel-running (distance/day)	0.39	NR	NR
Swallow et al. [43]	10 Generations (avg. n/gen=577)	Selectively bred mice	Wheel-running (revolutions/day)	0.28	NR	NR
Lightfoot et al. [41]	13 Inbred strains (total n=133)	Inbred mouse strain screen	Wheel-running (distance/day)	Males=0.31, females=0.12	NR	NR

Table 3.1 (continued)

Study author	Number of subjects	Design	Index of activity	Genetic influence	Common EI	Unique EI
Lightfoot et al. [38]	310 C57C3 F_2 Mice	F_2 intercross mouse cohort	Wheel-running (distance/day)	0.495	NR	NR
Turner et al. [46]	13 Inbred strains (total $n = 130$)	Inbred mouse strain screen	Wheel-running (distance/day)	0.41–0.764 (Age-related)	NR	NR

EI Environmental influence; *NR* not reported

[a]Genetic heritability estimate from 19 to 20-year-old age group; genetic heritability was less and environmental influence was higher in younger subjects

[b]Total numbers based on report of four to six animals used per strain

In one of the few family studies that present heritability estimates, Perusse et al. [31] collected 3-day activity records from 1,610 subjects from 375 different families from the Quebec area (Quebec Family Study) and estimated heritabilities of 20–29% (environmental effect 12%) for physical activity. These values were considerably lower than those from either Kaprio et al. [27] or Lauderdale et al. [28]. Interestingly, Perusse et al. [31] suggested while physical activity levels were heritable (including inactivity), exercise participation levels were not. They speculated the disposition toward moderate and more vigorous exercise was not influenced by activity. These conclusions conflict to some extent with Lauderdale et al. [28] and Stubbe et al. [30] who suggested moderate and vigorous activity levels and exercise participation were heritable. While all of these studies found significant heritability of activity, resolution of conflicts in the interpretation of their findings may actually lie in the limitations of the methods used to determine activity levels (see below).

Stubbe et al. [32] used survey data from 2,628 Dutch twin pairs between the ages of 13 and 20 years. They observed environmental influences on daily activity, while important during childhood and adolescence, cease to play a significant role after age 18 years. While environmental factors accounted for 78–84% of sports participation between the ages of 13 and 16 years, genetic influences accounted for 85% of variability in subjects' activity after the age of 18 years with environmental factors playing little role in activity determination after the age of 18 years. Thus, it appears the heritability of activity varies by age, with little influence before the late teen years, but then becoming the predominant determinant of activity levels after 18 years.

Of the available human studies, only Joosen et al. [33] have directly measured physical activity as opposed to using survey-based instruments to estimate activity levels. These investigators directly measured activity-induced energy expenditure and physical activity in 20 sets of twin pairs (12 MZ, 8 DZ). Physical activity energy expenditure was measured by doubly-labeled water over a 2-week period in conjunction with the use of an accelerometer. They found genetic factors explained 78% of the variance in free-living physical activity (i.e., outside the metabolic chamber during this 2-week period), while common environmental factors were responsible for none of the variance in physical activity and unique environmental factors were responsible for 22% of the variance. Of the available human studies, Joosen et al. [33] have reported the highest genetic contribution to physical activity. This higher estimate may be due to the smaller and potentially more homogenous subject pool or more likely due to the lower measurement error associated with direct measurement of activity versus estimation with surveys as evidenced by the extremely low variance noted in the daily activity counts, particularly in their MZ twin sets that averaged 8.5%.

From this brief review of the pertinent human studies, physical activity levels are clearly heritable (Table 3.1). While there is a wide heritability range reported, this variance is most likely due to a number of factors. The most prominent of these are the use of various statistical models used to estimate heritability and survey instruments to determine activity levels (with the exception of Joosen et al. [33]).

Numerous reviews have generally observed that survey estimations of physical activity typically overestimate actual activity levels. This overestimation was reinforced recently by Troiano et al. [13]. They measured daily activity in a large population using accelerometers and found only a small percentage ($3.5 \pm 0.3\%$) of adults completing moderate activity on a daily basis compared to survey estimates of adult activity levels (e.g., $45.4 \pm 0.2\%$ [34]). Two important factors that often lead to the least valid estimates of activity are the length of time separating subject recall from the activity and individuals who engage in lower levels of activity [35]. It is difficult to determine the possible effect of these two confounding factors on the results of any of the human studies of physical activity heritability. It should be noted, however, that the one study that directly measured activity [33] and thus removed the variation due to recall and measurement error, while admittedly limited in sample size power, still found some of the highest heritability estimates reported in the human literature.

Mouse Studies of Physical Activity Heritability

Measuring voluntary activity in animals, especially rodents such as mice, is relatively simple and largely standardizes environmental influences on activity levels – a design feature virtually impossible in human studies. Additionally, the use of inbred strains and selectively bred animals allows the consideration of large cohorts of animals with homozygous genomes, again a research design element that is impossible to impose in human studies. One of the most simple yet repeatable [36] forms of activity determination in mice is to measure running wheel behavior which appears to be particularly analogous to human voluntary activity [37]. There are a variety of activity indices that can be derived from running wheel behavior with the most common being the number of revolutions the wheel turns per day, the distance run per day, the duration of exercise, and/or the speed of exercise. It may be assumed that duration of activity and speed of activity may represent differing phenotypes; however, these two differing characteristics are indeed correlated and in some cases result in similar genomic associations (i.e., quantitative trait loci [QTL]). Thus, they may have common genetic background [38]. The reader is invited to peruse other discussions regarding appropriate physical activity phenotypes in mice for further discussion on this topic [36, 39].

From the available mouse running wheel studies much like the human studies, it is clear there is a significant genetic effect on physical activity (Table 3.1). Festing [40] noted the broad-sense heritability of daily distance run in 26 inbred strains ranged from 0.26 (7 day running) to 0.29 (48 h running). These results are similar to heritability estimates of 0.30 derived from a limited strain screen [41] for distance run in all of the mice, regardless of sex. Lerman et al. [42] reported significant heritability estimates for distance run (39–56%), duration of exercise (42–59%), and exercise speed (24–38%) in male mice in seven inbred strains.

Similarly, in a large F_2 cohort ($n = 310$) based on high-active C57L/J inbred mice and low-active C3H/HeJ mice [41], the coefficient for genetic determination (i.e., g^2 a measure not as liberal as common, broad-sense heritability estimates, but one not as conservative as narrow-sense approaches) was high for all activity indices (e.g., distance run per day $g^2 = 0.50 \pm 0.10$, duration $g^2 = 0.59 \pm 0.82$, and speed $g^2 = 0.47 \pm 0.11$) [38].

Swallow et al. [43] devised an interesting research design that made use of experimental evolution [44] by selectively breeding animals for high wheel-running activity over ten generations. They [43] reported a realized heritability (i.e., the degree to which a trait in a population can be pushed by selection) ranging from 0.18 to 0.32 in the animals selectively bred for high activity, while the founder population's wheel-running broad-sense heritability averaged 0.49. Uniquely, Garland's group [44] has observed as they have continued this experimental evolution trial, which is now at generation 57, that the animals appear to increase their wheel running primarily through increases in speed and not duration of activity [43, 45].

Using ten strains of inbred mice, Turner et al. [46] also noted significant heritability of physical activity, but suggested the heritability of activity may be dependent upon age. This hypothesis was also advanced almost simultaneously by Stubbe et al. [32] in a cohort of human twins. Turner et al. [46] found the heritability for distance per day was 40% at 12 weeks of age (roughly corresponding to a 15-year-old human), increased to approximately 75% at 21 weeks of age, and stayed above 60% until 36 weeks of age when the experiment was terminated. Much like Stubbe et al. [32] who observed a significant increase in the influence of genetic factors on activity levels after age 18 years, Turner et al. [46] data clearly indicated genetic mechanisms play a significant role in determining activity levels as the mouse aged from "adolescence" to "early adulthood" [46] and that the strength of influence of genetic factors changed during the early lifespan. Thus, not only are there copious data that show activity levels in mice are influenced significantly by heritability (Table 3.1), but also the influence of genetic factors change with age, especially over the earlier part of life in humans and animals.

All the available data in human and animal models show conclusively the physical activity level of an organism is significantly affected by heritage (Table 3.1). Whether there exists a general disposition toward a low level of activity being inherited – our so-called "couch potato" – or whether a high level of activity is passed from the parents is unknown. In the end, however, it may be unimportant to determine whether high or low levels of activity are passed from parents to their children. It is clear the magnitude of the genetic influence on activity exhibited by all of the described studies makes activity levels a "predisposition" rather than a "predestination," even though it may be a strong predisposition. Therefore, the critical question may not be whether you are "born a couch potato," but rather what are the genetic/biological mechanisms that predispose to a higher or lower level of activity and whether these mechanisms can be altered.

Tracking Down the Genetic Factors Involved in Regulating Physical Activity

There are approximately 19,000 genes in the human genome, a little over 20,200 genes in the mouse genome, and approximately 15,187 genes homologous between the two genomes [47]. The similarity in the mouse and human genomes (i.e., homology) facilitates translating research findings from murine models directly to the human genome. Nonetheless, it is still a sizeable task to determine which of the approximately 40,000 genes in the two genomes regulate physical activity, and whether the responsible genes are common to both species, unique in each species, or some unique mixture of responsible genes in each individual within each species. To narrow the number of genes that have to be considered, approaches called positional cloning/genome mapping and candidate gene studies have been traditionally employed [48]. These two approaches, while fundamentally helping the researcher arrive at genes that may be responsible for the trait of interest, take different approaches. In general, a positional cloning/genome mapping approach uses the genomic distribution of particular genetic markers such as single nucleotide polymorphisms (SNP) to determine genomic regions (QTL) within the genome associated with a particular phenotype. The identification of a QTL allows the researcher to narrow the genes that could be considered to just those contained within the genomic region of the QTL. While significantly reducing the number of potential genes to consider, the currently identified physical activity QTL studies still present QTL that could theoretically contain hundreds of genes (see below).

Conversely, the candidate gene approach selects particular genes for investigation based on their physiological and/or functional relevance to pathways known to be involved in determining/regulating the phenotype of interest. However, as one might have already concluded, the candidate gene approach is only as good as the initial gene selection, which depends on an understanding of the physiological pathway through which the phenotype is controlled. Given that there is little known regarding the physiologic pathways through which physical activity is regulated, the strict use of a candidate gene approach without integrating results from positional cloning approaches can lead to false positives as has been recently shown by De Moor et al. [49] Thus, determination of candidate genes for the regulation of physical activity requires the integration of both positional cloning and candidate gene approaches.

Positional Cloning Efforts

General Limitations of Positional Cloning

As noted earlier, the use of positional cloning approaches results in the identification of a genomic area – called a QTL – that is associated with the phenotype of interest. The determination of QTL is primarily statistical in nature, and in general, either regression [50–52] or Bayesian factor [53–56] approaches are used in their identification. There is extensive literature available to aid the researcher in determining the most appropriate approach for their positional cloning efforts [57, 58]. Of importance is the use of more stringent α values in positional cloning designs to aid in reducing the number of false positive QTL. Usually, $p < 0.05$ is considered "suggestive" of an association, $p < 0.01$ equals "significant" association, and $p < 0.001$ is considered "highly significant" [51]. Thus, the identification of a "significant" QTL requires a more stringent level of statistical proof than is normally observed in the physiological literature.

Positional cloning applied to human subjects is often called genome-wide association studies (GWAS). Because of the heterozygosity of the human genome, GWAS require multiple thousands of subjects to offset statistical power difficulties. The lack of power in human GWAS can lead to the nonidentification (i.e., false negatives) of QTL that may be associated with activity, but do not play a large role in the determination of the phenotype (i.e., areas that explain a small amount of variance). Most QTL thus far associated with physical activity have explained less than 6% of the variability in the phenotype. Thus, the concern regarding the power of a design to identify QTL is a valid one. Conversely, the use of animal models, and in particular inbred mice strains where the mice within each strain are virtual clones of each other due to the homozygosity of their genome [59], allows the use of positional cloning approaches with smaller cohorts of animals ($n = 300$–600) that are sensitive to QTL that explain less than 2% of the phenotypic variation.

Human or inbred mouse positional cloning techniques can result in QTL within which exist a gene or other genetic factor associated with physical activity. Because the resolution of the QTL results depends on the density of the genetic markers used, the area within a QTL may still be a significantly large genomic area containing hundreds of genes. There are a variety of techniques that can be used after a QTL study to further narrow the search area (e.g., congenic strains and local haplotype comparisons), but any genes uncovered with these approaches still suffer from the uncertainty of being a product of an associative research design. Without further hypothesis-driven testing with direct gene/protein manipulation, any genes discovered from a QTL cannot be considered the cause of any phenotypical characteristic.

Positional Cloning and Physical Activity in Mice

The application of positional cloning designs to identify the QTL associated with physical activity is still in its infancy with few studies available in either animal or human models (Table 3.2). The first direct-effect QTL [38] and epistatic QTL maps [60] associated with physical activity levels in mice were only published in 2008. Using a F_2 cohort ($n = 310$) derived from high-active C57L/J and low-active C3H/HeJ mice [38], four significant direct-effect QTL were identified associated with three running wheel activity indices (i.e., distance, duration, and speed). Because distance, duration, and speed indices were correlated in this cohort of animals, it was not surprising the significant QTL from each of these indices colocalized on

Table 3.2 Identified significant ($p < 0.01$) QTL associated with physical activity

Study	Model	Physical activity phenotype	QTL chromosome	Chromosome location	Confidence interval of QTL
Direct-effect QTL					
DeMoor et al. [49]	Human	Exercise participation (survey)	2	200.984 Mbp	200.865–200.984 Mbp
DeMoor et al. [49]	Human	Exercise participation (survey)	10	89.433 Mbp	89.400–89.435 Mbp
DeMoor et al. [49]	Human	Exercise participation (survey)	18	1.585 Mbp	1.585–1.591 Mbp
Cai et al. [69]	Human siblings	% Time in sedentary activities (accelerometry)	18	63–71 cM	Not reported
Simonen et al. [67]	Human families	Physical inactivity (survey)	2	50.12–59.6 cM	Not reported
Lightfoot et al. [38]	Inbred mouse – F_2 intercross	Running wheel distance/day	13	11 cM	1–15 cM
Lightfoot et al. [38]	Inbred mouse – F_2 intercross	Running wheel duration of exercise	13	11 cM	1–15 cM
Lightfoot et al. [38]	Inbred mouse – F_2 intercross	Running wheel speed of exercise	13	9 cM	1–17 cM
Lightfoot et al. [38]	Inbred mouse – F_2 intercross	Running wheel speed of exercise	9	7 cM	1–15 cM
Nehrenberg et al. [62]	Backcross of MM-HR with C57Bl/6J	Running wheel maximum speed and avg. speed	7	46.75–53.75 cM	26.75–77.99 cM
Nehrenberg et al. [62]	Backcross of MM-HR with C57Bl/6J	Running wheel maximum speed and avg. speed	5	9.21 cM	2.21–24.72 cM
Nehrenberg et al. [62]	Backcross of MM-HR with C57Bl/6J	Running wheel maximum speed	6	66.69 cM	38.00–78.00 cM
Nehrenberg et al. [62]	Backcross of MM-HR with C57Bl/6J	Running wheel duration	2	63.18 cM	39.18–74.19 cM

Epistatic QTL[a]

			Chromosome 1	Chromosome 2	
Leamy et al. [60]	Inbred mouse – F$_2$ intercross – epistatic	Running wheel distance/day	3 (62 cM)	10 (34 cM)	—
Leamy et al. [60]	Inbred mouse – F$_2$ intercross – epistatic	Running wheel distance/day	6 (80 cM)	15 (4 cM)	—
Leamy et al. [60]	Inbred mouse – F$_2$ intercross – epistatic	Running wheel duration of exercise	1 (107 cM)	8 (74 cM)	—
Leamy et al. [60]	Inbred mouse – F$_2$ intercross – epistatic	Running wheel duration of exercise	3 (68 cM)	10 (41 cM)	—
Leamy et al. [60]	Inbred mouse – F$_2$ intercross – epistatic	Running wheel duration of exercise	4 (110 cM)	14 (32 cM)	—
Leamy et al. [60]	Inbred mouse – F$_2$ intercross – epistatic	Running wheel duration of exericse	5 (19 cM)	11 (54 cM)	—
Leamy et al. [60]	Inbred mouse – F$_2$ intercross – epistatic	Running wheel duration of exercise	12 (17 cM)	14 (15 cM)	—
Leamy et al. [60]	Inbred mouse – F$_2$ intercross – epistatic	Running wheel speed of exercise	10 (80 cM)	11 (56 cM)	—
Leamy et al. [60]	Inbred mouse – F$_2$ intercross – epistatic	Running wheel speed of exercise	12 (25 cM)	15 (8 cM)	—

MM-HR high-running mice with mini-muscle phenotype
[a]Epistatic QTL are listed by the two interacting genomic areas involved in the epistatic relationship

chromosome 9 (7 cM, distance and speed) and on chromosome 13 (9–11 cM, distance, duration, and speed). The significant QTL located on chromosome 13 (11, 1–15 cM confidence interval) associated with all three traits was also confirmed using haplotype association mapping in 27 inbred strains of mice that identified an additional significant chromosome 13 QTL (40.8 cM) [38]. While significant in and of themselves, these QTL accounted for only 11–34% of the phenotypic variance (depending on the activity index used), indicating there were other QTL or genetic factors that explained additional variance in physical activity levels.

To account for other genetic factors responsible for the variance in activity levels in this model, Leamy et al. [60] conducted a genome-wide epistasis scan to determine if there were significant interactions between genes linked with physical activity levels. It had already been determined that the direct-effect QTL that were identified earlier did not exhibit epistatic interactions [38]. Therefore, the focus was to determine if there were combinations of the nonsignificant direct-effect QTL whose interactions might affect the physical activity traits. Through this effort, additional significant and suggestive epistatic QTL were identified (Table 3.2), associated with distance ($n=10$), duration ($n=12$), and speed ($n=8$) with chromosomes 2, 11, and 12 being involved in the most epistatic QTL pairs. Importantly, these additional epistatic QTL accounted for a sizeable portion of the total phenotypic variance of all three activity indices (distance 24%, duration 36%, and speed 18%) beyond that contributed by the direct-effect QTL. As a result, the total portion of the phenotypic variance accounted for by both direct-effect and epistatic QTL approached the broad-sense heritabilities estimated for those traits in this model (distance 47%, duration 59%, and speed 47%). Thus, the combined direct-effect and epistatic QTL maps appear to account for the large majority (80–100%) of heritable variation for physical activity in the F_2 model derived from high-active (C57L/J) and low-active (C3H/HeJ) progenitors indicating, at least in this model, the majority of genomic locations linked with physical activity were identified.

A unique approach recently taken by Hartmann et al. [61] and Nehrenberg et al. [62] using mice from Garland et al.'s [63] selective breeding experiments involved backcrossing high-running mice that have become fixed for what has been termed the "mini-muscle" phenotype [63]. This mini-muscle phenotype appears to arise from a simple recessive allele and is characterized by an approximately 50% reduction in the muscle mass of the triceps surae muscle complex with concomitant high-running behavior. The mini-muscles appear to have increased capillarity as well as increased capacity for glycogen synthesis [62, 64]. In both studies [61, 62], the high-running mouse line in which the mini-muscle phenotype became fixed in generation 36 was backcrossed (BC) with standard C57Bl/6J inbred mice. The BC and parental mice were then genotyped to determine the potential QTL that gave rise to the mini-muscle phenotype. Using this approach, Hartmann et al. [61] localized the genomic area containing the mini-muscle recessive allele to a 2.6336 Mbp interval on chromosome 11. As noted by these authors, this genomic region contains over 100 annotated genes, many of which are involved in muscle development. Thus, which of the genes within that region give rise to the mini-muscle phenotype or if the phenotype arises from a currently unknown gene in the region will have to await complete sequencing of that genomic interval.

Nehrenberg et al. [62] used the same backcross cohort and found QTL linked with speed and distance of wheel running colocalized with the mini-muscle QTL on chromosome 11 previously identified by Hartmann and colleagues [61]. The findings of Nehrenberg et al. [62] confirmed the pleiotropic effects of this mini-muscle QTL on chromosome 11. When the mini-muscle QTL was controlled for in the analysis, additional significant QTL affecting physical activity were identified on chromosomes 5, 6, and 7 (Table 3.2). Unlike other QTL/activity studies [38, 60], the majority of the identified QTL from Nehrenberg et al. [62] were linked with the speed phenotype as opposed to the distance phenotype. Interestingly, Nehrenberg et al. [62] were the first to identify a sex-linked QTL related to the duration of exercise in high-running male mice only (chromosome 2).

Thus, while few in number, the available animal data suggest several significant QTL associated with physical activity levels, and epistatic interactions are probably present explaining a good portion of the genetic influence on physical activity level. However, these studies, as do most traditional positional cloning studies, suffer from limitations due to the use of limited mouse strains (e.g., what if the QTL found are only responsible for physical activity in those strains) as well as rather wide QTL that contain hundreds of genes. To offset these limitations, future studies will need to employ a larger number of strains with denser genomic marker maps to provide more generalizable and narrower QTL. The 8.3 million SNP marker map for 56 inbred strains of mice [65] has been published, new computational algorithms that can efficiently handle this volume of data [53, 55, 56] now exist, and the Collaborative Cross mouse strains [66] will soon be available. Thus, more generalizable and narrower QTL should be available in the literature in a relatively short period of time.

Positional Cloning and Physical Activity in Humans

Much like the animal literature, positional cloning studies involving physical activity in humans are sparse. The first human study that attempted to localize the genetic factors responsible for physical activity was carried out as an extension of the Quebec Family Study [67]. These investigators genotyped DNA from 767 subjects in 207 families, a population for which heritabilities of daily activity indices previously had been estimated to be 17–25% [68]. The researchers identified one significant QTL linked with *inactivity* (chromosome 2 p22-p16; 50–59 cM) as well as nine suggestive QTL linked with other activity indices. While collecting data in any large-scale human study is difficult, it is possible that the lack of significant QTL associated with other indices of physical activity was related to the reduced statistical power of the research design attributable to the relatively small number of subjects and heterozygosity of the human genome.

In a slightly larger study on children, Cai et al. [69] genotyped DNA from 1,030 siblings from 319 Hispanic families after estimating physical activity using accelerometry. Interestingly, the only genomic area associated with any measure of physical activity was on chromosome 18q (between 63 and 71 cM). Thus, while this study may have missed QTL that contribute in smaller ways to activity, this was the first study to provide potential genetic areas for further investigation related to activity in children. However, Stubbe et al. [32] and Turner et al. [46] have shown the genetic influence on activity before early adulthood is minimal. Thus, the importance of this QTL found by Cai et al. [69] and the associated genes localized within it is unclear.

A more recent study from De Moor et al. [49] took great strides toward reducing the possible exclusion of smaller variance QTL by conducting a GWAS on 1,644 unrelated Dutch and 978 unrelated American adults. Investigating this large human cohort, they employed a dense SNP map of the human genome which included ≈1.6 million common SNP for the Dutch and American cohort. Even with the larger cohort and the denser genomic marker map, they identified only three significant QTL related to exercise participation (Table 3.2). None of these QTL localized with previously identified QTL in either human or animal models, representing additional possible genomic locations that may influence physical activity.

Figure 3.2 presents a visualization of the locations of the identified significant QTL as translated to the mouse genome. The number of identified QTL is somewhat less in number than what may be expected for the genetic control of a complex

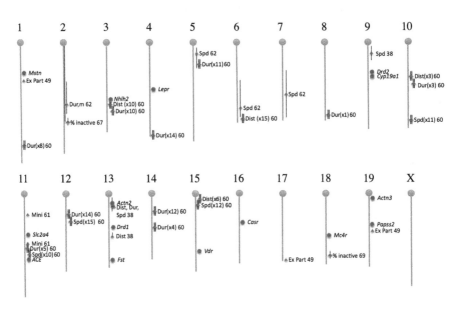

Fig. 3.2 All QTL and gene locations translated to the mouse genome with location in centimorgans. A *closed triangle* indicates the peak of the QTL with associated confidence intervals (CI) shown by the length of the line running through the QTL. If no CI line is shown, this indicates CI that are smaller than graph resolution. *Double lines* on QTL show epistatic QTL relating to the chromosome location that is indicated after "X" in designation. Each QTL designation lists activity index used and reference number of study. *Dist* distance/day; *Dur* duration of activity/day; *Spd* speed of activity (either maximal speed or average speed); *% inactive* percentage of time spent inactive; *Ex Part* exercise participation score; *Mini* mini-muscle phenotype. A *closed circle* indicates gene location according to Mouse Genomic Informatics database [84]

trait like physical activity and reflects the still-embryonic nature of work in this area. While these identified QTL are all reported to be significantly related to activity, given the generally lower phenotypic variance explained by these QTL (none have explained more than 6%), it is probable that other smaller-effect QTL associated with activity are yet to be uncovered, the discovery of which are complicated by the requirement of extremely large cohort sizes.

So, What Genes are Involved with Physical Activity?

Positional cloning approaches have identified QTL associated with physical activity; however, the width of the QTL can include many genes, leading to false positive classification of some genes as candidates for involvement in the phenotype. Moreover, a lack of power in these studies can lead to nonidentification of QTL that may play smaller but no less important roles in physical activity. These difficulties have led to less than stellar results when determining the genes underlying QTL, with some authors claiming less than 20 candidate genes have been identified from existing QTL studies [70]. Several authors [70, 71] and at least one scientific group [58] have recommended additional criteria to identify potential candidate genes to guard against false positive classification of genes as candidate genes linked to a phenotype. In particular, DiPetrillo et al. [71] recommend having at least three independent lines of evidence available before declaring a gene a candidate gene. These independent lines of evidence may arise from several experimental strategies including functional relevance, positional cloning (QTL) studies, combined geno-type studies (using several different intercrosses or cohorts of subjects), regional or genome-wide haplotype studies, gene expression differences, or gene manipulation studies. While there are literally hundreds of annotated genes contained in the identified physical activity QTL (Table 3.2), including many that appear to have functional relevance to activity (Table 3.3), there are currently only two genes that meet the criteria of having at least three independent lines of evidence to suggest candidacy as a regulatory gene of physical activity: dopamine receptor 1 (*Drd1*) and nescient helix-loop-helix 2 (*Nhlh2*).

   Rhodes and coworkers [72, 73] suggested based on the strength of two pharma-cological studies that the dopaminergic system was extensively involved in the regulation of physical activity. They noted that because of differential responses to various dopamine receptor agonists and antagonists [72], dopamine 1 (D1)-like receptors (both D1 and D5 receptors) had reduced function in mice that had been selectively bred to exhibit high wheel-running levels [72]. Supporting this finding, Knab et al. [74] noted the dopamine 1 receptor gene (*Drd1*) was underexpressed in high-active inbred mice (C57L/J) as compared to low-active inbred mice (C3H/HeJ). This underexpression was an independent factor in the determination of activity (i.e., not a result of exposure to wheel running). Further, Knab et al. [75] showed administration of a specific D1-receptor agonist (SKF-81297) caused significant decreases in the daily activity of high-active mice, suggesting manipulation

Table 3.3 Candidate and potential candidate genes associated with physical activity

Gene name (abbreviation)	*Evidence for/against candidacy
Candidate genes (those with three or more lines of evidence supporting candidacy)	
Dopamine receptor 1 (*DRD1*)	FR, QTLm, HD, ED, MD, noQTLh [38, 49, 65, 72–77]
Nescient helix-loop-helix 2 (*NHLH2*)	FR, QTLm, HD, MD, noQTLh [49, 60, 65, 77–79]
Potential candidate genes (those with at least two lines of evidence)	
Glucose transporter 4 (*SLC2A4*)	FR, QTL, within mini-muscle QTL, HD [38, 49, 60, 61, 64, 65, 83]
Myostatin (*MSTN*)	FR, QTL (both m & h), noHD [49, 60, 65]
Aromatase (*CYP19A1*)	FR, QTLm, noQTLh [17, 38, 49, 116]
3′-Phosphoadenosine 5′-phosphosulfate synthase 2 (*PAPSS2*)	≈FR, QTLh&m, partialHD [49, 60, 65]
Suggested genes with limited support for candidacy	
α Actinin 2 (*ACTN2*)	FR, QTLm, HD, noQTLh [38, 49, 60, 65]
α Actinin 3 (*ACTN3*)	FR, QTLm, HD, noQTLh [38, 49, 60, 65]
Angiotensin-converting enzyme (*ACE*)	≈FR, QTLm, noQTLh, noHD [38, 49, 60, 65, 117–119]
Dopamine receptor 2 (*DRD2*)	FR, HuP, QTLm, noQTLh, noED [38, 49, 74, 76, 120]
Follistatin (*FST*)	FR, noQTL, HD [38, 49, 60, 65, 121]
Melanocortin-4 receptor (*MC4R*)	FR, noQTL, HD, HuP [38, 49, 60, 65, 69, 122]
Leptin receptor (*LEPR*)	FR, QTLm, noQTLh, noHD [30, 49, 60, 65, 123]
Calcium-sensing receptor (*CASR*)	FR, noQTL, partialHD, HuP [38, 49, 60, 65, 124]
Vitamin D receptor (*VDR*)	FR, noQTL, partialHD, HuP [38, 49, 60, 65, 125]

*Lines of evidence: *FR* functionally relevant; *QTL* located in identified QTL; *HD* haplotype difference; *ED* gene expression difference; *MD* manipulation of gene causes difference in phenotype; *HuP* human polymorphism observed
Prefix of "no" on any evidence indicates that available evidence does not support this criteria being applied to candidacy of gene. For example: "noQTL" would indicate that this gene does not localize within any currently identified QTL associated with physical activity. Prefix of "m" or "h" refers to mouse or human model, respectively, where there is conflicting evidence between models. All HDs were determined in high vs. low inbred mouse strains using Perlegen Mouse Haplotype Browser [84]

of the D1-receptors could directly affect activity levels. Given *Drd1* has functional relevance to locomotor behavior [76], has been localized to a identified QTL by haplotype-mapping (chromosome 13; 32 cM [38]), exhibited haplotype and expression differences between high- and low-active strains of mice [74, 77], and activity levels are altered by manipulation of the gene product [75], there are at least four lines of evidence that *Drd1* is involved in the regulation of physical activity.

Nescient helix-loop-helix 2 (*Nhlh2*) is a gene shown to transcriptionally regulate both prohormone convertase 1 and 2 (PC1 and PC2) in addition to numerous other neuropeptide genes [78]. Good et al. [79] described an approximate 56% decrease in a 24-h wheel-running bout in *Nhlh2*-knockout mice when compared to wild-type mice with the *Nhlh2* genes intact. While it is not clear how *Nhlh2* functionally would regulate activity, Good et al. [79] suggested inhibition of *Nhlh2* would inhibit formation of β-endorphin, reducing the beneficial positive reinforcement of exercise, and thus decreasing physical activity. Supporting the potential candidacy of *Nhlh2* in the regulation of physical activity is its genomic location (chromosome 3; 101.8 Mbp), which falls almost directly under the peak of one of the significant epistatic activity-related QTL (Table 3.2 [60]). Additionally, when the haplotype structure of *Nhlh2* is considered [65], there are partial haplotype differences between the structure of *Nhlh2* in high-active inbred mice (C57L/J) and low-active inbred mice (C3H/HeJ) [77]. Thus, *Nhlh2* exhibits functional relevance [79], localizes with a known activity-related QTL [60], exhibits partial haplotype differences between animals with varying activity levels [65], and manipulation of the gene alters the phenotype [79]. These four independent lines of evidence suggest that *Nhlh2* is an appropriate candidate gene for the regulation of physical activity.

While not being supported by at least three lines of independent evidence, several other genes have been proposed as potential candidate genes involved in the regulation of physical activity primarily due to their relevance to proposed regulatory mechanisms of physical activity (Table 3.3). For example, there is a long history of investigating the effects of sex hormones on daily activity levels [17]. Specifically, estrogen administration, through the activation of the estrogen-α receptor pathway [80], will increase activity, especially in female animals [81]. In males, it has been suggested activity is also regulated through a similar central pathway after the conversion of testosterone to estrogen with the enzyme aromatase [82]. Interestingly, the aromatase gene (*CYP19*) colocalizes within one of the identified mouse activity QTL, but not in any human activity-related QTL. Thus, while not meeting the criteria of three lines of evidence, *CYP19* is an appropriate potential candidate gene for further investigations.

While the protein products of *Drd1*, *NHLH2*, and *CYP19* appear to have central (i.e., brain) effects, GLUT-4 has been suggested to regulate activity at a peripheral level (i.e., muscle). GLUT-4 is the primary glucose transporter isoform expressed in skeletal muscle, arises from the solute carrier family 2 facilitated glucose transporter, member 4 (*SLC2A4*) gene, and is critical in the regulation of glucose uptake in skeletal muscle and maintenance of glucose homeostasis. Tsao et al. [83] measured voluntary wheel exercise in control outbred male mice and transgenic mice overexpressing *Slc2a4* at 12–17 weeks of age. Over the 5-week period, the transgenic mice ran fourfold further on an average daily basis than did the control mice. While the mechanisms responsible for increased physical activity level with the *Slc2a4* overexpression were unknown, the authors suggested the increased glucose uptake due to the increased GLUT-4 resulted in less fatigue during exercise. Partially supporting this conclusion, Gomes et al. [64] found, after 5 days of access to running wheels, high-running mice selectively bred for activity increased their GLUT-4 levels approximately 2.5-fold higher than control mice (along with higher glycogen and glycogen-synthase activity). These investigators concluded that since the high-active mice did not have higher intrinsic levels of skeletal muscle GLUT-4, their activity levels were not solely predicated on glycogen availability. Nonetheless, the higher rates of glycogen synthesis and transport with activity indicated at least a partial role for peripheral factors in the regulation of activity [64]. Further strengthening the potential of *Slc2a4* as a candidate gene is the fact that *Slc2a4* colocalizes within two of the identified epistatic mouse activity QTL (chromosome 11; 40 cM; Table 3.2) and it localizes with the QTL that gives rise to the mini-muscle phenotype [61, 84]. Therefore, while currently lacking more than three lines of supporting lines of evidence, *Slc2a4* is a potential candidate gene for further investigation.

Several other potential candidate genes are speculated to be involved in the regulation of physical activity (Table 3.3). The candidacy of several of these genes has suffered because subsequent investigation has shown many of these genes do not colocate within either mouse or human activity QTL (e.g., angiotensin-converting enzyme [*ACE*], dopamine receptor 2 [*DRD2*], leptin receptor [*LEPR*], melanocortin-4 receptor [*MC4R*], or calcium-sensing receptor [*CASR*]). However, there are intriguing, new potential candidate genes that hold promise for further investigation. For example, De Moor et al. [49] identified several genomic markers significantly associated with exercise participation located within the intron region of the 3′-phosphoadenosine 5′-phosphosulfate synthase 2 (*PAPSS2*) gene. Given *PAPSS2* appears to be involved in initial skeletal development, its functional relevancy to physical activity is still unclear. However, supporting potential candidacy for *PAPSS2* is the homologous mouse gene *Papss2* that exhibits partial differences in haplotype structure between high-active inbred mice (C57L/J) and low-active inbred mice (C3H/HeJ) [65]. Thus, with potential functional relevance, inclusion in the human activity QTL, and partial haplotype differences in a mouse model, *PAPSS2* is certainly a potential candidate gene and awaits further experimental and independent lines of evidence.

Considering Table 3.3, it is obvious that the majority of the evidence available that has determined candidacy of genes associated with physical activity is whether or not the genes were functionally relevant and localized within a known activity QTL. Gene expression and manipulation data on any of these genes are sparse, and the determination of whether gene expression differences actually reflect a difference in protein production of any of these genes is currently not available. Expression and end-protein production differences should be a focus of future research in this area.

A Word About Physical Activity and Exercise Endurance

It is attractive to speculate that the genetic mechanisms regulating physical activity may also regulate exercise endurance and vice-versa. In fact, Novak et al. [85], based on rat and human models, suggested endurance capacity was the phenotype that actually determined physical activity levels. This suggestion, though intriguing, is not currently supported by other lines of research. First, several rodent studies have shown physical activity level and maximal aerobic capacity are not correlated and probably represent two distinct phenotypes [42, 86, 87]. Secondly, comparison of the limited inbred strain distribution patterns of exercise endurance [88] and wheel activity [40, 41] does not show similarity. Thirdly, while mice selectively bred for high wheel-running activity do show higher endurance capacities in general, their aerobic capacities are not completely distinct from the control lines [89]. In these same selectively bred animals, Rezende et al. [45] observed the aerobic capacity of the animals did not limit potential further increases in activity, and that "sometimes" increased physical activity appeared to evolve separately from the higher endurance of these animals. Lastly, comparisons [38] of the known QTL associated with activity (Table 3.2) with identified significant QTL linked with inherent exercise endurance or aerobic capacity [90–93] have shown little overlap among these QTL. There is the possible overlap of the MMU2 and MMU7 QTL identified by Nehrenberg et al. [62] with the rat chromosome 3 endurance QTL [93] and the human chromosome 11 maximal oxygen consumption (VO_{2max}) QTL [90], respectively. However, verification of these two possible overlaps awaits further resolution of the available rat/mouse/human homology maps in those specific QTL regions. It is probable that the genetic regulation of physical activity and exercise endurance will have some commonalities since there are functional physiological characteristics such as muscle capillarity that would lend themselves positively to higher physical activity levels and higher endurance capacity. Nonetheless, the preponderance of current evidence suggests physical activity and exercise endurance/aerobic capacity are two independent phenotypes linked to differing genomic loci.

It should be noted that the continuing rat selective breeding studies by Koch et al. [94] specifically deal with *maximal treadmill performance* (related to maximal aerobic capacity) and not physical activity levels. In a similar vein, it should be noted Evans' group has published several papers regarding the role of the peroxisome proliferative-activated receptor delta (PPARδ) pathway in regulating *maximal exercise endurance* as opposed to the regulation of daily physical activity [95–97]. While it is possible that PPARδ is involved in regulating activity, the PPARδ gene (mouse *Ppard*, chromosome 17; 13.5 cM; human *PPARD*, 6p21.2-p21.1) does not colocalize within any of the mouse or human QTL linked with physical activity (Table 3.2).

The Future?

From the available literature, it is clear that physical activity levels are heritable; however, understanding the genetic and biological mechanisms that control physical activity is at a very early stage. To this point, the available mapping studies have indicated few significant QTL involved in activity regulation. The small number of significant QTL make it possible that there are only a few genes involved, but the more probable scenario is that there are a large number of genes that play small roles in the ultimate determination of the complex trait we classify as physical activity as well as many "sets of genes" that through their interactions (i.e., epistasis) affect activity. Thus, completely understanding the underlying genetic mechanisms of physical activity may be a long, complex, confusing, and arduous journey for researchers interested in this area.

Besides the probability of many small-effect genes being involved in activity regulation, future investigations in this area must continue to be aware of the large advances that are taking place in the field of genetics. For example, the landmark study by Fire et al. [98] in 1998 – studies for which they subsequently won the Nobel Prize in Medicine in 2006 – generally elaborated the basic mechanism of RNA interference (RNAi). The evolving understanding of RNAi mechanisms [99, 100], how RNAi effectively regulates gene expression, and how RNAi arise from both "coding" and "non-coding" portions of the genome [101] require the consideration of how these novel RNAi mechanisms may affect the physiological processes that govern physical activity. Incorporation of potential regulation of physical activity arising from noncoding areas of the genome may be an important avenue for further consideration. To this end, it is interesting that two of the three identified QTL associated with physical activity in humans [49] localize within intergenic areas of the genome. Thus, future deliberations of the genetic control of physical activity may have to not only consider possible genes that alter protein structure and function, but also potential regulatory mechanisms arising from noncoding genomic regions.

Practical Applications

The consideration of the genetic/biological control of physical activity brings new techniques and research designs into the investigation of the factors that control physical activity level. Thus, "activity genetics" represents a unique approach to investigating the underlying cause of myriad diseases and conditions. Regardless of the genes and genetic mechanisms ultimately associated with the biological control of physical activity, the ultimate application of these findings must be considered. These types of "application" conversations are already taking place well in advance of any resolution of what genetic mechanisms are involved (see the Commentary and Responses by Roth [102]). The ultimate applications and significance of genetic results cannot be fully predicted presently. As progress is made with identifying genes and genetic mechanisms involved in regulating physical activity, any data that aid in understanding why individuals are not physically active will contribute to the understanding and possible prevention of the large number of conditions and diseases caused by physical inactivity [8] as well as decreasing the significant cost to health care from physical inactivity [103, 104].

Whether or not finding genetic influences on activity will give people another excuse to be inactive is a topic of debate. This chapter has emphasized that a *predisposition* to be active/inactive is not the same as a *predestination* to be active/inactive. All of the current estimates regarding the genetic influence on activity do not eliminate the significant, unique influence of environment on physical activity. Thus, while scientists are attempting to unravel the underinvestigated genetic piece of the regulation of activity, there remain other important factors that control activity. Investigating the integration of all the environmental, genetic, and the environmental/biologic interactions that influence activity is currently beyond the scope of the field of "physical activity genetics." And here may ultimately lay the real significance of understanding the genetic factors underlying physical activity – providing knowledge that can be used in future investigations that consider the interplay of all activity-regulating mechanisms in humans.

Acknowledgments A generous grant (R01AR050085) from the NIH National Institute of Arthritis and Musculoskeletal Diseases (NIAMS) supported the writing of this chapter and some of the data collected within.

References

1. Blair SN, LaMonte MJ, Nichaman MZ. The evolution of physical activity recommendations: how much is enough? Am J Clin Nutr. 2004;79(5):913S–20.
2. Chakravarthy MV, Booth FW. Eating, exercise, and "thrifty" genotypes: connecting the dots toward an evolutionary understanding of modern chronic diseases. J Appl Physiol. 2004;96(1):3–10.
3. Cooper DM, Nemet D, Galassetti P. Exercise, stress, and inflammation in the growing child: from the bench to the playground. Curr Opin Pediatr. 2004;16(3):286–92.
4. Lees SJ, Booth FW. Sedentary death syndrome. Can J Appl Physiol. 2004;29(4):447–60. discussion 444-6.
5. Manson JE, Skerrett PJ, Greenland P, VanItallie TB. The escalating pandemics of obesity and sedentary lifestyle. A call to action for clinicians. Arch Intern Med. 2004;164(3):249–58.
6. Roberts CK, Barnard RJ. Effects of exercise and diet on chronic disease. J Appl Physiol. 2005;98(1):3–30.
7. Mokdad AH, Marks JS, Stroup DF, Gerberding JL. Actual causes of death in the United States, 2000. JAMA. 2004;291(10):1238–45.
8. Booth FW, Gordon SE, Carlson CJ, Hamilton MT. Waging war on modern chronic diseases: primary prevention through exercise biology. J Appl Physiol. 2000;88(2):774–87.
9. Manson JE, Hu FB, Rich-Edwards JW, Colditz GA, Stampfer MJ, Willett WC, et al. A prospective study of walking as compared with vigorous exercise in the prevention of coronary heart disease in women. N Engl J Med. 1999;341(9):650–8.
10. Manson JE, Nathan DM, Krolewski AS, Stampfer MJ, Willett WC, Hennekens CH. A prospective study of exercise and incidence of diabetes among US male physicians. JAMA. 1992;268(1):63–7.
11. McTiernan A, Ulrich C, Slate S, Potter J. Physical activity and cancer etiology: associations and mechanisms. Cancer Causes Control. 1998;9(5):487–509.
12. Baumgartner RN, Waters DL, Gallagher D, Morley JE, Garry PJ. Predictors of skeletal muscle mass in elderly men and women. Mech Ageing Dev. 1999;107(2):123–36.
13. Troiano RP, Berrigan D, Dodd KW, Masse LC, Tilert T, McDowell M. Physical activity in the United States measured by accelerometer. Med Sci Sports Exerc. 2008;40(1):181–8.
14. Owen N, Leslie E, Salmon J, Fotheringham MJ. Environmental determinants of physical activity and sedentary behavior. Exerc Sport Sci Rev. 2000;28(4):153–8.
15. Dunton GF, Kaplan J, Wolch J, Jerrett M, Reynolds KD. Physical environmental correlates of childhood obesity: a systematic review. Obes Rev. 2009;10(4):393–402.
16. Rowland TW. The biological basis of physical activity. Med Sci Sports Exerc. 1998;30(3):392–9.
17. Lightfoot JT. Sex hormones' regulation of rodent physical activity: a review. Int J Biol Sci. 2008;4(3):126–32.
18. Eisenmann JC, Wickel EE, Kelly SA, Middleton KM, Garland Jr T. Day-to-day variability in voluntary wheel running among genetically differentiated lines of mice that vary in activity level. Eur J Appl Physiol. 2009;106(4):613–9.

19. Mattocks C, Leary S, Ness A, et al. Intraindividual variation of objectively measured physical activity in children. Med Sci Sports Exerc. 2007;39(4):622–9.
20. Wickel EE, Eisenmann JC. Within- and between-individual variability in estimated energy expenditure and habitual physical activity among young adults. Eur J Clin Nutr. 2006;60(4):538–44.
21. Wickel EE, Eisenmann JC, Pangrazi RP, Graser SV, Raustorp A, Tomson LM, et al. Do children take the same number of steps every day? Am J Hum Biol. 2007;19(4):537–43.
22. Wilkin TJ, Mallam KM, Metcalf BS, Jeffery AN, Voss LD. Variation in physical activity lies with the child, not his environment: evidence for an 'activitystat' in young children (EarlyBird 16). Int J Obes (Lond). 2006;30(7):1050–5.
23. Falconer DS, Mackay TFC. Introduction to quantitative genetics. 4th ed. Essex, England: Longman; 1996.
24. Sesardic N. Making sense of heritability: how not to think about behavior genetics. New York: Cambridge University Press; 2005.
25. Festing MFW. Strategy in the use of inbred strains. In: Festing MFW, editor. Inbred strains in biomedical research. New York: Oxford University Press; 1979. p. 122–31.
26. Festing MFW. Notes on genetic analysis. In: Festing MFW, editor. Inbred strains in biomedical research. New York: Oxford University Press; 1979. p. 80–98.
27. Kaprio J, Koskenvuo M, Sarna S. Cigarette smoking, use of alcohol, and leisure-time physical activity among same-sexed adult male twins. Prog Clin Biol Res. 1981;69:37–46.
28. Lauderdale DS, Fabsitz R, Meyer JM, Sholinsky P, Ramakrishnan V, Goldberg J. Familial determinants of moderate and intense physical activity: a twin study. Med Sci Sports Exerc. 1997;29(8):1062–8.
29. Carlsson S, Andersson T, Lichtenstein P, Michaelsson K, Ahlbom A. Genetic effects on physical activity: results from the Swedish twin registry. Med Sci Sports Exerc. 2006;38(8):1396–401.
30. Stubbe JH, Boomsma DI, Vink JM, Cornes BK, Martin NG, Skythe A, et al. Genetic influences on exercise participation in 37,051 twin pairs from seven countries. PLoS One. 2006;1:e22.
31. Perusse L, Tremblay A, Leblanc C, Bouchard C. Genetic and environmental influences on level of habitual physical activity and exercise participation. Am J Epidemiol. 1989;129(5):1012–22.
32. Stubbe JH, Boomsma DI, De Geus EJ. Sports participation during adolescence: a shift from environmental to genetic factors. Med Sci Sports Exerc. 2005;37(4):563–70.
33. Joosen AM, Gielen M, Vlietinck R, Westerterp KR. Genetic analysis of physical activity in twins. Am J Clin Nutr. 2005;82(6):1253–9.
34. Macera CA, Ham SA, Yore MM, Jones DA, Ainsworth BE, Kimsey CD, et al. Prevalence of physical activity in the United States: behavioral risk factor surveillance system, 2001. Prev Chronic Dis. 2005;2(2):A17.
35. Shephard RJ. Limits to the measurement of habitual physical activity by questionnaires. Br J Sports Med. 2003;37(3):197–206. discussion 206.
36. Knab AM, Bowen RS, Moore-Harrison T, Hamilton AT, Turner MJ, Lightfoot JT. Repeatability of exercise behaviors in mice. Physiol Behav. 2009;98(4):433–40.
37. Eikelboom R. Human parallel to voluntary wheel running: exercise. Anim Behav. 1999;57(3):F11–2.
38. Lightfoot JT, Turner MJ, Pomp D, Kleeberger SR, Leamy LJ. Quantitative trait loci for physical activity traits in mice. Physiol Genomics. 2008;32(3):401–8.
39. American Physiological Society. Resource book for the design of animal exercise protocols. 1887. http://www.the-aps.org.ezproxy.lib.uconn.edu/pa/action/exercise/book.pdf; http://www.the-aps.org.ezproxy.lib.uconn.edu/pa/action/exercise/book.pdf.
40. Festing MF. Wheel activity in 26 strains of mouse. Lab Anim. 1977;11(4):257–8.
41. Lightfoot JT, Turner MJ, Daves M, Vordermark A, Kleeberger SR. Genetic influence on daily wheel running activity level. Physiol Genomics. 2004;19(3):270–6.
42. Lerman I, Harrison BC, Freeman K, Hewett, TE, Allen DL, Robbins J, et al. Genetic variability in forced and voluntary endurance exercise performance in seven inbred mouse strains. J Appl Physiol. 2002;92(6):2245–55.
43. Swallow JG, Carter PA, Garland Jr T. Artificial selection for increased wheel-running behavior in house mice. Behav Genet. 1998;28(3):227–37.

44. Garland Jr T, Kelly SA. Phenotypic plasticity and experimental evolution. J Exp Biol. 2006;209(Pt 12):2344–61.

45. Rezende EL, Chappell MA, Gomes FR, Malisch JL, Garland Jr T. Maximal metabolic rates during voluntary exercise, forced exercise, and cold exposure in house mice selectively bred for high wheel-running. J Exp Biol. 2005;208(Pt 12):2447–58.

46. Turner MJ, Kleeberger SR, Lightfoot JT. Influence of genetic background on daily running-wheel activity differs with aging. Physiol Genomics. 2005;22(1):76–85.

47. Ponting CP, Goodstadt L. Separating derived from ancestral features of mouse and human genomes. Biochem Soc Trans. 2009;37(Pt 4):734–9.

48. Cho HY, Kleeberger SR. Genetic mechanisms of susceptibility to oxidative lung injury in mice. Free Radic Biol Med. 2007;42(4):433–45.

49. De Moor MH, Liu YJ, Boomsma DI, Li J, Hamilton JJ, Hottenga JJ, et al. Genome-wide association study of exercise behavior in Dutch and American adults. Med Sci Sports Exerc. 2009;41(10):1887–1895.

50. Haley CS, Knott SA. A simple regression method for mapping quantitative trait loci in line crosses using flanking markers. Heredity. 1992;69(4):315–24.

51. Lander E, Kruglyak L. Genetic dissection of complex traits: guidelines for interpreting and reporting linkage results. Nat Genet. 1995;11(3):241–7.

52. Lander ES, Botstein D. Mapping mendelian factors underlying quantitative traits using RFLP linkage maps. Genetics. 1989;121(1):185–99.

53. Wakefield J. Bayes factors for genome-wide association studies: comparison with P-values. Genet Epidemiol. 2009;33(1):79–86.

54. Guan Y, Stephens M. Practical issues in imputation-based association mapping. PLoS Genet. 2008;4(12):e1000279.

55. Servin B, Stephens M. Imputation-based analysis of association studies: candidate regions and quantitative traits. PLoS Genet. 2007;3(7):e114.

56. Varona L, Gomez-Raya L, Rauw WM, Clop A, Ovilo C, Noguera JL. Derivation of a Bayes factor to distinguish between linked or pleiotropic quantitative trait loci. Genetics. 2004;166(2):1025–35.

57. Broman KW. Review of statistical methods for QTL mapping in experimental crosses. Lab Anim (NY). 2001;30(7):44–52.

58. Abiola O, Angel JM, Avner P, Bachmanov AA, Belknap JK, Bennett B, et al. The nature and identification of quantitative trait loci: a community's view. Nat Rev Genet. 2003;4(11):911–6.

59. Silver LM. Mouse genetics: concepts and applications. New York: Oxford University Press; 1995.

60. Leamy LJ, Pomp D, Lightfoot JT. An epistatic genetic basis for physical activity traits in mice. J Hered. 2008;99(6):639–46.

61. Hartmann J, Garland Jr T, Hannon RM, Kelly SA, Munoz G, Pomp D. Fine mapping of "mini-muscle," a recessive mutation causing reduced hindlimb muscle mass in mice. J Hered. 2008;99(6):679–87.

62. Nehrenberg DL, Wang S, Hannon RM, Garland Jr T, Pomp D. QTL underlying voluntary exercise in mice: interactions with the "mini muscle" locus and sex. J Hered. 2010;101(1):42–53.

63. Garland Jr T, Morgan MT, Swallow JG, Rhodes JS, Girard I, Belter JG, et al. Evolution of a small-muscle polymorphism in lines of house mice selected for high activity levels. Evolution. 2002;56(6):1267–75.

64. Gomes FR, Rezende EL, Malisch JL, Lee SK, Rivas DA, Kelly SA, et al. Glycogen storage and muscle glucose transporters (GLUT-4) of mice selectively bred for high voluntary wheel running. J Exp Biol. 2009;212(Pt 2):238–48.

65. Frazer KA, Eskin E, Kang HM, Bogue MA, Hinds DA, Beilharz EJ, et al. A sequence-based variation map of 8.27 million SNPs in inbred mouse strains. Nature. 2007;448(7157):1050–3.

66. Churchill GA, Airey DC, Allayee H, Angel JM, Attie AD, Beatty J, et al. The collaborative cross, a community resource for the genetic analysis of complex traits. Nat Genet. 2004; 36(11):1133–7.

67. Simonen RL, Rankinen T, Perusse L, Rice T, Rao DC, Chagnon Y, et al. Genome-wide linkage scan for physical activity levels in the Quebec family study. Med Sci Sports Exerc. 2003; 35(8):1355–9.

68. Simonen RL, Perusse L, Rankinen T, Rice T, Rao DC, Bouchard C. Familial aggregation of physical activity levels in the Quebec family study. Med Sci Sports Exerc. 2002;34(7):1137–42.

69. Cai G, Cole SA, Butte N, Bacino C, Diego V, Tan K, et al. A quantitative trait locus on chromosome 18q for physical activity and dietary intake in Hispanic children. Obesity (Silver Spring). 2006;14(9):1596–604.

70. Flint J, Valdar W, Shifman S, Mott R. Strategies for mapping and cloning quantitative trait genes in rodents. Nat Rev Genet. 2005;6(4):271–86.

71. DiPetrillo K, Wang X, Stylianou IM, Paigen B. Bioinformatics toolbox for narrowing rodent quantitative trait loci. Trends Genet. 2005;21(12):683–92.

72. Rhodes JS, Garland T. Differential sensitivity to acute administration of ritalin, apomorphine, SCH 23390, but not raclopride in mice selectively bred for hyperactive wheel-running behavior. Psychopharmacology (Berl). 2003;167(3):242–50.

73. Rhodes JS, Hosack GR, Girard I, Kelley AE, Mitchell GS, Garland Jr T. Differential sensitivity to acute administration of cocaine, GBR 12909, and fluoxetine in mice selectively bred for hyperactive wheel-running behavior. Psychopharmacology (Berl). 2001;158(2):120–31.

74. Knab AM, Bowen RS, Hamilton AT, Gulledge AA, Lightfoot JT. Altered dopaminergic profiles: implications for the regulation of voluntary physical activity. Behav Brain Res. 2009;204(1):147–52.

75. Knab AM, Bowen RS, Hamilton AT, Moore-Harrison TL, Ferguson DP, Lightfoot JT. Central control of physical activity in mice is mediated by dopamine 1 (D1) receptors and the tyrosine hydroxylase enzyme. Med Sci Sports Exerc. 2009;41(5):S183.

76. Smith Y, Villalba R. Striatal and extrastriatal dopamine in the basal ganglia: an overview of its anatomical organization in normal and Parkinsonian brains. Mov Disord. 2008;23 Suppl 3:S534–47.

77. Ceaser T, Lightfoot JT. Interval specific haplotype analysis between high and low active mice within identified quantitative trait loci for physical activity [Masters]. Charlotte: University of North Carolina Charlotte; 2009.

78. Fox DL, Vella KR, Good DJ. Energy balance pathways converging on the Nhlh2 transcription factor. Front Biosci. 2007;12:3983–93.

79. Good DJ, Coyle CA, Fox DL. Nhlh2: a basic helix-loop-helix transcription factor controlling physical activity. Exerc Sport Sci Rev. 2008;36(4):187–92.

80. Morgan MA, Schulkin J, Pfaff DW. Estrogens and non-reproductive behaviors related to activity and fear. Neurosci Biobehav Rev. 2004;28(1):55–63.

81. Gorzek JF, Hendrickson KC, Forstner JP, Rixen JL, Moran AL, Lowe DA. Estradiol and tamoxifen reverse ovariectomy-induced physical inactivity in mice. Med Sci Sports Exerc. 2007;39(2):248–56.

82. Roy EJ, Wade GN. Role of estrogens in androgen-induced spontaneous activity in male rats. J Comp Physiol Psychol. 1975;89(6):573–9.

83. Tsao TS, Li J, Chang KS, Stenbit AE, Galuska D, Anderson JE, et al. Metabolic adaptations in skeletal muscle overexpressing GLUT4: effects on muscle and physical activity. FASEB J. 2001;15(6):958–69.

84. Bult CJ, Eppig JT, Kadin JA, Richardson JE, Blake JA, Mouse Genome Database Group. The mouse genome database (MGD): mouse biology and model systems. Nucleic Acids Res. 2008;36(Database issue):D724–8.

85. Novak CM, Escande C, Gerber SM, Chini EN, Zhang M, Britton SL, et al. Endurance capacity, not body size, determines physical activity levels: role of skeletal muscle PEPCK. PLoS One. 2009;4(6):e5869.

86. Friedman WA, Garland Jr T, Dohm MR. Individual variation in locomotor behavior and maximal oxygen consumption in mice. Physiol Behav. 1992;52(1):97–104.

87. Lambert MI, Van Zyl C, Jaunky R, Lambert EV, Noakes TD. Tests of running performance do not predict subsequent spontaneous running in rats. Physiol Behav. 1996;60(1):171–6.

88. Lightfoot JT, Turner MJ, Debate KA, Kleeberger SR. Interstrain variation in murine aerobic capacity. Med Sci Sports Exerc. 2001;33(12):2053–7.
89. Meek TH, Lonquich BP, Hannon RM, Garland Jr T. Endurance capacity of mice selectively bred for high voluntary wheel running. J Exp Biol. 2009;212(18):2908–17.
90. Bouchard C, Rankinen T, Chagnon YC, Rice T, Perusse L, Gagnon J, et al. Genomic scan for maximal oxygen uptake and its response to training in the HERITAGE family study. J Appl Physiol. 2000;88(2):551–9.
91. Rico-Sanz J, Rankinen T, Rice T, lean AS, Skinner JS, Wilmore JH, et al. Quantitative trait loci for maximal exercise capacity phenotypes and their responses to training in the HERITAGE family study. Physiol Genomics. 2004;16(2):256–60.
92. Ways JA, Smith BM, Barbato JC, Ramdath RS, Pettee KM, DeRaedt SJ, et al. Congenic strains confirm aerobic running capacity quantitative trait loci on rat chromosome 16 and identify possible intermediate phenotypes. Physiol Genomics. 2007;29(1):91–7.
93. Ways JA, Cicila GT, Garrett MR, Koch LG. A genome scan for loci associated with aerobic running capacity in rats. Genomics. 2002;80(1):13–20.
94. Koch LG, Meredith TA, Fraker TD, Metting PJ, Britton SL. Heritability of treadmill running endurance in rats. Am J Physiol. 1998;275(5 Pt 2):R1455–60.
95. Wang YX, Zhang CL, Yu RT, Cho HK, Nelson MC, Bayuaga-Ocampo CR, et al. Regulation of muscle fiber type and running endurance by PPARdelta. PLoS Biol. 2004; 2(10):e294.
96. Evans RM, Barish GD, Wang YX. PPARs and the complex journey to obesity. Nat Med. 2004;10(4):355–61.
97. Narkar VA, Downes M, Yu RT, Embler E, Wang YX, Banayo E, et al. AMPK and PPARdelta agonists are exercise mimetics. Cell. 2008;134(3):405–15.
98. Fire A, Xu S, Montgomery MK, Kostas SA, Driver SE, Mello CC. Potent and specific genetic interference by double-stranded RNA in *Caenorhabditis elegans*. Nature. 1998;391(6669):806–11.
99. Axtell MJ, Snyder JA, Bartel DP. Common functions for diverse small RNAs of land plants. Plant Cell. 2007;19(6):1750–69.
100. Siepel A. Darwinian alchemy: human genes from noncoding DNA. Genome Res. 2009; 19(10):1693–5.
101. Forrest AR, Abdelhamid RF, Carninci P. Annotating non-coding transcription using functional genomics strategies. Brief Funct Genomic Proteomic. 2009;8(6):437–43.
102. Roth SM. Last word on viewpoint: perspective on the future use of genomics in exercise prescription. J Appl Physiol. 2008;104(4):1254.
103. Chenoweth D, Leutzinger J. The economic cost of physical inactivity and excess weight in American adults. J Phys Act Health. 2006;3(2):148–63.
104. Centers for Disease Control and Prevention (U.S.). Chronic diseases and their risk factors: the nation's leading causes of death. Atlanta, GA: U.S. Department of Health and Human Services, Centers for Disease Control and Prevention; 1999.
105. Bronstein PM, Wolkoff FD, Levine WJ. Sex-related differences in rats open-field activity. Behav Biol. 1975;13(1):133–8.
106. Craft RM, Clark JL, Hart SP, Pinckney MK. Sex differences in locomotor effects of morphine in the rat. Pharmacol Biochem Behav. 2006;85(4):850–8.
107. Koteja P, Swallow JG, Carter PA, Garland Jr T. Energy cost of wheel running in house mice: implications for coadaptation of locomotion and energy budgets. Physiol Biochem Zool. 1999;72(2):238–49.
108. Leslie PW, Bindon JR, Baker PT. Caloric requirements of human populations: a model. Hum Ecol. 1984;12(2):137–62. http://www.jstor.org.ezproxy.lib.uconn.edu/stable/4602729.
109. Li JS, Huang YC. Early androgen treatment influences the pattern and amount of locomotion activity differently and sexually differentially in an animal model of ADHD. Behav Brain Res. 2006;175(1):176–82.
110. McCracken M, Jiles R, Blanck HM. Health behaviors of the young adult U.S. population: behavioral risk factor surveillance system, 2003. Prev Chronic Dis. 2007;4(2):A25.

111. Panter-Brick C. Seasonal and sex variation in physical activity levels among agro-pastoralists in Nepal. Am J Phys Anthropol. 1996;100(1):7–21.
112. Doran DM. Comparative locomotor behavior of chimpanzees and bonobos: the influence of morphology on locomotion. Am J Phys Anthropol. 1993;91(1):83–98.
113. Fox EA, van Schaik CP, Sitompul A, Wright DN. Intra-and interpopulational differences in orangutan (*Pongo pygmaeus*) activity and diet: implications for the invention of tool use. Am J Phys Anthropol. 2004;125(2):162–74.
114. Pontzer H, Wrangham RW. Climbing and the daily energy cost of locomotion in wild chimpanzees: implications for hominoid locomotor evolution. J Hum Evol. 2004;46(3): 317–35.
115. Mouse phenome database. http://www.jax.org/phenome. Accessed 1 Sept 2009.
116. Salmen T, Heikkinen AM, Mahonen A, Kroger H, Komulainen M, Pallonen H, et al. Relation of aromatase gene polymorphism and hormone replacement therapy to serum estradiol levels, bone mineral density, and fracture risk in early postmenopausal women. Ann Med. 2003;35(4):282–8.
117. Fuentes RM, Perola M, Nissinen A, Tuomilehto J. ACE gene and physical activity, blood pressure, and hypertension: a population study in Finland. J Appl Physiol. 2002;92(6):2508–12.
118. Winnicki M, Accurso V, Hoffmann M, Pawlowski R, Dorigatti F, Santonastaso M, et al. Physical activity and angiotensin-converting enzyme gene polymorphism in mild hypertensives. Am J Med Genet A. 2004;125A(1):38–44.
119. Roltsch MH, Brown MD, Hand BD, Kostek MC, Phares DA, Huberty A, et al. No association between ACE I/D polymorphism and cardiovascular hemodynamics during exercise in young women. Int J Sports Med. 2005;26(8):638–44.
120. Simonen RL, Rankinen T, Perusse L, Leon AS, Skinner JS, Wilmore JH, et al. A dopamine D2 receptor gene polymorphism and physical activity in two family studies. Physiol Behav. 2003;78(4–5):751–7.
121. Rose Jr FF, Mattis VB, Rindt H, Lorson CL. Delivery of recombinant follistatin lessens disease severity in a mouse model of spinal muscular atrophy. Hum Mol Genet. 2009;18(6):997–1005.
122. Loos RJ, Lindgren CM, Li S, Wheeler E, Zhao JH, Prokopenko I, et al. Common variants near MC4R are associated with fat mass, weight and risk of obesity. Nat Genet. 2008;40(6): 768–75.
123. Richert L, Chevalley T, Manen D, Bonjour JP, Rizzoli R, Ferrari S. Bone mass in prepubertal boys is associated with a Gln223Arg amino acid substitution in the leptin receptor. J Clin Endocrinol Metab. 2007;92(11):4380–6.
124. Lorentzon M, Lorentzon R, Lerner UH, Nordstrom P. Calcium sensing receptor gene polymorphism, circulating calcium concentrations and bone mineral density in healthy adolescent girls. Eur J Endocrinol. 2001;144(3):257–61.
125. Gentil P, de Lima Lins TC, Lima RM, de Abreu BS, Grattapaglia D, Bottaro M, et al. Vitamin-D-receptor genotypes and bone-mineral density in postmenopausal women: interaction with physical activity. J Aging Phys Act. 2009;17(1):31–45.

Chapter 4
Interaction Between Exercise and Genetics in Type 2 Diabetes Mellitus: An Epidemiological Perspective

Paul W. Franks and Ema C. Brito

Keywords Type 2 diabetes • Genetics • Genotype • Interaction • Effect-modification • Epidemiology • Clinical trials • Exercise • Physical activity

Introduction

Type 2 diabetes mellitus (T2D) is a heterogeneous disease that results from the interplay between environmental and genetic risk factors. The hallmark of diabetes is chronically elevated blood glucose concentrations. Prolonged hyperglycemia causes a range of complications including nephropathy, heart disease, blindness, and peripheral nerve damage. By consequence, three in four people with diabetes die from cardiovascular disease. According to the World Health Organization (WHO), the global burden of diabetes increased from 30 to 171 million between 1985 and 2000. These numbers are expected to rise to 366 million by 2030, which equates to an anticipated change in diabetes prevalence from 2.8% in 2000 to 5.8% in 2030 [1].

There are two major factors that underlie these alarming projections. The first is T2D is associated with age, and Western populations are aging rapidly. The second major explanation is our lifestyles have changed dramatically in recent years. Epidemiological studies have identified strong T2D risk relationships for obesity, sedentary behavior [2–4], and diets rich in energy [5], processed carbohydrates [6], and animal fats [7]. Collectively, these lifestyle factors impede the actions of insulin and raise hepatic glucose production, which can result in the diminution of endogenous insulin production and T2D. The strongest evidence for a causal relationship between adverse lifestyle behaviors and T2D comes from randomized controlled trials that show intensive lifestyle interventions involving structured exercise regimes which promote habitual physical activity (PA) and have a major beneficial impact on diabetes incidence in high-risk individuals [8, 9].

P.W. Franks (✉)
Genetic Epidemiology and Clinical Research Group, Department of Public Health and Clinical Medicine, Division of Medicine, Umeå University Hospital, Umeå, 90 187, Sweden
e-mail: paul.franks@medicin.umu.se

L.S. Pescatello and S.M. Roth (eds.), *Exercise Genomics*,
Molecular and Translational Medicine, DOI 10.1007/978-1-60761-355-8_4,
© Springer Science+Business Media, LLC 2011

Notwithstanding the important role lifestyle factors play in the etiology of T2D, persons living similar lifestyles can vary considerably in their susceptibility to the disease, with the variance being least among biologically related individuals, suggesting a genetic basis to the disease. In the past 4 years, major advances have been made in unraveling the genetic architecture of T2D. This search has cumulated in the discovery and confirmation of more than 30 common predisposing loci [10], but the variance in disease risk explained by these variants is much lower than predicted from heritability studies [11]. Thus, the genetic associations discovered to date are likely to represent no more than the tip of the iceberg with respect to the genetic landscape of T2D.

Lifestyle behaviors and genetic loci have clear and distinguishable effects on T2D risk; however, the pattern of disease occurrence within and between populations that differ in their genetic and environmental underpinnings suggests T2D is caused in part by the interaction between adverse lifestyle behaviors and the genetic profile of an individual. For many, this seems a reasonable assumption, but there is little robust empirical evidence supporting the presence of such interactions.

The availability of detailed information on gene×environment interactions may enhance our understanding of the molecular basis of T2D, elucidate the mechanisms through which lifestyle exposures influence diabetes risk, and possibly help to refine strategies for diabetes prevention or treatment. The ultimate hope is genetics might one day be used in primary care to inform the targeting of interventions that comprise exercise regimes and other lifestyle therapies for individuals most likely to respond well to them.

The overarching objective of this chapter is to describe existing examples of gene×exercise (or PA) interactions on T2D and related quantitative traits. "Exercise" is defined as structured PA, intended specifically to bring about a gain in health or performance. PA, on the other hand, is defined as any bodily movement produced by skeletal muscles which requires energy expenditure [12].

What is Diabetes?

Diabetes mellitus is a group of metabolic diseases characterized by hyperglycemia (elevated levels of glucose in the blood) resulting from defects in insulin secretion, insulin action, or both. There are two major types of diabetes mellitus: type 1 (T1D) and T2D, although several other rarer forms also exist [13]. T1D is an autoimmune disease that usually occurs in childhood, but the onset may occur at any age. T1D results from a cellular-mediated autoimmune destruction of the beta-cells in the pancreatic islets which usually leads to an absolute deficiency of endogenous insulin production. T2D on the other hand, which accounts for more than 90% of all forms of diabetes, is a metabolic disorder that generally appears later in life, but may occur in childhood and is characterized by the combination of insulin resistance and relative insulin secretion deficiency [13]. T2D usually begins predominantly with insulin resistance, which is a condition characterized by the inability of cells to respond to the action of insulin in transporting glucose from the bloodstream into muscle, fat, and liver cells [14]. This condition causes a compensatory increase in the secretion of insulin from the pancreatic beta-cells (hyperinsulinemia) in order to overcome the state of insulin resistance and thus help glucose enter the cells. The natural history of T2D in many individuals involves years of insulin resistance balanced by elevated insulin secretion. The pivotal point is when the beta-cells begin to fail and insulin production declines [15]. Thus, T2D is characterized by both defects in insulin secretion and by cellular insulin resistance.

T2D is diagnosed using either repeat fasting or 2-h plasma glucose concentrations following an oral glucose challenge (i.e., fasting blood glucose levels ≥126 mg/dL (≥7.1 mmol/L) without symptoms; 2 h glucose levels ≥200 mg/dL (≥11.1 mmol/L) after an oral glucose tolerance test (OGTT) without symptoms; or random blood glucose levels ≥200 mg/dL (≥11.1 mmol/L) with symptoms). These tests should be repeated on a separate day in order to confirm the diagnosis of T2D [16].

Because the progression from normoglycemia to hyperglycemia is often slow and gradual, there are usually intermediate stages. These intermediate stages are defined as impaired fasting glucose (IFG) and impaired glucose tolerance (IGT) where glucose values are considered to be above "normal" glucose tolerance, but below those used to diagnose diabetes. As a result, many individuals have "intermediate hyperglycemia" (sometimes referred to as "impaired glucose regulation," "prediabetes" [17], or "nondiabetic hyperglycemia" [18]). According to the criteria of the WHO, IFG and IGT are diagnosed when a person presents with fasting venous plasma glucose levels between 100–125 mg/dL (6.1–6.9 mmol/L) and 2-h blood glucose level between 140 and 199 mg/dL (7.8–11.1 mmol/L) during a 75 g OGTT. In 2003, the American Diabetes Association (ADA) recommended the IFG threshold should be lowered to 100 mg/dL (5.6 mmol/L) [19]. However, the WHO and some other agencies have not accepted this recommendation. The majority of those diagnosed with IFG and IGT (around 60%) do subsequently develop T2D [20]. It is for this reason that IFG and IGT are commonly used to identify high-risk groups for early intervention. For example, all-cause mortality rates in individuals with IFG or IGT are almost double those of persons with normal glucose levels [21], justifying early intervention.

Although the etiology of T2D has not been fully established, a number of risk factors are well defined. According to the ADA [22], the risk of developing T2D is associated with age (increased risk at ≥45 years), overweight/obesity, and lack of PA. T2D is more common in individuals with a family history of the disease, in certain ethnic groups (e.g., African–Americans, Hispanic–Americans, Native Americans, Asian–Americans, and Pacific Islanders), and in individuals with hypertension (≥140/90 mmHg in adults), dyslipidemia (high density lipoprotein cholesterol [HDL-C] 35 mg/dL (0.90 mmol/L) and/or a triglyceride level ≥250 mg/dL (2.82 mmol/L)), IFG, IGT, a history of vascular disease or gestational diabetes, or polycystic ovary syndrome. In addition, a range of common genetic variants are also known to raise the risk of T2D [23–25], of which some may interact with lifestyle factors to modify the risk of the disease [26]. Several examples are provided below.

The Global Burden of T2D

Over recent decades, the progressively increasing global prevalence of T2D [27] has created a major public health challenge. T2D is a major cause of premature morbidity and mortality and imposes a heavy burden on affected individuals and society as a whole. Furthermore, the disease is associated with long-term microvascular and macrovascular injury such as retinopathy (eye disease), nephropathy (kidney disease), neuropathy (damaged nerves), peripheral vascular disease, cerebrovascular disease (including hemorrhagic stroke), and atherosclerotic disease (often leading to myocardial infarcts) [16]. Mortality rates in adults with T2D are two- to four-fold higher than those observed in individuals without diabetes, with many premature deaths in people with diabetes being attributable to cardiovascular disease (CVD) [28, 29].

According to the WHO, the number of people with diabetes of all ages worldwide increased from 30 to 171 million between 1985 and 2000. These numbers are expected to increase to 366 million in 2030. The estimated prevalence of diabetes approximated 2.8% in 2000 and is predicted to be around 5.8% in 2030 [1]. In Sweden, it is estimated that diabetes affects ~350,000 people (2.2–4.5% of the population) [30–32]. Costs incurred from diabetes complications make up 1.6–6.6% of total health care spending in eight European countries including Sweden (~5%) [33].

Although T2D has traditionally been considered a disease of adult onset, in the past decade T2D incidence has increased rapidly in the young. In some aboriginal groups such as Pima Indians, T2D is as common in children as it is in middle-aged adults of lower-risk ethnic groups [34]. The explanations for the rising trends in pediatric T2D are likely to be attributable to changing lifestyles and the high prevalence of obesity in contemporary children [35, 36]. Data on T2D incidence in European children are scarce. Nevertheless, the proportion of children of European descent diagnosed with T2D appears to remain low. A French study [37] indicated a relatively low but increasing number of children with glucose levels exceeding the thresholds for T2D, and an Austrian population-based study [38] reported an incidence of 0.25/100,000/year. In the United Kingdom, the incidence of T2D was substantially higher in children from ethnic minority groups: 3.9 and 1.25/100,000/year for children of African and South Asian origin, respectively, compared to 0.35/100,000/year in ethnically European children [39].

Despite the increasing number of children with T2D, the WHO estimates that between 2000 and 2030 the most striking increase in T2D prevalence will be among persons aged 65 years and older. By 2030, it is estimated that more than 48 and 82 million older adults (>65 years) in developed and developing countries, respectively, will be afflicted with T2D [1]. The DECODE (Diabetes Epidemiology: Collaborative Analysis of Diagnostic Criteria in Europe) Study Group, which is comprised of nine European countries (including Sweden), estimates the prevalence of T2D will be <10% in persons younger than 60 years of age and 10–20% in persons aged 60–79 years [40]. The reason for this shift in the demographic distribution of affected individuals is threefold: first, global populations are aging; second, the complications of

T2D can be treated more efficiently than ever before which means that people are living longer with diabetes; and third, lifestyle behaviors that increase diabetes risk are becoming more common in all age groups [41, 42].

Physical Activity and T2D Risk

Training studies show aerobic exercise enhances insulin action [43] and glucose metabolism [44] in healthy individuals and those at high risk of T2D. Exercise often normalizes plasma glucose levels by improving insulin sensitivity and glucose transportation [45]. Exercise can also improve endothelial function, reduce inflammation, and beneficially affect the autonomic nervous system [46]. Even in the absence of weight loss, exercise can enhance insulin sensitivity [9] and glycemic control [47]. These findings are particularly relevant as they show regular exercise can be used effectively as a treatment for preventing T2D from developing in individuals with IFG/IGT and for improving insulin action in people with manifest diabetes.

One of the first lifestyle intervention studies from Sweden showed weight reduction and enhanced aerobic fitness improve glucose tolerance [48]. The intervention groups comprised 41 and 181 men with T2D and IGT, respectively, and the comparison groups comprised 79 and 114 men with IGT and normal glucose tolerance, respectively. Participants in the intervention groups received a 5-year protocol including dietary treatment and supervised exercise training. Follow-up measurements after 6 years revealed that body weight was reduced by 2.0–3.3 kg in the intervention groups, whereas body weight increased in the control groups by 0.2–2 kg. Participants from the intervention group who at baseline had IGT improved their glucose control by 75.8%, and 10.6% developed T2D. By contrast, those in the control group with baseline IGT experienced a 67.1% deterioration in glucose control, and 28.6% developed T2D. Weight reduction ($r=0.19$, $p<0.02$) and increased fitness ($r=0.22$, $p<0.02$) were positively correlated with improved glucose tolerance. This early study provided evidence changes in lifestyle might prevent diabetes even after the intervention ends.

In a second landmark study from Scandinavia called the Finnish Diabetes Prevention Study (DPS) [9], 522 overweight middle-aged adults with IFG/IGT were randomized either to receive intensive lifestyle intervention with exercise and diet modification or to a standard care control arm. Participants randomized to the lifestyle intervention arm received detailed advice regarding the five goals of the intervention: (1) weight loss, (2) reduced total fat intake, (3) reduced saturated fat intake, (4) increased fiber intake, and (5) exercise (for at least 30 min/day). After 1- and 2-year follow-up, there was a weight loss of 4.2 ± 5.1 and 3.5 ± 5.5 kg in the intervention group and 0.8 ± 3.7 and 0.8 ± 4.4 kg in the control group, respectively (both $p<0.001$). After an average of 3.2-year follow-up, the incidence of diabetes in the intervention group was 58% less than observed in the control group.

In the United States, a multicenter study similar in design to the Finnish DPS and called the Diabetes Prevention Program (DPP) was conducted [8]. The DPP involved an average follow-up of 3.2 years in 3,234 initially high risk individuals without diabetes who were randomized to receive an intensive lifestyle intervention or standard care. Unlike the Finnish DPS [9], the trial also included metformin and troglitazone arms. The intensive lifestyle modification arm included goals to achieve at least 7% weight loss, dietary modification, and at least 150 min of PA per week. As with the Finnish DPS, the reduction in diabetes incidence attributable to the lifestyle intervention was 58% when compared with the T2D incidence rate in the control group.

In Asia, the Da Qing Study [49] randomized 577 middle-aged Chinese adults with IGT to interventions comprising diet, exercise, diet+exercise, or a control intervention comprising standard care. The diabetes incidence rates at 6 years were significantly lower in the diet group (43.8%), the exercise group (41.1%), and the diet+exercise group (46%) than in the control group (67%). The Da Qing Study [50] is the only large-scale randomized controlled trial to date where the impact of diet and exercise interventions have been compared as separate and combined treatments for diabetes risk reduction. A second large-scale Asian DPS took place in India and was called the Indian DPP. The design of this study was similar to the DPP and involved an average follow-up duration of 3 years, where 531 middle-aged, overweight adults with IGT were randomized to one of four arms: (1) lifestyle modification, (2) metformin, (3) lifestyle modification+metformin, or (4) placebo control. At the end of the trial, the cumulative incidence of diabetes was 55.0% in the control group and 39.3% in the lifestyle intervention group. Similar effects were observed for metformin or metformin+lifestyle (40.5 and 39.5%, respectively).

One of the most well-known studies of exercise intervention and genetics is the *HE*ealth, *RI*sk factors, exercise *TrA*ining and *GE*netics (HERITAGE) Family Study [51]. Around 1,000 individuals from more than 300 North American nuclear families of European and African descent were enrolled into a noncontrolled exercise intervention study. The intervention included tightly monitored aerobic and resistance training sessions. This exceptionally well-phenotyped study has to date focused primarily on linkage scans and biologic candidate gene studies. HERITAGE is described in detail elsewhere in this book and in the sections below where specific results are documented.

Epidemiological studies examining the associations between lifestyle behaviors and diabetes risk have reached similar conclusions as the clinical trials described above. For example, the 14-year follow-up University of Pennsylvania Alumni Health Study [52] ($n=5,990$ men aged 39–68 years) showed PA (leisure time physical activity [LTPA] expressed in kcal expended per week through walking, stair climbing, and sports) was inversely associated with the incidence of T2D. Incidence rates declined as energy expenditure rose from 500 through 3,500 kcal/week. The age-adjusted relative risk ratio (RR) of T2D was reduced by about 6% for each 500 kcal increment increase in PA energy expenditure.

Similarly, in the 8-year follow-up of the Nurses' Health Study [53] ($n=87,253$ women aged 34–59 years), an inverse graded association between PA and incidence of T2D was observed. The age-adjusted risk of T2D was 0.67 (95% confidence interval [CI], 0.60–0.75) in women who engaged in vigorous exercise at least once a week compared with women who exercised less than once weekly. The same study also showed walking and vigorous activity are protective of T2D [54]. After adjustment for potential confounders and mediators, including body mass index (BMI), the risk of developing T2D across quintiles of PA (defined as metabolic energy equivalent (MET) hours per week, with the lowest MET quintile as the referent) yielded 0.84 (95% CI, 0.72–0.97), 0.87 (95% CI, 0.75–1.02), 0.77 (95% CI, 0.65–0.91), and 0.74 (95% CI, 0.62–0.89) fold reductions in T2D risk. Even in women who abstained from vigorous exercise, the reduction in risk across quintiles of PA was substantial.

In the 10-year follow-up of the Health Professional's Follow-up Study [55] ($n = 37,918$ men aged 40–75 years), sedentary lifestyle behaviors such as TV viewing were positively related with increased risk of T2D. After adjustment for potential confounders and mediators, the risk of developing T2D decreased in a dose–response manner across quintiles of PA (MET hours per week), with the most active men having roughly half the risk of T2D compared with the least active, i.e., 0.51 (95% CI, 0.41–0.63). In adjusted models including total PA, weekly TV viewing was associated in a dose-dependent manner with T2D risk. Diabetes risk increased in men who viewed more than 40 h of TV each week by 2.87 fold (95% CI, 1.46–5.65) compared with those who viewed <1 h/week. These data illustrate the complex and independent relationships of PA and sedentary behavior with T2D risk.

Genetic Factors in T2D

Heritability estimates provide an indication of the extent to which genetic and environmental factors influence the variance of specific traits (phenotypes) within populations. Heritability is formally defined as a ratio of variances, specifically as the proportion of total variance in a population for a particular measurement taken at a particular time or age is attributable to variation in additive genetic or total genetic values and is termed narrow-sense heritability (h^2) and broad-sense heritability (H^2), respectively [56]. The H^2 for T2D ranges from 26 to 75% [57–59].

The offspring RR is often used to express the heritable risk of developing a disease. In the Framingham Offspring Study, the RR in offspring with one diabetic parent was ~3.5, and when both parents had diabetes the RR increased to ~6.0 compared with the risk in offspring of parents without diabetes [60]. The heritable risk of diabetes extends beyond the influence of the parents to other family members. In the Framingham study, a history of diabetes in any biologic relative independently predicted diabetes risk in the proband [60].

Studies of twins also provide compelling evidence for a genetic component to T2D. Estimates for concordance rates range from 0.29 to 1.00 in monozygotic (MZ) twins, while in dizygotic (DZ) twins the range is 0.10–0.43 [57, 58, 61–64]. The high levels of heritability observed for insulin sensitivity and insulin secretion [65–67] further reinforce the role of genetics in diabetes and indicate the primary genetic lesions for diabetes are likely to localize to genes in beta-cell-centric pathways.

In 2001, the draft sequence of the human nuclear genome was published [68, 69]. The human genome consists of approximately 2.85 billion base pairs encoding about 20,000–25,000 genes [70]. Although 99.9% of the human DNA sequence is thought to be identical between unrelated individuals, about 0.1% of coded DNA differs between the two chromosomal strands at the same base [71]. It is these differences that account for some of the diversity in human phenotypes and their responsiveness to environmental exposures including, but by no means limited to, exercise and PA.

Over the past few years, genome-wide association studies (GWAS) have been extremely successful in detecting loci associated with complex disease traits such as obesity and T2D. GWAS is a hypothesis-free method where many genetic markers (usually more than one million single nucleotide polymorphisms [SNPs]) spread over the entire genome are tested for association with disease traits. This method differs from the traditional biologic candidate gene approach in that it is agnostic to prior biological knowledge about a specific gene's role in disease and is hence unbiased in this respect. This approach instead relies heavily on replication of association signals across multiple populations and generally requires very large sample sizes to overcome the power constraints inherent in conducting so many association tests [72]. GWAS have confirmed the three previously identified signals for T2D which localize to transcription factor 7-like 2 (*TCF7L2*), peroxisome proliferative activated receptor, gamma (*PPARG*), and potassium inwardly rectifying channel, subfamily J, member 11 (*KCNJ11*), and identified many new susceptibility loci [73–78]. More than 40 T2D loci have been discovered and replicated to date, most of which localize to genes that appear to influence beta-cell function [79]. These findings highlight the role of inherited defects in beta-cell function rather than defects in genes causing insulin resistance in the etiology of T2D [80, 81].

What is a Gene × Lifestyle Interaction?

In epidemiology, the term *interaction* implies a mutual dependency of two or more risk factors contributing to disease risk [82]. The use of the word *interaction* in biology sometimes differs from the epidemiological use of the word. In biology, an interaction is defined as the dependence of two or more factors that act together through the same pathway [83, 84]. This definition is somewhat similar to the concept of *effect-mediation* in epidemiology. The word *interaction* is often used in epidemiology to define a situation where the relationship between an environmental exposure and a disease outcome differs in magnitude between genotypes at a given (often SNP) locus (Fig. 4.1) [83]. The scenario where a gene variant exerts its effects on a disease trait via behavior (e.g., physical inactivity) does not necessarily involve *effect-modification* (interaction), but instead can represent *effect-mediation*. Although statistical and biologic definitions of interactions have important distinctions as outlined above, epidemiological models of interaction can sometimes be used to test biologically derived hypotheses of interaction and visa versa.

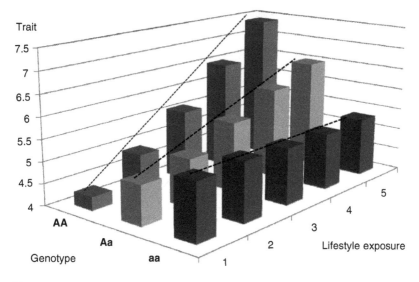

Fig. 4.1 In epidemiological studies, gene × lifestyle interactions are typically assessed by testing whether the magnitude of the association between the lifestyle exposure and the level of a quantitative disease trait (or relative risk of disease, if expressed as a binary or ordinal variable) differs in magnitude by genotype at a given locus. The figure illustrates this concept using simulated data. In the major homozygous genotype (AA) the association between the lifestyle exposure and the disease trait is positive in direction and strong in magnitude, but with each copy of the minor (a) allele, the magnitude of this association is progressively diminished toward the null. If the statistical comparison of magnitude of these slopes (coefficients) reveals that each is statistically different than the other, one would generally consider this evidence of an interaction

Different types of *interaction* exist in epidemiology. These can be divided into two basic classes termed removable, or *quantitative*, interactions and nonremovable, or *qualitative*, interactions. A removable interaction is dependent on the scale used to express the phenotype (e.g., additive or multiplicative scales), whereas a quantitative interaction is not [83]. For example, removable interactions may be evident when the data are expressed on the log scale, but are "removed" when the same data are shown on the normal scale. Assuming the choice of scale does not violate the assumptions of the statistical model, the design and purpose of the study influence the interpretation of interaction effects that are evident on one scale but not another [82].

Irrespective of the nature of the interaction effect, the most common statistical approach when testing for interactions involves fitting a product term (gene × environment) in addition to terms for the marginal effects to a regression model where the phenotype is fitted as the dependent variable. Several variations on these basic methods have been proposed [85], including the case-only design. Using this approach, a multiplicative model can be tested. A limitation of this method is that it does not allow for the estimation of the separate effects of high-risk environments or genotypes [86]. Where the case-only design is applied in family pedigrees [87],

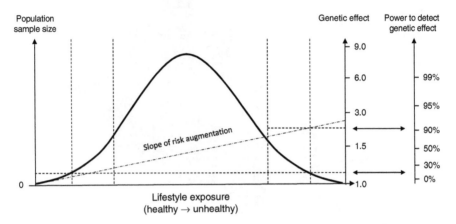

Fig. 4.2 A theoretical example of how, in the presence of a gene × lifestyle interaction, the relationship between gene variant and the disease trait is likely to vary in magnitude and how, for a given sample size, a study will be more or less powered to detect this effect across the spectrum of the lifestyle exposure

the log linear approach [88] or the transmission disequilibrium test can be used to test for interaction [89]. A more powerful method of testing for interactions involves a joint test of the genetic main effect and gene×environment interaction effects (also known as the two-degree of freedom model) [90].

Understanding the nature of gene×environment interactions may help improve the power of genetic prediction models. As shown in Fig. 4.2, where linear interaction effects occur, genetic risk varies across the spectrum of the environmental exposure. Selecting individuals from the extremes of the environmental distribution where genetic effects are of greatest magnitude could enhance the statistical power of genetic prediction models [91].

Confounding in genetic association studies is generally less of a problem than in studies evaluating disease associations for nongenetic exposures. The reason is DNA variants are fixed throughout life and are virtually unaffected by the level of other factors such as smoking, alcohol consumption, income, or social status which in nongenetic association studies may cause significant confounding. Nevertheless, at a population level, age (through survival bias) and ethnicity (through population stratification) can cause confounding in genetic association studies [92]. The latter can occur when allele frequencies and disease frequencies coincidently vary between ethnic subgroups, which when pooled for genetic association studies can lead to spurious conclusions about associations unless the models are appropriately controlled for ethnicity. It is important to bear in mind that even if genetic association studies are resilient to confounding, studies of gene×environment interactions are not, as they inherit the limitations and susceptibilities that beset both genetic and nongenetic association studies. Moreover, confounding by parallel interaction effects can also occur. Therefore, it may be necessary to include a range of potential confounders in interaction models, in addition to product terms comprised of the genotype of interest and putative environmental confounding variables.

Overview of Studies of Gene × Exercise Interactions

The following section reviews the published literature on gene × exercise/PA interactions on diabetes-related traits. Observational and interventional studies are described. Most of the genes described in the studies outlined below were selected as biologic candidate genes with a small number involving gene variants identified through GWAS.

Observational Studies

Several early studies of gene × PA interactions focused on variants in the adrenergic beta-2 receptor (*ADRB2*). One of the initial studies of interaction was undertaken in French males and focused on obesity as the outcome (BMI and waist circumference). In that study, Meirhaeghe et al. [93] reported a strong association between the *ADRB2* Gln27Glu variant and BMI and waist circumference in physically inactive men, but this effect was completely diminished in active men, which gave rise to a statistically significant gene × PA interaction. In a follow-up study conducted in white adults from the United Kingdom, Meirhaeghe et al. [94] reported gene × PA interactions for a different *ADRB2* variant (Gly16Arg) on obesity and nonesterified fatty acid (NEFA) levels. This was the first gene × environment interaction study to use objective assessments of PA in a population-based cohort. The *ADRB2* Gly16Arg variant was inversely related with fasting and postglucose challenge NEFA levels in the population as a whole. However, the magnitude of this association was greater in people with the *ADRB2* Arg16Arg genotype compared with carriers of the Gly16 allele. No evidence of interactions on obesity-related traits was reported. Elsewhere, Corbalan et al. [95] found recreational PA (ratio between MET-hours per week to time spent sitting down during leisure time) modulates the effect of the *ADRB2* Gln27Glu SNP on the risk of obesity in Spanish women.

One of the most widely studied genes in the context of gene × lifestyle interactions on obesity and T2D is *PPARG*. Several studies have reported interactions between dietary fat intake and the *PPARG* Pro12Ala variant on insulin resistance and obesity [96–100]. A number of subsequent studies examined the interaction between *PPARG* Pro12Ala and PA on these traits. For example, in a cross-sectional study of Caucasians from the United Kingdom, Franks et al. [101] reported PA and dietary fat composition (polyunsaturated to saturated fatty acid ratio) have an additive effect on fasting insulin levels in *PPARG* Pro12Pro homozygotes, but have a synergistic effect in carriers of at least one copy of the *PPARG* Ala12 allele. Elsewhere, in a cross-sectional study of 216 Hispanic pedigrees (1,850 nuclear families) and 236 non-Hispanic white pedigrees (1,240 families), Nelson et al. [102] found a significant interaction between the *PPARG* Pro12 allele and PA on T2D risk. The *PPARG* Pro12 allele was only associated with T2D risk in physically inactive individuals, with active individuals carrying the *PPARG* Pro12 allele being at a similar level of risk as Ala12 allele carriers.

A third class of biologic candidate genes widely studied for interactions with PA are the genes encoding uncoupling proteins (*UCP2* and *UCP3*). Two studies examining *UCP2* found no evidence of interactions with PA on obesity-related traits [103, 104]. Two other studies focusing on *UCP3* found no evidence of gene×PA interactions on obesity-related traits [103, 104].

Gene×PA interaction studies involving lipid enzyme encoding genes have also proven popular. For example, in the cross-sectional Inter99 study ($n=5,585$ Danish adults), Grarup et al. [105] observed an interaction ($p=0.002$) between the hepatic lipase gene (*LIPC*) −250G>A SNP and self-reported PA on serum HDL-C concentrations. The authors reported PA was more strongly associated with HDL-C levels in *LIP C/T* variant A allele carriers than in G allele homozygotes. In a study conducted in the United States with 14-year follow-up of Hispanics and non-Hispanic Whites, Hokanson et al. [106] found that the relationship between the *LIPC* −480C>T variant modified the association between PA and coronary heart disease (CHD). Overall, the *LIPC* TT genotype raised CHD risk, but this risk was offset in those reporting vigorous activity levels.

Several studies have tested for interactions between the ε2, ε3, and ε4 genotypes in the apolipoprotein E (*APOE*) gene and PA on plasma lipids. For example, in a Spanish study, Corella et al. [107] found that the relationship between *APOE* variants and levels of HDL-C differed when comparing physically active and inactive men. No interactions between *APOE* polymorphisms and PA were observed in women, suggesting additional sex-specific factors may further modify HDL-C levels, the analyses in women were underpowered to detect an interaction, and/or the findings in men were false-positive. In a study of Swiss men, Bernstein et al. [108] reported stronger associations between PA and HDL-C in the *APOE4* genotype group compared with the *APOE2* and *APOE3* genotype groups. Cross-sectional studies examining interactions and associations between levels of PA and lipoprotein lipase (*LPL*) polymorphisms on lipid profiles have yielded inconsistent results. In Dutch men and women, Boer et al. [109] found the *LPL* D9N missense SNP was associated with higher total cholesterol and lower HDL-C concentrations in physically inactive persons, but these relationships were not apparent in active individuals. In a study of Spanish men, Senti et al. [110] reported an absence of interaction between PA and the *LPL* HindIII variant on HDL-C and triglycerides levels.

In a cross-sectional study of African–Americans and Whites, Grove et al. [111] observed a significant interaction between the guanine nucleotide binding protein (G-protein) beta polypeptide 3 (*GNB3*) variant 825C>T and PA on obesity risk; this interaction was evident in Blacks but not in Whites. In physically active Blacks, each copy of the *GNB3* 825T allele was associated with a 20% lower prevalence of obesity, whereas in inactive individuals each copy of the *GNB3* 825T allele was associated with 23% increased prevalence of obesity. The authors also reported a three-way interaction between PA, obesity, and the *GNB3* 825C>T variant on hypertension risk.

Nitric oxide is a molecule central to numerous vascular and metabolic processes owing to its pivotal role in vasodilation. Variants in the genes encoding the molecule that synthesizes nitric oxide (nitric oxide synthase genes, *NOS1, NOS2, NOS3*) have been the focus of several interaction studies. For example, in Whites from the United Kingdom, Franks et al. [112] observed an interaction between PA energy expenditure and *NOS3* haplotypes (comprised of the rs2070744, IVS11-30, and rs3800787 variants) on 2-h glucose concentrations. Relative to the most common haplotype, the second most common haplotype was associated with a moderate increase in T2D risk, and the least common haplotype was associated with decreased T2D risk. PA was inversely associated with 2-h glucose concentrations within each of the three haplotypes, but the magnitude of this association was significantly greater in the least common haplotype which manifested as a statistically significant gene × PA interaction.

In a study of Japanese adults [113], an intron 4 *NOS3* variant modified the association between PA and systolic blood pressure levels. The authors reported a stronger inverse relationship between the intron 4 *NOS3* variant and blood pressure in physically inactive than in active individuals. Vimaleswaran et al. [114] also observed a significant interaction between PA and a *NOS3* gene variant (IVS25 + 15) on diastolic and systolic blood pressures. In each of the three genotype groups, PA was inversely related with blood pressures, but the association was stronger in people homozygous for the major allele than in carriers of the minor allele, indicating that blood pressures in people homozygous for the major allele may be resistant to the effects of exercise. Similar findings were reported in a study of gene × PA interactions at the G-protein-coupled receptor 10 (*GPR10*) locus [115]. In this study, PA was inversely related with blood pressure levels in individuals homozygous for the major allele (G62G), but there was no such association in carriers of the *GPR10* minor A62 allele.

Several studies have exploited the recent discoveries from GWAS for obesity-related traits to undertake studies of gene × lifestyle interactions. Possibly, the most striking example of a gene × PA interaction reported to date comes from a Danish study of the fat mass and obesity-associated (*FTO*) gene variants. In that study, Andreasen et al. [116] found an interaction between the *FTO* rs9939609 variant and self-reported PA on BMI levels in a large sample of treatment-naive Danish adults. Overall, they replicated the association between the *FTO* rs9939609 variant and obesity. However, when stratified by PA level, they observed the effect was substantially weaker in active compared with inactive individuals. In a report that emerged shortly after the Danish study from the Old Order Amish community, Rampersaud et al. [117] observed a statistically significant interaction between the *FTO* rs1861868 variant (in low linkage disequilibrium [LD] with the *FTO* rs9930969 variant) and objectively assessed PA on levels of BMI. Similar interaction effects were reported for the *FTO* rs1477196 variant. Since these initial studies, several other reports have emerged which reached variable conclusions regarding the interaction between PA and genetic variants in *FTO* on obesity predisposition [118–120].

The first GWAS report focusing specifically on obesity was conducted in the Framingham Heart Study [121]. The authors identified a variant in the insulin-induced gene 2 (*INSIG2*) that appeared to be associated with elevated BMI. Independent replication studies yielded conflicting results, with some suggesting that the *INSIG2* risk "C" allele reported in the original study was in fact protective in other populations [122]. These inconsistencies might be attributable to gene×environment interactions, a hypothesis that has been tested by several groups. For example, in the cross-sectional Danish Inter99 cohort study, Andreasen et al. [123] observed an interaction between self-reported PA and the *INSIG2* rs7566605 variant on BMI levels. The same authors conducted one of the largest studies of gene×PA interactions to date [122]. In that study the gene×PA interactions were examined for a variant at the phosphofructokinase, platelet (*PFKP*) gene locus on BMI levels in a 16,781 Danish adults; however, no evidence of an interaction was found.

Using GWAS results to guide the choice of SNPs, Brito et al. [124] recently reported a comprehensive analysis of gene×PA interactions on T2D risk. In this study variants in three genes were identified (i.e., *PPARG*, variant hepatic nuclear factor 1 beta [*HNF1B*], cyclin-dependent kinase inhibitor 2A/B [*CDKN2A/B*]), which showed at least nominal evidence of gene×PA interactions on either glucose homeostasis or T2D incidence. The strongest finding was for an *HNF1B* variant that appears to diminish the protective effects of PA on T2D risk.

Several of the *bona fide* T2D genes confirmed to date were initially identified for their roles in monogenic diabetes. One such example is the hepatocyte nuclear factor 4 alpha (*HNF4A*) gene. Stephanie-May et al. [125] investigated interactions between the *HNF4A* rs1885088 G>A and rs745975 C>T variants with PA in a cross-sectional study of 528 Canadians. Significant interactions between the *HNF4A* rs1885088 genotype and PA were found for both glucose area under the curve (AUC) and 2-h glucose levels independent of BMI. Higher levels of PA (>2 h/week) were associated with lower glucose AUC and 2-h glucose values in the *HNF4A* A/A, but not in G/A or in G/G genotype groups. The *HNF4A* A allele is generally perceived to be the T2D risk allele based on results from several large meta-analyses. Although Stephanie-May et al. [125] were unable to detect a significant main effect of the *HNF4A* rs1885088 G>A SNP on glucose levels possibly owing to the small sample, they did find modest evidence to suggest that carriers of the A allele may be more sensitive to the beneficial effects of PA on glucose homeostasis. In the same study, these authors reported significant gene×PA interactions for the *HNF4A* rs745975 C>T SNP and PA on fasting C peptide levels and insulin AUC.

Although many studies have been reported on gene×PA interactions during the past decade, rarely have the results from these studies been adequately replicated. This raises the possibility that many of these reports are false-positive. It is only recently that realistic estimates of genetic and interaction effect sizes have been established, which it transpires are much smaller than previously believed. With this new information in hand, it is now evident that most published studies of gene × PA interactions are probably statistically underpowered (i.e., the probability of detecting a true interaction effect is low). This emphasizes the need for future interaction studies to utilize large sample collections, well-measured exposures and phenotypes, appropriate analytic methods, and a conservative approach to the interpretation and reporting of results. Nevertheless, even the studies that are underpowered and may have reported false-positive results have provided the foundation for bigger and better future studies.

Clinical Trials and Other Experimental Studies

PPARG has been extensively investigated for its potential modifying role in exercise-induced changes in obesity, insulin resistance, and T2D. Most published studies have focused exclusively on the *PPARG* Pro12Ala SNP. Several studies have reported carriers of the *PPARG* Ala12 allele are more responsive to the effects of exercise training regarding improvements in insulin resistance and glucose homeostasis. For example, in a study of Japanese men, Kahara et al. [126] reported greater improvements in insulin action in carriers of the *PPARG* Ala12 allele than in people homozygous for the Pro12 allele after 3 months of aerobic exercise training. However, because the frequency of the *PPARG* Ala allele in this study population was very low and it was a small study, the findings should be interpreted with caution.

Elsewhere, Adamo et al. [127] reported that after 3 months of supervised exercise training, initially sedentary T2D patients with the *PPARG* Ala12 allele showed greater improvements in fasting plasma glucose homeostasis compared with those homozygous for the Pro12 allele. In White Americans (32 men and 41 women), Weiss et al. [128] reported men who were carriers of the *PPARG* Ala12 allele experienced significant improvements in insulin levels following 6 months of supervised exercise training. No such effects were found in women. A major limitation of this study is that all but four women in the trial were *PPARG* Pro12 homozygotes. Thus, the power to detect an interaction with exercise training on insulin levels in this trial is likely to be very low. Three randomized controlled trials have also assessed the interaction between the *PPARG* Pro12Ala SNP and PA on T2D risk [129]. The Finnish DPS involved a 3-year intensive lifestyle intervention in 490 overweight individuals with impaired fasting and 2-h glucose concentrations. In a report from this study, Lindi et al. [129] observed evidence of gene × treatment interactions on T2D incidence, where the *PPARG* Ala12 allele was apparently protected against developing diabetes within the lifestyle intervention arm, but not in the control arm of the study. These findings suggest that although the *PPARG* Ala12 allele may predispose to the development of T2D under normal conditions, it may be protective in the context of an intensive lifestyle intervention.

A limitation of the studies described above is that few appropriately tested for gene × exercise interactions. The DPP engaged a similar lifestyle intervention to the

Finnish DPS, but included a much larger US multiethnic cohort ($n=3{,}548$ participants without diabetes but with elevated fasting and 2-h glucose concentrations). In a report from this study, Florez et al. [130] reported an absence of statistical interaction between Pro12Ala (and five other *PPARG* variants) and intervention (lifestyle and metformin) on the incidence of T2D. However, statistically significant interactions between the Pro12Ala variant and dietary fat intake on weight change were observed in the DPP [131]. In another report from the Finnish DPS, Kilpelainen et al. [132] described statistical interactions between the *PPARG* rs17036314 and Pro12Ala SNPs with the change in total amount of self-report PA ($p=0.002$ and 0.031, respectively). In these observational analyses, increased PA tended to decrease the effect of the *PPARG* rs17036314 and Pro12Ala risk alleles on T2D incidence.

Inconsistent results have been reported regarding the interactions between the genes encoding the adrenergic receptors and PA. Two studies examining the *ADRB2* gene, including one randomized controlled trial, found no evidence of any interaction effects of PA and *ADRB2* Gln27Glu on plasma triglycerides and serum insulin [133] or T2D [134]. Similarly, four studies of *ADRB3* variants, including two randomized control trials, did not observe any statistical interactions between PA and the Trp64Arg polymorphism on fasting glucose [135], anthropometric measures of obesity, blood pressure [136], or T2D risk [134, 137]. In contrast, in the combined intervention and control groups of the Finnish DPS, Laaksonen et al. [138] observed a statistical interaction between changes in estimated total LTPA and the *ADRB2* 12Glu9 SNP ($p=0.033$). In that study, high levels of LTPA tended to decrease the risk of developing diabetes in carriers of the *ADRB2* 12Glu allele, but not in those homozygous for the 9Glu allele [138].

Numerous other genes have been studied in exercise or lifestyle intervention studies. These include *UCP1* for which results on gene×exercise interactions are inconclusive [135, 137]. As is the case with observational studies, several intervention studies have examined the interaction between exercise and *LIPC* variants. For example, in the Finnish DPS an interaction between the *LIPC* −250G>A SNP and lifestyle intervention was observed for T2D incidence, where the effect of the *LIPC* G-250 allele was more pronounced in the intervention group than in the control group [139]. In the control group, the cumulative incidence of diabetes was 23% in subjects with the *LIPC* G-250G genotype, whereas in the intervention group only one participant with the *LIPC* −250A allele developed diabetes. This finding suggests changes in lifestyle such as diet, PA, and weight loss modify diabetes risk predisposition in carriers of the *LIPC* −250A allele. However, in a follow-up observational analysis of the same cohort, Kilpelainen et al. [134] were unable to detect interactions between the *LIPC* −250G>A variants and changes in PA or body weight on the risk of T2D at 4.1 years of follow-up. The findings of Kilpelainen et al. [134] suggest the interaction effect reported in the initial study [139] was either false-positive or involved aspects of lifestyle other than PA (such as diet).

In one of the earliest studies of genes and exercise intervention, Hagberg et al. [140] reported that *APOE* genotypes influence the HDL-C response to exercise, with *APOE2* carriers being more responsive than *APOE3* and *APOE4* carriers following 9 months of endurance exercise. This was a small study ($n=51$), which lacked a control arm, and no formal tests of interaction were reported. Elsewhere, Garenc et al. [141] examined the *LPL* S447X SNP in the context of a 20-week exercise intervention study (the HERITAGE Study). White women with the *LPL* X447 allele exhibited greater reductions in BMI, fat mass, and percent body fat than Black women following the intervention. Whereas Black women with the *LPL* X447 allele showed a greater reduction in abdominal visceral fat and a larger increase in postheparin LPL activity than White women following the intervention. However, these effects were not apparent in the male participants in the study.

The recent advances in the genetics of obesity and T2D have prompted analyses exploring whether these confirmed disease predisposing loci modify the response to lifestyle interventions. In the DPP, for example, Florez et al. [142] showed that carriers of the T2D predisposing alleles at the transcription factor 7-like 2 (*TCF7L2*) gene (rs12255372 and rs7903146) experienced a similar reduction in diabetes risk following lifestyle intervention. In the same cohort, Franks et al. [143] previously analyzed two genes selected from obesity GWAS. These authors reported a positive association between the *FTO* rs9930969 variant and 1-year weight change in the placebo group, which was reversed in the lifestyle intervention group, suggesting a gene × treatment interaction. Similar analyses conducted in the Finnish DPS did not yield a significant gene × treatment interaction effect for this *FTO* variant [144]. A series of observational studies have since been published with inconsistent results [118–120, 145]. In the DPP, the *INSIG2* variant (rs7566605) initially identified in a GWAS conducted by Herbert et al. [121] was studied in relation to weight change and was found to convey discordant effects in the placebo and lifestyle intervention groups suggesting the presence of a gene × lifestyle interaction at this locus.

Another gene that has been the focus of studies of glucose homeostasis and has been studied in the Finnish DPS is the solute carrier family 2 (facilitated glucose transporter), member 2 (*SLC2A2*). Kilpelainen et al. [146] reported significant interactions between *SLC2A2* variants (rs5393, rs5394, and rs5404) and PA on T2D incidence. The same authors also found tentative evidence of gene × PA interactions on diabetes risk for the rs3758947 variant in the ATP-binding cassette, subfamily C (CFTR/MRP), member 8 (*ABCC8*) gene, and the E23K variant in the *KCNJ11* gene when analyzing observational data from the Finnish DPS. Kilpelainen et al. [134] also reported an absence of statistically significant gene × PA interactions for variants in the genes encoding the leptin receptor (*LEPR*), ghrelin/obestatin prepropeptide (*GHRL*), tumor necrosis factor alpha (*TNFA*), interleukin 6 (*IL6*), and insulin-like growth factor 1 receptor (*IGF1R*). These authors did, however, observe nominal interactions for the *GHRL* rs696217 variant and PA on changes in waist circumference, body weight, and HDL-C levels. They also reported interactions for the *LEPR* rs1137100 variant on systolic blood pressure during the first year of the trial. A major limitation of the results from the Finnish DPS is that the study is relatively small, few reported findings are statistically robust, and a wide range of hypotheses have been tested.

In the DPP, Moore et al. [147] undertook gene × treatment interaction analyses for ten previously confirmed T2D predisposing loci. The most promising finding emerged for a variant (rs10811661) proximal to the genes (*CDKN2A/B*) encoding the cyclin-dependent kinase inhibitor 2A (melanoma, p16, inhibits CDK4) and cyclin-dependent kinase inhibitor 2B (p15, inhibits CDK4) proteins. A significant interaction was observed between the *CDKN2A/B* rs10811661 variant and lifestyle intervention on beta-cell function after 1 year of treatment. A borderline significant gene × lifestyle interaction on diabetes incidence was also reported. A second study by Moore et al. [148] in the DPP examined interactions between the K121Q variant in the ectonucleotide pyrophosphatase/phosphodiesterase 1 (*ENPP1*) gene and lifestyle intervention. In that report, the increased risk of diabetes observed in carriers of the *ENPP1* Q121 allele in the placebo group was diminished in the lifestyle intervention group. As with observational studies, few reports of interactions from clinical trials have been adequately replicated and most, if not all, are underpowered for the detection of realistic interaction effects. The strength of randomized clinical trials is generally perceived to be their experimental design and their ability to control for confounding by evenly distributing all factors (observable and unobservable) other than the treatment that might affect the phenotype of interest. The strongest designs include a placebo control and ensure that the investigators and study participants are blinded to the allocation of treatments. However, it is impossible to blind the allocation of a lifestyle intervention; thus, results from lifestyle intervention trials may still be prone to the confounding effects of factors that correlate with the intervention. For example, in exercise intervention studies, participants may change their dietary behaviors even though this is not an explicit feature of the intervention. Such changes could confound the interpretation of the main effects of the intervention and gene × treatment interactions.

Methodological and Statistical Considerations in Studies of Gene × Physical Activity Interaction

The literature on gene × PA interactions on T2D and related traits is dominated by initial positive results which lack appropriate replication. A low level of statistical power would influence the reproducibility of a study's findings if (as is likely) this influences the way in which analyses are performed and reported. For example, investigators may be more likely to overanalyze data from small, poorly designed studies and selectively report these results.

Statistical power is defined as the probability that within a given sample a predefined effect will be detectable if it is present. Underpowered studies are more prone to type 2 error (i.e., accepting the null hypothesis when in fact it should be rejected). By convention, many consider a level of 80% power as a reasonable threshold with studies powered above this level being considered appropriately powered, although this threshold is arbitrary [149]. Studies that have simulated power to detect gene × environment interactions demonstrate that the sample size necessary to detect an interaction effect is generally larger than the sample size required to detect the genetic or environmental main effects [150, 151]. The main factors that affect power in studies of interaction are the magnitude of the association between exposure and outcome, the magnitude of the interaction effect, the frequency of the minor allele, sample size, and measurement error [149]. For example, a study of interaction with continuously distributed outcomes (e.g., glucose, insulin, or BMI) with accurate measurements of the exposures and outcomes would be equally powered to detect gene×lifestyle interactions as one 10–50 times larger which had incorporated weak measures of the exposures and outcomes [149].

Most epidemiological studies of gene×PA interactions on T2D or its antecedents have used questionnaires to characterize lifestyle behaviors. Although most of the commonly used PA questionnaires appropriately classify the behavior when compared with gold standard methods, the correlation between methods is usually low $r<0.25$ and reporting biases and heteroscadicity associated with disease outcomes can complicate the interpretation of results [152, 153]. On the other hand, objective measurements of PA (e.g., accelerometry) are generally more accurate $(r>0.5)$ [154–157]. Thus, studies of gene×PA interaction may benefit from the availability of objective assessment methods. However, it is important also to recognize that objective methods usually reflect a relatively short period of free living activity and may be prone to Hawthorne Effect (i.e., subjects will change their PA levels simply because they are being measured), whereas questionnaires often reflect activity levels during the past months or years.

In general, few studies of gene×PA interactions on T2D and related traits have corrected analyses for multiple testing (multiple statistical comparisons within the same sample). Multiple testing is a particular problem in studies of gene×environment interactions because such studies often involve the comparison of numerous genetic markers, environment factors, and outcomes. Such tests may also be performed at a secondary level and represent exploratory analyses, rather than those identified during the analysis planning stage. Generally, if this information is reported in the publications documenting the results, the results can be viewed in an appropriate context; however, this information is not always disclosed.

A number of methods have been proposed to be statistically correct for multiple testing. In studies of gene×PA interactions, the methods most used to date are the Bonferroni correction and the false discovery rate (FDR). The classical Bonferroni correction compensates for the number of independent tests performed and assumes each test is independent. Using this approach, one takes the observed p value and divides it by the number of tests performed. It is generally agreed this method is overly conservative, largely because it assumes each test is independent which is rarely true [158]. The FDR, on the other hand, is a study-specific estimate of type 1 error and may be more appropriate in studies of interaction where hypotheses are often closely related [159]. Applying the FDR method in studies of interaction may reduce false discovery and simultaneously preserve power to detect true effects.

The Future?

Detecting *bona fide* gene×exercise interactions, understanding how they affect disease susceptibility, and translating this information into a form where it can be used to prevent disease remains a vision for the future. The studies conducted to date have laid important and necessary groundwork, but in and of themselves they are insufficient to guide the implementation of exercise genomics into clinical practice. For this to be a realistic possibility requires a new era of studies that are specifically designed and powered for the detection of gene × lifestyle interactions and others which show how the implementation of such knowledge can be used to improve treatment outcomes, possibly by using personal genomics to guide the application of treatments in intervention studies. Many such studies are underway, and within the next few years, *bona fide* examples of gene × exercise interactions on T2D risk will almost certainly come to light; whether this information will translate to improvements in human health remains to be determined.

Practical Applications

As we have described in this chapter, an abundance of evidence supports the protective effects of health lifestyle behaviors on type 2 diabetes risk. However, population-wide programs of intensive lifestyle interventions are probably unrealistic owing to the costs involved in running such trials and the difficulties in recruiting participants and motivating them to adhere to the interventions. It may be more feasible to identify individuals at high risk of diabetes who, because of their genetic characteristics, are likely to respond well to exercise interventions, as an example, and target these persons. This does not of course mean that healthy lifestyle behaviors would be discouraged in the remainder of the population, but one might prioritize other, more effective, preventive strategies in these individuals while continuing to promote the virtues of active lifestyles. The benefits to this approach might include reduced overall costs and greater preventive success. Moreover, because those who receive the intervention are likely to respond well and by consequence maintain motivation, attrition rates may diminish and adherence improve. The actualization of this perspective will first require robust empirical evidence, most likely emerging from the combination of epidemiology for hypothesis generation and clinical trials to test those hypotheses and provide evidence of causality.

References

1. Wild S, Roglic G, Green A, Sicree R, King H. Global prevalence of diabetes: estimates for the year 2000 and projections for 2030. Diabetes Care. 2004;27(5):1047–53.
2. Hu FB, Manson JE, Stampfer MJ, Colditz G, Liu S, Solomon CG, et al. Diet, lifestyle, and the risk of type 2 diabetes mellitus in women. N Engl J Med. 2001;345(11):790–7.
3. Hu FB, Li TY, Colditz GA, Willett WC, Manson JE. Television watching and other sedentary behaviors in relation to risk of obesity and type 2 diabetes mellitus in women. JAMA. 2003;289(14):1785–91.
4. Dunstan DW, Salmon J, Healy GN, Shaw JE, Jolley D, Zimmet PZ, et al. Association of television viewing with fasting and 2-h postchallenge plasma glucose levels in adults without diagnosed diabetes. Diabetes Care. 2007;30(3):516–22.

5. Davis N, Forbes B, Wylie-Rosett J. Nutritional strategies in type 2 diabetes mellitus. Mt Sinai J Med. 2009;76(3):257–68.
6. Hu FB, van Dam RM, Liu S. Diet and risk of Type II diabetes: the role of types of fat and carbohydrate. Diabetologia. 2001;44(7):805–17.
7. Winzell MS, Ahren B. The high-fat diet-fed mouse: a model for studying mechanisms and treatment of impaired glucose tolerance and type 2 diabetes. Diabetes. 2004;53 Suppl 3:S215–9.
8. Knowler WC, Barrett-Connor E, Fowler SE, Hamman RF, Lachin JM, Walker EA, et al. Reduction in the incidence of type 2 diabetes with lifestyle intervention or metformin. N Engl J Med. 2002;346(6):393–403.
9. Tuomilehto J, Lindstrom J, Eriksson JG, Valle TT, Hamalainen H, Ilanne-Parikka P, et al. Prevention of type 2 diabetes mellitus by changes in lifestyle among subjects with impaired glucose tolerance. N Engl J Med. 2001;344(18):1343–50.
10. Voight BF, Scott LJ, Steinthorsdottir V, Morris AP, Dina C, Welch RP, et al. Nat Genet. 2010; 42(7):579–89.
11. Maher B. Personal genomes: the case of the missing heritability. Nature. 2008;456(7218): 18–21.
12. Physical activity and health: A Report of the Surgeon General (1996). U.S. Deparment of Health and Human Services, Atlanta, GA.
13. American Diabetes Association. Diagnosis and classification of diabetes mellitus. Diabetes Care. 2009;32 Suppl 1:S62–7.
14. Lillioja S, Mott DM, Spraul M, Ferraro R, Foley JE, Ravussin E, et al. Insulin resistance and insulin secretory dysfunction as precursors of non-insulin-dependent diabetes mellitus. Prospective studies of Pima Indians. N Engl J Med. 1993;329(27):1988–92.
15. Festa A, Williams K, D'Agostino Jr R, Wagenknecht LE, Haffner SM. The natural course of beta-cell function in nondiabetic and diabetic individuals: the Insulin Resistance Atherosclerosis Study. Diabetes. 2006;55(4):1114–20.
16. Expert Committee on the Diagnosis and Classification of Diabetes Mellitus. Report of the expert committee on the diagnosis and classification of diabetes mellitus. Diabetes Care. 2003;26 Suppl 1:S5–20.
17. The Expert Committee on the Diagnosis and Classification of Diabetes Mellitus. Report of the expert committee on the diagnosis and classification of diabetes mellitus. Diabetes Care. 1997;20(7):1183–97.
18. Forouhi NG, Balkau B, Borch-Johnsen K, Dekker J, Glumer C, Qiao Q, et al. The threshold for diagnosing impaired fasting glucose: a position statement by the European Diabetes Epidemiology Group. Diabetologia. 2006;49(5):822–7.
19. Genuth S, Alberti KG, Bennett P, Buse J, Defronzo R, Kahn R, et al. Follow-up report on the diagnosis of diabetes mellitus. Diabetes Care. 2003;26(11):3160–7.
20. Unwin N, Shaw J, Zimmet P, Alberti KG. Impaired glucose tolerance and impaired fasting glycaemia: the current status on definition and intervention. Diabet Med. 2002;19(9): 708–23.
21. Saydah SH, Loria CM, Eberhardt MS, Brancati FL. Subclinical states of glucose intolerance and risk of death in the U.S. Diabetes Care. 2001;24(3):447–53.
22. American Diabetes Association. Screening for type 2 diabetes. Diabetes Care. 2004;27 Suppl 1:S11–4.
23. Zeggini E, Scott LJ, Saxena R, Voight BF, Marchini JL, Hu T, et al. Meta-analysis of genome-wide association data and large-scale replication identifies additional susceptibility loci for type 2 diabetes. Nat Genet. 2008;40(5):638–45.
24. Lyssenko V, Jonsson A, Almgren P, Pulizzi N, Isomaa B, Tuomi T, et al. Clinical risk factors, DNA variants, and the development of type 2 diabetes. N Engl J Med. 2008;359(21):2220–32.
25. Lyssenko V, Almgren P, Anevski D, Orho-Melander M, Sjogren M, Saloranta C, et al. Genetic prediction of future type 2 diabetes. PLoS Med. 2005;2(12):e345.
26. Franks PW, Mesa JL, Harding AH, Wareham NJ. Gene-lifestyle interaction on risk of type 2 diabetes. Nutr Metab Cardiovasc Dis. 2007;17(2):104–24.

27. Zimmet PZ. Diabetes epidemiology as a tool to trigger diabetes research and care. Diabetologia. 1999;42(5):499–518.
28. Haffner SM, Lehto S, Ronnemaa T, Pyorala K, Laakso M. Mortality from coronary heart disease in subjects with type 2 diabetes and in nondiabetic subjects with and without prior myocardial infarction. N Engl J Med. 1998;339(4):229–34.
29. Fox CS, Coady S, Sorlie PD, D'Agostino RB, Pencina MJ, Vasan RS, et al. Increasing cardiovascular disease burden due to diabetes mellitus: the Framingham Heart Study. Circulation. 2007;115(12):1544–50.
30. Jansson SP, Andersson DK, Svardsudd K. Prevalence and incidence rate of diabetes mellitus in a Swedish community during 30 years of follow-up. Diabetologia. 2007;50(4): 703–10.
31. Eliasson M, Lindahl B, Lundberg V, Stegmayr B. No increase in the prevalence of known diabetes between 1986 and 1999 in subjects 25-64 years of age in northern Sweden. Diabet Med. 2002;19(10):874–80.
32. Berger B, Stenstrom G, Chang YF, Sundkvist G. The prevalence of diabetes in a Swedish population of 280,411 inhabitants. A report from the Skaraborg Diabetes Registry. Diabetes Care. 1998;21(4):546–8.
33. Jonsson B. Revealing the cost of Type II diabetes in Europe. Diabetologia. 2002;45(7): S5–12.
34. Franks PW, Looker HC, Kobes S, Touger L, Tataranni PA, Hanson RL, et al. Gestational glucose tolerance and risk of type 2 diabetes in young Pima Indian offspring. Diabetes. 2006;55(2):460–5.
35. Wiegand S, Maikowski U, Blankenstein O, Biebermann H, Tarnow P, Gruters A. Type 2 diabetes and impaired glucose tolerance in European children and adolescents with obesity – a problem that is no longer restricted to minority groups. Eur J Endocrinol. 2004;151(2): 199–206.
36. Singh R, Shaw J, Zimmet P. Epidemiology of childhood type 2 diabetes in the developing world. Pediatr Diabetes. 2004;5(3):154–68.
37. Ortega-Rodriguez E, Levy-Marchal C, Tubiana N, Czernichow P, Polak M. Emergence of type 2 diabetes in an hospital based cohort of children with diabetes mellitus. Diabetes Metab. 2001;27(5 Pt 1):574–8.
38. Rami B, Schober E, Nachbauer E, Waldhor T. Type 2 diabetes mellitus is rare but not absent in children under 15 years of age in Austria. Eur J Pediatr. 2003;162(12):850–2.
39. Haines L, Wan KC, Lynn R, Barrett TG, Shield JP. Rising incidence of type 2 diabetes in children in the U.K. Diabetes Care. 2007;30(5):1097–101.
40. DECODE Study Group. Age- and sex-specific prevalences of diabetes and impaired glucose regulation in 13 European cohorts. Diabetes Care. 2003;26(1):61–9.
41. Hussain A, Claussen B, Ramachandran A, Williams R. Prevention of type 2 diabetes: a review. Diabetes Res Clin Pract. 2007;76(3):317–26.
42. Colagiuri S, Borch-Johnsen K, Glumer C, Vistisen D. There really is an epidemic of type 2 diabetes. Diabetologia. 2005;48(8):1459–63.
43. Saltin B, Lindgarde F, Houston M, Horlin R, Nygaard E, Gad P. Physical training and glucose tolerance in middle-aged men with chemical diabetes. Diabetes. 1979;28 Suppl 1:30–2.
44. Holloszy JO, Schultz J, Kusnierkiewicz J, Hagberg JM, Ehsani AA. Effects of exercise on glucose tolerance and insulin resistance. Brief review and some preliminary results. Acta Med Scand Suppl. 1986;711:55–65.
45. Zierath JR, Wallberg-Henriksson H. Exercise training in obese diabetic patients. Special considerations. Sports Med. 1992;14(3):171–89.
46. Carnethon MR, Craft LL. Autonomic regulation of the association between exercise and diabetes. Exerc Sport Sci Rev. 2008;36(1):12–8.
47. Boule NG, Haddad E, Kenny GP, Wells GA, Sigal RJ. Effects of exercise on glycemic control and body mass in type 2 diabetes mellitus: a meta-analysis of controlled clinical trials. JAMA. 2001;286(10):1218–27.

48. Eriksson KF, Lindgarde F. Prevention of type 2 (non-insulin-dependent) diabetes mellitus by diet and physical exercise. The 6-year Malmo feasibility study. Diabetologia. 1991;34(12): 891–8.
49. Pan XR, Li GW, Hu YH, Wang JX, Yang WY, An ZX, et al. Effects of diet and exercise in preventing NIDDM in people with impaired glucose tolerance. The Da Qing IGT and Diabetes Study. Diabetes Care. 1997;20(4):537–44.
50. Ramachandran A, Snehalatha C, Mary S, Mukesh B, Bhaskar AD, Vijay V. The Indian Diabetes Prevention Programme shows that lifestyle modification and metformin prevent type 2 diabetes in Asian Indian subjects with impaired glucose tolerance (IDPP-1). Diabetologia. 2006;49(2):289–97.
51. Bouchard C, Leon AS, Rao DC, Skinner JS, Wilmore JH, Gagnon J. The HERITAGE family study. Aims, design, and measurement protocol. Med Sci Sports Exerc. 1995;27(5):721–9.
52. Helmrich SP, Ragland DR, Leung RW, Paffenbarger Jr RS. Physical activity and reduced occurrence of non-insulin-dependent diabetes mellitus. N Engl J Med. 1991;325(3):147–52.
53. Manson JE, Rimm EB, Stampfer MJ, Colditz GA, Willet WC, Krolewski AS, et al. Physical activity and incidence of non-insulin-dependent diabetes mellitus in women. Lancet. 1991;338(8770):774–8.
54. Hu FB, Sigal RJ, Rich-Edwards JW, Golditz GA, Solomon CG, Willet WC, et al. Walking compared with vigorous physical activity and risk of type 2 diabetes in women: a prospective study. JAMA. 1999;282(15):1433–9.
55. Hu FB, Leitzmann MF, Stampfer MJ, Colditz GA, Willett WC, Rimm EB. Physical activity and television watching in relation to risk for type 2 diabetes mellitus in men. Arch Intern Med. 2001;161(12):1542–8.
56. Visscher PM, Hill WG, Wray NR. Heritability in the genomics era – concepts and misconceptions. Nat Rev Genet. 2008;9(4):255–66.
57. Kaprio J, Tuomilehto J, Koskenvuo M, Romanov K, Reunanen A, Eriksson J, et al. Concordance for type 1 (insulin-dependent) and type 2 (non-insulin-dependent) diabetes mellitus in a population-based cohort of twins in Finland. Diabetologia. 1992;35(11):1060–7.
58. Poulsen P, Kyvik KO, Vaag A, Beck-Nielsen H. Heritability of type II (non-insulin-dependent) diabetes mellitus and abnormal glucose tolerance – a population-based twin study. Diabetologia. 1999;42(2):139–45.
59. Barroso I. Genetics of Type 2 diabetes. Diabet Med. 2005;22(5):517–35.
60. Meigs JB, Cupples LA, Wilson PW. Parental transmission of type 2 diabetes: the Framingham Offspring Study. Diabetes. 2000;49(12):2201–7.
61. Gottlieb MS, Root HF. Diabetes mellitus in twins. Diabetes. 1968;17(11):693–704.
62. Barnett AH, Eff C, Leslie RD, Pyke DA. Diabetes in identical twins. A study of 200 pairs. Diabetologia. 1981;20(2):87–93.
63. Newman B, Selby JV, King MC, Slemenda C, Fabsitz R, Friedman GD. Concordance for type 2 (non-insulin-dependent) diabetes mellitus in male twins. Diabetologia. 1987;30(10):763–8.
64. Medici F, Hawa M, Ianari A, Pyke DA, Leslie RD. Concordance rate for type II diabetes mellitus in monozygotic twins: actuarial analysis. Diabetologia. 1999;42(2):146–50.
65. Elbein SC, Hasstedt SJ, Wegner K, Kahn SE. Heritability of pancreatic beta-cell function among nondiabetic members of Caucasian familial type 2 diabetic kindreds. J Clin Endocrinol Metab. 1999;84(4):1398–403.
66. Elbein SC, Wegner K, Kahn SE. Reduced beta-cell compensation to the insulin resistance associated with obesity in members of Caucasian familial type 2 diabetic kindreds. Diabetes Care. 2000;23(2):221–7.
67. Gerich JE. The genetic basis of type 2 diabetes mellitus: impaired insulin secretion versus impaired insulin sensitivity. Endocr Rev. 1998;19(4):491–503.
68. Venter JC, Adams MD, Myers EW, Li PW, Mural RJ, Sutton GG, et al. The sequence of the human genome. Science. 2001;291(5507):1304–51.
69. Lander ES, Linton LM, Birren B, Nusbaum C, Zody MC, Baldwin J, et al. Initial sequencing and analysis of the human genome. Nature. 2001;409(6822):860–921.

70. International Human Genome Sequencing Consortium. Finishing the euchromatic sequence of the human genome. Nature. 2004;431(7011):931–45.
71. Kruglyak L, Nickerson DA. Variation is the spice of life. Nat Genet. 2001;27(3):234–6.
72. Hardy J, Singleton A. Genomewide association studies and human disease. N Engl J Med. 2009;360(17):1759–68.
73. Grarup N, Rose CS, Andersson EA, Andessen G, Nielsen AL, Albrechtsen A,et al. Studies of association of variants near the HHEX, CDKN2A/B, and IGF2BP2 genes with type 2 diabetes and impaired insulin release in 10, 705 Danish subjects: validation and extension of genome-wide association studies. Diabetes. 2007;56(12):3105–11.
74. Zeggini E, Weedon MN, Lindgren CM, Frayling TM, Elliot KS, Lango H, et al. Replication of genome-wide association signals in UK samples reveals risk loci for type 2 diabetes. Science. 2007;316(5829):1336–41.
75. Steinthorsdottir V, Thorleifsson G, Reynisdottir I, Benediktsson R, Jonsdottir T, Walters GB, et al. A variant in CDKAL1 influences insulin response and risk of type 2 diabetes. Nat Genet. 2007;39(6):770–5.
76. Sladek R, Rocheleau G, Rung J, Rocheleau G, Rung J, Dina C, et al. A genome-wide association study identifies novel risk loci for type 2 diabetes. Nature. 2007;445(7130):881–5.
77. Saxena R, Voight BF, Lyssenko V, Burtt NP, de Bakker PIW, Chen H, et al. Genome-wide association analysis identifies loci for type 2 diabetes and triglyceride levels. Science. 2007;316(5829):1331–6.
78. Scott LJ, Mohlke KL, Bonnycastle LL, Willer CJ, Li Y, Duren WL, et al. A genome-wide association study of type 2 diabetes in Finns detects multiple susceptibility variants. Science. 2007;316(5829):1341–5.
79. Voight BF, Scott LJ, Steinthorsdottir V, Morris AP, Dina C, Welch RP, et al. Twelve type 2 diabetes susceptibility loci identified through large-scale association analysis. Nat Genet. 2010;42(7):579–89.
80. Prokopenko I, McCarthy MI, Lindgren CM. Type 2 diabetes: new genes, new understanding. Trends Genet. 2008;24(12):613–21.
81. Florez JC. Newly identified loci highlight beta cell dysfunction as a key cause of type 2 diabetes: where are the insulin resistance genes? Diabetologia. 2008;51(7):1100–10.
82. Ottman R. Gene-environment interaction: definitions and study designs. Prev Med. 1996;25(6):764–70.
83. Rothman KJ, Greenland S, Walker AM. Concepts of interaction. Am J Epidemiol. 1980;112(4):467–70.
84. Yang Q, Khoury MJ. Evolving methods in genetic epidemiology. III. Gene-environment interaction in epidemiologic research. Epidemiol Rev. 1997;19(1):33–43.
85. Semenza JC, Ziogas A, Largent J, Peel D, Anton-Culver H. Gene-environment interactions in renal cell carcinoma. Am J Epidemiol. 2001;153(9):851–9.
86. Mucci LA, Wedren S, Tamimi RM, Trichopoulos D, Adami HO. The role of gene-environment interaction in the aetiology of human cancer: examples from cancers of the large bowel, lung and breast. J Intern Med. 2001;249(6):477–93.
87. Lake SL, Laird NM. Tests of gene-environment interaction for case-parent triads with general environmental exposures. Ann Hum Genet. 2004;68(Pt 1):55–64.
88. Umbach DM, Weinberg CR. The use of case-parent triads to study joint effects of genotype and exposure. Am J Hum Genet. 2000;66(1):251–61.
89. Khoury MJ, Flanders WD. Nontraditional epidemiologic approaches in the analysis of gene-environment interaction: case-control studies with no controls! Am J Epidemiol. 1996;144(3):207–13.
90. Kraft P, Yen YC, Stram DO, Morrison J, Gauderman WJ. Exploiting gene-environment interaction to detect genetic associations. Hum Hered. 2007;63(2):111–9.
91. Franks PW. Identifying genes for primary hypertension: methodological limitations and gene-environment interactions. J Hum Hypertens. 2009;23(4):227–37.
92. Clayton D, McKeigue PM. Epidemiological methods for studying genes and environmental factors in complex diseases. Lancet. 2001;358(9290):1356–60.

93. Meirhaeghe A, Helbecque N, Cottel D, Amouyel P. Beta2-adrenoceptor gene polymorphism, body weight, and physical activity. Lancet. 1999;353(9156):896.
94. Meirhaeghe A, Luan J, Franks PW, Hennings S, Mitchell J, Halsall D, et al. The effect of the Gly16Arg polymorphism of the beta(2)-adrenergic receptor gene on plasma free fatty acid levels is modulated by physical activity. J Clin Endocrinol Metab. 2001;86(12):5881–7.
95. Corbalan MS, Marti A, Forga L, Martinez-Gonzalez MA, Martinez JA. The 27Glu polymorphism of the beta2-adrenergic receptor gene interacts with physical activity influencing obesity risk among female subjects. Clin Genet. 2002;61(4):305–7.
96. Nemoto M, Sasaki T, Deeb SS, Fujimoto WY, Tajima N. Differential effect of PPARgamma2 variants in the development of type 2 diabetes between native Japanese and Japanese Americans. Diabetes Res Clin Pract. 2002;57(2):131–7.
97. Luan J, Browne PO, Harding AH, Halsall DJ, O'Rahilly S, Chatterjee VKK, et al. Evidence for gene-nutrient interaction at the PPARgamma locus. Diabetes. 2001;50(3):686–9.
98. Memisoglu A, Hu FB, Hankinson SE, Manson JE, De Vivo I, Willet WC, et al. Interaction between a peroxisome proliferator-activated receptor gamma gene polymorphism and dietary fat intake in relation to body mass. Hum Mol Genet. 2003;12(22):2923–9.
99. Robitaille J, Despres JP, Perusse L, Vohl MC. The PPAR-gamma P12A polymorphism modulates the relationship between dietary fat intake and components of the metabolic syndrome: results from the Quebec Family Study. Clin Genet. 2003;63(2):109–16.
100. Pisabarro RE, Sanguinetti C, Stoll M, Prendez D. High incidence of type 2 diabetes in peroxisome proliferator-activated receptor gamma2 Pro12Ala carriers exposed to a high chronic intake of trans fatty acids and saturated fatty acids. Diabetes Care. 2004;27(9): 2251–2.
101. Franks PW, Luan J, Browne PO, Harding AH, O'Rahilly S, Chatterjee VKK, et al. Does peroxisome proliferator-activated receptor gamma genotype (Pro12ala) modify the association of physical activity and dietary fat with fasting insulin level? Metabolism. 2004;53(1):11–6.
102. Nelson TL, Fingerlin TE, Moss LK, Barmada MM, Ferrell RE, Norris JM. Association of the peroxisome proliferator-activated receptor gamma gene with type 2 diabetes mellitus varies by physical activity among non-Hispanic whites from Colorado. Metabolism. 2007;56(3):388–93.
103. Otabe S, Clement K, Rich N, Warden C, Pecqueur C, Neverova M, et al. Mutation screening of the human UCP 2 gene in normoglycemic and NIDDM morbidly obese patients: lack of association between new UCP 2 polymorphisms and obesity in French Caucasians. Diabetes. 1998;47(5):840–2.
104. Berentzen T, Dalgaard LT, Petersen L, Pedersen O, Sorensen TI. Interactions between physical activity and variants of the genes encoding uncoupling proteins -2 and -3 in relation to body weight changes during a 10-y follow-up. Int J Obes (Lond). 2005;29(1):93–9.
105. Grarup N, Andreasen CH, Andersen MK, Albrechtsen A, Sandbaek A, Lauritzen T, et al. The -250G>A promoter variant in hepatic lipase associates with elevated fasting serum high-density lipoprotein cholesterol modulated by interaction with physical activity in a study of 16, 156 Danish subjects. J Clin Endocrinol Metab. 2008;93(6):2294–9.
106. Hokanson JE, Kamboh MI, Scarboro S, Eckel RH, Hamman RF. Effects of the hepatic lipase gene and physical activity on coronary heart disease risk. Am J Epidemiol. 2003;158(9): 836–43.
107. Corella D, Guillen M, Saiz C, Portolés O, Sabater A, Cortina S, et al. Environmental factors modulate the effect of the APOE genetic polymorphism on plasma lipid concentrations: ecogenetic studies in a Mediterranean Spanish population. Metabolism. 2001;50(8): 936–44.
108. Bernstein MS, Costanza MC, James RW, Morris MA, Cambien F, Raoux S, et al. Physical activity may modulate effects of ApoE genotype on lipid profile. Arterioscler Thromb Vasc Biol. 2002;22(1):133–40.
109. Boer JM, Kuivenhoven JA, Feskens EJ, Schouten EG, Havekes LM, Seidell JC, et al. Physical activity modulates the effect of a lipoprotein lipase mutation (D9N) on plasma lipids and lipoproteins. Clin Genet. 1999;56(2):158–63.

110. Senti M, Elosua R, Tomas M, Sala J, Masiá R, Ordovás JM, et al. Physical activity modulates the combined effect of a common variant of the lipoprotein lipase gene and smoking on serum triglyceride levels and high-density lipoprotein cholesterol in men. Hum Genet. 2001;109(4):385–92.

111. Grove ML, Morrison A, Folsom AR, Boerwinkle E, Hoelscher DM, Bray MS. Gene-environment interaction and the GNB3 gene in the atherosclerosis risk in communities study. Int J Obes (Lond). 2007;31(6):919–26.

112. Franks PW, Luan J, Barroso I, Brage S, Gonzalez Sanchez JL, Ekelund U, et al. Variation in the eNOS gene modifies the association between total energy expenditure and glucose intolerance. Diabetes. 2005;54(9):2795–801.

113. Kimura T, Yokoyama T, Matsumura Y, Yoshiike N, Date C, Muramatsu M, et al. NOS3 genotype-dependent correlation between blood pressure and physical activity. Hypertension. 2003;41(2):355–60.

114. Vimaleswaran KS, Franks PW, Barroso I, Brage S, Ekelund U, Wareham NJ, et al. Habitual energy expenditure modifies the association between NOS3 gene polymorphisms and blood pressure. Am J Hypertens. 2008;21(3):297–302.

115. Franks PW, Bhattacharyya S, Luan J, Montague C, Brennand J, Challis B, et al. Association between physical activity and blood pressure is modified by variants in the G-protein coupled receptor 10. Hypertension. 2004;43(2):224–8.

116. Andreasen CH, Stender-Petersen KL, Mogensen MS, Torekov SS, Wegner L, Andersen G, et al. Low physical activity accentuates the effect of the FTO rs9939609 polymorphism on body fat accumulation. Diabetes. 2008;57(1):95–101.

117. Rampersaud E, Mitchell BD, Pollin TI, Fu M, Shen H, O'Connell JR, et al. Physical activity and the association of common FTO gene variants with body mass index and obesity. Arch Intern Med. 2008;168(16):1791–7.

118. Vimaleswaran KS, Li S, Zhao JH, Luan J, Bingham SA, Khaw T, et al. Physical activity attenuates the body mass index-increasing influence of genetic variation in the FTO gene. Am J Clin Nutr. 2009;90(2):425–8.

119. Sonestedt E, Roos C, Gullberg B, Ericson U, Wirfalt E, Orho-Melander M. Fat and carbohydrate intake modify the association between genetic variation in the FTO genotype and obesity. Am J Clin Nutr. 2009;90(5):1418–25.

120. Cauchi S, Stutzmann F, Cavalcanti-Proenca C, Durand E, Pouta A, Hartikainen, et al. Combined effects of MC4R and FTO common genetic variants on obesity in European general populations. J Mol Med. 2009;87(5):537–46.

121. Herbert A, Gerry NP, McQueen MB, Heid IM, Pfeufer A, Illig T, et al. A common genetic variant is associated with adult and childhood obesity. Science. 2006;312(5771):279–83.

122. Heid IM, Huth C, Loos RJ, Kronenberg F, Adamkova V, Anand SS, et al. Meta-analysis of the INSIG2 association with obesity including 74, 345 individuals: does heterogeneity of estimates relate to study design? PLoS Genet. 2009;5(10):e1000694.

123. Andreasen CH, Mogensen MS, Borch-Johnsen K, Sandbaek A, Lauritzen T, Sorensen TI, et al. Non-replication of genome-wide based associations between common variants in INSIG2 and PFKP and obesity in studies of 18, 014 Danes. PLoS One. 2008;3(8): e2872.

124. Brito EC, Lyssenko V, Renstrom F, Berglund G, Nilsson PM, Groop L, et al. Previously associated type 2 diabetes variants may interact with physical activity to modify the risk of impaired glucose regulation and type 2 diabetes: a study of 16, 003 Swedish adults. Diabetes. 2009;58(6):1411–8.

125. Stephanie-May R, John WS, Tuomo R, Claude B, Marie-Claude V, Louis P. Interaction between HNF4A polymorphisms and physical activity in relation to type 2 diabetes-related traits: results from the Quebec Family Study. Diabetes Res Clin Pract. 2009;84(3): 211–8.

126. Kahara T, Takamura T, Hayakawa T, Nagai Y, Yamaguchi H, Katsuki T, et al. PPARgamma gene polymorphism is associated with exercise-mediated changes of insulin resistance in healthy men. Metabolism. 2003;52(2):209–12.

127. Adamo KB, Sigal RJ, Williams K, Kenny G, Prud'homme D, Tesson F. Influence of Pro12Ala peroxisome proliferator-activated receptor gamma2 polymorphism on glucose response to exercise training in type 2 diabetes. Diabetologia. 2005;48(8):1503–9.
128. Weiss EP, Kulaputana O, Ghiu IA, Brandauer J, Wohn CR, Phares DA, et al. Endurance training-induced changes in the insulin response to oral glucose are associated with the peroxisome proliferator-activated receptor-gamma2 Pro12Ala genotype in men but not in women. Metabolism. 2005;54(1):97–102.
129. Lindi VI, Uusitupa MI, Lindstrom J, Louheranta A, Eriksson JG, Valle YY, et al. Association of the Pro12Ala polymorphism in the PPAR-gamma2 gene with 3-year incidence of type 2 diabetes and body weight change in the Finnish Diabetes Prevention Study. Diabetes. 2002;51(8):2581–6.
130. Florez JC, Jablonski KA, Sun MW, Bayley N, Kahn SE, Shamoon H, et al. Effects of the type 2 diabetes-associated PPARG P12A polymorphism on progression to diabetes and response to troglitazone. J Clin Endocrinol Metab. 2007;92(4):1502–9.
131. Franks PW, Jablonski KA, Delahanty L, Hanson RL, Kahn SE, Altshuler D, et al. The Pro12Ala variant at the peroxisome proliferator-activated receptor gamma gene and change in obesity-related traits in the Diabetes Prevention Program. Diabetologia. 2007;50(12):2451–60.
132. Kilpelainen TO, Lakka TA, Laaksonen DE, Lindstrom J, Eriksson JG, Valle TT, et al. SNPs in PPARG associate with type 2 diabetes and interact with physical activity. Med Sci Sports Exerc. 2008;40(1):25–33.
133. Macho-Azcarate T, Marti A, Gonzalez A, Martinez JA, Ibanez J. Gln27Glu polymorphism in the beta2 adrenergic receptor gene and lipid metabolism during exercise in obese women. Int J Obes Relat Metab Disord. 2002;26(11):1434–41.
134. Kilpelainen TO, Lakka TA, Laaksonen DE, Mager U, Salopuro T, Kubaszek A, et al. Interaction of single nucleotide polymorphisms in ADRB2, ADRB3, TNF, IL6, IGF1R, LIPC, LEPR, and GHRL with physical activity on the risk of type 2 diabetes mellitus and changes in characteristics of the metabolic syndrome: The Finnish Diabetes Prevention Study. Metabolism. 2008;57(3):428–36.
135. Kahara T, Takamura T, Hayakawa T, Nagai Y, Yamaguchi H, Katsuki T, et al. Prediction of exercise-mediated changes in metabolic markers by gene polymorphism. Diabetes Res Clin Pract. 2002;57(2):105–10.
136. Shiwaku K, Nogi A, Anuurad E, Kitajima K, Enkhmaa B, Shimono K, et al. Difficulty in losing weight by behavioral intervention for women with Trp64Arg polymorphism of the beta3-adrenergic receptor gene. Int J Obes Relat Metab Disord. 2003;27(9):1028–36.
137. Salopuro T, Lindstrom J, Eriksson JG, Hamalainen H, Ilanne-Parikka P, Keinanen-Kiukaanniemi S, et al. Common variants in beta2- and beta3-adrenergic receptor genes and uncoupling protein 1 as predictors of the risk for type 2 diabetes and body weight changes. The Finnish Diabetes Prevention Study. Clin Genet. 2004;66(4):365–7.
138. Laaksonen DE, Siitonen N, Lindstrom J, Eriksson JG, Reunanen P, Tuomilehto J, et al. Physical activity, diet, and incident diabetes in relation to an ADRA2B polymorphism. Med Sci Sports Exerc. 2007;39(2):227–32.
139. Todorova B, Kubaszek A, Pihlajamaki J, Lindström J, Eriksson J, Valle TT, et al. The G-250A promoter polymorphism of the hepatic lipase gene predicts the conversion from impaired glucose tolerance to type 2 diabetes mellitus: the Finnish Diabetes Prevention Study. J Clin Endocrinol Metab. 2004;89(5):2019–23.
140. Hagberg JM, Ferrell RE, Katzel LI, Dengel DR, Sorkin JD, Goldberg AP. Apolipoprotein E genotype and exercise training-induced increases in plasma high-density lipoprotein (HDL)- and HDL2-cholesterol levels in overweight men. Metabolism. 1999;48(8):943–5.
141. Garenc C, Perusse L, Bergeron J, Gagnon J, Chagnon YC, Borecki IB, et al. Evidence of LPL gene-exercise interaction for body fat and LPL activity: the HERITAGE Family Study. J Appl Physiol. 2001;91(3):1334–40.
142. Florez JC, Jablonski KA, Bayley N, Pollin TI, de Bakker PIW, Shuldiner AR, et al. TCF7L2 polymorphisms and progression to diabetes in the Diabetes Prevention Program. N Engl J Med. 2006;355(3):241–50.

143. Franks PW, Jablonski KA, Delahanty LM, McAteer JB, Kahn SE, Knowler WC, et al. Assessing gene-treatment interactions at the FTO and INSIG2 loci on obesity-related traits in the Diabetes Prevention Program. Diabetologia. 2008;51(12):2214–23.
144. Lappalainen TJ, Tolppanen AM, Kolehmainen M, Schwab U, Lindström J, Tuomilehto J, et al. The common variant in the FTO gene did not modify the effect of lifestyle changes on body weight: the Finnish Diabetes Prevention Study. Obesity (Silver Spring). 2009;17(4): 832–6.
145. Hakanen M, Raitakari OT, Lehtimaki T, Peltonen N, Pahkala K, Sillanmäki L, et al. FTO genotype is associated with body mass index after the age of seven years but not with energy intake or leisure-time physical activity. J Clin Endocrinol Metab. 2009;94(4):1281–7.
146. Kilpelainen TO, Lakka TA, Laaksonen DE, Laukkanen O, Lindström J, Eriksson JG, et al. Physical activity modifies the effect of SNPs in the SLC2A2 (GLUT2) and ABCC8 (SUR1) genes on the risk of developing type 2 diabetes. Physiol Genomics. 2007; 31(2):264–72.
147. Moore AF, Jablonski KA, McAteer JB, Saxena R, Pollin TI, Franks PW, et al. Extension of type 2 diabetes genome-wide association scan results in the diabetes prevention program. Diabetes. 2008;57(9):2503–10.
148. Moore AF, Jablonski KA, Mason CC, McAteer JB, Goldstein BJ, Kahn SE, et al. The association of ENPP1 K121Q with diabetes incidence is abolished by lifestyle modification in the diabetes prevention program. J Clin Endocrinol Metab. 2009;94(2):449–55.
149. Wong MY, Day NE, Luan JA, Chan KP, Wareham NJ. The detection of gene-environment interaction for continuous traits: should we deal with measurement error by bigger studies or better measurement? Int J Epidemiol. 2003;32(1):51–7.
150. Smith PG, Day NE. The design of case-control studies: the influence of confounding and interaction effects. Int J Epidemiol. 1984;13(3):356–65.
151. Luan JA, Wong MY, Day NE, Wareham NJ. Sample size determination for studies of gene-environment interaction. Int J Epidemiol. 2001;30(5):1035–40.
152. Wareham NJ, Jakes RW, Rennie KL, Mitchell J, Hennings S, Day NE. Validity and repeatability of the EPIC-Norfolk Physical Activity Questionnaire. Int J Epidemiol. 2002;31(1):168–74.
153. Friedenreich CM, Courneya KS, Neilson HK, Matthews CE, Willis G, Irwin M, et al. Reliability and validity of the Past Year Total Physical Activity Questionnaire. Am J Epidemiol. 2006;163(10):959–70.
154. Trost SG, Way R, Okely AD. Predictive validity of three ActiGraph energy expenditure equations for children. Med Sci Sports Exerc. 2006;38(2):380–7.
155. Ceesay SM, Prentice AM, Day KC, Murgatroyd PR, Goldberg GR, Scott W, et al. The use of heart rate monitoring in the estimation of energy expenditure: a validation study using indirect whole-body calorimetry. Br J Nutr. 1989;61(2):175–86.
156. Brage S, Ekelund U, Brage N, Hennings MA, Froberg K, Franks PW, et al. Hierarchy of individual calibration levels for heart rate and accelerometry to measure physical activity. J Appl Physiol. 2007;103(2):682–92.
157. Wareham NJ, Young EH, Loos RJ. Epidemiological study designs to investigate gene-behavior interactions in the context of human obesity. Obesity (Silver Spring). 2008;16 Suppl 3:S66–71.
158. Balding DJ. A tutorial on statistical methods for population association studies. Nat Rev Genet. 2006;7(10):781–91.
159. Benjamini Y, Drai D, Elmer G, Kafkafi N, Golani I. Controlling the false discovery rate in behavior genetics research. Behav Brain Res. 2001;125(1–2):279–84.

Chapter 5
The Interaction Between Genetic Variation and Exercise and Physical Activity in the Determination of Body Composition and Obesity Status

Mary H. Sailors and Molly S. Bray

Keywords Obesity • Overweight • Body composition • Fat topography • Body weight • Genetic variation • Gene • Variant • Polymorphism • Sequence • DNA • Disease • Environment • Energy balance • Energy expenditure • Exercise • Physical activity • Inactivity • Risk • Heritability • Body mass index • Satiety • Feeding • Adipogenesis • Adipose • Differentiation • Metabolism • Lipid • Diet • Response • Hypothalamus • Gene map • Blood pressure • Thermogenesis • Catecholamine • Uncoupling • Sibutramine • Weight loss

Introduction

Obesity is a major health problem throughout the industrialized world. Behind smoking, it is the second most preventable cause of death in the United States [1]. Health officials warn, with the widespread pattern of unhealthy diets and physical inactivity, obesity is expected to overtake smoking as the leading preventable killer in the United States. Between 1980 and 2004, the prevalence of obesity in adults has grown from 15 to 33% [2]. Obesity in adults is associated with an increased risk of mortality and morbidity. Specifically, obesity increases the risk for a variety of health conditions such as type 2 diabetes mellitus, cardiovascular disease, stroke, gallbladder disease, respiratory problems, musculoskeletal disorders, and cancer [3–5]. Additionally, the distribution of fat deposits can affect many disease states. Abdominal obesity is associated with elevated triglycerides, insulin resistance, and hyperinsulinemia. Accumulation of fat in the abdominal area has also been linked to an increased incidence of type 2 diabetes, hypertension, and glucose tolerance [6–8]. This epidemic is not only an issue of health risk but it has recently come to light as an economic issue as well. Individuals who are overweight or obese incur healthcare expenses in the form of direct (diagnostic, treatment, or preventive

M.S. Bray (✉)
Department of Epidemiology, University of Alabama at Birmingham, 1530 3rd Avenue S, 35294, Birmingham, AL, USA
e-mail: mbray@uab.edu

L.S. Pescatello and S.M. Roth (eds.), *Exercise Genomics*, Molecular and Translational Medicine, DOI 10.1007/978-1-60761-355-8_5, © Springer Science+Business Media, LLC 2011 services) and indirect (decreased productivity, lost wages) costs. Obesity has become a tremendous economic liability in the healthcare system, with costs estimated to exceed $147 billion [9].

The purpose of this chapter is to provide an overview of the genetic components of body composition and obesity, and to discuss the role of physical activity (PA) and exercise in mediating and/or moderating this relationship. This chapter will discuss concepts of energy balance, the components of exercise, and the genetic and physiological basis of body size/mass regulation. In addition, a summary of published studies in which interactions between genetic variation and PA and/or exercise have been demonstrated to influence body size measures is presented.

Obesity and Energy Balance

Obesity is caused by a wide variety of factors including environmental, biological, social, nutritional, psychological, and genetic influences. Whatever may be the exact mechanism, obesity is primarily the result of an imbalance between energy intake and energy expenditure. The first law of thermodynamics states energy is neither created nor destroyed but is converted from one form to another. This law also applies to living organisms. The energy balance equation states body mass remains constant when caloric intake equals caloric expenditure. Any chronic imbalance (too much energy or a deficit of energy) can result in a change of body mass. If the caloric value of food intake exceeds the energy loss due to heat and work, it is converted to stored energy in endogenous stores such as glycogen, body protein, and fat. If the caloric intake of food is less than the energy output from work and heat, these endogenous stores will be utilized, resulting in a loss of body mass. A primary cause of this energy imbalance in an obese state is the combination of low levels of PA and/or excessive caloric consumption.

Relationship Between Body Composition and Exercise and Physical Activity

Although the energy balance equation appears very simplistic in nature, in reality it is extraordinarily complex when considering all of the underlying mechanisms involving biological, social, nutritional, psychological, and genetic influences that potentially affect both sides of the energy balance equation and the complex interrelation among these factors. The two variables under an individual's control on a daily basis are energy expended during PA and dietary energy intake. PA is defined as "any bodily movement produced by skeletal muscles that result in energy expenditure" [10]. The energy expended in PA can be quantified in kilojoules (kJ) or kilocalories (kcal). Exercise is a subcategory of PA and differentiates itself from the broad category of PA by specifying that the activity be "planned, structured, repetitive, and purposive in the sense that improvement or maintenance of one or more of the components of physical fitness is an objective" [10].

Exercise is comprised of four main components: frequency, intensity, type, and time (FITT). Frequency of exercise indicates the number of exercise sessions performed in a specified time period, while intensity refers to how vigorously the exercise is performed or the level of physical exertion [11]. Type of exercise refers to the kind of exercise activity being performed, and time refers to the duration of the exercise bout. For most adults, the American College of Sports Medicine (ACSM) recommends both moderate intensity exercise (exercise that noticeably increases heart rate and breathing or 40–60% of maximal oxygen consumption [VO_2 max]) and vigorous exercise (exercise that substantially increases heart rate and breathing or >60% VO_2 max) [11]. Overweight and obese individuals should perform aerobic exercise involving the large muscle groups for a minimum of 5 days/week; initial exercise training should begin with moderate exercise, progressing to more vigorous intensity (50–70% VO_2 max), and each exercise session should last 30–60 min [11].

In today's society, fewer jobs require strenuous activity, and fewer people compensate for this decrease in job-related activity level with regular voluntary PA. A critical risk factor for obesity is a sedentary lifestyle. Considerable weight gain can occur in individuals who have reduced their level of energy expended without compensating for energy intake. Many studies have shown those who are more physically active are less likely to gain weight. Di Pietro et al. [12] reported calculated PA levels (amount of PA expressed in multiples of daily resting metabolic rate) in over 2,500 males over 5 years were inversely associated with weight gain. Donnelly et al. [13] conducted a randomized control trial to examine the effects of exercise on weight gain over a 16 month period. The investigators determined an exercise protocol of 45 min/day, 5 times a week resulted in weight maintenance or weight loss. Male subjects who expended over 3,300 kcal/week experienced approximately 5 kg of weight lost, while females expended over 2,100 kcal/week maintained weight over the 16 month study period. Sedentary male controls maintained weight, while sedentary female controls experienced approximately 3 kg of weight gain over the 16 month study period [13].

Schmitz et al. [14] extracted data from the Coronary Artery Risk Development in Young Adults (CARDIA) study to examine the relationship between weight gain and PA in over 5,000 black and white men and women aged 18–30 years over a 10 year period. These investigators showed change in PA was inversely associated with body weight over a 10 year period. They also indicated increasing PA during the first 2–3 years of the study attenuated weight gain assessed at year 5, whether or not PA was maintained [14]. Similarly, Haapanen et al. [15] found those who decreased PA or were inactive over a 10 year observation period were more likely to gain weight compared to those who were active at the end of the 10 year period. In addition, Williamson et al. [16] found those who reported low levels of PA at follow-up in the National Health and Nutrition Examination Survey (NHANES-I) were three to four times as likely to have a weight gain over 13 kg as compared to those who reported high PA.

According to the ACSM [17], moderate intensity PA between 150 and 250 min/week is associated with only modest weight loss but greater amounts of PA (>250 min/week) have been reported to produce clinically significant weight loss.

In addition, ACSM recommends moderate intensity PA between 150 and 250 min/ week should be performed to prevent weight gain following a weight loss intervention [17]. The combination of moderate dietary restriction and moderate intensity PA has been shown to achieve greater weight loss than either strategy alone. These studies suggest a sedentary lifestyle leads to weight gain while as little as 45 min of PA on most days of the week can promote weigh loss or weight maintenance throughout life. All of the studies summarized above demonstrate the importance of exercise in preventing and attenuating obesity.

Genetics of Body Composition

Heritability of Body Composition

Obesity and body mass related phenotypes have long been recognized to cluster in families. Quantifying the specific contribution of genes to obesity and other body mass/composition phenotypes requires partitioning of the variability in body size measures accounted for by genes from the variance in body size attributed to both shared environmental factors within the family and external environmental factors. Substantial effort has been made to quantify the genetic contribution of body mass/ composition in the form of family studies, twin studies, and adoption studies. After adjusting for the contribution of shared familial environment, family based studies (e.g., parent-offspring, sibling–sibling, adopted family members, and twins) estimate the heritability (i.e., the amount of variance in a trait that can be accounted for by variation in genes) of several measures of body mass, percent body fat, and fat patterning to range from 0.37 to 0.78 [18–24].

Genetic studies of extreme body types suggest an even stronger degree of familiality among those with clinically severe obesity (body mass index (BMI >40 kg/m^2)) compared to those with moderate levels of obesity. In a sample of 1,841 relatives of severely obese (BMI >40 kg/m^2) bariatric surgery patients and 1,059 relatives of normal weight controls, patients with obesity were 24.5 times more likely to have a clinically severe or super obese (BMI >50 kg/m^2) first degree relative compared to controls [25]. Adams et al. [26] conducted a study in 221 non-Hispanic white families ($N=1,560$ individuals) ascertained through one morbidly obese family member who was at least 45.5 kg over his/her ideal weight. The risk of clinically severe obesity was eight times higher in these families compared to the general population, and families in which one or both parents were morbidly obese had 2.6 times the risk of having one or more offspring with obesity [26]. Based on these and similar studies, both early onset and clinically severe obesity appear to have a substantially greater genetic component underlying the obese phenotype compared to more common forms of obesity.

Although the heritability of body composition and related traits indicates there is a genetic component to these measures, the heritability estimates do not specify which genes confer a genetic susceptibility to obesity. Obesity is a complex disease in which multiple genes are likely to be responsible for genetic susceptibility. Recent years have been an exciting time in the field of obesity research with the discovery of several genes in which mutations that eliminate or greatly diminish the function of their protein products give rise to syndromic forms of obesity in humans [27]. A discussion of the specific genes associated with human obesity is provided below. Nearly all of the genes identified for human obesity to date appear to produce obesity both through alterations in feeding behavior as well as impaired energy metabolism.

Physiologic and Genetic Basis for Obesity

The discovery of the leptin gene in late 1994 has been heralded as a breakthrough in obesity research, moving our understanding of energy balance and satiety signaling forward in a significant way [28]. We now know a complex, highly regulated, and redundant system exists that controls feeding behavior and energy homeostasis. Obesity can result from defects in any part of this feedback system. Leptin serves as a powerful regulator of feeding behavior, an "energy sensor," and a component of lipid and glucose metabolism and insulin signaling [29–32]. The leptin receptor gene was characterized shortly after the discovery of leptin and is expressed in a complex network of hypothalamic neurons regulating adiposity, substrate utilization, and reproduction [33].

The melanocortin system, a neuronal pathway in the hypothalamus that regulates energy homeostasis and interacts with the leptin signaling system to regulate fat storage and utilization, contains additional genes that influence appetite and basal metabolism, including agouti related protein (*AGRP*), pro-opiomelanocortin (*POMC*), melanocortin 4 receptor (*MC4R*), and melanocortin concentrating hormone (*MCH*) [34–36]. Other genes demonstrated to interact with this neural system include neuropeptide Y (*NPY*), cocaine-amphetamine related transcript (*CART*), orexin (*OX*), glucagon-like peptide 1 (*GLP1*), cholecystekinin (*CCK*), corticotrophin releasing factor (*CRF*), ghrelin (*GHRL*), and brain-derived neurotrophic factor (*BDNF*). The dopaminergic and serotonergic systems, neuronal pathways in the brain associated with reward and pleasure, also regulate appetite. The release of dopamine has been proposed as the neural mechanism that makes food intake a rewarding process [37, 38]. In addition, serotonin has been demonstrated to act upon POMC neurons in the arcuate nucleus to inhibit food intake.

Defects in *LEP*, *LEPR*, *POMC*, *MC4R*, and proconvertase 1 (*PC1*, which encodes the enzyme that cleaves POMC into its constituent peptides) have all been shown to produce early onset morbid obesity, hyperphagia, hyperinsulinemia, and hyperglycemia in humans [39–48]. All adults with leptin or leptin receptor deficiencies have also demonstrated impaired reproductive function and hypogonadism, suggesting leptin also plays a role in pubertal development. Of all genetic defects identified to date in early onset, morbid human obesity, the most compelling are found within the *MC4R* gene. Numerous studies have identified DNA sequence variation/mutation within *MC4R*. Many of these DNA sequence variants have been shown to alter function of the receptor protein by changing binding affinity or receptor activation. Most of these *MC4R* mutations are associated with extreme obesity and overeating resulting from haploinsufficiency of the receptor protein [39–43]. In addition, it is estimated that up to 4% of severe obesity may be accounted for by these common variants in the *MC4R* gene [49].

While single gene defects have revealed new insight into the physiology of energy balance, common forms of obesity likely result from more complex interactions between multiple genes and the environment. The latest published version of the Human Obesity Map has reported in 426 studies, 127 candidate genes that are potentially associated with an obesity phenotype [27]. This report has identified 22 genes shown in at least five published studies to have associations with obesity related phenotypes. According to Bouchard, these genes fall into five major categories: (1) thriftiness (beta adrenergic receptors 2 and 3 [*ADRB2, ADRB3*], uncoupling proteins 1, 2, and 3 [*UCP1, UCP2, UCP3*]); (2) hyperphagia (dopamine D2 receptor [*DRD2*], 5 hydroxytryptamine (serotonin) receptor 2C [*HTR2C*], leptin and its receptor [*LEP, LEPR*], *MC4R*, nuclear receptor subfamily 3, group C, member 1 [*NR3C1*]); (3) low lipid oxidation (angiotensin converting enzyme [*ACE*], adiponectin [*ADIPOQ*], guanine nucleotide binding protein, beta 3 subunit [*GNB3*], hormone sensitive lipase [*LIPE*], low density lipoprotein receptor [*LDLR*]); (4) adipogenesis (peroxisome proliferator activated receptor gamma [*PPARG*], vitamin D receptor [*VDR*], resistin [*RETN*], interleukin 6 [*IL6*], tumor necrosis factor alpha [*TNF*]); and (5) low PA (*DRD2, MC4R*) [50]. While the genes listed above have been most consistently associated with obesity related measures, this list is not meant to imply that there are not other genes that may play a role in the determination of body mass/composition. Since PA and exercise are such critical components of energy balance, it is not surprising that many of the genes identified to date for obesity and body composition have also been shown to interact with or be modified by exercise and/or PA.

Physiological Mechanisms Linking Exercise and Physical Activity to Obesity

As illustrated above, exercise and PA are key factors in the ability to lose and/or maintain body weight. Understanding the mechanistic link between exercise and both body weight and adiposity has ultimately informed the identification of genes that affect body weight and adiposity. The primary ways in which exercise leads to reduced risk for obesity are through its effect on energy expenditure, utilization of specific fuel types, and adiposity. Chronic exercise training stimulates expression of key regulators of fatty acid metabolism and is associated with increased plasma high density lipoprotein cholesterol (HDL-C) and reduced fasting and postprandial triglyceride, with concurrent changes in lipoprotein lipase (LPL) activity [51, 52]. Exercise is also associated with increases in mitochondrial number primarily via the induction of the peroxisome proliferator activated receptor gamma, coactivator

1 alpha (*PPARGC1*) gene in human skeletal muscle, which translates to an improvement in the functional aerobic capacity and metabolism of skeletal muscle [53].

Exercise has been shown to play a role in overall adiposity by inhibiting transcription of adipocyte differentiation pathways, in addition to its role in energy expenditure. Exercise in rats fed a high fat diet was associated with significantly reduced visceral fat mass and adipocyte size compared to nonexercise controls, which was accompanied by significantly reduced cannabinoid receptor type 1 (CB1) expression within adipose tissue [54]. In addition, expression of the peroxisome proliferative activated receptor gamma (*PPARG*) gene, an important factor in adipocyte differentiation, is markedly reduced in skeletal muscle by chronic exercise, suggesting a reduced capacity for adipocyte formation proximal to exercising muscles [52]. Leptin, a key marker of adiposity, has been shown to decrease in response to acute, prolonged exercise (i.e., 3 h of stationary cycling), primarily at the level of protein [55]. mRNA levels of adiponectin, another important component of insulin sensitivity, were elevated within adipose tissue following chronic exercise in rodents, and adiponectin receptor 1 mRNA levels increased up to four times in skeletal muscle in response to chronic exercise [56, 57]. In humans, exercise is independently associated with an increase in skeletal muscle cytokines, including IL6, which has been shown to stimulate lipolysis and fat oxidation. During exercise, IL6 acts in a hormone like manner to mobilize extracellular substrates and enhance substrate delivery [58]. As the studies described in this section indicate, the relationships between exercise/PA, body composition, and the physiological mechanisms linking them are extremely complex. Underlying variation in genes associated with the intermediate physiologic alterations that occur in response to exercise training and PA may contribute to the variability in the response of body mass and adiposity to exercise/PA.

Gene and Exercise and Physical Activity Interactions in Obesity and Body Composition

In addition to identifying genetic variation associated with obesity and the exercise response, great strides have been made in establishing the relationship among genes, PA, and their interactions in determining how these factors influence body composition. Beginning in 2000, and updated annually, Bouchard and coworkers [59–65] began compiling the reports of genes and exercise interactions and related physiologic outcomes in a document entitled, *The Human Gene Map for Performance and Health-Related Fitness Phenotypes.* In the final update of that report, the authors described 23 autosomal genes that significantly interacted with PA or exercise to influence body composition [65]. Since this last update, one additional gene, the fat mass and obesity associated gene (*FTO*), has also been found to significantly differentiate between exercise responders and exercise nonresponders in relation to body composition [66–69]. A summary of these studies is presented in Table 5.1.

Table 5.1 Genes and variants identified to interact with exercise training to influence body size measures

Gene	Location	References	Variant	Subjects	Exercise/physical activity	Body composition phenotype	p-Value
Appetite regulation							
FTO	16q12.2	Rankinen et al. [67]	rs805136	481 Sedentary white males and females	20 Weeks endurance exercise	% Body fat	0.026
						Fat mass	0.026
		Mitchell et al. [68]	rs8050136	234 White females	6 Months moderate intensity exercise	Body mass	<0.05
		Vimaleswaran et al. [69]	rs1121980	20,374 Males and females	Self-report by questionnaire	BMI	0.004
						Waist circumference	0.02
		Andreasen et al. [66]	rs9939609	17,162 Middle aged Danes	Self-report by questionnaire	BMI	0.007
Adipogenesis							
PPARG	3p25	Lindi et al. [85]	Pro12Ala	490 Males and females	3 Year exercise	Body weight	0.04
		Ostergard et al. [87]	Pro12Ala	29 Healthy offspring of type 2 diabetes	10 Weeks endurance training	Body weight	0.05
Energy and lipid metabolism							
ADRB2	5q31-q32	Meirhaeghe et al. [89]	Gln27Glu	420 Males	Self-report by questionnaire	Body weight	0.0001
						BMI	0.0001
						Waist circumference	0.0001
						Hip circumference	0.0007
						WHR	0.02
		Macho-Azcarate et al. [90]	Gln27Glu	12 Obese females	Maximal exercise treadmill test	Respiratory exchange ratio	<0.05
		Garenc et al. [91]	Gln27Glu	482 White males and females	20 Week endurance exercise	Fat mass	0.02
		Phares et al. [92]	Gln27Glu	70 Males and females	24 Weeks aerobic exercise	% Body fat	0.0154
						Trunk fat	0.0154
		Corbalan et al. [93]	Gln27Glu	252 Females	Self-report by questionnaire	BMI	0.005
		Garenc et al. [91]	Arg16Gly	482 White males and females	20 Week endurance exercise	BMI	0.04
						Fat mass	0.0008
						% Body fat	0.0003
						Subcutaneous fat	0.03

Gene	Locus	Reference	Polymorphism	Sample	Intervention	Outcome	p
ADRA2B	2p13-q13	Yao et al. [94]	Glu^{12}/Glu^9	98 Males and females	10-Week single leg strength training	Intermuscular fat	0.04
GNB3	12p13	Rankinen et al. [97]	C825T	255 Black males and females	20 Weeks endurance exercise	Fat mass	0.012
						% Body fat	0.006
		Grove et al. [98]	C825T	3,728 AA male and females	Self-report by questionnaire	Obesity	<0.001
ADRB3	8p12-p11.2	Sakane et al. [100]	Trp64Arg	61 Obese diabetic females	3 Months exercise program	Body weight	<0.001
						BMI	<0.001
						WHR	<0.001
		Shiwaku et al. [101]	Trp64Arg	76 Females	3 Month exercise program	Body weight	0.001
						BMI	0.002
						Waist circumference	0.02
		Kahara et al. [102]	Trp64Arg	106 Males	3 Months low intensity exercise	Serum leptin	<0.05
		Marti et al. [103]	Trp64Arg	313 Spanish males and females	Self-report by questionnaire	BMI	0.05
		Phares et al. [92]	Trp64Arg	70 Males and females	24 Weeks aerobic exercise	% Body fat	0.0265
						Fat mass	0.0368
						Trunk fat	0.0311
COMT	22q11.21-q11.23	Tworoger et al. [105]	Val158Met	173 Postmenopausal females	1 Year moderate aerobic exercise	% Body fat	<0.05
CYP19A1	15q21.1	Tworoger et al. [105]	$(TTTA)_n$ $(n=7-13)$	173 Postmenopausal females	1 Year moderate aerobic exercise	BMI	0.04
						% Body fat	0.02
						Fat mass	0.03
ACE	17q23	Montgomery et al. [117]	I/D	81 Males	10-Week physical training	Body weight	0.001
						Fat mass	0.04
						Fat free mass	0.01
		Kritchevsky et al. [120]	I/D	3,075 Older adults	Self-report by questionnaire	Intermuscular thigh fat	0.02
						% Body fat	0.02
		Moran et al. [119]	I/D	481 Greek adolescent females	Self-report by questionnaire	Tricep skinfold	0.012
						Subscapular skinfold	0.001

(continued)

Table 5.1 (continued)

Gene	Location	References	Variant	Subjects	Exercise/physical activity	Body composition phenotype	p-Value
UCP3	11q13	Otabe et al. [124]	C-55T	368 Morbidly obese	Self-report by questionnaire	BMI	0.015
		Lanouette et al. [125]	GAIVS6	503 White males and females	20 Weeks endurance exercise	Subcutaneous fat	0.0006
LPL	8p22	Garenc et al. [129]	S447X	249 White females	20 Weeks endurance exercise	BMI	0.01
						Fat mass	0.01
						% body fat	0.03
IL15RA	10p15-p14	Reichman et al. [130]	PstI	153 Males and females	10 Weeks resistance exercise	Lean mass	<0.05
						Arm circumference	<0.05
						Leg circumference	<0.05
		Reichman et al. [130]	BstI:HpaII haplotype	153 Males and females	10 Weeks resistance exercise	Lean mass	<0.05
PNMT	17q21-q22	Peters et al. [131]	G-148A	149 Females	Self-report by questionnaire	Body weight	0.002
IGF1	12q22-q23	Sun et al. [132]	189 bp Repeat in 5' UTR	502 Caucasian males and females	20 Week endurance exercise	Fat free mass	0.005
ENPP1	6q22-q23	Park et al. [133]	K121Q	84 Korean females	12 Weeks aerobic exercise	Body weight	0.02
						BMI	0.03
PPARA	22q13.31	Uthurralt et al. [137]	L162V	146 Males	12 Weeks unilateral resistance training	Upper arm subcutaneous fat	0.002

Appetite Regulation Genes and Body Composition Change from Exercise and Physical Activity

Although great progress has been made in elucidating the mechanisms regulating satiety and eating behavior, few genes within these pathways have been demonstrated to interact with or be influenced by PA. The *FTO* gene is one notable exception. The *FTO* gene was originally identified through whole genome association mapping and has been one of the most robustly reproducible genetic associations with obesity and type 2 diabetes mellitus yet reported [70–73]. Scientists quickly discovered *FTO* mRNA is highly expressed in the hypothalamus of humans and mice and *FTO* mRNA fluctuated in a manner dependent upon the fed state of the animals [74–76]. It was also shown *FTO* mRNA expression was correlated with *NPY* mRNA expression further implicating that the primary action of *FTO* may be through the hypothalamus [74]. However, it has been shown the expression of *FTO* is not mediated through leptin; therefore *FTO* may yet be another control mechanism within the hypothalamus [74–76]. Identifying the role of *FTO* in energy balance is still the early stages of research, but new findings may shed additional light on the complex mechanism within the hypothalamus that regulates energy balance.

Among the most exciting and robust gene×PA interactions reported in the scientific literature are the reports of interactions between *FTO* variation and exercise/PA in influencing obesity and body composition [66–69]. Since the discovery of *FTO*, several groups have demonstrated the deleterious effects of obesity risk raising *FTO* alleles may be exacerbated in low physically active individuals, and individuals without the risk raising alleles may be more responsive to exercise training. For example, in 481 previously sedentary white subjects from the *HE*alth, *RI*sk factors, exercise *TrA*ining, and *GE*netics (HERITAGE) study, the *FTO* rs8050136 polymorphism was associated with fat mass loss following 20 weeks of aerobic exercise training [67]. Carriers of the C allele lost significantly more fat mass and percent body fat than those with the AA genotype, after adjusting for age, gender, and baseline fat mass or percent body fat [67].

In the Dose-Response to Exercise Women (DREW) Trial, 234 white females underwent 6 months of moderate intensity exercise. Subjects with the *FTO* rs8050136 AA genotype lost significantly more weight than carriers of the C allele, among those who adhered to or exceeded the recommended dosage of moderate intensity exercise [68]. Vimaleswaran et al. [69] examined the *FTO* rs1121980 polymorphism, which is in strong linkage disequilibrium with the *FTO* rs8050136 variant, in 20,374 subjects from the European Prospective Investigation into Cancer and Nutrition Norfolk Study. These authors demonstrated that increased risk of obesity with the presence of the *FTO* rs1121980 T allele can potentially be attenuated by PA; active individuals with the T allele had significantly lower BMI and waist circumference as compared to inactive individuals with the T allele [69]. In another large study conducted in 17,162 middle-aged Danes, Andreason et al. [66] reported carriers of the A allele of the rs9939609 *FTO* variant (also in strong linkage disequilibrium with the previously mentioned *FTO* variants) who were inactive had a significantly higher BMI than those individuals who were homozygous for the T allele and were also inactive.

Although PA has been reliably demonstrated to moderate the effects of the *FTO* gene on obesity and diabetes related outcomes, the *FTO* gene does not appear to influence PA levels directly. While the exact function of *FTO* has yet to be identified, animal studies have provided evidence *FTO* as a key regulator of energy metabolism. It remains to be determined exactly how the physiologic alterations that occur during exercise may interact at a molecular level with the FTO protein [77, 78]. Nevertheless, all of these studies provide compelling evidence variation found within the *FTO* gene may alter exercise induced changes in adiposity and body mass. While many other strong obesity candidate genes exist within pathways regulating feeding behavior (as described above), no other genes within these pathways have been examined or reported to interact with PA or exercise in influencing body composition.

Adipogenesis Genes and Body Composition Change from Exercise and Physical Activity

Genes that regulate the initiation of preadipocyte differentiation into mature adipocytes and the formation and storage of lipids within the adipose tissue comprise critical mechanisms underlying the control of body mass and fat storage. These genes include peroxisome proliferator receptor gamma (*PPARG*), diacylglycerol transferase 1 and 2 (*DGAT1, DGAT2*), perilipin (*PLIN*), CCAAT/enhancer-binding protein (*C/EBP*), sterol regulatory element binding protein (*SREBP/ADD1*), and preadipocyte differentiation factor 1 (*PREF1*). Though it was originally thought total adipocyte number was determined early in life, preadipocytes have been successfully extracted and cultured into mature adipocytes from individuals up to 78 years of age, suggesting adipocyte precursors remain functional throughout life [79]. Lean individuals have both smaller and fewer adipocytes than their obese counterparts [79], and the increase in body weight normally occurs with aging is primarily due to an increase in body fat mass [80].

Much progress has been made in identifying the key genes for the induction of preadipocyte differentiation, and several transcription factors have been elucidated that work in concert to stimulate the differentiation pathway. An early signal of adipocyte differentiation is the expression of the CCAAT/enhancer-binding protein (C/EBP) family of transcription factors [81], which are stimulated by adipogenic molecules such as insulin, glucocorticoids, insulin like growth factor (IGF1) and other growth factors, and fatty acids. Mice lacking both C/EBP β (beta) and C/EBP δ (delta), early differentiation factors, show poor development of adipose tissue, while mice lacking either of the two transcription factors alone have well differentiated fat cells, suggesting a cooperative action for the two molecules [82]. Another key regulator of differentiation is PPARG, which has been shown to independently induce preadipocyte differentiation in cell culture [83]. Each of the genes listed above plays a critical role in the development and maturation of adipocytes. Genetic variation that impairs the action of adipogenic genes or promotes the activity of negative regulatory molecules is likely to provide a powerful mechanism for regulating fat mass both at baseline and subsequent to exercise.

Of all adipocyte differentiation factors identified to date, PPARG has been most robustly associated with the exercise response. The well studied Pro12Ala polymorphism within *PPARG* has been robustly demonstrated to be associated with obesity and diabetes as well as to obesity and diabetes interventions. Lindi et al. [84] reported *PPARG* Ala12 carriers gained significantly more weight over a 10 year period of follow-up than noncarriers, while subjects homozygous for the Ala12 allele had lower fasting plasma insulin than noncarriers at baseline and after 10 years, despite significant weight gain. In a separate study, Lindi et al. [85] investigated the association of the *PPARG* Pro12Ala polymorphism and the response to a dietary and exercise intervention in 490 subjects with impaired glucose tolerance. Upon entry into the study, subjects were randomized into either a control group, which received information on diet and exercise, or an intervention group, which received guidance to increase PA and a dietary plan aimed at decreasing weight. After 3 years of enrollment in the study, the authors showed individuals in the intervention who were homozygous for the Ala12 allele lost significantly more weight than those who were also enrolled in the intervention and homozygous for the Pro12 allele; no differences in response by genotype were noted for those in the control group [85].

Consistent with the findings for a significant interaction between *PPARG* and response to weight loss interventions, Nicklas et al. [86] reported *PPARG* Ala12 carriers undergoing a 6 month hypocaloric diet lost a similar amount of weight compared to those homozygous for the *PPARG* Pro12 allele , yet gained significantly more weight following completion of the intervention. Ostregard et al. [87] reported similar findings for the *PPARG* Pro12Ala polymorphism in 29 healthy offspring of type 2 diabetic probands who underwent 10 weeks of aerobic exercise; significantly greater weight loss was observed in Ala12 carriers compared to those homozygous for the *PPARG* Pro12 allele. These studies serve to illustrate, genetic variation within adipocyte differentiation pathways can have significant impact on both weight loss and weight maintenance following an exercise based obesity intervention [84–86].

Energy Metabolism Genes and Body Composition Change from Exercise and Physical Activity

Catecholamine and cytokine activity are a critical part of the maintenance of appropriate energy homeostasis. Among the most frequently reported gene×exercise interactions that affect body composition are those of the adrenergic receptor family. Genetic variants in the *ADRB3*, *ABDR2*, and adrenergic alpha 2A receptor (*ADRA2B*) has been reported to alter physiologic change in body composition from exercise and PA. A mediator of the catecholamine induced signaling of adenylate cyclase is the well characterized β2 (beta 2) adrenergic receptor (ADRB2). This activation follows a G protein ternary complex formation and subsequent adenylyl cyclase activation that is triggered by epinephrine [88]. Polymorphisms within *ADRB2* have been associated with asthma and obesity in several studies. More recently, *ADRB2* variation has also been shown to interact with PA and exercise to influence body size measures.

The *ADRB2* Gln27Glu polymorphism has been reported in several studies to have a gene×exercise interaction effect on body composition. Meirhaeghe et al. [89] conducted one of the first studies reporting gene×exercise interactions involving 1,152 men and women. They reported sedentary males with the Glu27 allele had significantly lower body mass, BMI, waist circumference, hip circumference, and waist hip ratio compared to noncarriers. There were no significant differences in body size measures for noncarriers of the Glu27 allele among active individuals, suggesting the deleterious effect of the Glu27 allele may be attenuated by PA. Macho-Azcarante et al. [90] investigated the effect of the *ADRB2* Gln27Glu polymorphism in 12 obese females, six of whom were homozygous for the Glu27 allele while the remaining six were homozygous for the Gln27 allele. Women who were homozygous for the Glu27 allele had a significantly higher respiratory exchange ratio (RER) following a maximal exercise treadmill test than those women homozygous for the Gln27 allele. This finding suggest women homozygous for the Glu27 allele had a lower postexercise fat oxidation which may translate to less fat mass loss from regular aerobic exercise.

Garenc et al. [91] enrolled 482 white and 260 black subjects from the HERITAGE study to investigate the effect of the *ADRB2* Gln27Glu polymorphism in body composition change after 20 weeks of aerobic exercise training. They showed in white, obese males homozygous for the Glu27 allele, more fat mass was lost after the exercise protocol than in white, obese males homozygous for the Gln27 allele. No gene effects for body composition were observed in blacks or females after exercise training. Phares et al. [92] also reported ADRB2 Glu27 allele carriers had a greater reduction of total percent body fat and percent trunk fat after a 24 week exercise program when compared to noncarriers of the Glu27 allele.

There are also studies which do not replicate the findings mentioned previously regarding the *ADRB2* Gln27Glu polymorphism. Corbalan et al. [93] investigated the *ADRB2* Gln27Glu polymorphism in 113 healthy controls and 139 obese females. These authors in contrast to those previously mentioned, demonstrated carriers of the Glu27 allele who were also physically active had a higher BMI than noncarriers who were also physically active, suggesting *ADRB2* Glu27 allele carriers may not see as much beneficial improvement on body composition when increasing PA level as noncarriers.

An additional *ADRB2* variant, Arg16Gly, has also been shown to affect physiologic response to aerobic exercise [91]. White females from the HERITAGE study who were homozygous for the Arg16 allele exhibited a greater reduction in BMI, percent fat, and fat mass compared to white females who were homozygous for the Gly16 allele following 20 weeks of aerobic exercise training. Additionally, white males who were homozygous for the Arg16 allele also exhibited greater reductions in subcutaneous fat depots than those homozygous for the Gly16 allele following the training protocol [91]. One additional study reported an interaction with a variant in the *ADRA2B* gene (*ADRA2B* Glu^{12}/Glu^9), in which 98 men and women engaged in 10 weeks of single leg strength training exercise [94]. In this study, Yao et al. [94] showed Glu^9 allele carriers significantly decreased intermuscular fat while non carriers exhibited no change in intermuscular fat.

The guanine nucleotide binding protein beta polypeptide 3 (*GNB3*) gene, a key component in adrenergic signaling, has been associated with hypertension, obesity, and adipogenesis [95, 96]. Two separate studies have reported significant associations between the *GNB3* C825T polymorphism in the *GNB3* gene and body composition in black populations. Rankinen et al. [97] conducted the first study from HERITAGE in 473 whites and 255 blacks who participated in 20 weeks of aerobic exercise training. In blacks, those with the T825T genotype saw a significantly greater reduction in percent body fat and total body fatness than those who were carriers of the C825 allele. No *GNB3* C825T genotype effects were observed in whites. In the second study, Grove et al. [98] reported in large cohort of individuals from the atherosclerosis risk in communities (ARIC) Study, involving 10,988 whites and 3,728 blacks, the T825 allele differentially affected the incidence of obesity by PA level. The authors demonstrated African-American carriers of the T825 allele who were physically active had a significantly lower risk for obesity compared to those homozygous for the C825 allele; while the presence of the T825 allele in African-Americans who reported they were physically inactive had an increased risk for obesity [98]. The findings from these two studies suggest in African-Americans, the T allele in the C825T *GNB3* polymorphism may confer a higher risk for increased adiposity and obesity, but individuals with the T allele can greatly benefit from regular bouts of PA [97, 98].

Coincident with the action of ADRB2 and GNB3 is the β (beta) 3 adrenergic receptor (ADRB3), which functions in the regulation of lipolysis and thermogenesis [99]. One of the first and most consistently reported gene×exercise interaction is with the Trp64Arg polymorphism in the *ADRB3* gene [100]. Sakane et al. [100] assessed 61 obese diabetic women at baseline and after a 3 month exercise and low calorie diet intervention. Women who were carriers of the *ADRB3* Arg64 allele were found to lose significantly less weight and had smaller changes in waist hip ratio than those who were homozygous for the Trp64 allele. Shiwaku et al. [101] investigated the effects of the *ADRB3* Try64Arg *ADRB3* polymorphism and weight loss among 76 middle-aged women enrolled in a 3 month weight loss program that included diet, exercise, and a behavioral component. Significantly more women homozygous for the Trp64 allele lost weight than did carriers of the Arg64 allele (69 vs. 48%) [101]. Additionally, significant body mass, BMI and waist circumference changes were only seen in women with the Trp64Try genotype. Kahara et al. [102] investigated the effects of a 3 month low intensity exercise training program on serum leptin levels in 106 Japanese men. These authors reported *ADRB3* Arg64 allele carriers did not significantly reduce serum leptin levels after the exercise protocol, but those with the Try64Trp genotype did have significantly reduced serum leptin levels consistent with a greater reduction in fat mass [102].

Additional studies have reported that carriers of the *ADRB3* Arg64 allele can benefit substantially from exercise. Marti et al. [103] employed a case/control design among 313 physically active and sedentary Spanish individuals. These authors demonstrated among physically active individuals, there was no *ADRB3* Try64 genotype differences in BMI, while among sedentary individuals those with the Arg64 allele had a significantly higher BMI compared to those homozygous for the Try64 allele [103]. Phares et al. [92] reported among 41 postmenopausal females and 29 sedentary males, a twofold greater percent fat loss after 24 weeks of aerobic exercise in carriers of the Arg64 allele compared to those homozygous for the Trp64 allele. Differences in populations (e.g., men vs. women, diabetics vs. healthy individuals, premenopausal vs. postmenopausal women, etc.) and study design (e.g., exercise alone vs. combinations of exercise, diet, and behavior interventions, case/control vs. cohort studies, etc.) may account for the discrepancies reported for this variant. One of the difficulties in definitively determining the effects of any genetic variant on the exercise response in terms of body composition is the wide variety of "replication" studies reported.

The catechol-O-methyltransferase (*COMT*) gene encodes a key enzyme involved in the degradation of catecholamines such as dopamine, epinephrine, and norepinephrine, and as such, acts as a component of feeding motivation and reward related systems [104]. Since catecholamine release is a key component of exercise, it is not surprising variation in the *COMT* gene has been shown to interact with exercise training to influence body mass. Tworoger et al. [105] investigated the change in body composition following a 1 year exercise training protocol that included 225 min/week of moderate intensity exercise in 173 postmenopausal women genotyped for the *COMT* Val158Met variant. The authors demonstrated that after 1 year, those subjects homozygous for the Val158 allele had a significantly greater reduction in percent body fat than those homozygous for the Met158 allele [105].

The findings for the *COMT* gene may result from multiple mechanisms related to both eating behavior and/or fat deposition. COMT catalyzes 2-methoxyestradiol which has been shown to influence body fatness by inhibiting preadipocyte proliferation and differentiation in vitro [106, 107]. The *COMT* Val58Met variant alters the activity of the COMT enzyme thus potentially altering processes such as degradation of catecholamines and catalyzation of two methoxyestradiol, which may influence the rewarding effect of food and inhibit preadipocyte differentiation. Variation in the *COMT* gene has been associated with eating disorders [108–110] and obesity [111–113] in multiple studies [114]. In the Tworoger et al. [105] study described above, subjects were also genotyped for a tetranucleotide repeat polymorphism $[(TTTA)_n \ (n=7–13)]$ in the cytochrome p450 family 19 subfamily A polypeptide 1 (*CYP19A1*) gene. *CYP19A1* encodes the protein aromatase which modulates the ratio of androgens to estrogens in adipose tissue and may ultimately affect body fat regulation and distribution [106, 115, 116]. Those individuals homozygous for the 11 repeat allele had significantly larger decreases in percent body fat and total fat mass than subjects with no 11 repeat alleles [105]. Exercisers with the *COMT* Val/Val genotype and at least one copy of the *CYP19A1* 11r allele experienced significantly greater percentage and total fat loss and a larger reduction in BMI than exercisers without this genotype/allele providing evidence for an additive effect of the two variants [105].

The angiotensin I converting enzyme (*ACE*) gene, which encodes one of the key factors in blood pressure regulation, has been shown to interact with exercise to affect body composition. The *ACE* gene was among the first reported to influence performance traits [117]. All of the significant findings are for the insertion/deletion (I/D) polymorphism in the *ACE* gene, a variant that has been proposed to be a marker of ACE activity in body tissues [118]. It has been hypothesized that a reduction in ACE activity could cause the differential usage of fat stores in the body due to the presence of renin angiotensin systems in adipose tissue [119]. The first report of a significant gene×exercise interaction was carried out in 81 British army recruits who underwent 10 weeks of physical training [117]. Montgomery et al. [117] showed those with the *ACE* I/I genotype had significantly greater increases in body mass, fat mass, and fat free mass than carriers of the D allele. An additional study, conducted in a large sample of older adults (70–79 years, $n = 3,000$) from the Healthy Aging and Body Composition Cohort Study, reported the *ACE* I/I genotype was associated with higher intramuscular thigh fat and percent body fat [120]. This finding was only observed in physically active subjects. These two findings support the idea that the *ACE* I/I genotype may enhance metabolic efficiency by creating a positive energy balance during PA. Moran et al. [119] reported the D allele was associated with increased body fatness in 1,016 Greek adolescent boys and girls (age 11–18 years), which is in opposition to the two previously mentioned studies [117, 120]. Moran et al. [119] demonstrated inactive girls with the *ACE* I/I genotype had significantly lower tricep and subscapular skinfold thickness than inactive girls who were carriers of the ACE D allele. No ACE I/D genotype association were reported for boys or active girls [119].

Uncoupling proteins are another important factor in energy balance. By uncoupling the proton gradient in mitochondria, energy is effectively dissipated as heat. Recently, it has been demonstrated humans possess substantial stores of brown fat, a metabolically active tissue in which protein gradient uncoupling acts to stimulate nonshivering thermogenesis primarily through the action of UCP1 [121, 122]. UCP2, primarily expressed in white adipose tissue and skeletal muscle, and UCP3, expressed only in skeletal muscle and heart, are also involved in uncoupling the proton gradient in mitochondria [123]. The *UCP3* gene, a key component of energy balance, has been shown to also interact with PA to influence body composition. Otabe et al. [124] reported an interaction between a polymorphism in the 5′ flanking region of the *UCP3* gene among 368 individuals with morbid obesity. In these individuals, BMI was negatively associated with PA among those with the CC genotype, while there were no associations between PA and BMI among T allele carriers. In a sample of 276 blacks and 503 whites from the HERITAGE study, a microsatellite repeat polymorphism in intron 6 of the *UCP3* gene was investigated for its association with training induced changes in adiposity [125]. Whites who were homozygous for the 240 bp allele had the greatest reduction in subcutaneous adiposity as determined by sum of eight skinfolds. Whites who were carriers of the

238 bp allele had an intermediate reduction in the skinfold sum, while Whites with the 242 bp allele (240/242 and 242/242) experienced an increase in skinfolds sum following 20 weeks of aerobic exercise. No associations were reported with the microsatellite repeat polymorphism in intron 6 of the UCP3 gene for the black population [125].

Metabolic activity is a critical factor in the natural balance of energy consumption and expenditure. Insulin and catecholamines have pronounced metabolic effects on human adipose tissue metabolism. Insulin stimulates LPL and inhibits hormone sensitive lipase (LIPE), while the opposite is true for catecholamines secreted subsequent to exercise [126]. LIPE plays a critical role in the mobilization of fatty acids from triacylglyceride stores and shows a marked decrease in hydrolytic activity when either of the lipid stabilizing proteins, adipose differentiation related protein (ADRP) or PLIN, are covering the lipid droplets [127]. LPL functions to catalyze the breakdown of triacylglycerol into diacylglycerol and fatty acids and convert chylomicrons and VLDL into LDL and IDL [128]. Garenc et al. [129] reported that the *LPL* S447X polymorphism was associated with reduction in BMI, percent fat, fat mass, and abdominal visceral fat following exercise. Specifically, results from 741 subjects from the HERITAGE study demonstrated carriers of the *LPL* X447 allele had greater reduction in abdominal visceral fat in black females and significantly greater decreases in BMI, percent body fat, and fat mass in white females after 20 weeks of aerobic exercise as compared to those with the *LPL* S447S genotype.

The interleukin 15 receptor alpha (*IL15RA*) gene has also been found to be associated with change in body composition in response to exercise training [130]. Reichman et al. [130] concluded a *IL15RA* variant (*Pst*I) in exon 7 and a haplotype (*Bst*NI:*Hpa*II) in exon 4 were associated with the muscle mass response in 153 males and females following 10 weeks of resistance exercise training. Those individuals with the A allele in the *Pst*I polymorphism and the C:A haplotype in the *Bst*NI:*Hpa*II haplotype had significantly higher increases in lean mass when compared to all other individuals. The phenylethanolamine N-methyltransferase (*PNMT*) gene has also been shown to be associated with exercise mediated body composition change [131]. Peters et al. [131] employed use of the weight loss drug, sibutramine, in a 6 month weight loss trial that included behavioral modification aimed at increasing healthy eating and daily exercise in 149 obese females. At the end of the trial, females with the AA or GG genotype in the *PNMT* G-148A promoter polymorphism had significantly greater weight loss compared to those with the AG genotype.

As a member of a family of proteins involved in mediating growth and development, IGF1 is a key factor in cellular growth, including skeletal muscle growth following exercise. A two base pair microsatellite repeat marker (i.e., two nucleotides that repeat a variable number of times in the DNA sequence of this gene) in the 5' region of *IGF1* has been associated with changes in body fatness following a 20 week exercise protocol in 502 white subjects from the HERITAGE study [132]. Prior to the exercise intervention, the 189 bp allele was associated with fat mass, fat free mass, and percent fat. Following exercise training, individuals homozygous for the 189 bp allele gained half the amount of fat free mass compared to the other two genotypes [132].

More recently, there have been reports of significant exercise×gene interactions for the Plasma cell 1 glycoprotein (*PC-1*, also known as *ENPP1*) gene, which is also associated with insulin sensitivity and body composition. Park et al. [133] enrolled 84 Korean women with abdominal obesity in a 12 week aerobic exercise program and assessed the *PC-1* K121Q polymorphism for its association with body composition change. The authors found women with the *PC-1* Q121 allele lost significantly less weight and experienced a smaller decrease in BMI than those who were homozygous for the K121 allele. Others have reported that the K121Q variant is associated with insulin resistance [134], BMI [135], and both childhood and adult obesity [136]. The effect of the *PC-1* genotype specific improvement in body weight following the exercise program may be through the combination of both PC-1 mediated and exercise mediated upregulation of insulin signaling pathways, which in turn would be associated with improved body adiposity [133].

Peroxisome proliferative activated receptor alpha (PPARA) is a key regulator of lipid metabolism. It is expressed primarily in the liver, adipose tissue, kidney, heart, skeletal muscle, and large intestine where it has been shown to regulate fatty acid synthesis and oxidation, gluconeogenesis, ketogenesis, and lipoprotein assembly. Uthurralt et al. [137] investigated the influence of the *PPARA* L162V polymorphism on change in adiposity following 12 weeks of unilateral upper body resistance training among 610 young men and women. The authors demonstrated men who were carriers of the *PPARA* V162 allele had increased fat volume in the untrained arm while men who were homozygous for the *PPARA* L162 allele had a decrease in the fat volume of the untrained arm.

Exercise produces profound effects on global metabolism by altering fuel utilization, enhancing sensitivity to the effects of catecholamines, altering cardiovascular physiology, enhancing insulin sensitivity, and/or altering mechanisms that regulate energy balance. Thus, it is not surprising that many of the genes demonstrated to interact with exercise in influencing body weight and composition are key components of metabolic pathways controlling blood pressure, fuel partitioning, insulin signaling, and other related pathways. As described above, genetic variation within the energy metabolism genes *ADRB3*, *ARDB2*, *ADRA2B*, *GNB3*, *COMT*, *CYP19A1*, *ACE*, *UCP3*, *LPL*, *IL15RA*, *IGF1*, *PC-1*, and *PPARA* has been shown to influence the manner in which body weight and body fatness is altered by exercise training or PA. Though exercise has predictable effects on metabolism, it has long been recognized such effects can be highly variable among individuals. Understanding how genetic variation in genes related to energy metabolism influences overall adiposity or body composition following exercise training or PA is a critical component in our ability to design effective programs focused on healthy energy balance.

The Future?

An excellent foundation has already been laid by the previously mentioned studies in the search for genetic markers. In order to build upon this foundation, prospective studies in which individuals are selected on the basis of genotype and undergo an exercise intervention, would be useful to establish and verify genetic markers that can predict body composition change following exercise. Additionally, the development of robust statistical techniques that can handle numerous genetic markers and environmental factors will be crucial to the progressive movement to personalized genetic exercise prescriptions. Given the progress made to date and these special considerations, there is future hope for successful exercise interventions that employ the use of genetic information to elicit the best response possible from each individual.

Practical Applications

This chapter has provided a brief overview of the published studies to date in which interactions between genetic variation and PA and/or exercise have been demonstrated to influence body size measures. These studies provide considerable evidence the effects of genetic variants on body mass and composition can be substantially modified by PA and/or exercise. For complex traits such as obesity and body size, most genetic variants account for only a small portion of the total variance in the trait. Although genetic variation has been estimated to account for up to half of the population variance in body size, environmental and behavioral factors explain the rest of the variance. Thus, an important concept to glean from studies of gene × environment interaction is that most genetic variation is not deterministic, i.e., the effects attributed to any given variant are often modifiable, depending on both the physiologic and physical environments associated with the gene action. The genes listed in Table 5.1 identified to interact with PA and/or exercise by no means comprise a comprehensive list. Most studies do not test for such interactions and few studies to date have examined the body composition response to exercise in the context of genetic variation, and further research in this area is certainly warranted.

The potential benefits gained from regular exercise on reducing risk of obesity are well described in the literature. However, most studies report and emphasize mean changes in body composition from a PA or exercise intervention. What may be of great importance is further investigation of those individuals who achieve a differential change in body composition from exercise based on genetic variation at specific loci. While the average physiological response to an exercise training protocol is decreased body weight, decreased fat mass, and favorable changes in adipose distribution, some individuals do not respond in a similar manner to a given amount of exercise. By setting PA guidelines based solely on the mean response across subjects, one may fail to recognize these guidelines may be highly efficacious for some individuals and ineffective for others. Identifying genetic variation that moderates or mediates the effect of exercise and PA may be the first step in formulating more efficacious recommendations for exercise and PA.

The challenge remains in utilizing this information about specific gene × exercise interactions and how one should go about doing so. Several recommendations for the utilization of genetic information have been provided to improve intervention strategies that include PA or exercise [138]. First, genetic markers that are highly replicable and strongly predict the body composition response to exercise must be identified. This will require prospective exercise intervention by genotype studies that focus primarily on body composition change to identify potential genetic markers. Second, the ability to quantify the genetic markers must be accurate, affordable, and practical. Technology for assessing genomic information is quickly becoming faster and less expensive; therefore it will be plausible in the future to rapidly assess an individual for his/her particular genetic information. Third, the assessment of genetic markers needs to be acceptable to a population. Individuals should view the assessment of genetic markers as another form of health screening. Finally, assurance against misuse of genetic information must be of utmost importance. Currently, concerns over the misuse of genetic information plague many individuals, therefore safeguards to ensure the integrity of this information need to be in place [138].

References

1. Mokdad AH, Marks JS, Stroup DF, Gerberding JL. Actual causes of death in the united states, 2000. JAMA. 2004;291(10):1238–45.
2. Ogden CL, Carroll MD, Curtin LR, McDowell MA, Tabak CJ, Flegal KM. Prevalence of overweight and obesity in the united states, 1999–2004. JAMA. 2006;295(13):1549–55.
3. Adams KF, Schatzkin A, Harris TB, Kipnis V, Mouw T, Ballard-Barbash R, et al. Overweight, obesity, and mortality in a large prospective cohort of persons 50 to 71 years old. N Engl J Med. 2006;355(8):763–78.
4. Calle EE, Rodriguez C, Walker-Thurmond K, Thun MJ. Overweight, obesity, and mortality from cancer in a prospectively studied cohort of U.S. adults. N Engl J Med. 2003;348(17):1625–38.
5. WHO Consultation on Obesity: preventing and managing the global epidemic. report of a WHO consultation on Obesity. World Health Organ Tech Rep Ser. 2000;894:i–xii, 1–253.
6. Carey VJ, Walters EE, Colditz GA, Solomon CG, Willett WC, Rosner BA, et al. Body fat distribution and risk of non-insulin-dependent diabetes mellitus in women. the nurses' health study. Am J Epidemiol. 1997;145(7):614–9.
7. Folsom AR, Prineas RJ, Kaye SA, Munger RG. Incidence of hypertension and stroke in relation to body fat distribution and other risk factors in older women. Stroke. 1990;21(5):701–6.
8. Despres JP, Moorjani S, Lupien PJ, Tremblay A, Nadeau A, Bouchard C. Regional distribution of body fat, plasma lipoproteins, and cardiovascular disease. Arteriosclerosis. 1990;10(4):497–511.
9. Finkelstein EA, Trogdon JG, Cohen JW, Dietz W. Annual medical spending attributable to obesity: payer-and service-specific estimates. Health Aff (Millwood). 2009;28(5):w822–31.
10. Caspersen CJ, Powell KE, Christenson GM. Physical activity, exercise, and physical fitness: definitions and distinctions for health-related research. Public Health Rep. 1985;100(2):126–31.
11. Thompson WR, Gordon NF, Pescatello LS, American College of Sports Medicine. ACSM's guidelines for exercise testing and prescription. 8th ed. Philadelphia: Lippincott Williams & Wilkins; 2009.
12. Di Pietro L, Dziura J, Blair SN. Estimated change in physical activity level (PAL) and prediction of 5-year weight change in men: the aerobics center longitudinal study. Int J Obes Relat Metab Disord. 2004;28(12):1541–7.

13. Donnelly JE, Hill JO, Jacobsen DJ, Potteiger J, Sullivan DK, Johnson SL, et al. Effects of a 16-month randomized controlled exercise trial on body weight and composition in young, overweight men and women: The midwest exercise trial. Arch Intern Med. 2003;163(11): 1343–50.
14. Schmitz KH, Jacobs Jr DR, Leon AS, Schreiner PJ, Sternfeld B. Physical activity and body weight: associations over ten years in the CARDIA study. Coronary artery risk development in young adults. Int J Obes Relat Metab Disord. 2000;24(11):1475–87.
15. Haapanen N, Miilunpalo S, Pasanen M, Oja P, Vuori I. Association between leisure time physical activity and 10-year body mass change among working-aged men and women. Int J Obes Relat Metab Disord. 1997;21(4):288–96.
16. Williamson DF, Madans J, Anda RF, Kleinman JC, Kahn HS, Byers T. Recreational physical activity and ten-year weight change in a US national cohort. Int J Obes Relat Metab Disord. 1993;17(5):279–86.
17. Donnelly JE, Blair SN, Jakicic JM, Manore MM, Rankin JW, Smith BK. American College of Sports Medicine. American college of sports medicine position stand. appropriate physical activity intervention strategies for weight loss and prevention of weight regain for adults. Med Sci Sports Exerc. 2009;41(2):459–71.
18. Rice T, Borecki IB, Bouchard C, Rao DC. Segregation analysis of body mass index in an unselected French-Canadian sample: the Quebec family study. Obes Res. 1993;1(4):288–94.
19. Comuzzie AG, Blangero J, Mahaney MC, Mitchell BD, Hixson JE, Samollow PB, et al. Major gene with sex-specific effects influences fat mass in mexican americans. Genet Epidemiol. 1995;12(5):475–88.
20. Bouchard C, Rice T, Lemieux S, Despres JP, Perusse L, Rao DC. Major gene for abdominal visceral fat area in the Quebec family study. Int J Obes Relat Metab Disord. 1996;20(5):420–7.
21. Maes HH, Neale MC, Eaves LJ. Genetic and environmental factors in relative body weight and human adiposity. Behav Genet. 1997;27(4):325–51.
22. Borjeson M. The aetiology of obesity in children. A study of 101 twin pairs. Acta Paediatr Scand. 1976;65(3):279–87.
23. Stunkard AJ, Foch TT, Hrubec Z. A twin study of human obesity. JAMA. 1986;256(1): 51–4.
24. Sorensen TI, Holst C, Stunkard AJ, Skovgaard LT. Correlations of body mass index of adult adoptees and their biological and adoptive relatives. Int J Obes Relat Metab Disord. 1992;16(3):227–36.
25. MacLean L, Rhode B. Does genetic predisposition influence surgical results of operations for obesity? Obes Surg. 1996;6(2):132–7.
26. Adams TD, Hunt SC, Mason LA, Ramirez ME, Fisher AG, Williams RR. Familial aggregation of morbid obesity. Obes Res. 1993;1(4):261–70.
27. Rankinen T, Zuberi A, Chagnon YC, Weisnagel SJ, Argyropoulos G, Walts B, et al. The human obesity gene map: The 2005 update. Obesity (Silver Spring). 2006;14(4):529–644.
28. Zhang Y, Proenca R, Maffei M, Barone M, Leopold L, Friedman JM. Positional cloning of the mouse obese gene and its human homologue. Nature. 1994;372(6505):425–32.
29. Chen G, Koyama K, Yuan X, Lee Y, Zhou YT, O'Doherty R, et al. Disappearance of body fat in normal rats induced by adenovirus-mediated leptin gene therapy. Proc Natl Acad Sci U S A. 1996;93(25):14795–9.
30. Cohen B, Novick D, Rubinstein M. Modulation of insulin activities by leptin. Science. 1996;274(5290):1185–8.
31. Collins S, Kuhn CM, Petro AE, Swick AG, Chrunyk BA, Surwit RS. Role of leptin in fat regulation. Nature. 1996;380(6576):677.
32. Muoio DM, Dohm GL, Fiedorek Jr FT, Tapscott EB, Coleman RA. Leptin directly alters lipid partitioning in skeletal muscle. Diabetes. 1997;46(8):1360–3.
33. Israel D, Chua Jr S. Leptin receptor modulation of adiposity and fertility. Trends Endocrinol Metab. 2010;21(1):10–6.

34. Banks WA, Kastin AJ, Huang W, Jaspan JB, Maness LM. Leptin enters the brain by a saturable system independent of insulin. Peptides. 1996;17(2):305–11.
35. Elmquist JK. Hypothalamic pathways underlying the endocrine, autonomic, and behavioral effects of leptin. Int J Obes Relat Metab Disord. 2001;25 Suppl 5:S78–82.
36. Zamorano PL, Mahesh VB, De Sevilla LM, Chorich LP, Bhat GK, Brann DW. Expression and localization of the leptin receptor in endocrine and neuroendocrine tissues of the rat. Neuroendocrinology. 1997;65(3):223–8.
37. Kelley AE, Berridge KC. The neuroscience of natural rewards: relevance to addictive drugs. J Neurosci. 2002;22(9):3306–11.
38. Kelley AE, Baldo BA, Pratt WE, Will MJ. Corticostriatal-hypothalamic circuitry and food motivation: integration of energy, action and reward. Physiol Behav. 2005;86(5):773–95.
39. Vaisse C, Clement K, Durand E, Hercberg S, Guy-Grand B, Froguel P. Melanocortin-4 receptor mutations are a frequent and heterogeneous cause of morbid obesity. J Clin Invest. 2000;106(2):253–62.
40. Farooqi IS, Yeo GS, Keogh JM, Aminian S, Jebb SA, Butler G, et al. Dominant and recessive inheritance of morbid obesity associated with melanocortin 4 receptor deficiency. J Clin Invest. 2000;106(2):271–9.
41. Hinney A, Schmidt A, Nottebom K, Heibult O, Becker I, Ziegler A, et al. Several mutations in the melanocortin-4 receptor gene including a nonsense and a frameshift mutation associated with dominantly inherited obesity in humans. J Clin Endocrinol Metab. 1999;84(4):1483–6.
42. Vaisse C, Clement K, Guy-Grand B, Froguel P. A frameshift mutation in human MC4R is associated with a dominant form of obesity. Nat Genet. 1998;20(2):113–4.
43. Yeo GS, Farooqi IS, Aminian S, Halsall DJ, Stanhope RG, O'Rahilly S. A frameshift mutation in MC4R associated with dominantly inherited human obesity. Nat Genet. 1998;20(2):111–2.
44. O'Rahilly S, Gray H, Humphreys PJ, Krook A, Polonsky KS, White A, et al. Brief report: Impaired processing of prohormones associated with abnormalities of glucose homeostasis and adrenal function. N Engl J Med. 1995;333(21):1386–90.
45. Krude H, Biebermann H, Luck W, Horn R, Brabant G, Gruters A. Severe early-onset obesity, adrenal insufficiency and red hair pigmentation caused by POMC mutations in humans. Nat Genet. 1998;19(2):155–7.
46. Clement K, Vaisse C, Lahlou N, Cabrol S, Pelloux V, Cassuto D, et al. A mutation in the human leptin receptor gene causes obesity and pituitary dysfunction. Nature. 1998;392(6674): 398–401.
47. Strobel A, Issad T, Camoin L, Ozata M, Strosberg AD. A leptin missense mutation associated with hypogonadism and morbid obesity. Nat Genet. 1998;18(3):213–5.
48. Montague CT, Farooqi IS, Whitehead JP, Soos MA, Rau H, Wareham NJ, et al. Congenital leptin deficiency is associated with severe early-onset obesity in humans. Nature. 1997;387(6636):903–8.
49. Govaerts C, Srinivasan S, Shapiro A, Zhang S, Picard F, Clement K, et al. Obesity-associated mutations in the melanocortin 4 receptor provide novel insights into its function. Peptides. 2005;26(10):1909–19.
50. Bouchard C. The biological predisposition to obesity: beyond the thrifty genotype scenario. Int J Obes (Lond). 2007;31(9):1337–9.
51. Katsanos CS. Prescribing aerobic exercise for the regulation of postprandial lipid metabolism: current research and recommendations. Sports Med. 2006;36(7):547–60.
52. Tunstall RJ, Mehan KA, Wadley GD, Collier GR, Bonen A, Hargreaves M, Cameron-Smith D. Exercise training increases lipid metabolism gene expression in human skeletal muscle. Am J Physiol Endocrinol Metab. 2002;283(1):E66–72.
53. Pilegaard H, Saltin B, Neufer PD. Exercise induces transient transcriptional activation of the PGC-1alpha gene in human skeletal muscle. J Physiol. 2003;546(Pt 3):851–8.
54. Yan ZC, Liu DY, Zhang LL, Shen CY, Ma QL, Cao TB, et al. Exercise reduces adipose tissue via cannabinoid receptor type 1 which is regulated by peroxisome proliferator-activated receptor-delta. Biochem Biophys Res Commun. 2007;354(2):427–33.

55. Keller P, Keller C, Steensberg A, Robinson LE, Pedersen BK. Leptin gene expression and systemic levels in healthy men: effect of exercise, carbohydrate, interleukin-6, and epinephrine. J Appl Physiol. 2005;98(5):1805–12.
56. Zeng Q, Fu L, Takekoshi K, Kawakami Y, Isobe K. Effects of short-term exercise on adiponectin and adiponectin receptor levels in rats. J Atheroscler Thromb. 2007;14(5):261–5.
57. Zeng Q, Fu L, Takekoshi K, Kawakami Y, Isobe K. Effects of exercise on adiponectin and adiponectin receptor levels in rats. Life Sci. 2007;80(5):454–9.
58. Berggren JR, Hulver MW, Houmard JA. Fat as an endocrine organ: influence of exercise. J Appl Physiol. 2005;99(2):757–64.
59. Rankinen T, Perusse L, Rauramaa R, Rivera MA, Wolfarth B, Bouchard C. The human gene map for performance and health-related fitness phenotypes. Med Sci Sports Exerc. 2001;33(6):855–67.
60. Rankinen T, Perusse L, Rauramaa R, Rivera MA, Wolfarth B, Bouchard C. The human gene map for performance and health-related fitness phenotypes: the 2001 update. Med Sci Sports Exerc. 2002;34(8):1219–33.
61. Perusse L, Rankinen T, Rauramaa R, Rivera MA, Wolfarth B, Bouchard C. The human gene map for performance and health-related fitness phenotypes: the 2002 update. Med Sci Sports Exerc. 2003;35(8):1248–64.
62. Rankinen T, Perusse L, Rauramaa R, Rivera MA, Wolfarth B, Bouchard C. The human gene map for performance and health-related fitness phenotypes: the 2003 update. Med Sci Sports Exerc. 2004;36(9):1451–69.
63. Wolfarth B, Bray MS, Hagberg JM, Perusse L, Rauramaa R, Rivera MA, et al. The human gene map for performance and health-related fitness phenotypes: The 2004 update. Med Sci Sports Exerc. 2005;37(6):881–903.
64. Rankinen T, Bray MS, Hagberg JM, Perusse L, Roth SM, Wolfarth B, Bouchard C. The human gene map for performance and health-related fitness phenotypes: The 2005 update. Med Sci Sports Exerc. 2006;38(11):1863–88.
65. Bray MS, Hagberg JM, Perusse L, Rankinen T, Roth SM, Wolfarth B, Bouchard C. The human gene map for performance and health-related fitness phenotypes: The 2006-2007 update. Med Sci Sports Exerc. 2009;41(1):35–73.
66. Anderson LA, McTernan PG, Barnett AH, Kumar S. The effects of androgens and estrogens on preadipocyte proliferation in human adipose tissue: Influence of gender and site. J Clin Endocrinol Metab. 2001;86(10):5045–51.
67. Rankinen T, Rice T, Teran-Garcia M, Rao DC, Bouchard C. FTO genotype is associated with exercise training-induced changes in body composition. Obesity (Silver Spring). 2010;18(2):322–6.
68. Mitchell JA, Church TS, Rankinen T, Earnest CP, Sui X, Blair SN. FTO genotype and the weight loss benefits of moderate intensity exercise. Obesity (Silver Spring). 2010;18(3):641–3.
69. Vimaleswaran KS, Li S, Zhao JH, Luan J, Bingham SA, Khaw KT, et al. Physical activity attenuates the body mass index-increasing influence of genetic variation in the FTO gene. Am J Clin Nutr. 2009;90(2):425–8.
70. Frayling TM, Timpson NJ, Weedon MN, Zeggini E, Freathy RM, Lindgren CM, et al. A common variant in the FTO gene is associated with body mass index and predisposes to childhood and adult obesity. Science. 2007;316(5826):889–94.
71. Price RA, Li WD, Zhao H. FTO gene SNPs associated with extreme obesity in cases, controls and extremely discordant sister pairs. BMC Med Genet. 2008;9:4.
72. Scuteri A, Sanna S, Chen WM, Uda M, Albai G, Strait J, et al. Genome-wide association scan shows genetic variants in the FTO gene are associated with obesity-related traits. PLoS Genet. 2007;3(7):e115.
73. Wardle J, Carnell S, Haworth CM, Farooqi IS, O'Rahilly S, Plomin R. Obesity associated genetic variation in FTO is associated with diminished satiety. J Clin Endocrinol Metab. 2008;93(9):3640–3.
74. Fredriksson R, Hagglund M, Olszewski PK, Stephansson O, Jacobsson JA, Olszewska AM, et al. The obesity gene, FTO, is of ancient origin, up-regulated during food deprivation and

expressed in neurons of feeding-related nuclei of the brain. Endocrinology. 2008;149(5):2062–71.

75. Gerken T, Girard CA, Tung YC, Webby CJ, Saudek V, Hewitson KS, et al. The obesity-associated FTO gene encodes a 2-oxoglutarate-dependent nucleic acid demethylase. Science. 2007;318(5855):1469–72.

76. Stratigopoulos G, Padilla SL, LeDuc CA, Watson E, Hattersley AT, McCarthy MI, et al. Regulation of Fto/Ftm gene expression in mice and humans. Am J Physiol Regul Integr Comp Physiol. 2008;294(4):R1185–96.

77. Fischer J, Koch L, Emmerling C, Vierkotten J, Peters T, Bruning JC, Ruther U. Inactivation of the fto gene protects from obesity. Nature. 2009;458(7240):894–8.

78. Church C, Lee S, Bagg EA, McTaggart JS, Deacon R, Gerken T, et al. A mouse model for the metabolic effects of the human fat mass and obesity associated FTO gene. PLoS Genet. 2009;5(8):e1000599.

79. Prins JB, O'Rahilly S. Regulation of adipose cell number in man. Clin Sci (Lond). 1997;92(1):3–11.

80. Kyle UG, Gremion G, Genton L, Slosman DO, Golay A, Pichard C. Physical activity and fat-free and fat mass by bioelectrical impedance in 3853 adults. Med Sci Sports Exerc. 2001;33(4):576–84.

81. Darlington GJ, Ross SE, MacDougald OA. The role of C/EBP genes in adipocyte differentiation. J Biol Chem. 1998;273(46):30057–60.

82. Wu Z, Puigserver P, Spiegelman BM. Transcriptional activation of adipogenesis. Curr Opin Cell Biol. 1999;11(6):689–94.

83. Rangwala SM, Lazar MA. Transcriptional control of adipogenesis. Annu Rev Nutr. 2000;20:535–59.

84. Lindi V, Sivenius K, Niskanen L, Laakso M, Uusitupa MI. Effect of the Pro12Ala polymorphism of the PPAR-gamma2 gene on long-term weight change in finnish non-diabetic subjects. Diabetologia. 2001;44(7):925–6.

85. Lindi VI, Uusitupa MI, Lindstrom J, Louheranta A, Eriksson JG, Valle TT, et al. Association of the Pro12Ala polymorphism in the PPAR-gamma2 gene with 3-year incidence of type 2 diabetes and body weight change in the finnish diabetes prevention study. Diabetes. 2002;51(8):2581–6.

86. Nicklas BJ, van Rossum EF, Berman DM, Ryan AS, Dennis KE, Shuldiner AR. Genetic variation in the peroxisome proliferator-activated receptor-gamma2 gene (Pro12Ala) affects metabolic responses to weight loss and subsequent weight regain. Diabetes. 2001;50(9):2172–6.

87. Ostergard T, Ek J, Hamid Y, Saltin B, Pedersen OB, Hansen T, Schmitz O. Influence of the PPAR-gamma2 Pro12Ala and ACE I/D polymorphisms on insulin sensitivity and training effects in healthy offspring of type 2 diabetic subjects. Horm Metab Res. 2005;37(2):99–105.

88. Liggett SB. Plastic adenylyl cyclase. Am J Respir Cell Mol Biol. 1999;21(5):564–6.

89. Meirhaeghe A, Helbecque N, Cottel D, Amouyel P. Beta2-adrenoceptor gene polymorphism, body weight, and physical activity. Lancet. 1999;353(9156):896.

90. Macho-Azcarate T, Calabuig J, Marti A, Martinez JA. A maximal effort trial in obese women carrying the beta2-adrenoceptor Gln27Glu polymorphism. J Physiol Biochem. 2002;58(2):103–8.

91. Garenc C, Perusse L, Chagnon YC, Rankinen T, Gagnon J, Borecki IB, et al. Effects of beta2-adrenergic receptor gene variants on adiposity: The HERITAGE family study. Obes Res. 2003;11(5):612–8.

92. Phares DA, Halverstadt AA, Shuldiner AR, Ferrell RE, Douglass LW, Ryan AS, et al. Association between body fat response to exercise training and multilocus ADR genotypes. Obes Res. 2004;12(5):807–15.

93. Corbalan MS, Marti A, Forga L, Martinez-Gonzalez MA, Martinez JA. The 27Glu polymorphism of the beta2-adrenergic receptor gene interacts with physical activity influencing obesity risk among female subjects. Clin Genet. 2002;61(4):305–7.

94. Yao L, Delmonico MJ, Roth SM, Hand BD, Johns J, Conway J, et al. Adrenergic receptor genotype influence on midthigh intermuscular fat response to strength training in middle-aged and older adults. J Gerontol A Biol Sci Med Sci. 2007;62(6):658–63.
95. Siffert W, Rosskopf D, Siffert G, Busch S, Moritz A, Erbel R, et al. Association of a human G-protein beta3 subunit variant with hypertension. Nat Genet. 1998;18(1):45–8.
96. Siffert W, Forster P, Jockel KH, Mvere DA, Brinkmann B, Naber C, et al. Worldwide ethnic distribution of the G protein beta3 subunit 825T allele and its association with obesity in caucasian, chinese, and black african individuals. J Am Soc Nephrol. 1999;10(9):1921–30.
97. Rankinen T, Rice T, Leon AS, Skinner JS, Wilmore JH, Rao DC, Bouchard C. G protein beta 3 polymorphism and hemodynamic and body composition phenotypes in the HERITAGE family study. Physiol Genomics. 2002;8(2):151–7.
98. Grove ML, Morrison A, Folsom AR, Boerwinkle E, Hoelscher DM, Bray MS. Gene-environment interaction and the GNB3 gene in the atherosclerosis risk in communities study. Int J Obes (Lond). 2007;31(6):919–26.
99. Collins S, Surwit RS. The beta-adrenergic receptors and the control of adipose tissue metabolism and thermogenesis. Recent Prog Horm Res. 2001;56:309–28.
100. Sakane N, Yoshida T, Umekawa T, Kogure A, Takakura Y, Kondo M. Effects of Trp64Arg mutation in the beta 3-adrenergic receptor gene on weight loss, body fat distribution, glycemic control, and insulin resistance in obese type 2 diabetic patients. Diabetes Care. 1997;20(12):1887–90.
101. Shiwaku K, Nogi A, Anuurad E, Kitajima K, Enkhmaa B, Shimono K, Yamane Y. Difficulty in losing weight by behavioral intervention for women with Trp64Arg polymorphism of the beta3-adrenergic receptor gene. Int J Obes Relat Metab Disord. 2003;27(9):1028–36.
102. Kahara T, Takamura T, Hayakawa T, Nagai Y, Yamaguchi H, Katsuki T, et al. Prediction of exercise-mediated changes in metabolic markers by gene polymorphism. Diabetes Res Clin Pract. 2002;57(2):105–10.
103. Marti A, Corbalan MS, Martinez-Gonzalez MA, Martinez JA. TRP64ARG polymorphism of the beta 3-adrenergic receptor gene and obesity risk: effect modification by a sedentary lifestyle. Diabetes Obes Metab. 2002;4(6):428–30.
104. Rask-Andersen M, Olszewski PK, Levine AS, Schioth HB. Molecular mechanisms underlying anorexia nervosa: focus on human gene association studies and systems controlling food intake. Brain Res Rev. 2010;62(2):147–64.
105. Tworoger SS, Chubak J, Aiello EJ, Yasui Y, Ulrich CM, Farin FM, et al. The effect of CYP19 and COMT polymorphisms on exercise-induced fat loss in postmenopausal women. Obes Res. 2004;12(6):972–81.
106. Anderson LA, McTernan PG, Barnett AH, Kumar S. The effects of androgens and estrogens on preadipocyte proliferation in human adipose tissue: influence of gender and site. J Clin Endocrinol Metab. 2001;86(10):5045–51.
107. Dieudonne MN, Pecquery R, Leneveu MC, Giudicelli Y. Opposite effects of androgens and estrogens on adipogenesis in rat preadipocytes: evidence for sex and site-related specificities and possible involvement of insulin-like growth factor 1 receptor and peroxisome proliferator-activated receptor gamma2. Endocrinology. 2000;141(2):649–56.
108. Mikolajczyk E, Grzywacz A, Samochowiec J. The association of catechol-O-methyltransferase genotype with the phenotype of women with eating disorders. Brain Res. 2010;1307:142–8.
109. Frieling H, Romer KD, Wilhelm J, Hillemacher T, Kornhuber J, de Zwaan M, et al. Association of catecholamine-O-methyltransferase and 5-HTTLPR genotype with eating disorder-related behavior and attitudes in females with eating disorders. Psychiatr Genet. 2006;16(5):205–8.
110. Hersrud SL, Stoltenberg SF. Epistatic interaction between COMT and DAT1 genes on eating behavior: a pilot study. Eat Behav. 2009;10(2):131–3.
111. Annerbrink K, Westberg L, Nilsson S, Rosmond R, Holm G, Eriksson E. Catechol O-methyltransferase val158-met polymorphism is associated with abdominal obesity and blood pressure in men. Metabolism. 2008;57(5):708–11.

112. Kring SI, Werge T, Holst C, Toubro S, Astrup A, Hansen T, et al. Polymorphisms of serotonin receptor 2A and 2C genes and COMT in relation to obesity and type 2 diabetes. PLoS One. 2009;4(8):e6696.
113. Wang SS, Morton LM, Bergen AW, Lan EZ, Chatterjee N, Kvale P, et al. Genetic variation in catechol-O-methyltransferase (COMT) and obesity in the prostate, lung, colorectal, and ovarian (PLCO) cancer screening trial. Hum Genet. 2007;122(1):41–9.
114. Lachman HM, Papolos DF, Saito T, Yu YM, Szumlanski CL, Weinshilboum RM. Human catechol-O-methyltransferase pharmacogenetics: description of a functional polymorphism and its potential application to neuropsychiatric disorders. Pharmacogenetics. 1996;6(3):243–50.
115. Armellini F, Zamboni M, Bosello O. Hormones and body composition in humans: clinical studies. Int J Obes Relat Metab Disord. 2000;24 Suppl 2:S18–21.
116. McTernan PG, Anwar A, Eggo MC, Barnett AH, Stewart PM, Kumar S. Gender differences in the regulation of P450 aromatase expression and activity in human adipose tissue. Int J Obes Relat Metab Disord. 2000;24(7):875–81.
117. Montgomery H, Clarkson P, Barnard M, Bell J, Brynes A, Dollery C, et al. Angiotensin-converting-enzyme gene insertion/deletion polymorphism and response to physical training. Lancet. 1999;353(9152):541–5.
118. Rigat B, Hubert C, Alhenc-Gelas F, Cambien F, Corvol P, Soubrier F. An insertion/deletion polymorphism in the angiotensin I-converting enzyme gene accounting for half the variance of serum enzyme levels. J Clin Invest. 1990;86(4):1343–6.
119. Moran CN, Vassilopoulos C, Tsiokanos A, Jamurtas AZ, Bailey ME, Wilson RH, Pitsiladis YP. Effects of interaction between angiotensin I-converting enzyme polymorphisms and lifestyle on adiposity in adolescent greeks. Obes Res. 2005;13(9):1499–504.
120. Kritchevsky SB, Nicklas BJ, Visser M, Simonsick EM, Newman AB, Harris TB, et al. Angiotensin-converting enzyme insertion/deletion genotype, exercise, and physical decline. JAMA. 2005;294(6):691–8.
121. Virtanen KA, Lidell ME, Orava J, Heglind M, Westergren R, Niemi T, et al. Functional brown adipose tissue in healthy adults. N Engl J Med. 2009;360(15):1518–25.
122. Cypess AM, Lehman S, Williams G, Tal I, Rodman D, Goldfine AB, et al. Identification and importance of brown adipose tissue in adult humans. N Engl J Med. 2009;360(15):1509–17.
123. Dulloo AG, Samec S. Uncoupling proteins: their roles in adaptive thermogenesis and substrate metabolism reconsidered. Br J Nutr. 2001;86(2):123–39.
124. Otabe S, Clement K, Dina C, Pelloux V, Guy-Grand B, Froguel P, Vasseur F. A genetic variation in the 5' flanking region of the UCP3 gene is associated with body mass index in humans in interaction with physical activity. Diabetologia. 2000;43(2):245–9.
125. Lanouette CM, Chagnon YC, Rice T, Perusse L, Muzzin P, Giacobino JP, et al. Uncoupling protein 3 gene is associated with body composition changes with training in HERITAGE study. J Appl Physiol. 2002;92(3):1111–8.
126. Poirier P, Despres JP. Exercise in weight management of obesity. Cardiol Clin. 2001;19(3):459–70.
127. Martinez-Botas J, Anderson JB, Tessier D, Lapillonne A, Chang BH, Quast MJ, et al. Absence of perilipin results in leanness and reverses obesity in lepr(db/db) mice. Nat Genet. 2000;26(4):474–9.
128. Kanadys WM, Oleszczuk J. Pathophysiological aspects of adipose tissue development in women. Ginekol Pol. 1999;70(6):456–63.
129. Garenc C, Perusse L, Bergeron J, Gagnon J, Chagnon YC, Borecki IB, et al. Evidence of LPL gene-exercise interaction for body fat and LPL activity: The HERITAGE family study. J Appl Physiol. 2001;91(3):1334–40.
130. Reichman SE, Balasekaran G, Roth SM, Ferrell RE. Association of interleukin-15 protein and interleukin-15 receptor genetic variation with resistance exercise training responses. J Appl Physiol. 2004;97(6):2214–9.

131. Peters WR, MacMurry JP, Walker J, Giese Jr RJ, Comings DE. Phenylethanolamine N-methyltransferase G-148A genetic variant and weight loss in obese women. Obes Res. 2003;11(3):415–9.
132. Sun G, Gagnon J, Chagnon YC, Perusse L, Despres JP, Leon AS, et al. Association and linkage between an insulin-like growth factor-1 gene polymorphism and fat free mass in the HERITAGE family study. Int J Obes Relat Metab Disord. 1999;23(9):929–35.
133. Park S, Han T, Son T, Kang HS. PC-1 genotype and IRS response to exercise training. Int J Sports Med. 2008;29(4):294–9.
134. Pizzuti A, Frittitta L, Argiolas A, Baratta R, Goldfine ID, Bozzali M, et al. A polymorphism (K121Q) of the human glycoprotein PC-1 gene coding region is strongly associated with insulin resistance. Diabetes. 1999;48(9):1881–4.
135. Matsuoka N, Patki A, Tiwari HK, Allison DB, Johnson SB, Gregersen PK, et al. Association of K121Q polymorphism in ENPP1 (PC-1) with BMI in caucasian and african-american adults. Int J Obes (Lond). 2006;30(2):233–7.
136. Meyre D, Bouatia-Naji N, Tounian A, Samson C, Lecoeur C, Vatin V, et al. Variants of ENPP1 are associated with childhood and adult obesity and increase the risk of glucose intolerance and type 2 diabetes. Nat Genet. 2005;37(8):863–7.
137. Uthurralt J, Gordish-Dressman H, Bradbury M, Tesi-Rocha C, Devaney J, Harmon B, et al. PPARalpha L162V underlies variation in serum triglycerides and subcutaneous fat volume in young males. BMC Med Genet. 2007;8:55.
138. Bray MS. Implications of gene-behavior interactions: prevention and intervention for obesity. Obesity (Silver Spring). 2008;16 Suppl 3:S72–8.

Chapter 6

Interactive Effects of Genetics and Acute Exercise and Exercise Training on Plasma Lipoprotein-Lipid and Blood Pressure Phenotypes

James M. Hagberg

Keywords Exercise • Exercise training • Genetics • Genotype • Blood pressure • Plasma lipoprotein-lipids • Cholesterol • Angiotensin converting enzyme • Angiotensinogen • Apolipoprotein E • Cholesteryl ester transfer protein

Introduction

Plasma lipoprotein-lipid levels and blood pressure (BP) were among the first risk factors identified for cardiovascular (CV) disease. Since then they have remained a major focus for CV disease prevention. Plasma lipoprotein-lipid and BP profiles clearly vary substantially among individuals, with some having very low risk BP and plasma lipoprotein-lipid profiles, with others having BP and plasma lipoprotein-lipids associated with high risk for CV disease. A portion of this interindividual variation in plasma lipoprotein-lipid levels and BP is clearly the result of environmental factors. However, substantial research over the last 2–3 decades indicates genetic factors also contribute to the differences among individuals in these critical CV disease risk factors [1].

More recently, it has also become evident that the responses of plasma lipoprotein-lipids and BP to even a highly standardized endurance training program vary substantially among individuals. For example, in the 675 participants in the *HE*ealth, *RI*sk factors, exercise *TrA*ining and *GE*netics or HERITAGE Family Study, Leon et al. reported an overall significant 3.6% increase in plasma high-density lipoprotein cholesterol (HDL-C) levels with exercise training [1]. However, the lowest 25% of responders actually experienced a 9.3% average *decrease*, while the highest quartile of responders had an 18% average *increase*, in plasma HDL-C levels with training. In our laboratory in response to a highly standardized 26 weeks exercise training program

J.M. Hagberg (✉)
Department of Kinesiology, School of Public Health, University of Maryland,
College Park, MD 20742-2611, USA
e-mail: Hagberg@umd.edu

L.S. Pescatello and S.M. Roth (eds.), *Exercise Genomics*,
Molecular and Translational Medicine, DOI 10.1007/978-1-60761-355-8_6,
© Springer Science+Business Media, LLC 2011

combined with a low-fat isocaloric diet, we also found substantial variability in the changes in both BP and the different components of the plasma lipoprotein-lipid profile [2–4]. For example, in terms of HDL-C changes with training, we saw an overall significant 3.3 ± 0.5 mg/dL increase with training; however, the range of individual changes was again substantial, with ~33% of individuals actually decreasing or not changing their plasma HDL-C levels with exercise training, while another ~33% each increased his or her HDL-C levels with training by >7 mg/dL (Fig. 6.1). We also found substantial interindividual variation in systolic BP changes with exercise training in hypertensives or prehypertensives (Fig. 6.2) with a majority of them decreasing their systolic BP with training although a significant proportion saw no change or an actual increase with training. Similar interindividual variability in the response of diastolic BP to exercise training was also evident in these same individuals. In the last 10 years, it has also become evident that genetic variations account for some of the interindividual differences in the responses of virtually all CV disease risk factors to exercise training. The purpose of this chapter is to summarize all of the previous English literature relative to the genetic basis for the interindividual differences in plasma lipoprotein-lipid profile and BP responses to exercise training.

Thus, there are clearly substantial interindividual differences in baseline lipoprotein-lipid and BP and in their responses to exercise training. This is a critical initial step when attempting to assess whether a phenotype may have some genetic

Fig. 6.1 Individual data for the changes in HDL-C with a highly standardized 26-week exercise training intervention while participants were maintained relatively weight stable on an isocaloric low-fat diet. Each *vertical bar* indicates the response of a single individual, with those experiencing the smallest increases in HDL-C with training (which are actually decreases) on the *left* and those demonstrating the largest HDL-C increases with training on the *right* of the x-axis (unpublished data from Hagberg)

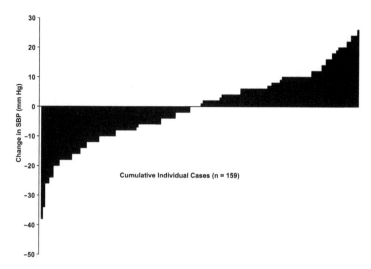

Fig. 6.2 Individual data for the changes in systolic BP with a highly standardized 26-week exercise training intervention while participants were maintained relatively weight stable on an isocaloric low-fat diet. Each *vertical bar* indicates the response of a single individual, with those experiencing the largest decreases in systolic BP with training on the *left* and those demonstrating the smallest systolic BP decreases with training (which were actually increases in systolic BP with training) on the *right* of the x-axis (unpublished data from Hagberg)

underpinnings because if there is no, or minimal, interindividual variability, there is little reason to assess any potential genetic basis for that phenotype. The next step in attempting to identify the genetic basis underlying any phenotype is to determine if the trait is heritable. If the trait is heritable, this suggests that genetic variations passed from one generation to the next within a family might account for at least a portion of the interindividual variation in that phenotype.

Heritability of Resting Plasma Lipoprotein-Lipid and Blood Pressure Levels

Numerous studies over the past 2–3 decades have quantified the heritability of the different components of the plasma lipoprotein-lipid profile. It appears that the first study on the genetics of plasma lipoprotein-lipid levels in humans was by Heiberg in 1974 [5]. He studied 50 pairs of young normolipidemic twins and found heritability values of 0.24–0.79 for a range of components of the plasma lipoprotein-lipid profile, many of which have been renamed and are now isolated via much different methods. In a follow-up to this study 2 years later, Weinberg et al. [6] used newer methods for that time to also quantify heritability of plasma lipoprotein-lipid levels. In fact, they used the data from the previous Heiberg study and with these newer methods found the heritability values ranged from 0.06 to

0.84, with some of the values increasing and some decreasing from the initial estimates provided by Heiberg [5].

Namboodiri et al. [7] conducted one of the first large studies assessing the heritability of plasma lipoprotein-lipid levels in 1983. They found the heritability of plasma HDL-C levels in the Lipid Research Clinic (LRC) cohort to be 0.2–0.3, which was within the range for heritability previously reported for plasma HDL-C levels. A year later, a second study in ~5,000 whites from the LRC cohort, Namboodiri et al. [8] reported plasma total and low-density lipoprotein cholesterol (LDL-C) had significant within-family correlations, whereas triglycerides (TG) and very-low-density lipoprotein cholesterol (VLDL-C) generally did not. In a much smaller set of blacks (~320), they found some within-family correlations for total and LDL-C, but again not for TG or VLDL-C. A third LRC study another year later reported heritability of 0.56, 0.54, 0.49, and 0.36 for total cholesterol, LDL-C, HDL-C, and TG levels, respectively, in ~5,100 Caucasian individuals from 1,336 families [9].

Claude Bouchard's HERITAGE Family Study also quantified the heritability of baseline plasma lipoprotein-lipids and found values of 0.62, 0.83, 0.50, and 0.55 for total cholesterol, HDL-C, LDL-C, and TG levels, respectively [10]. A recent study from Framingham also reported very high levels of heritability of 0.66, 0.69, and 0.58 for plasma LDL-C, HDL-C, and TG, respectively [11]. Interestingly, these high levels of heritability were based on long-term averages of plasma lipoprotein-lipid measures, in fact up to 30-year averages, which would clearly result in a more stable phenotype that would be influenced to a substantially lesser degree by measurement errors and environmental variability. In fact, in this study the heritability of these plasma lipoprotein-lipid levels were somewhat lower, ranging from 0.48 to 0.59, when the relationships were based on single time point measurements.

Blood Pressure

Numerous studies over the past 20 years have assessed the heritability of BP. These studies generally find heritability for systolic, diastolic, and mean BP to be in the range of 0.20–0.50 [12, 13]. For example, in 2005 Mitchell et al. reported a heritability of 0.33 for mean BP in ~1,500 individuals from 204 Framingham families [14]. DeStefano et al. [15] found heritability of 0.51 for pulse pressure in ~6,400 individuals from ~1,600 Framingham families. More recently, de Oliveira et al. [13] reported heritability of 0.26 for systolic and diastolic BP in ~1,700 individuals from 81 Brazilian families after accounting for the effects of other covariates.

Thus, a large and ever increasing body of literature has found substantial heritability for the different components of the plasma lipoprotein-lipid profile and for BP. Since it is clear that these critical CV disease risk factors are heritable, the next step is to identify the genetic loci that might underlie these phenotypes.

Genome-Wide Linkage and Association Studies for Resting Plasma Lipoprotein-Lipids and Blood Pressure Levels

One method for identifying the chromosomal loci underlying a phenotype is to perform a genome-wide linkage or association study. The initial studies of this type were completed 2–3 decades ago and assessed linkage in families between specific phenotypes and general chromosomal loci using 400–800 polymorphic markers across the genome. Today, 500k/1M, and some even larger, single nucleotide polymorphisms (SNP) chips are used for this purpose, allowing genome-wide association studies (GWAS) to be undertaken in large populations.

Lipoprotein-Lipid

The first linkage or association study for plasma lipoprotein-lipid levels appears to have been published in 1992 in which Nishina et al. [16] assessed five different genetic markers in a likely "candidate" region in 51 relatives of nine probands who had what at the time was called an "atherogenic lipoprotein phenotype." They found one locus within the LDL receptor (*LDLR*) gene demonstrated a logarithm of differences (LOD) of ~4.2 for this phenotype. In what appears to be the first genome-wide linkage study for plasma lipoprotein-lipid levels, Rainwater et al. [17] in 1999 assessed 331 microsatellite markers and various measures relative to small LDL-C particles in 470 Hispanic-Americans. They first found heritability values of 0.22–0.37 for the four LDL size fractions they assessed and 0.54 for total LDL-C. Rainwater et al. [17] also found two chromosomal loci linked with varying plasma levels of small LDL particles (chromosome (chr) 3 at 244 cM, chr 4 at 126 cM, both LOD = 4.11) with genes coding for apolipoprotein D and microsomal TG transfer protein lying adjacent to these loci. In 2000, Shearman et al. [18] reported heritabilities of 0.40 and 0.49 for plasma TG and TG/HDL-C ratio, respectively, among the largest 332 families in the Framingham population. They then typed 399 microsatellite markers and found the highest linkages (LOD 1.8–2.5) for these two lipid phenotypes at chromosomal locus 7q32.3. Also in 2000, Imperatore et al. [19] reported linkages after typing 516 microsatellite markers in 998 siblings from 292 Pima Indian nuclear families. The strongest linkage for cholesterol levels was on chromosome 19p (LOD = 3.89), for HDL-C levels 3q (LOD = 2.64), and for TG 2p (LOD = 1.70) and 3p (LOD = 1.77).

More recently, Sandhu et al. [20] genotyped ~290,000 SNPs on ~11,700 subjects across five studies, as well as a replication cohort of ~5,000 subjects, to assess genome-wide associations with plasma LDL-C levels. In their initial scan, they found two highly significant SNPs at 1p13.3 (both $p < 3 \times 10^{-11}$). In the replication group, another SNP at the same locus had a $p < 4.3 \times 10^{-9}$. Pooling the results showed two of these SNPs had $p < 1 \times 10^{-20}$ and explained ~1% of the interindividual variation in plasma LDL-C levels. In a Japanese population of 900 men and women, Hiura et al. [21] genotyped ~370,000 SNPs to quantify associations with plasma

HDL-C levels. They found 43 SNPs with LOD scores >4.0 and the highest LOD score was evident at a SNP in close proximity to the cholesteryl ester transfer protein (*CETP*) gene (LOD = 6.17). This locus was replicated in a follow-up sample of 1,810 men and women genotyped for the 22 SNPs with the highest LOD scores in the initial GWAS. Importantly, plasma HDL-C levels increased by 6.2 mg/dL for each minor allele an individual carried at the *CETP* locus.

Blood Pressure

Numerous studies have identified chromosomal loci that are linked or associated with resting BP. In what appears to be the first genome-wide linkage study for BP in humans, Rice et al. [22] genotyped 420 markers across the genome in 125 randomly selected and 81 obese Quebec families. In the combined sample, they found loci on chromosomes 1, 2, 3, 5, 7, 14, and 19 that were linked with systolic BP at $p < {\sim}0.01$; however, they found only minimal linkages for diastolic BP in this population. In the same year, Levy et al. [23] genotyped a genome-wide polymorphic set of markers in 1,585 individuals from 332 families from Framingham. For systolic BP, they found two highly significant linkages on chromosome 17 (67 cM, LOD = 4.7; 94 cM, LOD = 2.2) and two significant linkages for diastolic BP (chr 17 74 cM, LOD = 2.1; chr 18 7 cM, LOD = 2.1). In 2004, DeStefano et al. [15] reported linkage at four chromosomal loci for pulse pressure in the Framingham population (chr 15 122 cM, LOD = 2.94; chr 7 71 cM, LOD = 2.42; chr 5 53 cM, LOD = 2.03; chr 10 81 cM, LOD = 1.83). Also from Framingham, in a GWAS Levy et al. [24] in 2007 identified seven SNPs that had $p < 1 \times 10^{-5}$ for their relationships with systolic and diastolic BP, with the two strongest loci having $p = 3.3 \times 10^{-6}$ and 1.7×10^{-6}. In a more recent study, Adeyemo et al. [12] assessed ~800,000 SNPs in African Americans. The ten best associations had $p < 1.12 \times 10^{-6}$ for systolic BP, $p < 4.47 \times 10^{-6}$ for diastolic BP, and $p < 1.03 \times 10^{-5}$ for hypertension. Newton-Chen et al. [25] recently assessed 2.5 million SNPs in ~34,000 Europeans and in three additional replication cohorts totaling ~110,000 individuals. They found eight loci associated with either systolic or diastolic BP with $p < 1 \times 10^{-8}$. While the results of these five examples are very promising, it is also important to keep in mind that the first two GWAS for BP-related phenotypes [26, 27] did not identify significant relationships with *any* chromosomal loci. Furthermore, even the SNPs found to replicate relationships with BP account for only a small proportion of the interindividual variation in BP.

Thus, genome-wide linkage and association studies have identified several chromosomal loci related to different components of the plasma lipoprotein-lipid profile and BP levels. However, in general, these studies have not identified novel genes that have subsequently been shown to play a powerful role in determining these phenotypes, perhaps because there are a substantial number of genes involved in the regulation of BP and each of them plays only a minimal role, making them very hard to detect and substantiate.

Candidate Gene Association Studies of Resting Plasma Lipoprotein-Lipid Levels and Blood Pressure Levels

The majority of studies relating genes to plasma lipoprotein-lipid and BP pheno-types are candidate gene association studies. The first of these studies was pub-lished ~30 years ago, and it capitalized on the recent development, at that time, of relatively time- and cost-efficient assays for single SNPs [26]. As a result, it became possible to genotype a small number of SNPs in cohorts with measured phenotypes. Genes and SNPs were selected as "candidates" because they could plausibly be proposed to impact the phenotype of interest. Examples of such candidates would be the lipoprotein lipase (*LPL*) or *CETP* genes for plasma lipoprotein-lipid levels or the genes within the renin-angiotensin (angiotensin converting enzyme [ACE], angiotensinogen [AGT]) or adrenergic (various adrenergic-responsive receptors) systems for BP phenotypes.

Lipoprotein-Lipid

Numerous studies in the last 25 years have investigated the effect of specific candi-date gene variants on different components of the plasma lipoprotein-lipid profile. In fact, a PubMed search for the phrase "genotype and lipids in humans" on 15 February 2010 resulted in >10,000 citations. Thus, there is clearly a very long list of candidate SNPs that have been significantly associated with different components of the plasma lipoprotein-lipid profile. It is beyond the scope of this review to address this issue in detail. Thus, only the results relative to two genes that appear to have the largest effect on plasma lipoprotein-lipid levels will be summarized briefly as examples. These two genes are apolipoprotein E (*APOE*), which codes for a protein that binds to receptors in the liver to mediate VLDL and chylomicron clearance from the bloodstream, and *CETP*, which codes for an enzyme that enhances the exchange of cholesteryl esters between various components of the plasma lipoprotein-lipid profile. These biological actions would clearly make these genes plausible candi-dates to affect components of the plasma lipoprotein-lipid profile.

Apolipoprotein E (APOE)

The *APOE* gene was first hypothesized by Havekes et al. [28] in 1980 to affect plasma lipoprotein-lipid levels in a case study of a woman with homozygous familial hypercholesterolemia. In that same year, Utermann et al. [29] reported on the genetics of *APOE* polymorphisms. This gene has remained at the forefront of potential lipid candidate genes as best exemplified by a PubMed search conducted on 15 February 2010 for the search phrase "*APOE* genotype and lipids and humans" that resulted in ~4,200 citations. A classic 1985 paper by Sing and Davignon [30] reported common variations at the *APOE* gene locus accounted for as much as 16% of the genetic variance, and 8% of the total variance, in plasma LDL-C levels in normolipidemic Canadians, with the E2 allele decreasing and E4 allele increasing plasma cholesterol and LDL-C levels. A second study by this group found each E2 allele reduced plasma cholesterol levels by 18 mg/dL and each E4 allele increased them by 9 mg/dL compared to APOE E3/E3 individuals, resulting in a difference of ~50 mg/dL between E2 and E4 homozygotes [31].

A 2007 meta-analysis by Bennet et al. [32] used a final data set based on 82 studies with *APOE* genotype and plasma lipoprotein-lipid data. They found those with the *APOE* E2/E2 genotype had 44 and 31 mg/dL lower plasma LDL-C and total cholesterol levels, respectively, and ~3 mg/dL higher plasma HDL-C levels than those with the *APOE* E4/E4 genotype. These authors indicated the magnitude of these lipid-lipoprotein *APOE* genotype dependent differences were similar to those resulting from a statin medication. Relative to more common APOE genotypes (i.e., E3/E3, E4/E4), they found individuals with the *APOE* E2/E3 genotype had 20 and 17 mg/dL lower plasma LDL-C and total cholesterol levels, respectively, and ~3 mg/dL higher plasma HDL-C levels than individuals with the APOE E3/4 genotype. Overall there was a negative relationship between the number of E2 alleles, and a positive relationship between the number of E4 alleles, and plasma LDL-C levels. Thus a substantial evidence base clearly indicates *APOE* genotype is probably one of the strongest predictors of plasma lipoprotein-lipid levels.

Cholesteryl Ester Transfer Protein (CETP)

The *CETP* gene appears to have been first investigated by Koizumi et al. [33] in 1985 in a case study of a Japanese male with familial hyperalphalipoproteinemia. In fact, the mutation present in this individual resulted in a complete deficiency of serum CETP activity, and the individual had a plasma HDL-C level of 301 mg/dL. This report was followed by numerous similar case studies where the level of CETP activity was strongly and negatively associated with plasma HDL-C and HDL_2-C levels. Not surprisingly, none of the cases in these studies with an absolute or relative CETP activity deficiency had any evidence of CV disease in their family history. A recent meta-analysis by Thompson et al. [34] summarized the results of 92 studies assessing the impact of *CETP* genotype on plasma lipoprotein-lipid levels. Based on results from ~114,000 individuals across these studies, they concluded that for each A allele a person had at the *CETP* Taq1B locus, their plasma HDL-C levels were ~6% higher than common (G allele) homozygote individuals. Somewhat smaller effects on plasma HDL-C levels were evident as a function of the number of rare alleles present at the *CETP* I405V and C-629A loci. Some effects of these different genotypes were also evident on other components of the plasma lipoprotein-lipid profile, but the effects were not as substantial and were less consistent. Thus, common SNPs at the *CETP* locus also appear to have substantial effects on a person's plasma HDL-C levels.

Interactive Lipoprotein-Lipid Gene Effects

These studies investigating the impact of single genes, and often times only one SNP, on plasma lipoprotein-lipid levels are clearly over-simplistic, as these pheno-types are obviously influenced by numerous genes. A small number of studies have assessed the impact of multiple genes and genetic variations on the different com-ponents of the plasma lipoprotein-lipid profile. The first of these appears to be an investigation by Heiba et al. [35] from a large pedigree within the Bogalusa Heart Study. They found on a univariate basis, i.e., when the impact of each gene was assessed independently without accounting for the effects of other genes, the *CETP*, *LPL*, haptoglobin (*HP*), and apolipoprotein B (*APOB*) genes had significant effects on plasma LDL-C, HDL-C, VLDL-C, and TG levels. While this study rep-resents an important step forward, it is limited because these genes do not function independently, but are highly dependent and influenced by other genes involved in the metabolism of plasma lipoprotein-lipids.

In 2002, Knoblauch et al. [36] took these candidate gene association studies to a new level by using differential equations to model the impact of six lipid metabolism-related genes on plasma lipoprotein-lipid profiles in 732 individuals from 184 German families. On a univariate basis, they found haplotypes within the *CETP*, *LPL*, *APOE*, *LDLR*, and hepatic lipase (*LIPC*) genes all significantly influenced various components of the plasma lipoprotein-lipid profile. When haplotypes in all genes were included in the same model, the models were highly significant and accounted for more variability than when only single genes were considered for HDL-C and LDL-C, but not for TG and total cholesterol, with *APOE* genotype having an especially strong effect. In a follow-up study, the same group investigated the effects of SNPs and haplotypes in 13 lipid metabolism-related genes on plasma lipoprotein-lipid profiles in 1,054 individuals from 250 German families [37]. They concluded that the 13 selected genes accounted for 67% of the genetic variance in plasma LDL-C levels and 58% for HDL-C. Furthermore, for LDL-C, *APOE* geno-type accounted for 33% of the total genetic variance with *CETP*, *LIPC*, *APOB*, and *LDLR* accounting for another 17, 7, 6, and 3%, respectively. For HDL-C, *LIPC*, *CETP*, ATPase binding cassette A1 (*ABCA1*), *LPL*, and *LDLR* accounted for 30, 15, 6, 4, and 4%, respectively. Thus, these genes highly relevant to plasma lipoprotein-lipid metabolism appear to explain a very large percent of the overall variation among individuals and a majority of the total variance attributed to genetic factors.

Blood Pressure

Angiotensin Converting Enzyme (ACE)

The first large scale studies that assessed candidate gene associations with BP investigated hypertension relative to *ACE* genotype. In 1991, Jacob et al. [38] iden-tified a locus containing the *ACE* gene that was linked to hypertension, and Nara et al. [39] found an *ACE* gene microsatellite cosegregated with BP, with both studies done in spontaneously hypertensive rats. In 1992, Zee et al. [40] and in 1993, Harrap et al. [41] reported a 287 base pair (bp) insertion (I)/deletion (D) in the *ACE* gene associated with hypertension in humans. Although this variant is intronic, it does alter plasma ACE activity levels and, thus, may well play a functional role [42]. *ACE* has remained a high profile BP candidate gene as evidenced by a recent PubMed search for "*ACE* genotype and hypertension" that resulted in 716 citations. While results are not completely consistent, this variant has been shown to be related to a wide range of CV phenotypes, including physiological, structural, and pathological outcomes.

Angiotensinogen (AGT)

An M>T substitution at bp 235 in the *AGT* gene appears to be the second genetic variant studied relative to BP phenotypes. In 1992, Jeunemaitre et al. [43] reported a highly significant association between this variant and hypertension in Caucasians. This was followed in 1993–1994 by similar reports by Bennett et al. [44] in severe familial hypertension, Hata et al. [45] in Japanese hypertensives, and Hegele et al. [46] in a Canadian isolate group. The M>T *AGT* 235 variant has also been shown to affect plasma AGT levels [43]. A recent PubMed search generated 261 citations for "*AGT* genotype and hypertension." In addition to these two BP candidate genes that have been studied intensely, there have been a large number of other candidate genes/SNPs that have been investigated relative to BP, e.g., aldosterone synthase (*CYP11B2*), angiotensin II type 1 receptor (*AGTR1*).

Thus, there is a growing body of literature that provides substantial and replicated evidence of at least two key genes (*APOE* and *CETP*) that contribute in a quantitative fashion to the interindividual variations in the different components of the plasma lipoprotein-lipid profile. Furthermore, another substantial body of literature has shown that two key genes (*ACE* and *AGT*) involved in BP regulation also appear to be statistically and quantitatively important in terms of interindividual variations in BP.

Heritability of Blood Pressure Responses to Acute Interventions

While the genetics underlying resting phenotypes are important to understand, physiologists would much rather study the genetics of the *response* of different phenotypes to interventions. Plasma lipoprotein-lipid profiles respond only very minimally to acute exercise, unless it is of very long duration; thus, this review will not concern itself with these responses. Recently, a small number of studies have begun to quantify the heritability of BP responses to acute (i.e., immediate or short-term) interventions. Gu et al. [47] quantified the heritability of BP responses to altered Na$^+$ and K$^+$ intake. Heritability for baseline BP was 0.31–0.34; and the heritability of the BP measures increased to 0.47–0.53 after the interventions.

The BP responses to the dietary interventions also had relatively high heritability, ranging from 0.20 to 0.33. Roy-Gagnon et al. [48] in extended Amish families found heritability of 0.14–0.27 for systolic and diastolic BP responses to and during recovery from a cold pressor test.

Unfortunately, relatively few studies have assessed the heritability of BP responses to acute exercise. In one of the first such studies in 1989, Hunt et al. [49] found heritability of 0.32 and 0.42 for systolic and diastolic BP, respectively, during cycle ergometer exercise, and 0.19 and 0.35 for systolic and diastolic BP, respectively, during isometric hand grip. However, in 1991 Bielen et al. [50] found BP responses during supine cycle ergometer exercise to be only minimally heritable. Ingelsson et al. [51] from Framingham found systolic and diastolic BP responses during exercise and recovery had heritability of 0.13–0.26. In a smaller subset of the Framingham study, Vasan et al. [52] reported heritability was 0.16–0.40 for systolic and diastolic BP during and after a treadmill exercise test.

These data represent the entire body of literature on the heritability of BP responses to acute exercise. These data clearly do not quantify the heritable aspects of anywhere near all of the BP responses to the numerous forms of acute exercise. However, they generally show that the BP responses to acute exercise are moderately heritable with estimates ranging from 0.13 to 0.42.

Heritability of Plasma Lipoprotein-Lipid and Blood Pressure Responses to Exercise Training

The next question to address in this progression is whether the plasma lipoprotein-lipid and BP responses to more long-term exercise training are heritable. Unfortunately, again, very few studies have addressed this issue. In fact, only the HERITAGE Family Study has an appropriate sample size and study design to assess the heritability of these responses to endurance exercise training. HERITAGE Family Study investigators [53] implemented a highly standardized 20-week endurance exercise training intervention in sedentary individuals in 113 black and 99 white two-generation families.

In the first such study published in 2000, An et al. [54] provided some evidence that the plasma apolipoprotein A-1 (APOA1) and B-100 responses to exercise training were heritable in the white HERITAGE families. In 2000, Hong et al. [55] in the second such study from HERITAGE reported the heritability of the changes in TG and postheparin LPL activity with exercise training in the white families to be 0.22 and 0.15, respectively. In an impressive study from HERITAGE in 2002, Rice et al. [56] assessed the heritability of the responses of a number of components of the plasma lipoprotein-lipid profile to exercise training in white and black families (Table 6.1). Of the changes in eight different components of the plasma lipoprotein-lipid profile they measured with training in blacks and whites, only the change in LDL-C with training in blacks was not significantly heritable. Virtually all of the heritability values were in the range of 0.25–0.38, except for the change in HDL_2-C

Table 6.1 Heritability of the responses of plasma lipoprotein-lipid levels to exercise training in the HERITAGE Family Study

Group	Cholesterol	TG	LDL-C	ApoB	HDL-C	ApoA-1	HDL$_2$-C	HDL$_2$-C
White families	0.29	0.39	0.34	0.26	0.29	0.33	0.64	0.31
Black families	0.32	0.32	----	0.59	0.26	0.38	0.29	0.25

Adapted from Rice et al. [56]
--- indicates not significantly heritable

in whites ($h=0.64$) and the change in ApoB in blacks ($h=0.59$). In another study from HERITAGE, Feitosa et al. [57] reported heritability of 0.18–0.49 for the changes with exercise training in ten different components of the plasma lipoprotein-lipid profile in whites (all $p<0.05$), while in blacks eight of the ten changes with training were heritable ($h=0.25$–0.59, all $p<0.05$), although in blacks two components were not significantly heritable ($h=0.14$ for ΔLDL-C, 0.21 for ΔApoA-1).

Rice et al. [58] in another report from HERITAGE found systolic and diastolic BP changes at rest following exercise training had heritability of 0.14–0.24. However, in those with normal BP only diastolic BP was heritable ($h=0.19$), whereas in the elevated BP group only systolic BP responses to training were heritable ($h=0.20$). An et al. [59] also reported heritability in the white HERITAGE families of 0.22 for the change in systolic BP during submaximal exercise with exercise training.

Thus, very little is known about the heritability of the plasma lipoprotein-lipid and BP responses to endurance training. Clearly, substantially more studies are required to provide the data necessary to verify that all of these responses to training are heritable. However, the available data all consistently demonstrate that, at least for the limited plasma lipoprotein-lipid and BP phenotypes studied to date, these responses are moderately heritable. This provides a strong rationale to pursue more detailed studies to identify the specific genetic loci underlying this heritability.

Genome-Wide Linkage and Association Studies of Plasma Lipoprotein-Lipid and Blood Pressure Responses to Acute Exercise and Exercise Training

Acute Blood Pressure Studies

Not surprisingly, relatively few studies have assessed genome-wide linkage or association of chromosomal loci with BP responses to acute exercise. Furthermore, as is true for the other phenotypes discussed above, most of the data on BP responses to acute exercise are from the HERITAGE Family Study. In the first genome-wide linkage results from HERITAGE for CV phenotypes during exercise, Rankinen et al. [60] in 2001 found linkage for submaximal exercise systolic BP in the sedentary state in whites at chromosomal locus 10q23-q24, while in blacks two loci were identified for submaximal exercise diastolic BP (11q13-q21, 18p11.2). They also identified seven loci with "suggestive" evidence for linkage with submaximal exercise BP in whites and another 11 in blacks. A number of years later, Vasan et al. [52] assessed ~71,000 SNPs in the Framingham population and found two SNPs on chromosomes 8 and 11 that were associated with exercise and recovery BP with $p < 4.88 \times 10^{-6}$.

Exercise Training Studies

Very few studies have assessed genome-wide linkage or association with plasma lipoprotein-lipid or BP responses to exercise training. In terms of plasma lipoprotein-lipid responses to exercise training, it appears only two studies have assessed genome-wide linkage and both are from the HERITAGE Family Study [61, 62]. In the first such study published in 2005, Feitosa et al. [62] assessed 654 polymorphic markers across the genome in relation to plasma LDL-C levels at baseline and their changes with 20 weeks of exercise training. Although they found a number of strong linkages (LOD > 2.5) for various baseline LDL measures, they found no linkages for training-induced changes in any of these LDL phenotypes. In a second study published in 2006, Feitosa and HERITAGE coworkers [60] also found no significant bivariate linkages for the change in TG with exercise training, again despite the fact they found strong bivariate linkages in the sedentary state prior to exercise training. This study accounted for training-induced changes in BMI, total body fat mass, % body fat, and abdominal subcutaneous skinfold thickness.

Rankinen et al. [60] in 2001 presented the first complete genome-wide linkage study for BP responses to exercise training. They found one locus linked to the training-induced change in submaximal exercise systolic BP in whites (8q21), while in blacks the training-induced change in submaximal exercise diastolic BP was linked to 10q21-q23. Numerous linkages with "suggestive" evidence were found for the training-induced changes in submaximal exercise BP. In 2002, Rice et al. [63] from HERITAGE found very few suggestive or promising linkages for the change in resting BP following exercise training.

Thus, it appears that only four studies have assessed genome-wide linkage for plasma lipoprotein-lipid and BP responses to exercise training, and only one of these four studies found *any* significant linkages for these important CV disease risk factor responses to training. Also, no GWAS utilizing large SNP chips have yet been done for these phenotypes, which may be a major reason why no likely candidate loci have yet been identified for these phenotype responses to exercise training. Clearly, substantially more studies are required to potentially identify novel chromosomal loci that are robustly linked with these CV disease risk factor responses to exercise training.

Candidate Gene Studies of Blood Pressure Responses to Acute Exercise

Candidate gene studies, once again, provide most of our knowledge relative to the genetics of BP responses to acute exercise. By the end of 2009, it appears 23 studies reporting significant results have addressed this issue [64]. Just as for candidate gene studies for resting BP, the *ACE* gene variant is the most frequently, and was the first polymorphism, studied relative to BP responses to exercise [64]. To date five studies have assessed the impact of the *ACE* variant on BP responses to exercise. In the first such study in 1996, Friedl et al. [65] found that diastolic BP during and following exercise varied by *ACE* genotype with DD, ID, and II individuals having maximal exercise diastolic BP of 93 ± 10, 85 ± 10, and 82 ± 8 mmHg, respectively, with there also being a dose-dependent reduction in diastolic BP evident during recovery as a function of the number of ACE I alleles an individual carried. Two studies from another group [66, 67] have found significant effects of the *ACE* variant on ambulatory systolic and diastolic BP following submaximal exercise as a function of genotype, Ca^{2+} intake, and exercise intensity. The final two studies, both from Framingham [51, 52], found associations between *ACE* genotype and BP during exercise and recovery, but the direction and magnitude of the effects could not be ascertained.

The effects of only three other genes on BP responses to acute exercise have been assessed in more than a single study (*AGT*, adrenergic receptor beta 2 [*ADRB2*], and endothelial nitric oxide synthase [*NOS3*]). Four studies have reported significant effects of the *AGT* M235T variant on BP responses to exercise [64]. In the first study, Krizanova et al. [68] in 1998 found diastolic BP during exercise was lower in *AGT* TT individuals, but there was no effect on systolic BP. In 1999–2000, two HERITAGE studies by Rankinen et al. [69, 70] reported no overall effect of *AGT* M235T genotype on exercise BP. However, in white men performing maximal exercise, Rankinen et al. [69] reported diastolic BP was significantly higher by 6–9 mmHg in *AGT* TT individuals. In two studies from Framingham [51, 52], significant associations were found between *AGT* genotypes and BP during exercise and recovery, but it was not possible to quantify the effect.

Another plausible mechanism that could affect BP responses to exercise would be the sympathetic nervous system, especially the adrenergic receptor (*ADR*) genes. In fact, genetic variations in a number of *ADR* alpha and beta genes have been assessed in this regard [64]. However, one study assessed the impact of an *ADRA2B* variant, one investigated an *ADRB1* variant, and two assessed *ADRB2* variants. Furthermore, half of these studies assessed the impact of these *ADR* variants on BP responses to isometric handgrip rather than endurance exercise. Again, two studies from Framingham [51, 52] found significant associations between *ADRA1A*, *ADRA1B*, *ADRA1D*, and *ADRB2* genetic variations and BP during exercise and recovery.

The nitric oxide (NO) pathway is another mechanism that regulates BP responses to exercise. Kim et al. [71] reported that Korean *NOS3* 894T allele carriers were significantly less likely to develop a hypertensive response to maximal exercise.

A second study [72] reported that C allele carriers at the *NOS3* T-786C locus had significantly lower systolic BP during ambulatory recordings following submaximal exercise.

The remainder of the genes studied and found to be significantly related to BP responses to acute exercise is from single studies that have not been replicated [64, 73]. These genes include adenosine monophosphate deaminase 1 (*AMPD1*), adducin 1 (*ADD1*), *AGTR1*, endothelin 1 (*EDN1*), guanine nucleotide binding protein beta polypeptide 3 (*GNB3*), angiogenin ribonuclease (*ANG*), solute carrier family 4, sodium bicarbonate cotransporter, member 5 (*SLC4A5*), and transforming growth factor beta 1 (*TGFB1*) genes. These genes clearly span a wide array of plausible pathways that could affect BP responses to acute exercise. However, since each of these genes has only been assessed in a single study and the results have not been replicated, it is obviously premature to draw any conclusions from them at this point.

Thus, in summary, the most frequently studied genes with respect to BP responses to acute exercise are the *ACE*, *AGT*, *ADR*, and *NOS3* genes. The best conclusion at this point is that common variants in these genes appear to affect BP responses to acute exercise. However, it is not possible at this time to generate a more precise conclusion because the very small number of studies that have addressed this issue have small sample sizes and small numbers of polymorphisms. In addition, these studies have measured different BP phenotypes in response to different types and amounts of exercise.

Candidate Gene Studies of Plasma Lipoprotein-Lipid and Blood Pressure Responses to Exercise Training

Lipoprotein-Lipids

There are relatively few studies that have assessed the impact of genetic variants on plasma lipoprotein-lipid responses to exercise training. The latest version of the Human Gene Map for Performance and Health-Related Fitness Phenotypes: The 2006–2007 Update [64] indicated there were only 26 exercise training studies that had reported significant genotype-dependent effects. Since then it appears that another five studies have been published addressing this issue. While 31 studies may seem like a substantial evidence base from which to derive robust conclusions, it should be kept in mind that these studies assessed the impact of 14 different genes. Thus, there is currently not very much replicated data available to support very strong conclusions for most of these genes.

Similar to other candidate gene studies addressing plasma lipoprotein-lipid phenotypes, the two most studied genes relative to training-induced plasma lipoprotein-lipid changes are *APOE* and *CETP*, with 12 studies assessing the impact of *APOE* and four quantifying the effect of *CETP*. Following these two most popular genes, there are only three other genes that have been the focus of more than a single study (*LPL*, *LIPC*, *LIPG*).

Apolipoprotein E (APOE)

Taimela et al. [74] in 1996 were the first to provide evidence of a potential genotype-dependent effect of exercise training on plasma lipoprotein-lipids for *APOE*. In young Finns, they found that habitual physical activity levels and plasma lipoprotein-lipids were not related in *APOE* E4/4 males, were moderately related in *APOE* E3/4 and 3/3 males, and were strongly associated with plasma lipoprotein-lipid levels in *APOE* E2/3 males. St-Amand et al. [75] reported generally similar findings in a second cross-sectional study concluding *APOE* E2 carriers may be especially responsive to exercise training in terms of plasma lipoprotein-lipids. Conversely, in another cross-sectional study, Bernstein et al. [76] reported plasma lipoprotein-lipid levels were related to the amount of high intensity physical activity in middle-aged men and women who were carriers of *APOE* E4 but not *APOE* E2. In another cross-sectional study, Corella et al. [77] found a significant *APOE* genotype × physical activity interaction, with *APOE* E4 carriers having the lowest HDL-C levels among sedentary men, whereas *APOE* E4 carriers had the highest HDL-C levels among physically active men. Schmitz et al. [78] found that CV fitness did not influence the associations between *APOE* genotype and plasma LDL-C and HDL-C levels. More recently, Bernstein et al. [76] and Pisciotta et al. [79] in cross-sectional studies found that the benefits of high levels of physical activity on plasma lipoprotein-lipid levels were evident in *APOE* E4 carriers but not in E2 or E3 carriers.

The first study to assess the impact of *APOE* genotype on the plasma lipoprotein-lipid responses to an endurance exercise training intervention was conducted in 1999. Hagberg et al. [80] found *APOE* E2 individuals improved their plasma HDL-C and HDL_2-C more, by 5–6 and 4 mg/dL, respectively, with exercise training than *APOE* E4 carriers. In 2004, Thompson et al. [81] found that total cholesterol/HDL-C and LDL-C/HDL-C ratios decreased significantly in individuals with the *APOE* E2/3 and E3/3 genotypes, but not the *APOE* E3/4 genotype after 6 months of endurance exercise training. Also in 2004 from HERITAGE, Leon et al. [82] reported significant effects of the *APOE* genotype on the training-induced changes in 10 of 16 plasma lipoprotein-lipid levels they measured in white men and women. In the black men and women in HERITAGE, they found only 2 of the 16 plasma lipoprotein-lipid changes with training differed significantly as a function of *APOE* genotype.

Interestingly, Obisesan et al. [83] recently reported a significant interactive effect between *APOE* genotype, race, and exercise training on plasma lipoprotein-lipid profiles. They reported that black individuals with the *APOE* E2/3 genotype increased plasma HDL particle size by ~1.5 times more with training than white individuals with the *APOE* E2/3 genotype, while both white and black individuals who were carriers of the *APOE* E4 allele responded similarly to exercise training. These results are contrasted with those from Leon et al. [82] from a much larger group of whites and blacks from the HERITAGE Family Study who found plasma HDL-C and HDL_2-C levels increased less in blacks with the *APOE* E2/2 and E2/3 genotypes compared to whites, though this difference did not appear to be statistically significant. In another study from the Thompson group [84], small LDL particles decreased and medium LDL particles increased with training only in the *APOE* E3/3 genotype group, with these responses being in the opposite direction to those with the E2/3 and E3/4 genotypes.

Cholesteryl Ester Transfer Protein (CETP)

In 2002, Wilund et al. [4] reported that *CETP* Taq1 B1B2 heterozygotes responded to training better in terms of antiatherogenic HDL subfractions measured by nuclear magnetic resonance (NMR) than B1B1 genotype. In 2004, Mukherjee and Shetty [85] reported in a cross-sectional study that there was a significant interactive effect between *CETP* Taq1 genotype and habitual physical activity levels, with the most active individuals exhibiting higher plasma HDL-C levels than the inactive individuals only in the B1B1 genotype group. In 2005, Ayyobi et al. [86] reported in a cardiac rehabilitation program which also included weight loss, individuals with the B1B1 genotype improved total cholesterol, HDL-C, and TG more than individuals carrying at least one B2 allele at this locus. In 2007, Spielman et al. [87] from HERITAGE reported women who were homozygous for the A allele at a different *CETP* locus (−629) had the largest training-induced improvements in plasma HDL_3-C and Apolipoprotein A1 levels.

Lipoprotein Lipase (LPL)

In 1999, Hagberg et al. [88] reported in a study with a small sample size older men with the *LPL* PvuII −/+ genotype increased plasma HDL-C and HDL_2-C levels with exercise training 8–9 mg/dL more than men carrying at least one + allele at this locus. Also in 1999, Boer et al. [90] in a cross-sectional study found that the *LPL* D9N variant was significantly associated with plasma lipoprotein-lipid profiles in sedentary men and women. However, in physically active individuals this same variant was not associated with plasma lipoprotein-lipid levels. In 2001, Senti et al. [92] in another cross-sectional study reported that the *LPL* HindIII +/+ genotype had an adverse relationship with plasma TG and HDL-C levels, but this relationship was significantly attenuated in persons with higher habitual levels of physical activity.

Hepatic Lipase (LIPC)

LIPC is a biologically plausible candidate gene because of its involvement in lipoprotein metabolism, especially related to HDL-C. Pisciotta et al. [79] in 2003 found that the *LIPC* G-250A genotype interacted with habitual physical activity levels to affect plasma HDL-C levels on a cross-sectional basis. In 2005, Teran-Garcia et al. [89]

reported that in the blacks in the HERITAGE cohort, *LIPC* C-514T genotype affected the response of plasma ApoB levels to exercise training.

Endothelial Lipase (LIPG)

In 2003, Halverstadt et al. [3] first reported the common Thr111Ile variation in the *LIPG* gene affected the plasma lipoprotein-lipid responses to exercise training. They found with training, HDL-C levels increased twice as much, HDL_3-C levels increased almost twofold greater, and the cardioprotective HDL_5 levels measured by NMR increased more than 4 times as much in the CC genotype group compared to the CT/TT group. In 2009 in a cross-sectional study, Smith et al. [92] found the *LIPG* i24582 SNP interacted significantly with a sedentary lifestyle to affect plasma HDL-C, large HDL, small LDL, and large HDL concentrations and HDL and LDL particle size.

Other Genetic Variants

The remaining evidence for genotype effects on the plasma lipoprotein-lipid responses to exercise training consists of only single studies that found significant effects of different candidate genes [64], including the *APOA1*, apolipoprotein A-2 (*APOA2*), apolipoprotein A-5 (*APOA5*), interleukin 6 (*IL6*), fatty acid binding protein2 (*FABP2*), ghrelin (*GHRL*), hormone sensitive lipase (*LIPE*), peroxisome proliferator activated receptor alpha (*PPARA*) and delta (*PPARD*), and paraoxonase 1 (*PON1*) genes. Thus, clearly more studies are necessary to assess the impact of the numerous potential candidate genes that could affect plasma lipoprotein-lipid responses to exercise training.

At this time, it is difficult to draw any conclusions relative to genetic variants affecting plasma lipoprotein-lipid responses to exercise training. Although a substantial number of studies have addressed this effect as a function of *APOE* genotype, the results as summarized above are not at all consistent, with about an equal number of studies indicating that either *APOE* E2 or E4 individuals responded best to training. For the four studies addressing the impact of *CETP* genotype, two different variants were studied but two studies found that Taq1 B1 homozygotes responded better to exercise training. For the three studies quantifying the effect of *LPL* gene variants on training-induced changes in plasma lipoprotein-lipid profiles, each study assessed the impact of different *LPL* variants. For *LIPC*, the two studies also investigated different gene variants and the same is true for *LIPG*. Thus, it is really not possible to generate any robust conclusions because of the lack of consistency in the results of the previous studies and even within the same gene, often times the impact of different variants were quantified.

Blood Pressure

There also are relatively few studies that have assessed the impact of genetic variants on the BP responses to exercise training. In fact, in the last version of the Human Gene Map for Performance and Health-Related Fitness Phenotypes: The 2006–2007 Update [1] there were only 18 such studies that had reported significant genotype-dependent effects. Since then it appears another three studies have been published addressing the effects of genetic variations on BP responses to exercise training or a significant gene×physical activity interaction. Similar to acute exercise candidate gene studies addressing BP phenotypes, the three most studied genes relative to training-induced BP changes are *ACE*, *AGT*, and *NOS3*, with three studies each assessing their effects, followed by *EDN1* and *GNB3*, which were both the focus of two separate studies.

Angiotensin Converting Enzyme (ACE)

In 1999, Hagberg et al. [88] reported in a small population of people with hypertension that the *ACE* I allele carriers reduced diastolic BP more with training than men with the *ACE* DD genotype (−10 vs. −1 mmHg) with there being a tendency for I allele carriers to also reduce systolic BP more with training than those with the *ACE* DD genotype (−10 vs. −5 mmHg). In 2000, Rankinen et al. [69] from HERITAGE reported white men with the *ACE* DD genotype reduced their submaximal exercise diastolic BP more with training than *ACE* I allele carriers (−4.4 vs. −2.6 mmHg). Zhang et al. [93] in 2002 found systolic and diastolic BP decreased with training in *ACE* I allele carriers with hypertension from Japan, but did not change in those with the *ACE* DD genotype.

Angiotensin (AGT)

In 2000, Rankinen et al. [69] in white men from HERITAGE found *AGT* M235T M allele carriers reduced submaximal exercise diastolic BP with training by ~3.5 mmHg, while the reduction was less in those with the *AGT* TT genotype (−0.4 mmHg). They also reported a significant gene interaction as individuals carrying the *AGT* TT genotype and the *ACE* D allele did not reduce submaximal exercise diastolic BP with training. Rauramaa et al. [94] found that individuals with the *AGT* M235T MM genotype undergoing 6 years of exercise training decreased resting systolic BP by 1 mmHg, while sedentary MM genotype controls increased systolic BP by ~15 mmHg over the same time period. Delmonico et al. [95] found differences in the resting BP responses to strength training as a function of two renin angiotensin system genetic variants, i.e., the *AGT* A-20C genotype for systolic BP, and the *AGTR1* A1166C genotype for diastolic BP.

Endothelial Nitric Oxide Synthase (ENOS)

In 2000, Rankinen et al. [96] showed in HERITAGE individuals with the *NOS3* G894T GG genotype had a ~3 mmHg greater reduction in submaximal exercise diastolic BP with training than TT homozygotes independent of gender. Individuals with the *NOS3* Glu298Glu genotype also tended to reduce submaximal exercise systolic BP response and submaximal exercise rate pressure product more with training than carriers of the *NOS3* Asp allele. Vimaleswaran et al. [97] assessed the impact of habitual levels of physical activity on the relationship between *NOS3* polymorphisms and BP. They found that the relationships between the intronic IVS25+15 G>A polymorphism and systolic and diastolic BP were significantly affected by habitual physical activity level, with the beneficial effects of one specific genotype only evident in the most active individuals with the benefits averaging 3–5 mmHg for systolic and diastolic BP. Kimura et al. [98] in a cross-sectional study in a Japanese population found significant interactions between the *NOS3* T-786C polymorphism, habitual physical activity levels, systolic BP, and the presence of systolic hypertension.

Endothelin 1 (EDN1)

In 2007, Rankinen et al. [99] published an important paper relative to *EDN1* genotype, physical activity, and CV phenotypes. In the HERITAGE population, they first found that *EDN1* haplotypes did not relate to BP phenotypes at baseline prior to training. However, various *EDN1* haplotypes were significantly associated with a number of BP responses to exercise training. Then in another independent cohort, they again found *EDN1* genotypes did not differ between those with hypertension and normal BP. However, two *EDN1* SNPs interacted significantly with CV fitness levels to impact the risk for developing hypertension. These *EDN1* SNPs only exerted their effects on the risk of developing hypertension in low fit individuals with the risk roughly doubling in those carrying the risk allele.

Guanine Nucleotide Binding Protein Beta Polypeptide 3 (GNB3)

Rankinen et al. [100] found effects of the *GNB3* C825T variant on BP responses to training in HERITAGE Family Study cohort. They found that black women with the CC genotype reduced resting systolic and diastolic BP more with training than black women with the TT genotype. Grove et al. [101] in the Atherosclerosis Risk in Communities cohort also found that the *GNB3* variant interacted with habitual physical activity levels and obesity to affect the prevalence of hypertension, such that TT homozygotes who were obese and sedentary had a 2.7 times greater risk of having hypertension compared to CC homozygotes who were nonobese and physically active.

Other Genetic Variants

The remaining evidence for genotype-dependent effects on BP responses to exercise training consists of only single studies that assessed the effects of different candidate genes [64, 73], including the *AMPD1*, *FABP2*, G-protein-coupled receptor 10 (*GPR10*), *AGTR1*, *LPL*, leptin receptor (*LEPR*), *APOE*, and *SLC4A5* genes. Clearly, more studies are needed to assess the impact of the myriad potential candidate genes that could be involved in regulating BP responses to exercise training.

Some tentative conclusions can be drawn from the data that are available addressing genetic variants and BP responses to exercise training. For *ACE* genotype, the two studies that assessed resting BP changes with training indicate that II homozygotes or I allele carriers decreased their BP to a greater extent than those with the *ACE* DD genotype. For the common *AGT* M235T variant, the two available studies indicate that M allele carriers had the best resting BP response to exercise training. For *NOS3*, three studies have been published but they each addressed different SNPs within this gene, so no conclusions can be made. It also appears that generally consistent results were evident for the effect of *GNB3* and *EDN1* variants on BP responses to exercise training. Thus, it appears, common variants in the *ACE*, *AGT*, *GNB3*, and *EDN1* genes may possibly affect BP responses to endurance exercise training, although these conclusions are still based on very minimal data.

Relative to candidate gene studies addressing the responses of plasma lipoprotein-lipid levels and BP to exercise training, at present, it is difficult to draw any definitive conclusions, especially with regard to genetic variants affecting plasma lipoprotein-lipid responses to exercise training. There is some evidence indicating specific candidate gene variants that may impact the responses of BP to exercise training. Our inability to generate strong conclusions at this time is the result of (a) a generally small set of previously published data, (b) the huge number of potential candidate genes most of which have not been examined, (c) the inconsistency of SNPs that have been studied in the few candidate genes that have been investigated, (d) the generally small sample sizes used in most studies, and (e) the inconsistency of the results to date.

The Future?

Clearly, substantially more data are needed before strong conclusions can be drawn relative to the genetics underlying the plasma lipoprotein-lipid and BP responses to acute exercise and exercise training. While on first pass it would appear that there have been a relatively "large" pool of studies focusing on these issues, the number is actually very small compared to the number of candidate genes available for study.

A major problem for the future of this area of investigation is that most disease gene discovery and disease susceptibility genetic studies have sample sizes well in excess of those usually included in acute or long-term exercise intervention studies, and large replication cohorts are often included in the same study. Such requirements are clearly difficult to implement relative to the genetics underlying the plasma lipoprotein-lipid and BP responses to acute exercise and exercise training because of the large number of candidate genes to be investigated, the absolutely essential need to measure highly standardized phenotypes, and the need for highly standardized acute exercise or exercise training interventions. It should be acknowledged that the inclusion of precisely measured phenotypes in exercise genomics studies (e.g., HR, BP, and VO_2 max at baseline and their changes with exercise training) and the repeated measures aspect of assessing a phenotype before and after training in the same individual, markedly enhance the statistical power for detecting SNPs related to these exercise-related phenotypes as compared to disease gene discovery and disease susceptibility genetic studies. However, unless another large trial like HERITAGE is initiated, it is hard to see how repli-cated, definitive evidence will be generated to validly quantify the effect of genetic variations on plasma lipoprotein-lipid and BP responses, especially regarding their responses to exercise training.

Practical Applications

Personalized medicine proposes a specific profile containing some minimal number of gene variants would optimize the application of medical interventions, whether they are pharmacologic or lifestyle to maximize a person's health. However, the sequencing of genomes has taught us that we and all higher life forms are very complex in terms of the number of genes responsible for virtually any phenotype. All critical physiological phenotypes are determined by numerous redundant signaling pathways involving a substantial number of genes. A potentially very complex genetic variation profile across these numerous loci impacts the final phenotype. Our complexity is highlighted further by the current estimate that there are ~10 million SNPs across the human genome [102]. In reality, if we and all higher life forms were not this complex, by now we would have become extinct. Thus, our initial hope of finding a small number of genetic variations that have substantial independent effects on any phenotype, including those discussed in this chapter and any phenotypes related to acute exercise or exercise training, was clearly overly simplistic. The evidence summarized in this chapter should indicate that we have taken only very small steps toward deriving robust conclusions relative to the genetic factors that underlie the interindividual differences in the responses of plasma lipoprotein-lipids and BP to acute exercise and exercise training. Some evidence is available concerning highly plausible candidate genes that might influ-ence these responses. However, at the present, these results are "not ready for prime time" in terms of identifying specific genetic screening panels that would robustly predict optimal responders to acute exercise or exercise training in terms of plasma lipoprotein-lipid or BP.

References

1. Leon AS, Gaskill SE, Rice T, Bergeron J, Gagnon J, Rao DC, et al. Variability in the response of HDL cholesterol to exercise training in the HERITAGE family study. Int J Sports Med. 2002;23(1):1–9.
2. Obisesan TO, Leeuwenburgh C, Phillips T, Ferrell RE, Phares DA, Prior SJ, Hagberg JM. C-reactive protein genotypes affect baseline, but not exercise training-induced changes, in C-reactive protein levels. Arterioscler Thromb Vasc Biol. 2004;24(10):1874–9.
3. Halverstadt A, Phares DA, Ferrell RE, Wilund KR, Goldberg AP, Hagberg JM. High-density lipoprotein-cholesterol, its subfractions, and responses to exercise training are dependent on endothelial lipase genotype. Metabolism. 2003;52(11):1505–11. Accessed 24 June 2010.
4. Wilund KR, Ferrell RE, Phares DA, Goldberg AP, Hagberg JM. Changes in high-density lipoprotein-cholesterol subfractions with exercise training may be dependent on cholesteryl ester transfer protein (CETP) genotype. Metabolism. 2002;51(6):774–8.
5. Heiberg A. The heritability of serum lipoprotein and lipid concentrations. A twin study. Clin Genet. 1974;6(4):307–16.
6. Weinberg R, Avet LM, Gardner MJ. Estimates of the heritability of serum lipoprotein and lipid concentrations. Clin Genet. 1976;9(6):588–92.
7. Namboodiri KK, Green PP, Kaplan EB, Tyroler HA, Morrison JA, Chase GA, et al. Family aggregation of high density lipoprotein cholesterol. collaborative lipid research clinics program family study. Arteriosclerosis. 1983;3(6):616–26.
8. Namboodiri KK, Green PP, Kaplan EB, Morrison JA, Chase GA, Elston RC, et al. The collaborative lipid research clinics program family study. IV. familial associations of plasma lipids and lipoproteins. Am J Epidemiol. 1984;119(6):975–96.
9. Namboodiri KK, Kaplan EB, Heuch I, Elston RC, Green PP, Rao DC, et al. The collaborative lipid research clinics family study: Biological and cultural determinants of familial resemblance for plasma lipids and lipoproteins. Genet Epidemiol. 1985;2(3):227–54.
10. Perusse L, Rice T, Despres JP, Rao DC, Bouchard C. Cross-trait familial resemblance for body fat and blood lipids: familial correlations in the quebec family study. Arterioscler Thromb Vasc Biol. 1997;17(11):3270–7.
11. Kathiresan S, Manning AK, Demissie S, D'Agostino RB, Surti A, Guiducci C, et al. A genome-wide association study for blood lipid phenotypes in the framingham heart study. BMC Med Genet. 2007;8 Suppl 1:S17.
12. Adeyemo A, Gerry N, Chen G, Herbert A, Doumatey A, Huang H, et al. A genome-wide association study of hypertension and blood pressure in african americans. PLoS Genet. 2009;5(7):e1000564.
13. de Oliveira CM, Pereira AC, de Andrade M, Soler JM, Krieger JE. Heritability of cardiovascular risk factors in a Brazilian population: Baependi heart study. BMC Med Genet. 2008;9:32.
14. Mitchell GF, DeStefano AL, Larson MG, Benjamin EJ, Chen MH, Vasan RS, et al. Heritability and a genome-wide linkage scan for arterial stiffness, wave reflection, and mean arterial pressure: The framingham heart study. Circulation. 2005;112(2):194–9.
15. DeStefano AL, Larson MG, Mitchell GF, Benjamin EJ, Vasan RS, Li J, et al. Genome-wide scan for pulse pressure in the national heart, lung and blood institute's framingham heart study. Hypertension. 2004;44(2):152–5.
16. Nishina PM, Johnson JP, Naggert JK, Krauss RM. Linkage of atherogenic lipoprotein phenotype to the low density lipoprotein receptor locus on the short arm of chromosome 19. Proc Natl Acad Sci U S A. 1992;89(2):708–12.
17. Rainwater DL, Almasy L, Blangero J, Cole SA, VandeBerg JL, MacCluer JW, Hixson JE. A genome search identifies major quantitative trait loci on human chromosomes 3 and 4 that influence cholesterol concentrations in small LDL particles. Arterioscler Thromb Vasc Biol. 1999;19(3):777–83.

18. Shearman AM, Ordovas JM, Cupples LA, Schaefer EJ, Harmon MD, Shao Y, et al. Evidence for a gene influencing the TG/HDL-C ratio on chromosome 7q32.3-qter: A genome-wide scan in the framingham study. Hum Mol Genet. 2000;9(9):1315–20.
19. Imperatore G, Knowler WC, Pettitt DJ, Kobes S, Fuller JH, Bennett PH, Hanson RL. A locus influencing total serum cholesterol on chromosome 19p: Results from an autosomal genomic scan of serum lipid concentrations in pima indians. Arterioscler Thromb Vasc Biol. 2000;20(12):2651–6.
20. Sandhu MS, Waterworth DM, Debenham SL, Wheeler E, Papadakis K, Zhao JH, et al. LDL-cholesterol concentrations: A genome-wide association study. Lancet. 2008;371(9611): 483–91.
21. Hiura Y, Shen CS, Kokubo Y, Okamura T, Morisaki T, Tomoike H, et al. Identification of genetic markers associated with high-density lipoprotein-cholesterol by genome-wide screening in a japanese population: The suita study. Circ J. 2009;73(6):1119–26.
22. Rice T, Rankinen T, Province MA, Chagnon YC, Perusse L, Borecki IB, et al. Genome-wide linkage analysis of systolic and diastolic blood pressure: The quebec family study. Circulation. 2000;102(16):1956–63.
23. Levy D, DeStefano AL, Larson MG, O'Donnell CJ, Lifton RP, Gavras H, et al. Evidence for a gene influencing blood pressure on chromosome 17. genome scan linkage results for longitudinal blood pressure phenotypes in subjects from the framingham heart study. Hypertension. 2000;36(4):477–83.
24. Levy D, Larson MG, Benjamin EJ, Newton-Cheh C, Wang TJ, Hwang SJ, et al. Framingham heart study 100K project: Genome-wide associations for blood pressure and arterial stiffness. BMC Med Genet. 2007;8 Suppl 1:S3.
25. Newton-Cheh C, Johnson T, Gateva V, Tobin MD, Bochud M, Coin L, et al. Genome-wide association study identifies eight loci associated with blood pressure. Nat Genet. 2009;41: 666–76.
26. Diabetes Genetics Initiative of Broad Institute of Harvard and MIT, Lund University, and Novartis Institutes of BioMedical Research, Saxena R, Voight BF, Lyssenko V, Burtt NP, de Bakker PI, et al. Genome-wide association analysis identifies loci for type 2 diabetes and triglyceride levels. Science. 2007;316(5829):1331–6.
27. Wellcome Trust Case Control Consortium. Genome-wide association study of 14,000 cases of seven common diseases and 3,000 shared controls. Nature. 2007;447(7145):661–78.
28. Havekes L, Vermeer BJ, de Wit E, Emeis JJ, Vaandrager H, van Gent CM, Koster JF. Suppression of cholesterol synthesis in cultured fibroblasts from a patient with homozygous familial hypercholesterolemia by her own low density lipoprotein density fraction. A possible role of apolipoprotein E. Biochim Biophys Acta. 1980;617(3):529–35.
29. Utermann G, Langenbeck U, Beisiegel U, Weber W. Genetics of the apolipoprotein E system in man. Am J Hum Genet. 1980;32(3):339–47.
30. Sing CF, Davignon J. Role of the apolipoprotein E polymorphism in determining normal plasma lipid and lipoprotein variation. Am J Hum Genet. 1985;37(2):268–85.
31. Boerwinkle E, Visvikis S, Welsh D, Steinmetz J, Hanash SM, Sing CF. The use of measured genotype information in the analysis of quantitative phenotypes in man. II. The role of the apolipoprotein E polymorphism in determining levels, variability, and covariability of cholesterol, betalipoprotein, and triglycerides in a sample of unrelated individuals. Am J Med Genet. 1987;27(3):567–82.
32. Bennet AM, Di Angelantonio E, Ye Z, Wensley F, Dahlin A, Ahlbom A, et al. Association of apolipoprotein E genotypes with lipid levels and coronary risk. JAMA. 2007;298(11): 1300–11.
33. Koizumi J, Mabuchi H, Yoshimura A, Michishita I, Takeda M, Itoh H, et al. Deficiency of serum cholesteryl-ester transfer activity in patients with familial hyperalphalipoproteinaemia. Atherosclerosis. 1985;58(1–3):175–86.
34. Thompson A, Di Angelantonio E, Sarwar N, Erqou S, Saleheen D, Dullaart RP, et al. Association of cholesteryl ester transfer protein genotypes with CETP mass and activity, lipid levels, and coronary risk. JAMA. 2008;299(23):2777–88.

35. Heiba IM, DeMeester CA, Xia YR, Diep A, George VT, Amos CI, et al. Genetic contributions to quantitative lipoprotein traits associated with coronary artery disease: Analysis of a large pedigree from the bogalusa heart study. Am J Med Genet. 1993;47(6):875–83.
36. Knoblauch H, Bauerfeind A, Krahenbuhl C, Daury A, Rohde K, Bejanin S, et al. Common haplotypes in five genes influence genetic variance of LDL and HDL cholesterol in the general population. Hum Mol Genet. 2002;11(12):1477–85.
37. Knoblauch H, Bauerfeind A, Toliat MR, Becker C, Luganskaja T, Gunther UP, et al. Haplotypes and SNPs in 13 lipid-relevant genes explain most of the genetic variance in high-density lipoprotein and low-density lipoprotein cholesterol. Hum Mol Genet. 2004;13(10): 993–1004.
38. Jacob HJ, Lindpaintner K, Lincoln SE, Kusumi K, Bunker RK, Mao YP, et al. Genetic mapping of a gene causing hypertension in the stroke-prone spontaneously hypertensive rat. Cell. 1991;67(1):213–24.
39. Nara Y, Nabika T, Ikeda K, Sawamura M, Endo J, Yamori Y. Blood pressure cosegregates with a microsatellite of angiotensin I converting enzyme (ACE) in F2 generation from a cross between original normotensive wistar-kyoto rat (WKY) and stroke-prone spontaneously hypertensive rat (SHRSP). Biochem Biophys Res Commun. 1991;181(3):941–6.
40. Zee RY, Lou YK, Griffiths LR, Morris BJ. Association of a polymorphism of the angiotensin I-converting enzyme gene with essential hypertension. Biochem Biophys Res Commun. 1992;184(1):9–15.
41. Harrap SB, Davidson HR, Connor JM, Soubrier F, Corvol P, Fraser R, et al. The angiotensin I converting enzyme gene and predisposition to high blood pressure. Hypertension. 1993;21(4):455–60.
42. Tiret L, Rigat B, Visvikis S, Breda C, Corvol P, Cambien F, Soubrier F. Evidence, from combined segregation and linkage analysis, that a variant of the angiotensin I-converting enzyme (ACE) gene controls plasma ACE levels. Am J Hum Genet. 1992;51(1):197–205.
43. Jeunemaitre X, Soubrier F, Kotelevtsev YV, Lifton RP, Williams CS, Charru A, et al. Molecular basis of human hypertension: Role of angiotensinogen. Cell. 1992;71(1): 169–80.
44. Bennett CL, Schrader AP, Morris BJ. Cross-sectional analysis of Met235–>Thr variant of angiotensinogen gene in severe, familial hypertension. Biochem Biophys Res Commun. 1993;197(2):833–9.
45. Hata A, Namikawa C, Sasaki M, Sato K, Nakamura T, Tamura K, Lalouel JM. Angiotensinogen as a risk factor for essential hypertension in japan. J Clin Invest. 1994;93(3):1285–7.
46. Hegele RA, Brunt JH, Connelly PW. A polymorphism of the angiotensinogen gene associated with variation in blood pressure in a genetic isolate. Circulation. 1994;90:2207–12.
47. Gu D, Rice T, Wang S, Yang W, Gu C, Chen CS, et al. Heritability of blood pressure responses to dietary sodium and potassium intake in a chinese population. Hypertension. 2007;50(1):116–22.
48. Roy-Gagnon MH, Weir MR, Sorkin JD, Ryan KA, Sack PA, Hines S, et al. Genetic influences on blood pressure response to the cold pressor test: Results from the heredity and phenotype intervention heart study. J Hypertens. 2008;26(4):729–36.
49. Hunt SC, Hasstedt SJ, Kuida H, Stults BM, Hopkins PN, Williams RR. Genetic heritability and common environmental components of resting and stressed blood pressures, lipids, and body mass index in Utah pedigrees and twins. Am J Epidemiol. 1989;129(3):625–38.
50. Bielen EC, Fagard RH, Amery AK. Inheritance of blood pressure and haemodynamic phenotypes measured at rest and during supine dynamic exercise. J Hypertens. 1991;9(7):655–63.
51. Ingelsson E, Larson MG, Vasan RS, O'Donnell CJ, Yin X, Hirschhorn JN, et al. Heritability, linkage, and genetic associations of exercise treadmill test responses. Circulation. 2007;115(23):2917–24.
52. Vasan RS, Larson MG, Aragam J, Wang TJ, Mitchell GF, Kathiresan S, et al. Genome-wide association of echocardiographic dimensions, brachial artery endothelial function and treadmill exercise responses in the framingham heart study. BMC Med Genet. 2007;8 Suppl 1:S2.

53. Bouchard C, Leon AS, Rao DC, Skinner JS, Wilmore JH, Gagnon J. family study. aims, design, and measurement protocol. Med Sci Sports Exerc. 1995;27(5):721–9.

54. An P, Rice T, Gagnon J, Borecki IB, Bergeron J, Despres JP, et al. Segregation analysis of apolipoproteins A-1 and B-100 measured before and after an exercise training program: The HERITAGE family study. Arterioscler Thromb Vasc Biol. 2000;20(3):807–14.

55. Hong Y, Rice T, Gagnon J, Perusse L, Province M, Bouchard C, et al. Familiality of triglyceride and LPL response to exercise training: The HERITAGE study. Med Sci Sports Exerc. 2000;32(8):1438–44.

56. Rice T, Despres JP, Perusse L, Hong Y, Province MA, Bergeron J, et al. Familial aggregation of blood lipid response to exercise training in the health, risk factors, exercise training, and genetics (HERITAGE) family study. Circulation. 2002;105(16):1904–8.

57. Feitosa MF, Rice T, Rankinen T, Almasy L, Leon AS, Skinner JS, et al. Common genetic and environmental effects on lipid phenotypes: The HERITAGE family study. Hum Hered. 2005;59(1):34–40.

58. Rice T, An P, Gagnon J, Leon AS, Skinner JS, Wilmore JH, et al. Heritability of HR and BP response to exercise training in the HERITAGE family study. Med Sci Sports Exerc. 2002;34(6):972–9.

59. An P, Perusse L, Rankinen T, Borecki IB, Gagnon J, Leon AS, et al. Familial aggregation of exercise heart rate and blood pressure in response to 20 weeks of endurance training: The HERITAGE family study. Int J Sports Med. 2003;24(1):57–62.

60. Rankinen T, An P, Rice T, Sun G, Chagnon YC, Gagnon J, et al. Genomic scan for exercise blood pressure in the health, risk factors, exercise training and genetics (HERITAGE) family study. Hypertension. 2001;38(1):30–7.

61. Feitosa MF, Rice T, North KE, Kraja A, Rankinen T, Leon AS, et al. Pleiotropic QTL on chromosome 19q13 for triglycerides and adiposity: The HERITAGE family study. Atherosclerosis. 2006;185(2):426–32.

62. Feitosa MF, Borecki IB, Rankinen T, Rice T, Despres JP, Chagnon YC, et al. Evidence of QTLs on chromosomes 1q42 and 8q24 for LDL-cholesterol and apoB levels in the HERITAGE family study. J Lipid Res. 2005;46(2):281–6.

63. Rice T, Rankinen T, Chagnon YC, Province MA, Perusse L, Leon AS, et al. Genomewide linkage scan of resting blood pressure: HERITAGE family study. health, risk factors, exercise training, and genetics. Hypertension. 2002;39(6):1037–43.

64. Bray MS, Hagberg JM, Perusse L, Rankinen T, Roth SM, Wolfarth B, Bouchard C. The human gene map for performance and health-related fitness phenotypes: The 2006-2007 update. Med Sci Sports Exerc. 2009;41(1):35–73.

65. Friedl W, Krempler F, Sandhofer F, Paulweber B. Insertion/deletion polymorphism in the angiotensin-converting-enzyme gene and blood pressure during ergometry in normal males. Clin Genet. 1996;50(6):541–4.

66. Pescatello LS, Turner D, Rodriguez N, Blanchard BE, Tsongalis GJ, Maresh CM, et al. Dietary calcium intake and renin angiotensin system polymorphisms alter the blood pressure response to aerobic exercise: A randomized control design. Nutr Metab (Lond). 2007;4:1.

67. Blanchard BE, Tsongalis GJ, Guidry MA, LaBelle LA, Poulin M, Taylor AL, et al. RAAS polymorphisms alter the acute blood pressure response to aerobic exercise among men with hypertension. Eur J Appl Physiol. 2006;97(1):26–33.

68. Krizanova O, Koska J, Vigas M, Kvetnansky R. Correlation of M235T DNA polymorphism with cardiovascular and endocrine responses during physical exercise in healthy subjects. Physiol Res. 1998;47(2):81–8.

69. Rankinen T, Gagnon J, Perusse L, Chagnon YC, Rice T, Leon AS, et al. AGT M235T and ACE ID polymorphisms and exercise blood pressure in the HERITAGE family study. Am J Physiol Heart Circ Physiol. 2000;279(1):H368–74.

70. Rankinen T, Gagnon J, Perusse L, Rice T, Leon AS, Skinner JS, et al. Body fat, resting and exercise blood pressure and the angiotensinogen M235T polymorphism: The heritage family study. Obes Res. 1999;7(5):423–30.

71. Kim JS, Cho JR, Park S, Shim J, Kim JB, Cho DK, et al. Endothelial nitric oxide synthase Glu298Asp gene polymorphism is associated with hypertensive response to exercise in well-controlled hypertensive patients. Yonsei Med J. 2007;48(3):389–95.
72. Augeri AL, Tsongalis GJ, Van Heest JL, Maresh CM, Thompson PD, Pescatello LS. The endothelial nitric oxide synthase -786 T>C polymorphism and the exercise-induced blood pressure and nitric oxide responses among men with elevated blood pressure. Atherosclerosis. 2009;204(2):e28–34.
73. Taylor JY, Maddox R, Wu CY. Genetic and environmental risks for high blood pressure among African American mothers and daughters. Biol Res Nurs. 2009;11(1):53–65.
74. Taimela S, Lehtimäki T, Porkka KVK, Räsänen L, Viikari JSA. The effect of physical activity on serum total and low-density lipoprotein cholesterol concentrations varies with apolipoprotein E phenotype in male children and young adults: the cardiovascular risk in young Finns study. Metab Clin Exp. 1996;45(7):797–803.
75. St-Amand J, Prud'homme D, Moorjani S, Nadeau A, Tremblay A, Bouchard C, et al. Apolipoprotein E polymorphism and the relationships of physical fitness to plasma lipoprotein-lipid levels in men and women. Med Sci Sports Exerc. 1999;31(5):692–7.
76. Bernstein MS, Costanza MC, James RW, Morris MA, Cambien F, Raoux S, Morabia A. Physical activity may modulate effects of ApoE genotype on lipid profile. Arterioscler Thromb Vasc Biol. 2002;22(1):133–40.
77. Corella D, Guillen M, Saiz C, Portoles O, Sabater A, Cortina S, et al. Environmental factors modulate the effect of the APOE genetic polymorphism on plasma lipid concentrations: Ecogenetic studies in a mediterranean spanish population. Metabolism. 2001;50(8):936–44.
78. Schmitz KH, Schreiner PJ, Jacobs DR, Leon AS, Liu K, Howard B, Sternfeld B. Independent and interactive effects of apolipoprotein E phenotype and cardiorespiratory fitness on plasma lipids. Ann Epidemiol. 2001;11(2):94–103.
79. Pisciotta L, Cantafora A, Piana A, Masturzo P, Cerone R, Minniti G, et al. Physical activity modulates effects of some genetic polymorphisms affecting cardiovascular risk in men aged over 40 years. Nutr Metab Cardiovasc Dis. 2003;13(4):202–10.
80. Hagberg JM, Ferrell RE, Katzel LI, Dengel DR, Sorkin JD, Goldberg AP. Apolipoprotein E genotype and exercise training-induced increases in plasma high-density lipoprotein (HDL)- and HDL2-cholesterol levels in overweight men. Metabolism. 1999;48(8):943–5.
81. Thompson PD, Tsongalis GJ, Seip RL, Bilbie C, Miles M, Zoeller R, et al. Apolipoprotein E genotype and changes in serum lipids and maximal oxygen uptake with exercise training Metabolism. 2004;53(2):193–202.
82. Leon AS, Togashi K, Rankinen T, Despres JP, Rao DC, Skinner JS, et al. Association of apolipoprotein E polymorphism with blood lipids and maximal oxygen uptake in the sedentary state and after exercise training in the HERITAGE family study. Metabolism. 2004;53(1): 108–16.
83. Obisesan TO, Ferrell RE, Goldberg AP, Phares DA, Ellis TJ, Hagberg JM. APOE genotype affects black-white responses of high-density lipoprotein cholesterol subspecies to aerobic exercise training. Metabolism. 2008;57(12):1669–76.
84. Seip RL, Otvos J, Bilbie C, Tsongalis GJ, Miles M, Zoeller R, et al. The effect of apolipoprotein E genotype on serum lipoprotein particle response to exercise. Atherosclerosis. 2006;188(1):126–33.
85. Mukherjee M, Shetty KR. Variations in high-density lipoprotein cholesterol in relation to physical activity and taq 1B polymorphism of the cholesteryl ester transfer protein gene. Clin Genet. 2004;65(5):412–8.
86. Ayyobi AF, Hill JS, Molhuizen HO, Lear SA. Cholesterol ester transfer protein (CETP) Taq1B polymorphism influences the effect of a standardized cardiac rehabilitation program on lipid risk markers. Atherosclerosis. 2005;181(2):363–9.
87. Spielmann N, Leon AS, Rao DC, Rice T, Skinner JS, Bouchard C, Rankinen T. CETP genotypes and HDL-cholesterol phenotypes in the HERITAGE family study. Physiol Genomics. 2007;31(1):25–31.

88. Hagberg JM, Ferrell RE, Dengel DR, Wilund KR. Exercise training-induced blood pressure and plasma lipid improvements in hypertensives may be genotype dependent. Hypertension. 1999;34(1):18–23.
89. Teran-Garcia M, Santoro N, Rankinen T, Bergeron J, Rice T, Leon AS, et al. Hepatic lipase gene variant -514C>T is associated with lipoprotein and insulin sensitivity response to regular exercise: The HERITAGE family study. Diabetes. 2005;54(7):2251–5.
90. Boer JM, Kuivenhoven JA, Feskens EJ, Schouten EG, Havekes LM, Seidell JC, et al. Physical activity modulates the effect of a lipoprotein lipase mutation (D9N) on plasma lipids and lipoproteins. Clin Genet. 1999;56(2):158–63.
91. Senti M, Elosua R, Tomas M, Sala J, Masia R, Ordovas JM, et al. Physical activity modulates the combined effect of a common variant of the lipoprotein lipase gene and smoking on serum triglyceride levels and high-density lipoprotein cholesterol in men. Hum Genet. 2001;109(4):385–92.
92. Smith CE, Arnett DK, Tsai MY, Lai CQ, Parnell LD, Shen J, et al. Physical inactivity interacts with an endothelial lipase polymorphism to modulate high density lipoprotein cholesterol in the GOLDN study. Atherosclerosis. 2009;206(2):500–4.
93. Zhang B, Sakai T, Miura S, et al. Association of angiotensin-converting-enzyme gene polymorphism with the depressor response to mild exercise therapy in patients with mild to moderate essential hypertension. Clin Genet. 2002;62(4):328–33.
94. Rauramaa R, Kuhanen R, Lakka TA, Vaisanen SB, Halonen P, Alen M, et al. Physical exercise and blood pressure with reference to the angiotensinogen M235T polymorphism. Physiol Genomics. 2002;10(2):71–7.
95. Delmonico MJ, Ferrell RE, Meerasahib A, Martel GF, Roth SM, Kostek MC, Hurley BF. Blood pressure response to strength training may be influenced by angiotensinogen A-20C and angiotensin II type I receptor A1166C genotypes in older men and women. J Am Geriatr Soc. 2005;53(2):204–10.
96. Rankinen T, Rice T, Perusse L, Chagnon YC, Gagnon J, Leon AS, et al. NOS3 Glu298Asp genotype and blood pressure response to endurance training: The HERITAGE family study. Hypertension. 2000;36(5):885–9.
97. Vimaleswaran KS, Franks PW, Barroso I, Brage S, Ekelund U, Wareham NJ, Loos RJ. Habitual energy expenditure modifies the association between NOS3 gene polymorphisms and blood pressure. Am J Hypertens. 2008;21(3):297–302.
98. Kimura T, Yokoyama T, Matsumura Y, Yoshiike N, Date C, Muramatsu M, Tanaka H. NOS3 genotype-dependent correlation between blood pressure and physical activity. Hypertension. 2003;41(2):355–60.
99. Rankinen T, Church T, Rice T, Markward N, Leon AS, Rao DC, et al. Effect of endothelin 1 genotype on blood pressure is dependent on physical activity or fitness levels. Hypertension. 2007;50(6):1120–5.
100. Rankinen T, Rice T, Leon AS, Skinner JS, Wilmore JH, Rao DC, Bouchard C. G protein beta 3 polymorphism and hemodynamic and body composition phenotypes in the HERITAGE family study. Physiol Genomics. 2002;8(2):151–7.
101. Grove ML, Morrison A, Folsom AR, Boerwinkle E, Hoelscher DM, Bray MS. Gene-environment interaction and the GNB3 gene in the atherosclerosis risk in communities study. Int J Obes (Lond). 2007;31(6):919–26.
102. International HapMap Consortium, Frazer KA, Ballinger DG, Cox DR, Hinds DA, Stuve LL, et al. A second generation human haplotype map of over 3.1 million SNPs. Nature. 2007;449(7164):851–61.

Chapter 7
Genetic Aspects of Muscular Strength and Size

Monica J. Hubal, Maria L. Urso, and Priscilla M. Clarkson

Keywords Hypertrophy • Resistance training • Genetic variants • Genotype association • Single nucleotide polymorphism • Adaptation • Fiber type • Alpha-actinin 3 • Protein synthesis • Growth factors • Phosphatidylinositol-3-kinase • Protein kinase B • Mammalian target of rapamycin • Insulin-like growth factor • Mechano growth factor • Myostatin • Inflammatory factors • Cytokines • Tumor necrosis factor alpha • Interleukin-6 • Interleukin-15 • Exercise genomics • Polygenic traits • Genome wide association study • Next generation sequencing • Genetic testing • Angiotensin converting enzyme • Protein phosphatase 3 regulatory subunit B • Insulin-like growth factor binding protein

Introduction

Skeletal muscle strength is important to athletic success and is a key component of physical fitness in all people contributing significantly to quality of life. While elite athletes train to maximize muscle strength for competition purposes, maximizing capabilities in nonathletes increases a person's ability to perform activities of daily living, decreases incidence of injury, and speeds recovery from illness or injury.

One of the primary functions of skeletal muscle is to produce force, and the ability to produce force at a given speed defines muscle strength [1]. Resistance training or "strength training" can affect muscle strength by improving neuromuscular efficiency and stimulating muscle hypertrophy via increased protein synthesis. Correlations between strength and size gains during the first several weeks of training are weak, indicating neural changes drive much of early strength gains [2]. After this initial period of training, however, significant gains in muscle mass are

M.J. Hubal (✉)
Department of Integrative Systems Biology, George Washington University School of Medicine, Research Center for Genetic Medicine, Children's National Medical Center, Washington, DC 20010, USA
e-mail: mhubal@cnmcresearch.org

L.S. Pescatello and S.M. Roth (eds.), *Exercise Genomics*,
Molecular and Translational Medicine, DOI 10.1007/978-1-60761-355-8_7,
© Springer Science+Business Media, LLC 2011

typically seen, although a great deal of variation in both strength and size gain exists among individuals [3].

Variations in the ability to adapt to a training program are influenced by many factors, including genetic factors, ethnic influences, sex, age, physical activity history, type of strength training (e.g., plyometric vs. weight training), and the muscle groups trained (e.g., arm vs. leg). While each of these factors is known to add to variability in exercise responses, this chapter highlights genetic contributions, focusing specifically on influences of genetic background on training induced variations in muscle strength and size. Observed variations in the amount of strength and muscle size gains were found to be 5–150 and 5–40%, respectively, over the course of a standardized strength training intervention [3]. Others have estimated 35–85% of strength gains can be attributed to inheritance [4–6]. Furthermore, twin studies have documented greater than 50% of the variation in baseline strength and lean body mass is heritable [7–10].

A basic review of genetic variation and considerations for exercise genomics studies can be found in the first two and last chapters of this volume. The most common type of genetic variation tested for association with expressed traits like strength is a single nucleotide polymorphism (SNP). Millions of SNPs exist across the human population, and these SNPs range in how they affect proteins from positive (increasing protein levels or activity) to negative (decreasing protein levels or activity) with most being neutral (no significant effect on protein levels or activity). Studies of genetic variants with regard to muscle traits rely on associations between trait (phenotype) variability and genotype information (genotype) measured from DNA isolated from blood. Direct testing of SNP function on mRNA and protein levels has been utilized, although less so in human studies due to the invasiveness of collecting muscle biopsies.

The key focus of this chapter is to review what we know regarding those SNPs in or near genes that have the potential to influence skeletal muscle phenotypes. Most of the SNPs investigated to date for association with muscle strength and size and responses to resistance exercise fall into three general categories: (1) muscle structure, (2) growth factors, and (3) inflammatory factors. This chapter has been organized into three sections to cover each of these categories. Within each section, basic biological processes known to drive skeletal muscle development or adaptation are first explained as a background so that the SNP associations can be understood in context. Variations in a few additional key genes that are outside of these three functional categories are also discussed briefly. Finally, we provide insight into future directions and practical applications for muscle genomics research.

Genetics of Muscle Structure Adaptation to Resistance Exercise

Muscle is particularly sensitive to the mechanical forces placed upon it, as happens in resistance exercise. Tension and load trigger increases in the anabolic signaling cascades that promote protein synthesis within each muscle fiber, eventually resulting in hypertrophy and increased muscle force [11]. Tension is defined as the force exerted within a contracting or stretched muscle. Load is defined as the force exerted on the muscle by a weight or force. The primary modifiers of muscle force production are muscle size (amount of contractile and supporting/structural protein) and muscle composition (muscle fiber type).

Muscle Structure

Each skeletal muscle fiber is a multinucleated cell and represents the smallest complete contractile system with specific subsystems designed for metabolism, excitation, and contraction. Cellular components regulating these processes include the mitochondria, T-tubule/sarcoplasmic reticulum system, and contractile proteins, respectively. The contractile proteins primarily consist of actin, myosin, tropomyosin, and troponin; and the structural support proteins including Z-line proteins, M-line proteins, nebulin, titin, desmin, and the alpha-actinins. The nuclei direct protein synthesis, and the DNA in the nuclei includes genes that code for all structural and functional proteins.

Skeletal muscle is composed of different types of fibers that vary in neural innervations, metabolic characteristics, protein isoforms (e.g., myosin heavy chain [MHC] isoforms), and force generating capacity. This chapter uses the simplified classification of muscle fibers into two basic fiber types. Type I fibers are oxidative, fatigue resistant, slow contracting, and predominantly recruited during endurance activities. Type II fibers are less oxidative, more fatigable, fast contracting, and predominantly recruited during high force contractions. To determine fiber types, researchers typically use antibodies specific for protein isoforms with the most common being those of the contractile protein MHC. The majority of Type I fibers express the slow Type I MHC, while the majority of Type II fibers express different fast MHC isoforms (e.g., the Type IIx and Type IIa) [12].

Muscle Structural Protein Genomic Influences

Because structural proteins are important to muscle size and integrity of the fiber, mutations in their encoding genes might be expected to produce alterations in muscle size and performance. There is very little information on the genomics of skeletal muscle structure. The only structural protein to receive attention regarding associations among SNPs and muscle traits is alpha-actinin 3 (ACTN3). ACTN3, one of several alpha-actinins, anchors actin to the Z proteins in a sarcomere. It is found only in Type II muscle fibers and is thus implicated in fast contraction ability.

Several large scale investigations in humans have attempted to link SNPs in the *ACTN3* gene with individual differences in athletic phenotypes [13–17]. A common mutation in the *ACTN3* gene received much attention after initial reports suggested it might be linked to athletic performance. The R577X (rs1815739) mutation in *ACTN3* causes no functional *ACTN3* protein to be made because of a premature stop codon. Individuals who possess the XX (nonancestral) genotype have no ACTN3 protein being synthesized. While no ACTN3 protein is found in Type I fibers, the ubiquitous expression of a similar gene (i.e., *ACTN2*), found across all fiber types, could partially compensate for ACTN3-deficiency in Type II fibers, thereby avoiding exaggerated structural deficits [15, 16].

In a cross-sectional examination of an Australian cohort of athletes and controls, Yang et al. [18] found the *ACTN3* XX genotype (no ACTN3 protein) was less frequent in power athletes and more frequent in endurance athletes as compared to nonathlete controls. Several other groups have since attempted to validate this association, with mixed results often stratified by sex [15, 16]. Several studies suggested the *ACTN3* genotype affects muscle strength in women, while fewer studies have reported significant effects in men. Clarkson et al. [17] reported lower baseline isometric strength in XX vs. RX women, but greater increases in 1-RM after 12 weeks of resistance training. Delmonico et al. [13] reported higher baseline peak power in older women with the XX genotype and higher gains in power following 10 weeks of knee extensor resistance training, while no significant differences in peak power were found in older men (Fig. 7.1).

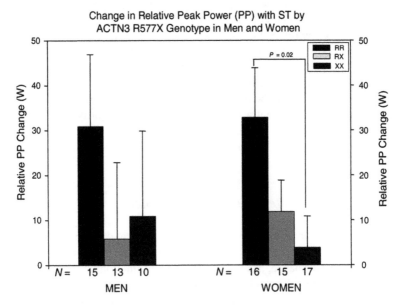

Fig. 7.1 Changes in knee extensor relative (70% of one-repetition maximum [1-RM] to baseline and after strength training [ST]) peak power (PP) with ST by alpha-actinin-3 (*ACTN3*) R577X genotype in men and women. When covarying for age and changes in the untrained leg, there was a significantly greater increase in relative PP in the RR group than in the XX group with ST in women ($p = 0.02$). There were no significant differences in relative PP change among genotype groups in men. Values are least-square means ± standard error of the mean. Figure reprinted with permission from Delmonico et al. [13]

Norman et al. [16] reported no differences in baseline power, torque-velocity relationship and fatigability among *ACTN3* genotype groups across young men and women. A subset of men ($N=21$) underwent two isokinetic exercise bouts within 1 week, which induced gains in peak torque only in RR men. The Norman et al. [16] data suggest an impaired responsiveness to training in XX men (women were not included in the training subcohort), which does not align with the greater increases in strength [13] and relative power [17] in XX genotype in women found by others [13, 17]. However, this study recruited previously trained subjects, and only employed two exercise bouts, while the Clarkson et al. [17] and Delmonico et al. [13] studies employed much longer supervised exercise training programs (10–12 weeks) in untrained subjects.

Yang et al. [18] suggested *ACTN3* SNPs may contribute to the distribution of Type I and Type II muscle fibers, thereby explaining the association of the *ACTN3* SNP with muscle power. In its role in binding to Z-line protein, ACTN3 colocalizes with calsarcins. Calsarcins are proteins that bind to calcineurin, which is hypothesized to play a role in determination of fiber types [19]. Two studies have examined the effects of ACTN3 deficiency on associations between *ACTN3* genotype and fiber type composition in men [19] and men and women [16]. Vincent et al. [19] reported men who were homozygous for the X allele and consequently deficient in the ACTN3 protein had significantly fewer Type IIx fibers as compared to those homozygous for the R allele. Also, ACTN3 protein content was higher in the Type IIx compared with Type IIa fibers. Vincent et al. [19] suggested the mechanism by which *ACTN3* SNPs influence muscle power is through control of fiber type distribution. However, Norman et al. [16] reported no difference in fiber type composition between XX and RR genotype groups.

To understand better the effects of a particular gene and its protein product on physiological function, it is possible to systematically eliminate single genes in animal models subsequently resulting in the loss of a protein. A mouse *Actn3* knockout model demonstrated functional and metabolic differences from normal littermates, while overall muscle morphology appeared unchanged [20–22]. Grip strength, body mass, and lean body mass were generally lower in the ACTN3 deficient mice, although mass differences were muscle specific. Increased aerobic enzyme expression, reduced fatigability, and altered contractile properties suggest a shift in muscle fibers towards oxidative rather than glycolytic metabolism in the ACTN3 deficient mice. ACTN3 may thus regulate fiber size and metabolic pathways rather than MHC composition, which is how muscle fiber type is classified in most human studies.

Strenuous resistance exercise results in damage to muscle fibers that is most evident in myofibrillar Z-line streaming in Type II fibers [23, 24]. The role of ACTN3 as a structural myofibrillar protein localized to the Z-disk suggests the *ACTN3* genotype may also affect the degree of physical damage that occurs in response to intense exercise. Specifically, without the stabilizing influence of ACTN3 in subjects homozygous for the X allele, Clarkson et al. [25] theorized these individuals would be more susceptible to Z-line disruption and exercise induced muscle damage. They therefore examined the association between indicators of muscle damage pre-and posteccentric exercise and the *ACTN3* R577X genotypes. They found no association of *ACTN3* genotype with postexercise indirect markers of muscle damage (i.e., muscle strength loss, blood creatine kinase [CK] activity, and blood myoglobin content). The lack of association may be explained by compensation of ACTN2 to stabilize the fibers.

In summary, ACTN3 is an important protein that contributes to skeletal muscle structural integrity. The R577X mutation in *ACTN3* causes no functional ACTN3 protein to be made in individuals possessing the XX genotype. The equivocal findings regarding the *ACTN3* genotype and skeletal muscle phenotype relationships may be due to interstudy variability in experimental design, sample size, and training programs. However, the preponderance of the data suggests the *ACTN3* R577X SNP is associated with skeletal muscle function. Further studies are needed to definitively document these associations and to determine the mechanisms to explain them.

Effects of Resistance Exercise and Genomics on Growth Factors

The functional link between strength training and muscle size gain is explained at the cellular level by the balance of protein synthesis and breakdown. Resistance exercise increases protein synthesis and breakdown, but increases in protein synthesis greatly outpace protein breakdown, producing net gains in protein accretion. For example, resistance exercise causes a rapid increase in protein synthesis within 1–2 h of a single bout, and this increased rate of synthesis typically persists for 24–48 h depending on the individual's training status [26–28]. Molecular pathways have been identified that are regulated by tension/load and growth factors and have been found to play key roles in the regulation of protein synthesis and degradation, leading to increased muscle size.

Growth Factor Effects on Protein Synthesis

The key pathway for protein synthesis and skeletal muscle growth is the phosphatidylinositol-3-kinase (PI3K)/protein kinase B (AKT)/mammalian target of rapamycin (mTOR) pathway. However, other pathways, notably the mitogen activated protein kinase (MAPK) pathway, also influence anabolic signaling. All of these pathways are modified by mechanical factors such as tension and load and growth factors such as insulin-like growth factor (IGF-I), mechano growth factor (MGF), and myostatin (MSTN).

Figure 7.2 presents a detailed schematic highlighting the specific proteins involved in protein synthesis and how increased mechanical tension and load activates the PI3K/AKT/mTOR pathway and subsequently protein synthesis. Essentially, this process is controlled through the activation of stimulus sensing proteins (IGF-I and MSTN), signal transduction proteins (AKT/PKB), and effector proteins (4E-BP1).

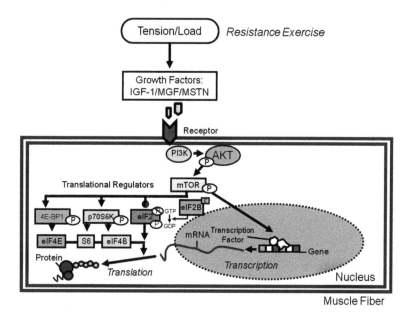

Fig. 7.2 Mechanisms of activation of protein synthesis in response to resistance training induced increase in growth factors. Tension and load increase growth factors such as insulin-like growth factor type I (IGF-I) and mechano growth factor (MGF), while decreasing the negative regulator of muscle growth, myostatin (MSTN). When IGF-I and MGF bind to their respective receptors, they activate, via phosphorylation, protein kinase B (AKT), which in turn phosphorylates mammalian target of rapamycin (mTOR). mTOR affects the phosphorylation of the translational regulators, eukaryotic translation initiation factor 4E-binding protein 1 (4E-BP1), ribosomal protein S6 kinase (p70S6K), and eukaryotic translation initiation factor 2Beta (eIF2B) resulting in increased translation and protein synthesis. MSTN, on the other hand, inhibits activation of the AKT/mTOR pathways

While Fig. 7.2 is in no way comprehensive regarding the necessary components for protein synthesis, the molecules listed are essential modifiers of the protein synthesis pathway and skeletal muscle hypertrophy. Much research has focused on the role of IGF-I and MGF in skeletal muscle hypertrophy because of the predominant role these sensor proteins play in regulating the activity of the PI3K/AKT/mTOR pathway and downstream signal transduction molecules and effector proteins (Fig. 7.2) [29–32]. For IGF-I and MSTN (and related growth factors), there is genomic evidence that genetic variation in their encoding gene affects the response of skeletal muscle to resistance exercise. For the other molecules, including AKT and mTOR, there are no published data to support a role of SNPs in the activity or abundance of these proteins in skeletal muscle.

IGF-I is a muscle growth factor that is produced by the liver and skeletal muscle in response to growth hormone secretion, and when increased beyond resting levels in skeletal muscle, stimulates protein synthesis [33–35]. Skeletal muscle IGF-I mRNA has been shown by some groups to increase in response to resistance exercise [32, 36, 37], while others have shown no change [38], or even a decrease [39].

Therefore, while IGF-I is a growth factor that promotes protein synthesis, the link between the resistance exercise signal and changes in IGF-I mRNA expression is not well response to increased load.

Other molecules that interact with IGF-I include calcineurin B, IGF-II and the binding proteins, such as IGF binding protein 3 (IGFBP3). In skeletal and cardiac muscle, IGF-I induced muscle hypertrophy is partially influenced by the calcium dependent calcineurin signaling pathway. Calcineurin is a protein phosphatase with two subunits, a catalytic subunit known as calcineurin A, and a regulatory calcium binding subunit, calcineurin B, the protein product of the protein phosphatase 3 regulatory subunit B (*PPP3R1*) gene [40]. The function of IGFBP3 is to prolong the half-life of IGF-I and IGF-II in the plasma, assisting with their interaction with cell surface receptors at the muscle site [41, 42]. IGF-II is a protein with a dual role in skeletal muscle depending on age. In the fetus, IGF-II is a major determinant of skeletal muscle growth. Once development is complete, IGF-II functions in skeletal muscle regeneration, specifically through its effects on satellite cell (muscle progenitor cell) proliferation [43]. For this reason, IGF-II gene expression during development is thought to influence age associated losses in muscle mass and strength [44].

MSTN is a negative regulator of skeletal muscle growth [30]. In skeletal muscle, MSTN has been reported to inhibit activation of the PI3K/AKT/mTOR signaling pathway [30]. This is evidenced by the double muscling phenotype in naturally occurring or genetically engineered *Mstn* knockout animals [45, 46]. MSTN protein levels have also been inversely correlated with muscle size in healthy and HIV affected men [47]. In response to resistance exercise in humans, Roth et al. [48] found a 37% decrease in MSTN mRNA levels following a heavy resistance training program among adults. However, MSTN mRNA levels were not associated with any size or strength measure, likely due to the small sample size ($N=15$). Although, MSTN is produced primarily in skeletal muscle cells, it also circulates in the blood and imposes its action on skeletal muscle through binding to activin receptors (ACVR2A and ACVR2B) on skeletal muscle cells. Follistatin (FST) is a glycoprotein that inhibits MSTN activity through regulating activin-receptor activity and by binding to the MSTN peptide in skeletal muscle preventing its binding to ACVR2B.

Genomic Influences on Growth Factors

Genetic variants in several hypertrophy-related growth factors have been associated with muscle traits and can be generally classified into two related pathways: IGF related genes (*IGF1, IGF2, IGFBP3* and *PPP3R1*) and myostatin-related genes (*MSTN, FST* and *ACVR2B*).

The IGF genes (*IGF1* and *IGF2*) are well known quantitative trait loci for growth and body composition in breeding animal stocks. The *IGF1* gene has a variable length sequence (rs10665874) located within its promoter region that is thought to influence *IGF1* transcription rate and IGF related phenotypes. In humans, the *IGF1* cytosine-adenosine (CA) 192 allele was associated with greater dynamic strength gains than noncarriers in a population of 67 comprising middle to old age men and women [49]. A later study from this group [50] reported an interaction effect between two genetic variations (the *IGF1* CA repeat and a small insertion/deletion variation in the promoter of the *PPP3R1* gene) on changes in muscle strength and muscle quality (strength per unit size) in 128 older individuals following resistance training. However, in this analysis, neither gene variant on its own was significantly associated with muscle traits. This gene×gene interaction suggests while each SNP might not account for enough variability to achieve a significant association level, variation across multiple variants could be additive, producing significant associations that could be further elucidated using a higher throughput approach (i.e., statistical models with a higher number of genotypes per trait) along with a larger sample size.

The *IGF2* ApaI polymorphism (rs680) has been associated with strength and fat free mass in two studies [51, 52]. Sayer et al. [51] showed men with the GG genotype had lower strength than men with the AA genotype, with no associations found in women. Conversely, Schrager et al. [52], who tested subjects from the Baltimore Longitudinal Study of Aging, reported the AA genotype was associated with lower strength in men and lower strength and fat free mass in women at the age of 35 years, an effect maintained in women aged 65 year. Devaney et al. [53] found no association of *IGF2* ApaI genotype on baseline muscle strength, but did find exaggerated strength loss following maximal eccentric exercise in individuals with the AA genotype ($N=12$) vs. G allele carriers. These subjects also had higher levels of CK activity 7 days postexercise suggesting they are more susceptible to exertional muscle damage. In response to eccentric or strenuous resistance exercise, satellite cells are activated and proliferated assisting in skeletal muscle repair [54–56]. Increased muscle damage in individuals with AA genotype may result in an accelerated and more efficient repair process with the end result being greater hypertrophy. However, until a clear relationship between the *IGF2* ApaI polymorphism and muscle strength or size has been established, these conclusions are speculative.

MSTN's effects on skeletal muscle have been observed from studies of naturally bred or genetically engineered animal models that produce no, or greatly reduced, MSTN protein. Only one report to date has described a similar condition in humans, the case study of a boy with a mutation in the *MSTN* gene [57], which was associated with reduced MSTN levels and gross muscle hypertrophy. More common SNPs in *MSTN* include two SNPs (rs1805086 and rs1805065) that result in a change in MSTN amino acid sequence modifying the ratio between latent and active MSTN protein levels [58]. Increased amounts of active MSTN inhibit muscle growth and development, which would ultimately affect muscle size and strength.

Early work [58] found no significant associations between *MSTN* SNPs and muscle size in 40 individuals, with the authors concluding that the skewed allelic frequencies in that population made detecting small effects improbable. Ivey et al. [59] subsequently found women in possession of the 2379G (nonancestral) allele ($N=5$) demonstrated a 68% greater increase in muscle size response to strength training as compared to women with the AA genotype ($N=15$), while no associations were found for men. Other studies of *MSTN* and *FST* polymorphisms have generated mixed results. For example, Walsh et al. [60] found no genetic associations of muscle traits with *FST* genotypes, but did find a significant association between *ACVR2B* (MSTN's receptor) and knee extensor concentric peak torque in women but not men.

The frequencies of these *MSTN* SNP alleles are higher in populations of African ancestry [61], as compared to Caucasians or Asians, suggesting the lack of associations between *MSTN* and muscle traits in populations not of African ancestry could be due to insufficient statistical power. Kostek et al. [62] found no significant associations between *MSTN* genotypes and muscle traits in a primarily Caucasian study population ($N=645$), but greater baseline maximal isometric strength in African-American carriers of the *MSTN* 2379G allele ($N=15$) as compared to individuals with the AA genotype ($N=8$). Kostek et al. [62] also found associations in this African-American subcohort among strength and SNPs in the *FST* gene, which produces a MSTN inhibiting hormone, theoretically releasing inhibition of muscle growth.

In summary, changes in the levels of mRNA and protein of growth factors affect anabolic signaling in skeletal muscle. In some cases, variations in the *IGF* and *MSTN* related genes are reported to have significant associations with skeletal muscle phenotypes. There appears to be a combined effect of variations in both the *IGF1* and *PPP3R1* genes that contribute to advantageous adaptations in baseline and training induced gains in skeletal muscle strength. The *IGF2* ApaI polymorphism, however, has shown equivocal results in regard to its effect on skeletal muscle strength and size. Associations between variations in the *MSTN* gene have shown promise in animals, but only a single case study in humans supports the role of a *MSTN* mutation contributing to significant muscle hypertrophy, and results of growth inhibitor SNP association studies are equivocal. Furthermore, demonstrated relationships between variations in the *MSTN* and *FST* genes and baseline muscle strength are largely reported to occur in African-American populations. There is not yet enough evidence to conclude common growth inhibitor polymorphisms play significant roles in modifying muscle strength or size at baseline or in response to training, likely due to skewed allelic distribution of these SNPs across ethnicities and possible sex differences, as well as limited sample sizes in the few studies that have been reported.

Effects of Resistance Exercise and Genomics on Inflammatory Factors

In addition to the growth factors, discussed in the previous section that promote increased muscle size by enhancing muscle protein synthesis, various inflammatory factors, called cytokines, can also contribute to skeletal muscle growth via various cellular mechanisms. Some inflammatory cytokines inhibit muscle cell growth by promoting protein breakdown or inhibiting protein synthesis [63]. Others promote cell growth, for example, by stimulating satellite cells proliferation and differentiation, a requisite for muscle repair following damage from resistance exercise [64].

Inflammatory Cytokine Responses to Resistance Exercise

Key inflammatory cytokines that respond to resistance exercise and have been shown to play roles in muscle protein balance include tumor necrosis factor alpha (TNF-alpha), interleukin-6 (IL-6), and interleukin-15 (IL-15). Each cytokine can have distinct roles and targets, but also interacts with other cytokines, growth hormones, and growth factors in the overall inflammatory process.

The cytokine TNF-alpha promotes skeletal muscle proteolysis [65], as inhibition of TNF-alpha reduces skeletal muscle wasting in animals with sepsis or cancer cachexia [66, 67]. TNF-alpha has been shown to inhibit the expression and activity of proteins such as growth hormone and IGF-I that are important contributors to skeletal muscle growth [68, 69]. Circulating and muscle TNF-alpha levels decrease with resistance training [70], with a generally inverse correlation between blood TNF-alpha and strength gains [71]. Although, a high degree of variability exists between cytokine levels and response to resistance training [72]. TNF-alpha is a potent activator of nuclear factor kappa B (NF-kB), which deactivates transcription factors and genes involved in MAPK pathway upregulation, the heat shock response (a subset of genes responsive to temperature or other stress), and release of inflammatory cytokines such as IL-6 [73–76]. Decreased phosphorylation of the MAPK pathway inhibits protein synthesis [77, 78].

IL-6 is produced and released from skeletal muscle following resistance exercise [79], and the magnitude of the IL-6 increase is dependent on exercise mode, intensity, and duration [80]. IL-6 expression is regulated by many stress responsive proteins, including TNF-alpha and NF-kB. While IL-6 may be indirectly associated with overall protein balance based on its interactions with proteins such as TNF-alpha, the primary roles of IL-6 are participating in the acute phase of stress response and regulation of muscle metabolism [81].

Ciliary neurotrophic factor (CNTF), a cytokine that is similar in structure to IL6 and shares a common receptor subunit, has also been proposed to be related to muscle traits based on its strong growth and cell survival effects in neurons [82]. Most studies of CNTF protein have focused on neuronal cell types rather than skeletal muscle fibers, although expression of CNTF mRNA in muscle was positively related to resistance training strength gains in an older population [83]. No studies to date have directly investigated the relationship of CNTF levels in muscle with muscle size.

IL-15 can increase in skeletal muscle following resistance exercise [84], although not all resistance exercise protocols evoke IL-15 increases. Overexpression of IL-15 in cell culture increases myofibrillar protein accretion [85, 86], which seems to be independent of satellite cell activation [85]. These effects found in in vitro experiments have not been demonstrated to date in in vivo human studies.

While TNF-alpha, IL-6, and IL-15 are known key regulators of growth and have been explored in many studies, other inflammatory factors could also play roles in determining muscle size. The inflammatory response is comprised of many elements, some of which simply have not yet been selected for study. An example of another potential inflammatory mediator of muscle growth is chemokine (C-C motif) ligand 2 (CCL2). CCL2 mRNA is dramatically upregulated following eccentric exercise [87, 88], and CCL2 is a key element in the interaction between macrophages and satellite cells [89]. Increased CCL2 expression could lead to enhanced recruitment of macrophages to the site of tissue injury, and greater expression of CCL2 by additional macrophages could enhance stimulation of satellite cells. Gene sequence variants in *CCL2* that alter CCL2 levels [90] would be particularly interesting SNPs to evaluate with respect to muscle size and strength gain in response to resistance exercise, given that satellite cell activation by macrophages is a critical step in muscle repair and subsequent growth.

Inflammatory Cytokine Genomic Influences

As mentioned above, inflammatory cytokines can have various roles in skeletal muscle, including regulating protein balance and satellite cell signaling. Given these roles, there are potential genetic variations in several cytokines and related genes could be associated with muscle strength and size traits in humans. The following section reviews the associations published to date on the TNF-alpha (*TNF*), *IL6*, *CNTF* and *IL15* genes.

It would be expected that individuals with genetic variants that elevate TNF-alpha levels (promoting proteolysis) would have a hard time maintaining a positive protein balance. In fact, several SNPs in the promoter region (i.e., area of the DNA sequence with potential to alter transcription levels) of *TNF* have been tested. Liu et al. [91] reported lower muscle mass in men with variants in two SNPs (rs1799964 and rs1800630) that increase TNF-alpha mRNA expression, while SNP associations with strength varied with selected loci and sex/ethnicity subpopulations in that same study.

The C (minor) allele of a SNP (rs1800795) in the *IL6* promoter has been associated with higher plasma IL-6 levels in a cohort of ~1,000 myocardial infarction survivors [92]. Testing the hypothesis individuals with the variant associated with elevated IL-6 could have smaller muscles (theoretically from increased stimulation of proteolysis via TNF-alpha), Roth et al. [93] found lower fat free mass in men (but not women) with the CC genotype at the *IL6* rs1800795 locus. Furthermore, Ruiz et al. [94] found the frequency of the GG genotype at the rs1800795 locus was significantly higher in elite power athletes (odds ratio of 2.4) than in elite endurance athletes or nonathlete controls. However, studies of *IL6* genotypes with muscle strength have found limited association, with Walston et al. [95] finding no associations with *IL6* promoter SNPs and muscle strength in older adults. In addition, Roth et al. [93] found no associations with strength across a large age span (20–92 years).

Based on the stimulatory effect of IL-15 on protein accretion in cell culture, polymorphisms in *IL15* and its receptor (*IL15RA*) have been hypothesized to be associated with muscle traits. However, only two *IL15* association studies have been published to date. Pistilli et al. [96] found associations between the *IL15RA* rs2228059 genotype and baseline muscle size and quality (strength/size) in men but not women. This report also showed associations between the *IL15* rs1057972 genotype and training induced strength gains in men, and between the *IL15RA* rs2296135 genotype and training induced strength gains in women. In an earlier study, Riechman et al. [97] found associations between *IL15RA* rs2296135 and lean body mass in men and women after resistance training, but no associations with strength.

Several studies that examined muscle strength and size in association with variants in the *CNTF* gene and its receptor (*CNTFR*) have generated mixed results. Roth et al. [98] associated *CNTFR* genotype with both fat free mass and strength, while Arking et al. [99] and De Mars et al. [100] did not find size differences across various *CNTF* and *CNTFR* genotypes. Association studies between baseline strength with *CNTF* and *CNTFR* genotypes have yielded equivocal, often with sex specific, results. Only one study examined the effect of resistance training and *CNTF* genotype on muscle. Walsh et al. [101] reported strength, but not size, differences in women between rs1800169 *CNTF* genotypes, with G allele carriers stronger at baseline and gaining more strength with resistance training. These strength gains were seen in both arms following unilateral resistance training, suggesting a neuromuscular signaling mechanism rather than local muscular adaptations. This is a hypothesis supported by data from Conwit et al. [102] showing differences in motor unit activation between *CNTF* genotype groups.

In summary, a number of associations between variations in genes coding for cytokines and muscle traits have been investigated. Results to date show variants in *TNFA* and *IL6* (in men) are associated with lower muscle mass, although effects on muscle strength are not clear. Variants in *CNTF* and its receptor likely do not affect muscle size but may be related to neuromuscular signaling. Two studies suggest muscle size may be related to *IL15* genotype, while strength results are again equivocal. It is possible that the higher sensitivity of size measures vs. the more variable nature of strength measures could account for these equivocal results. Differences in experimental groups and protocols used to investigate genetic associations of inflammatory genes with skeletal muscle traits also make it difficult to definitively conclude how much trait variability might be explained by inflammatory gene variations.

Genomics of Resistance Exercise, Strength, and Muscle Mass in Genes Outside of Traditional Hypertrophy Pathways

In the previous sections, three main categories of genes were explored in relation to strength and size muscle traits: structural genes, growth factors, and inflammatory factors. While most strength and size related loci studied to date fit into one of these three categories, a few gene associations with muscle traits have been found in genes outside of the normal hypertrophy pathways [103]. These include angiotensin 1 converting enzyme (*ACE*) and the vitamin D receptor (*VDR*).

ACE typically affects blood flow, therefore *ACE* variations have most often been related to endurance muscle traits [103]. Associations between *ACE* genotype and strength have been investigated, yielding equivocal results [103–106]. VDR acts as a transcription factor and a nonhypertrophy related steroid receptor and is thought to relate to baseline muscle traits via effects on early muscle development [107]. As such, *VDR* polymorphisms have been related to baseline muscle strength [108, 109], but have not been studied in relation to changes following strength training. Even when associations are found between variants in these "orphan" genes and muscle traits, very small amounts of variability are explained. While it is biologically plausible, multiple SNPs in related genes (such as those within biological pathways such as AKT) may have additive effects (i.e., epistasis or multigene interactions); it is less plausible that variants in orphan genes such as *ACE* and *VDR* would contribute to additive effects, making their individual contributions to strength and size gains following resistance training marginal at best. At the current time, insufficient data exist to say these genes link to known strength and hypertrophy pathways.

The Future

While the field of exercise genomics is young, the studies reviewed in this chapter demonstrate that various genes can harbor genetic polymorphisms explaining some of the large variability in muscle strength and size traits. However, in most cases, single variants and single genes do not account for high percentages of trait variability on their own and few interactions between multiple genetic variations have been investigated to date. Based on the rare instances where interactions among genes in similar biological pathways have been tested, it appears that effects across multiple variants could be additive. A higher throughput research approach (i.e., statistical models with a higher number of genotypes per trait) would enable identification of these multiple gene/loci associations in studies with adequate statistical power (i.e., sample size).

The vast majority of published genomics studies have used a candidate gene approach, where investigators select genes and variants of interest for study. A key problem with this approach is the current lack of knowledge about underlying mechanisms driving each trait, making candidate gene selection difficult. For skeletal muscle strength and size traits, candidate genes have typically been identified from known anabolic pathways or via expression profiling studies. However, multiple physiological adaptations occur within skeletal muscle in response to specific training programs, each regulated by specific genes and their respective gene products. Skeletal muscle strength and size are polygenic traits, arising from the input of many genes and proteins, of which some are poorly defined. Therefore, many potentially regulatory DNA variations in candidate genes simply have yet to be selected for study. This limitation should be minimized as higher throughput genotyping methods become more cost effective and commonplace.

The use of genome wide association studies (GWAS) [110] has emerged as an alternate, higher throughput approach that avoids the gene selection issues that limit the candidate gene approach. The latest GWAS platforms can screen over one million loci simultaneously for associations with traits of interest, and some are coupled with technologies that can also read epigenetic modifications (nonheritable DNA regulation). In a GWAS study, Liu et al. [111] reported two loci in the thyrotropin-releasing hormone receptor (*TRHR*) gene that are associated with lean body mass. TRHR stimulates cascades via thyroxin that enable the anabolic effects of IGF-I. Liu et al. [111] speculated the association of *TRHR* and lean body mass could be driven by modification of the IGF-I pathway. While only two loci achieved statistical significance in this GWAS, an additional 146 loci demonstrated "suggestive" associations with lean body mass. These findings highlight a key limitation of GWAS studies: multiple testing corrections necessitate very stringent filters for significance (typically $p < 10^{-7}$ or 10^{-8}). Given the stringency of these filters, GWAS studies often require thousands to tens of thousands of subjects to find significant loci in cross sectional designs.

Although GWAS is touted as an "agnostic" approach to loci discovery, where variant selection for study is random and not informed by a priori hypotheses, there also is the potential for bias in the selection of the million loci represented on the GWAS arrays [112]. This limitation can be avoided by fully sequencing the genome via highly parallel ("next generation") sequencing techniques [113]. The predicted cost of sequencing all three billion base pairs will drop towards $1,000 per subject over the next decade, which is nearly the current cost per sample for GWAS studies examining 500K to 1M variations. Despite the fact that declining costs make highly parallel sequencing an appealing alternative to GWAS, technical and statistical concerns still exist with this technology.

While technologies push forward, knowing full genetic sequences for all people still does not address key questions regarding the nature of relationships between traits and underlying genetic variations. These relationships need to be addressed using multiple layers of data that cover both molecular and functional data, as well as environmental information. It is clear from the genetic variation literature summarized in this chapter that not only are the mechanisms driving strength and size variability not fully understood, but studies done to date have also varied widely in many confounding factors such as different exercise regimens, muscle groups, or populations tested. To address these issues, it is important future studies utilize muscle samples from various study designs (exercise regimens, muscle groups and populations) to elucidate molecular consequences of candidate SNPs determining if chosen variations affect mRNA levels, splicing of transcripts, and/or protein levels.

It is also possible that variations in one gene can control expression of other genes and related proteins, which can be explored using software that indexes known gene and protein relationships, commonly referred to as network or pathway analysis. Future studies should incorporate sequence information, transcriptional and translational data, protein localization, tissue characteristics (muscle composition

---

and size), and environmental data like training status. Methods of systems biology modeling of gene networks are just being developed and applied to different diseases, and in the future could be applied to muscle traits like strength and size.

Practical Applications

Skeletal muscle function is critical to athletes and nonathletes alike as a major contributor to quality of life, as well as athletic performance. Better understanding of the genetics underlying muscle strength and size could have several practical applications, including the advancement of personal genomics that can be used to predict who will respond positively and negatively to different interventions like exercise and drug therapy. For example, a genetic test for the *ACTN3* R577X variant has been commercially available for years claiming to help people predict their "innate sports performance abilities," including responsiveness to training. Thousands of these tests have been sold, often to parents who want to predict their children's "athletic ability." While current data do not support a high predictability of existing genetic tests for muscle traits such as *ACTN3*, improved test development with a better knowledge base could enable performance prediction capabilities.

In addition to the use of exercise genomics to predict athletic performance, knowledge of muscle trait related loci could have more direct impact on current athletes if scientists determine how to exploit "good genes." One example of this exploitation would be the development of a successful MSTN inhibitor, which does not currently exist on the market, but is in strong demand. How to prevent or regulate genetic manipulations or gene "doping" is an emerging field, tied to the advancement of knowledge of muscle related genes.

While personalized training and gene doping are key applications of exercise genomics to current and future athletes, optimization of muscle health has applications to athletes and nonathletes alike. For example, individuals who have genetic backgrounds that are associated with lower strength may want to adopt strength training regimens, especially as they age to maintain healthy muscle function, which can influence other factors, such as body weight regulation and bone health. Another example would be the tailoring of rehabilitation programs after injury, based on genetic associations with strength development. Overall, musculoskeletal health across the population can be enhanced in the future with greater knowledge of genomic contributors to these health related traits.

References

1. Baechle T, Earle R, editors. Essentials of Strength Training and Conditioning: Human Kinetics, 2008.
2. Sale DG. Neural adaptation to resistance training. Med Sci Sports Exerc. 1988;20 (5 Suppl):S135–45.

3. Hubal MJ, Gordish-Dressman H, Thompson PD, Price TB, Hoffman EP, Angelopoulos TJ, et al. Variability in muscle size and strength gain after unilateral resistance training. Med Sci Sports Exerc. 2005;37(6):964–72.
4. Thomis MA, Beunen GP, Van Leemputte M, Maes HH, Blimkie CJ, Claessens AL, et al. Inheritance of static and dynamic arm strength and some of its determinants. Acta Physiol Scand. 1998;163(1):59–71.
5. Thomis MA, Beunen GP, Maes HH, Blimkie CJ, Van Leemputte M, Claessens AL, et al. Strength training: importance of genetic factors. Med Sci Sports Exerc. 1998;30(5): 724–31.
6. Perusse L, Lortie G, Leblanc C, Tremblay A, Theriault G, Bouchard C. Genetic and environmental sources of variation in physical fitness. Ann Hum Biol. 1987;14(5):425–34.
7. Seeman E, Hopper JL, Young NR, Formica C, Goss P, Tsalamandris C. Do genetic factors explain associations between muscle strength, lean mass, and bone density? A twin study. Am J Physiol. 1996;270(2 Pt 1):E320–7.
8. Nguyen TV, Howard GM, Kelly PJ, Eisman JA. Bone mass, lean mass, and fat mass: same genes or same environments? Am J Epidemiol. 1998;147(1):3–16.
9. Forbes GB, Sauer EP, Weitkamp LR. Lean body mass in twins. Metabolism. 1995;44(11):1442–6.
10. Calvo M, Rodas G, Vallejo M, Estruch A, Arcas A, Javierre C, et al. Heritability of explosive power and anaerobic capacity in humans. Eur J Appl Physiol. 2002;86(3):218–25.
11. Baar K, Nader G, Bodine S. Resistance exercise, muscle loading/unloading and the control of muscle mass. Essays Biochem. 2006;42:61–74.
12. Weiss A, Leinwand LA. The mammalian myosin heavy chain gene family. Annu Rev Cell Dev Biol. 1996;12:417–39.
13. Delmonico MJ, Kostek MC, Doldo NA, Hand BD, Walsh S, Conway JM, et al. Alpha-actinin-3 (ACTN3) R577X polymorphism influences knee extensor peak power response to strength training in older men and women. J Gerontol A Biol Sci Med Sci. 2007;62(2):206–12.
14. MacArthur DG, North KN. A gene for speed? The evolution and function of alpha-actinin-3. Bioessays. 2004;26(7):786–95.
15. MacArthur DG, North KN. ACTN3: A genetic influence on muscle function and athletic performance. Exerc Sport Sci Rev. 2007;35(1):30–4.
16. Norman B, Esbjornsson M, Rundqvist H, Osterlund T, von Walden F, Tesch PA. Strength, power, fiber types, and mRNA expression in trained men and women with different ACTN3 R577X genotypes. J Appl Physiol. 2009;106(3):959–65.
17. Clarkson PM, Devaney JM, Gordish-Dressman H, Thompson PD, Hubal MJ, Urso M, et al. ACTN3 genotype is associated with increases in muscle strength in response to resistance training in women. J Appl Physiol. 2005;99(1):154–63.
18. Yang N, MacArthur DG, Gulbin JP, Hahn AG, Beggs AH, Easteal S, et al. ACTN3 genotype is associated with human elite athletic performance. Am J Hum Genet. 2003;73(3):627–31.
19. Vincent B, De Bock K, Ramaekers M, Van den Eede E, Van Leemputte M, Hespel P, et al. ACTN3 (R577X) genotype is associated with fiber type distribution. Physiol Genomics. 2007;32(1):58–63.
20. MacArthur DG, Seto JT, Chan S, Quinlan KG, Raftery JM, Turner N, et al. An Actn3 knock-out mouse provides mechanistic insights into the association between alpha-actinin-3 deficiency and human athletic performance. Hum Mol Genet. 2008;17(8):1076–86.
21. MacArthur DG, Seto JT, Raftery JM, Quinlan KG, Huttley GA, Hook JW, et al. Loss of ACTN3 gene function alters mouse muscle metabolism and shows evidence of positive selection in humans. Nat Genet. 2007;39(10):1261–5.
22. Chan S, Seto JT, MacArthur DG, Yang N, North KN, Head SI. A gene for speed: contractile properties of isolated whole EDL muscle from an alpha-actinin-3 knockout mouse. Am J Physiol Cell Physiol. 2008;295(4):C897–904.
23. Friden J. Changes in human skeletal muscle induced by long-term eccentric exercise. Cell Tissue Res. 1984;236(2):365–72.

24. Friden J, Sjostrom M, Ekblom B. Myofibrillar damage following intense eccentric exercise in man. Int J Sports Med. 1983;4(3):170–6.
25. Clarkson PM, Hoffman EP, Zambraski E, Gordish-Dressman H, Kearns A, Hubal M, et al. ACTN3 and MLCK genotype associations with exertional muscle damage. J Appl Physiol. 2005;99(2):564–9.
26. Phillips SM, Tipton KD, Aarsland A, Wolf SE, Wolfe RR. Mixed muscle protein synthesis and breakdown after resistance exercise in humans. Am J Physiol. 1997;273(1 Pt 1):E99–107.
27. Biolo G. Increased rates of muscle protein turnover and amino acid transport after resistance exercise in humans. Am J Physiol Endocrinol Metab. 1995;268:E514–E20.
28. Macdougall JD, Gibala, MJ, Tarnapolsky, MA. The time course for elevated muscle protein synthesis following heavy resistance exercise. Can J Appl Physiol. 1995;20:480–6.
29. Zanchi NE, Lancha AH, Jr. Mechanical stimuli of skeletal muscle: implications on mTOR/p70s6k and protein synthesis. Eur J Appl Physiol. 2008;102(3):253–63.
30. Trendelenburg AU, Meyer A, Rohner D, Boyle J, Hatakeyama S, Glass DJ. Myostatin reduces Akt/TORC1/p70S6K signaling, inhibiting myoblast differentiation and myotube size. Am J Physiol Cell Physiol. 2009;296(6):C1258–70.
31. Sacheck JM, Ohtsuka A, McLary SC, Goldberg AL. IGF-I stimulates muscle growth by suppressing protein breakdown and expression of atrophy-related ubiquitin ligases, atrogin-1 and MuRF1. Am J Physiol Endocrinol Metab. 2004;287(4):E591–601.
32. Deldicque L, Louis M, Theisen D, Nielens H, Dehoux M, Thissen JP, et al. Increased IGF mRNA in human skeletal muscle after creatine supplementation. Med Sci Sports Exerc. 2005;37(5):731–6.
33. Latres E, Amini AR, Amini AA, Griffiths J, Martin FJ, Wei Y, et al. Insulin-like growth factor-1 (IGF-1) inversely regulates atrophy-induced genes via the phosphatidylinositol 3-kinase/Akt/mammalian target of rapamycin (PI3K/Akt/mTOR) pathway. J Biol Chem. 2005;280(4):2737–44.
34. Goldspink G. Mechanical Signals, IGF-I Gene Splicing, and Muscle Adaptation. Physiology. 2005;20(4):232–8.
35. Cheema U, Brown R, Mudera V, Yang SY, McGrouther G, Goldspink G. Mechanical signals and IGF-I gene splicing in vitro in relation to development of skeletal muscle. J Cell Physiol. 2005;202(1):67–75.
36. Bamman MM, Petrella JK, Kim JS, Mayhew DL, Cross JM. Cluster analysis tests the importance of myogenic gene expression during myofiber hypertrophy in humans. J Appl Physiol. 2007;102(6):2232–9.
37. Greig CA, Hameed M, Young A, Goldspink G, Noble B. Skeletal muscle IGF-I isoform expression in healthy women after isometric exercise. Growth Horm IGF Res. 2006;16 (5-6):373–6.
38. Psilander N, Damsgaard R, Pilegaard H. Resistance exercise alters MRF and IGF-I mRNA content in human skeletal muscle. J Appl Physiol. 2003;95(3):1038–44.
39. Coffey VG, Reeder DW, Lancaster GI, Yeo WK, Febbraio MA, Yaspelkis BB, 3rd, et al. Effect of high-frequency resistance exercise on adaptive responses in skeletal muscle. Med Sci Sports Exerc. 2007;39(12):2135–44.
40. Musaro A, McCullagh KJ, Naya FJ, Olson EN, Rosenthal N. IGF-1 induces skeletal myocyte hypertrophy through calcineurin in association with GATA-2 and NF-ATc1. Nature. 1999;400(6744):581–5.
41. Ferry RJ, Jr., Katz LE, Grimberg A, Cohen P, Weinzimer SA. Cellular actions of insulin-like growth factor binding proteins. Horm Metab Res. 1999;31(2-3):192–202.
42. Jones JI, Clemmons DR. Insulin-like growth factors and their binding proteins: biological actions. Endocr Rev. 1995;16(1):3–34.
43. Goldberg AL, Etlinger JD, Goldspink DF, Jablecki C. Mechanism of work-induced hypertrophy of skeletal muscle. Med Sci Sports. 1975;7(3):185–98.
44. Marsh DR, Criswell DS, Hamilton MT, Booth FW. Association of insulin-like growth factor mRNA expressions with muscle regeneration in young, adult, and old rats. Am J Physiol. 1997;273(1 Pt 2):R353–8.

45. McPherron AC, Lawler AM, Lee SJ. Regulation of skeletal muscle mass in mice by a new TGF-beta superfamily member. Nature. 1997;387(6628):83–90.
46. Grobet L, Martin LJ, Poncelet D, Pirottin D, Brouwers B, Riquet J, et al. A deletion in the bovine myostatin gene causes the double-muscled phenotype in cattle. Nat Genet. 1997;17(1):71–4.
47. Gonzalez-Cadavid NF, Taylor WE, Yarasheski K, Sinha-Hikim I, Ma K, Ezzat S, et al. Organization of the human myostatin gene and expression in healthy men and HIV-infected men with muscle wasting. Proc Natl Acad Sci. 1998;95(25):14938–43.
48. Roth SM, Martel GF, Ferrell RE, Metter EJ, Hurley BF, Rogers MA. Myostatin gene expression is reduced in humans with heavy-resistance strength training: a brief communication. Exp Biol Med. 2003;228(6):706–9.
49. Kostek MC, Delmonico MJ, Reichel JB, Roth SM, Douglass L, Ferrell RE, et al. Muscle strength response to strength training is influenced by insulin-like growth factor 1 genotype in older adults. J Appl Physiol. 2005;98(6):2147–54.
50. Hand BD, Kostek MC, Ferrell RE, Delmonico MJ, Douglass LW, Roth SM, et al. Influence of promoter region variants of insulin-like growth factor pathway genes on the strength-training response of muscle phenotypes in older adults. J Appl Physiol. 2007;103(5): 1678–87.
51. Sayer AA, Syddall H, O'Dell SD, Chen XH, Briggs PJ, Briggs R, et al. Polymorphism of the IGF2 gene, birth weight and grip strength in adult men. Age Ageing. 2002;31(6): 468–70.
52. Schrager MA, Roth SM, Ferrell RE, Metter EJ, Russek-Cohen E, Lynch NA, et al. Insulin-like growth factor-2 genotype, fat-free mass, and muscle performance across the adult life span. J Appl Physiol. 2004;97(6):2176–83.
53. Devaney JM, Hoffman EP, Gordish-Dressman H, Kearns A, Zambraski E, Clarkson PM. IGF-II gene region polymorphisms related to exertional muscle damage. J Appl Physiol. 2007;102(5):1815–23.
54. Clarkson PM, Hubal MJ. Exercise-induced muscle damage in humans. Am J Phys Med Rehabil. 2002;81(11 Suppl):S52–69.
55. Yu JG, Carlsson L, Thornell LE. Evidence for myofibril remodeling as opposed to myofibril damage in human muscles with DOMS: an ultrastructural and immunoelectron microscopic study. Histochem Cell Biol. 2004;121(3):219–27.
56. Yu JG, Furst DO, Thornell LE. The mode of myofibril remodelling in human skeletal muscle affected by DOMS induced by eccentric contractions. Histochem Cell Biol. 2003; 119(5):383–93.
57. Schuelke M, Wagner KR, Stolz LE, Hubner C, Riebel T, Komen W, et al. Myostatin mutation associated with gross muscle hypertrophy in a child. N Engl J Med. 2004;350(26):2682–8.
58. Ferrell RE, Conte V, Lawrence EC, Roth SM, Hagberg JM, Hurley BF. Frequent sequence variation in the human myostatin (GDF8) gene as a marker for analysis of muscle-related phenotypes. Genomics. 1999;62(2):203–7.
59. Ivey FM, Roth SM, Ferrell RE, Tracy BL, Lemmer JT, Hurlbut DE, et al. Effects of age, gender, and myostatin genotype on the hypertrophic response to heavy resistance strength training. J Gerontol A Biol Sci Med Sci. 2000;55(11):M641–8.
60. Walsh S, Metter EJ, Ferrucci L, Roth SM. Activin-type II receptor B (ACVR2B) and follistatin haplotype associations with muscle mass and strength in humans. J Appl Physiol. 2007;102(6):2142–8.
61. Saunders MA, Good JM, Lawrence EC, Ferrell RE, Li WH, Nachman MW. Human adaptive evolution at Myostatin (GDF8), a regulator of muscle growth. Am J Hum Genet. 2006;79(6):1089–97.
62. Kostek MA, Angelopoulos TJ, Clarkson PM, Gordon PM, Moyna NM, Visich PS, et al. Myostatin and follistatin polymorphisms interact with muscle phenotypes and ethnicity. Med Sci Sports Exerc. 2009;41(5):1063–71.
63. Frost RA, Lang CH. Protein kinase B/Akt: a nexus of growth factor and cytokine signaling in determining muscle mass. J Appl Physiol. 2007;103(1):378–87.

64. Tidball JG. Inflammatory processes in muscle injury and repair. Am J Physiol Regul Integr Comp Physiol. 2005;288(2):R345–53.

65. Pahl HL. Activators and target genes of Rel/NF-kappaB transcription factors. Oncogene. 1999;18(49):6853–66.

66. Costelli P, Carbo N, Tessitore L, Bagby GJ, Lopez-Soriano FJ, Argiles JM, et al. Tumor necrosis factor-alpha mediates changes in tissue protein turnover in a rat cancer cachexia model. J Clin Invest. 1993;92(6):2783–9.

67. Breuille D, Farge MC, Rose F, Arnal M, Attaix D, Obled C. Pentoxifylline decreases body weight loss and muscle protein wasting characteristics of sepsis. Am J Physiol. 1993;265 (4 Pt 1):E660–6.

68. Fernandez-Celemin L, Pasko N, Blomart V, Thissen JP. Inhibition of muscle insulin-like growth factor I expression by tumor necrosis factor-alpha. Am J Physiol Endocrinol Metab. 2002;283(6):E1279–90.

69. Langen RC, Schols AM, Kelders MC, Wouters EF, Janssen-Heininger YM. Inflammatory cytokines inhibit myogenic differentiation through activation of nuclear factor-kappaB. Faseb J. 2001;15(7):1169–80.

70. Greiwe JS, Cheng B, Rubin DC, Yarasheski KE, Semenkovich CF. Resistance exercise decreases skeletal muscle tumor necrosis factor alpha in frail elderly humans. Faseb J. 2001;15(2):475–82.

71. Bruunsgaard H, Bjerregaard E, Schroll M, Pedersen BK. Muscle strength after resistance training is inversely correlated with baseline levels of soluble tumor necrosis factor receptors in the oldest old. J Am Geriatr Soc. 2004;52(2):237–41.

72. Malm C, Nyberg P, Engstrom M, Sjodin B, Lenkei R, Ekblom B, et al. Immunological changes in human skeletal muscle and blood after eccentric exercise and multiple biopsies. J Physiol. 2000;529 Pt 1:243–62.

73. Dahlman JM, Wang J, Bakkar N, Guttridge DC. The RelA/p65 subunit of NF-kappaB specifically regulates cyclin D1 protein stability: implications for cell cycle withdrawal and skeletal myogenesis. J Cell Biochem. 2009;106(1):42–51.

74. Grounds MD, Radley HG, Gebski BL, Bogoyevitch MA, Shavlakadze T. Implications of cross-talk between tumour necrosis factor and insulin-like growth factor-1 signalling in skeletal muscle. Clin Exp Pharmacol Physiol. 2008;35(7):846–51.

75. Guttridge DC, Albanese C, Reuther JY, Pestell RG, Baldwin AS, Jr. NF-kappaB controls cell growth and differentiation through transcriptional regulation of cyclin D1. Mol Cell Biol. 1999;19(8):5785–99.

76. Guttridge DC, Mayo MW, Madrid LV, Wang CY, Baldwin AS, Jr. NF-kappaB-induced loss of MyoD messenger RNA: possible role in muscle decay and cachexia. Science. 2000;289(5488):2363–6.

77. Millino C, Fanin M, Vettori A, Laveder P, Mostacciuolo ML, Angelini C, et al. Different atrophy-hypertrophy transcription pathways in muscles affected by severe and mild spinal muscular atrophy. BMC Med. 2009;7:14.

78. Vary TC, Deiter G, Lang CH. Diminished ERK 1/2 and p38 MAPK phosphorylation in skeletal muscle during sepsis. Shock. 2004;22(6):548–54.

79. Buford TW, Cooke MB, Willoughby DS. Resistance exercise-induced changes of inflammatory gene expression within human skeletal muscle. Eur J Appl Physiol. 2009;107(4): 463–71.

80. Febbraio MA, Pedersen BK. Muscle-derived interleukin-6: mechanisms for activation and possible biological roles. Faseb J. 2002;16(11):1335–47.

81. Pedersen BK, Febbraio MA. Muscle as an endocrine organ: focus on muscle-derived interleukin-6. Physiol Rev. 2008;88(4):1379–406.

82. Ip NY, Yancopoulos GD. Ciliary neurotrophic factor and its receptor complex. Prog Growth Factor Res. 1992;4(2):139–55.

83. Dennis RA, Zhu H, Kortebein PM, Bush HM, Harvey JF, Sullivan DH, et al. Muscle expression of genes associated with inflammation, growth, and remodeling is strongly correlated in older adults with resistance training outcomes. Physiol Genomics. 2009;38(2):169–75.

84. Nielsen AR, Mounier R, Plomgaard P, Mortensen OH, Penkowa M, Speerschneider T, et al. Expression of interleukin-15 in human skeletal muscle effect of exercise and muscle fibre type composition. J Physiol. 2007;584 (Pt 1):305–12.

85. Furmanczyk PS, Quinn LS. Interleukin-15 increases myosin accretion in human skeletal myogenic cultures. Cell Biol Int. 2003;27(10):845–51.

86. Quinn LS, Anderson BG, Drivdahl RH, Alvarez B, Argiles JM. Overexpression of interleukin-15 induces skeletal muscle hypertrophy in vitro: implications for treatment of muscle wasting disorders. Exp Cell Res. 2002;280(1):55–63.

87. Hubal MJ, Chen TC, Thompson PD, Clarkson PM. Inflammatory gene changes associated with the repeated-bout effect. Am J Physiol Regul Integr Comp Physiol. 2008;294(5): R1628–37.

88. Chen YW, Hubal MJ, Hoffman EP, Thompson PD, Clarkson PM. Molecular responses of human muscle to eccentric exercise. J Appl Physiol. 2003;95(6):2485–94.

89. Chazaud B, Sonnet C, Lafuste P, Bassez G, Rimaniol AC, Poron F, et al. Satellite cells attract monocytes and use macrophages as a support to escape apoptosis and enhance muscle growth. J Cell Biol. 2003;163(5):1133–43.

90. McDermott DH, Yang Q, Kathiresan S, Cupples LA, Massaro JM, Keaney JF, Jr., et al. CCL2 polymorphisms are associated with serum monocyte chemoattractant protein-1 levels and myocardial infarction in the Framingham Heart Study. Circulation. 2005;112(8):1113–20.

91. Liu D, Metter EJ, Ferrucci L, Roth SM. TNF promoter polymorphisms associated with muscle phenotypes in humans. J Appl Physiol. 2008;105(3):859–67.

92. Ljungman P, Bellander T, Nyberg F, Lampa E, Jacquemin B, Kolz M, et al. DNA variants, plasma levels and variability of interleukin-6 in myocardial infarction survivors: results from the AIRGENE study. Thromb Res. 2009;124(1):57–64.

93. Roth SM, Schrager MA, Lee MR, Metter EJ, Hurley BF, Ferrell RE. Interleukin-6 (IL6) genotype is associated with fat-free mass in men but not women. J Gerontol A Biol Sci Med Sci. 2003;58(12):B1085–8.

94. Ruiz JR, Buxens A, Artieda M, Arteta D, Santiago C, Rodriguez-Romo G, et al. The -174 G/C polymorphism of the IL6 gene is associated with elite power performance. J Sci Med Sport. 2009.

95. Walston J, Arking DE, Fallin D, Li T, Beamer B, Xue Q, et al. IL-6 gene variation is not associated with increased serum levels of IL-6, muscle, weakness, or frailty in older women. Exp Gerontol. 2005;40(4):344–52.

96. Pistilli EE, Devaney JM, Gordish-Dressman H, Bradbury MK, Seip RL, Thompson PD, et al. Interleukin-15 and interleukin-15R alpha SNPs and associations with muscle, bone, and predictors of the metabolic syndrome. Cytokine. 2008;43(1):45–53.

97. Riechman SE, Balasekaran G, Roth SM, Ferrell RE. Association of interleukin-15 protein and interleukin-15 receptor genetic variation with resistance exercise training responses. J Appl Physiol. 2004;97(6):2214–9.

98. Roth SM, Metter EJ, Lee MR, Hurley BF, Ferrell RE. C174T polymorphism in the CNTF receptor gene is associated with fat-free mass in men and women. J Appl Physiol. 2003;95(4):1425–30.

99. Arking DE, Fallin DM, Fried LP, Li T, Beamer BA, Xue QL, et al. Variation in the ciliary neurotrophic factor gene and muscle strength in older Caucasian women. J Am Geriatr Soc. 2006;54(5):823–6.

100. De Mars G, Windelinckx A, Beunen G, Delecluse C, Lefevre J, Thomis MA. Polymorphisms in the CNTF and CNTF receptor genes are associated with muscle strength in men and women. J Appl Physiol. 2007;102(5):1824–31.

101. Walsh S, Kelsey BK, Angelopoulos TJ, Clarkson PM, Gordon PM, Moyna NM, et al. CNTF 1357 G -> A polymorphism and the muscle strength response to resistance training. J Appl Physiol. 2009;107(4):1235–40.

102. Conwit RA, Ling S, Roth S, Stashuk D, Hurley B, Ferrell R, et al. The relationship between ciliary neurotrophic factor (CNTF) genotype and motor unit physiology: preliminary studies. BMC Physiol. 2005;5:15.

103. Bray MS, Hagberg JM, Perusse L, Rankinen T, Roth SM, Wolfarth B, et al. The human gene map for performance and health-related fitness phenotypes: the 2006-2007 update. Med Sci Sports Exerc. 2009;41(1):35–73.
104. Folland J, Leach B, Little T, Hawker K, Myerson S, Montgomery H, et al. Angiotensin-converting enzyme genotype affects the response of human skeletal muscle to functional overload. Exp Physiol. 2000;85(5):575–9.
105. Pescatello LS, Kostek MA, Gordish-Dressman H, Thompson PD, Seip RL, Price TB, et al. ACE ID genotype and the muscle strength and size response to unilateral resistance training. Med Sci Sports Exerc. 2006;38(6):1074–81.
106. McCauley T, Mastana SS, Hossack J, Macdonald M, Folland JP. Human angiotensin-converting enzyme I/D and alpha-actinin 3 R577X genotypes and muscle functional and contractile properties. Exp Physiol. 2009;94(1):81–9.
107. Pfeifer M, Begerow B, Minne HW. Vitamin D and muscle function. Osteoporos Int. 2002;13(3):187–94.
108. Windelinckx A, De Mars G, Beunen G, Aerssens J, Delecluse C, Lefevre J, et al. Polymorphisms in the vitamin D receptor gene are associated with muscle strength in men and women. Osteoporos Int. 2007;18(9):1235–42.
109. Grundberg E, Brandstrom H, Ribom EL, Ljunggren O, Mallmin H, Kindmark A. Genetic variation in the human vitamin D receptor is associated with muscle strength, fat mass and body weight in Swedish women. Eur J Endocrinol. 2004;150(3):323–8.
110. Manolio TA, Collins FS, Cox NJ, Goldstein DB, Hindorff LA, Hunter DJ, et al. Finding the missing heritability of complex diseases. Nature. 2009;461(7265):747–53.
111. Liu XG, Tan LJ, Lei SF, Liu YJ, Shen H, Wang L, et al. Genome-wide association and replication studies identified TRHR as an important gene for lean body mass. Am J Hum Genet. 2009;84(3):418–23.
112. Tucker T, Marra M, Friedman JM. Massively parallel sequencing: the next big thing in genetic medicine. Am J Hum Genet 2009;85(2):142–54.
113. Schadt EE. Molecular networks as sensors and drivers of common human diseases. Nature. 2009;461(7261):218–23.

Chapter 8
Genomics of Aerobic Capacity and Endurance Performance: Clinical Implications

Yannis Pitsiladis, Guan Wang, and Bernd Wolfarth

Keywords Body mass index • Coronary artery disease • Genome-wide association study • Knockout • Linkage disequilibrium • Maximal oxygen consumption ($\dot{V}O_2$max) • Odds ratio • Performance-associated polymorphism • Recombinant human erythropoietin • One-repetition maximum • Single nucleotide polymorphism • Triglyceride • Type 2 diabetes mellitus

Introduction

In this chapter the genomics of health-related fitness including physical performance and training is reviewed in light of the extensive data from relatively small single gene association studies but also incorporating findings from more recent studies involving larger cohorts and multiple genes as well as a limited number of studies using genome-wide approaches. Despite numerous attempts in recent years to discover genes associating with health-related fitness including aerobic capacity and endurance performance, there has been limited progress due to few coordinated research efforts involving major funding initiatives/consortia and the use primarily of the candidate gene approach involving a small number of single nucleotide polymorphisms (SNPs). Much of the genetic data relating to human performance has been generated while exploring the etiology of lifestyle-related disorders such as obesity and type 2 diabetes mellitus (T2DM). As of 2008, 214 autosomal gene entries and quantitative trait loci, 18 mitochondrial genes and seven genes on the X chromosome have been reported to be significantly associated with some component(s) of performance and health-related fitness [1]. Three genomic hits in the first genome-wide association study (GWAS) applied to assess exercise behavior (i.e., type, frequency and duration of exercise in Dutch and American adults [2])

Y. Pitsiladis (✉)
College of Medicine, Veterinary and Life Sciences, Institute of Cardiovascular and Medical Sciences, University of Glasgow, Glasgow G12 8QQ, Scotland, UK
e-mail: yannis.pitsiladis@glasgow.ac.uk

L.S. Pescatello and S.M. Roth (eds.), *Exercise Genomics*,
Molecular and Translational Medicine, DOI 10.1007/978-1-60761-355-8_8,
© Springer Science+Business Media, LLC 2011

are of particular interest especially in how the findings reveal interactions with leisure time exercise behavior. However, most genetic findings to date are inconclusive due to studies employing relatively small sample sizes and predominantly single gene approaches which are especially prone to type 1 errors. It is widely acknowledged that there will be many interacting genes involved in health-related fitness phenotypes and hence it is timely that genetic research has moved to the genomics era, i.e., the simultaneous testing of multiple genes is now possible. New approaches involving large well-funded consortia and utilizing well-phenotyped large cohorts and genome-wide technologies will be necessary for meaningful progress to be made with reference to clinical significance. This chapter summarizes most recent and significant findings from exercise genetics and explores future trends and possibilities.

Study Designs, Strategies, and Methodologies

Scientific Strategies and Study Designs

Similar to many other areas of research, family and/or twin studies were initially the main focus investigating the genetic basis of human performance. The first studies in the 1970s assessed indirectly the genetic basis of human performance using twin models and comparing the intrapair variation between monozygotic (MZ) and dizygotic (DZ) twins; a concept referred to as the heritability estimate (h^2), which is defined as the proportion of a phenotypic variance attributable to genotypic variance and calculated by dividing the difference of the variance between DZ and MZ twins by the variance of DZ twins. When this approach was applied to maximal oxygen consumption, ($\dot{V}O_2$max) using 25 pairs of twins (15 MZ and 10 DZ preadolescent boys), high heritability estimates were reported (e.g., $h^2=93.4\%$) [3]. In other words, genetics could explain as much as 93.4% of the phenotypic variation in $\dot{V}O_2$max. Furthermore, DZ twins had a significantly higher intrapair difference when compared to MZ twins [4]. Similarly, high heritability estimates were reported in 15 MZ and 16 DZ twins of both genders ($h^2=96.5\%$) by Komi et al. [5] for the variation in skeletal muscle fiber composition. Genetic influences on other performance-related attributes such as body composition and motor activities (e.g., walking, running, throwing and balancing) as well as training-induced improvements in $\dot{V}O_2$max were also reported using similar methods [6–10]. Given these exceptionally high heritability estimates, this concept has received considerable criticism with arguments that the very high heritability estimates were due to low twin numbers and the near identical social environment of the studied twins [11, 12]. More recent studies continue to report high heritability estimates for neuromuscular performance and body composition [13–15].

Despite some interesting findings, the limitations and criticisms of the early indirect methods required the focus to be shifted to the continuously developing molecular-based laboratory methods to test directly the interaction between genetic and environmental factors, not only in family or twin studies, but also in studies involving populations of interest. A more contemporary view based on results from molecular studies is that genetics can explain 40–50% of $\dot{V}O_2$max when adjusted for age, body mass, and body composition [16]; substantially lower than heritability estimates. Acknowledging the different determinants of $\dot{V}O_2$max (i.e., cardiovascular, skeletal muscle and central nervous systems limitations) and the limitations of $\dot{V}O_2$max to predict exercise performance has urged most investigators to move from a focus on single phenotypes such as $\dot{V}O_2$max (despite being the most investigated performance-related phenotype to date) to more complex phenotypes such as athlete status where interindividual phenotypic variations are caused by a heterogeneous, polygenic model with several gene variants involved and interacting with environmental factors [1, 17, 18].

A number of different methodological approaches within the field of genetic epidemiology have been utilized to unravel the genetic basis of human performance and health-related fitness in general. Following the initial indirect/theoretical approaches involving for example, heritability estimates, advances in molecular understanding and techniques were applied to a variety of different experimental approaches. These included linkage and association studies, the data of which was built on segregation analysis [19–22]. The most popular gene discovery methods for polygenic traits are summarized in Fig. 8.1. The basic family/twin study approach has provided useful and, to some extent, reliable genetic data. For example, a recent twin study, which comprised of 37,051 twin pairs from seven countries: Australia, Denmark, Finland, the Netherlands, Norway, Sweden, and United Kingdom, suggested additive genetic variants contribute significantly to exercise participation among the twin pairs (i.e., $h^2 = 62\%$) [23]. To date, no similar studies of such magnitude have been conducted in the area of human performance. Due to the development of more advanced gene discovery techniques, genetic studies are no longer restricted to family/twin studies but expanded to include the assessment of genetic variants within a population of interest. Population-based studies are

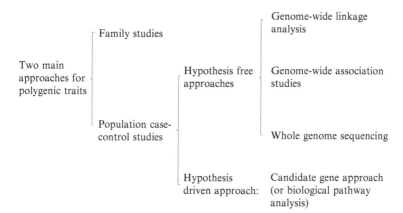

Fig. 8.1 Popular gene discovery methods for polygenic traits

extensively being used at present, particularly involving two groups – cases and controls in order to make comprehensive comparisons. Population case-control studies can be further differentiated into hypothesis-free (sometimes referred to as a "fishing trip," i.e., no assumptions made about the location of associated variants relative to genes) and the more commonly used hypothesis-driven approaches.

Further advances in molecular technologies enabled researchers to apply genome-wide approaches to the field. The GWAS is a newly developed hypothesis-free approach used to detect the common variants underlying complex diseases and traits so as to help predict the disease risk and develop targeted therapy. GWAS has been successful in identifying novel genetic variants for age-related macular degeneration, T2DM [24] and the interleukin 23 (IL-23) pathway in Crohn's disease [25]. This promising new approach is not without important limitations. For example, human height is a highly heritable quantitative trait (up to 90% of variation most likely explained by genetic factors) [26–30] as well as stable and easy to measure. In theory, the application of GWAS would be suitable in finding height-related genes. However, despite significant investment and large sample numbers (i.e., a study involved more than 30,000 individuals [31]), GWAS results have been disappointing as only 5% of phenotypic variation in height can be explained from the 47 identified SNPs [32]. Notably, the largest cohort to date ($n = 183,727$) identified at least 180 associated loci to adult height (explaining as much as 10% of the phenotypic variation in height) and indicated that GWAS could detect many loci that implicate biologically related genes and pathways [33]. The occurrence of rare variants which are not well captured by GWAS may partly explain this limited success in determining the genomics of adult height. It has been suggested that it would be more efficient both in terms of cost and time to combine GWAS with sequencing as this technology becomes cheaper so as to target the rarer genetic variants [34]. Nonetheless, the hypothesis-free GWAS design is the most powerful of the current widespread approaches as with this approach one can: (1) detect smaller gene effects by narrowing down the genomic target region precisely with new chips; (2) maximize the amount of variation captured per SNP with the fixed set of markers; and (3) reduce genotyping costs, which make this approach attractive [35]. Other factors relating to the sample population (e.g., family history of disease or traits, ethnically homogeneous populations, sample size of at least several thousands) and analytical approaches (e.g., the conservative Bonferroni correction for multiple testing or the nonconservative false discovery rate (FDR) correction as well as the application of permutation testing approaches) need to be carefully considered in order to ensure successful application of the GWAS approach [24]. The application of the genome-wide linkage analysis approach has been successful in identifying disease genes related to monogenic disorders [36] but only partially successful in detecting complex genetic traits related to multiple genes. The lack of greater success is probably due to the low heritability of the examined complex traits (common variants with modest effect) [37, 38]. Using this approach, over 100 hypertension-related quantitative trait locus (QTLs) have been identified, with loci on chromosomes 1, 2, 3, 17, and 18 containing multiple QTLs with often overlapping confidence limits. These results suggested only a few variants to be responsible for the common forms of hypertension [39]. Nevertheless, major endeavor has gone into locating QTLs for hypertension in human population by genome-wide linkage analysis [40–42]. Genetic heterogeneity and ethnic diversity complicate replication and therefore the overall effectiveness of linkage studies [39].

The most extensively used candidate gene association study approach requires a prior hypothesis that the genetic polymorphisms of interest are causal variants or in strong linkage disequilibrium (LD) with a causal variant. This population-based genetic approach aims to define alleles or markers that segregate with a particular phenotype or disease at a significantly higher rate than predicted by chance alone, by genotyping the variants in both affected and unaffected individuals [39]. This approach is effective in detecting genetic variants with small or modest influence on common disease or complex traits. Functional SNPs with tag SNPs which would cover the entire candidate gene have been used in many candidate gene association studies [35]. However, in this approach, candidate genes ought to be selected if there was good evidence that (1) the proposed candidate gene is biologically relevant to main phenotype/complex trait of interest (e.g., physical performance/ aerobic capacity, obesity/body mass index [BMI]); (2) the variants of the candidate gene influences the overall function of the gene (e.g., variation in physiological angiotensin converting enzyme (ACE) activity levels are linked to polymorphisms in the *ACE* gene; see section on the *ACE* gene); and (3) the polymorphisms of the selected candidate gene are frequent enough in the population to allow meaningful statistical analysis (e.g., typical allele frequencies for the I/D polymorphism in a European population are frequency (D)=0.57 and frequency (I)=0.43). When these criteria are not fulfilled and candidate genes are selected based primarily on the interest of the research group, this approach generates conflicting results with low statistical power and difficulty to be replicated in other populations [39]. Furthermore, a major limitation of the indirect candidate gene approach is the need to genotype larger numbers of SNPs than the direct candidate SNP analysis [43].

Major Study Cohorts

The number of large genetic cohorts with extensive health-related and physical performance phenotypes is limited due to the high costs involved in creating and maintaining such cohorts. The leading studies and the most significant cohorts based on current publication outcomes are shown in Table 8.1 and also briefly described below.

The HERITAGE Family Study

The HERITAGE Family Study is the largest family intervention study to standardize the exercise training intervention [44]. In total, almost 750 partici- pants from approximately 300 families were studied before and after a 20-week exercise intervention to assess the familial and genetic effects to regular exercise.

Table 8.1 Leading genetic studies in the field of exercise and training

Authors	Study	Design	Subjects	Intervention
Bouchard et al.	HERITAGE	Prospective Training Study Family Study	App. 100 white families App. 200 Afro-American families	20 weeks controlled endurance training
Defoor et al.	CAREGENE	Prospective Training Study	1,095 men and women with coronary artery disease	3 months graded exercise with achieving evident exhaustion
Hagberg et al.	GERS	Prospective Training Study	225 sedentary, healthy men and women (50–75 years)	24 weeks endurance training
Bouchard et al. Wolfarth et al.	GENATHLETE	Case-control-study, elite endurance athletes ($\dot{V}O_2$ max > 75 mL/kg) vs. untrained controls ($\dot{V}O_2$ max < 50 mL/kg)	App. 300 endurance athletes App. 300 untrained controls	
Ahmetov et al.	Elite Russian athlete	Case-control study, elite athletes from mixed sport's disciplines vs. healthy controls	786 elite Russian endurance athletes 1,242 healthy controls	
Scott et al.	Elite East African athlete	Case-control study	291 elite Kenyan endurance athletes 85 controls	
Yang et al.	Elite Australian athlete	Case-control study, elite athletes from different sports vs. controls	429 elite Australian athletes, 436 unrelated controls	
Montgomery et al.	British military recruit	Prospective Training Study	App. 140 army recruits	10 weeks standardized physical fitness program
Cerit et al.	Turkish military recruit	Prospective Training Study	186 Caucasian men	6 months training program
He et al.	Chinese military recruit	Prospective Training Study	102 healthy and untrained military personnel	18 weeks exercise training program

$\dot{V}O_2$ max maximal oxygen consumption

Each participant was required to attend three controlled training sessions per week for 20 weeks conducted on a cycle ergometer. Apart from performance measures such as $\dot{V}O_2$max pre- and post-training, several cardiovascular risk factors and extensive data on body composition were assessed. This unique study design involving entire families allows both cross-sectional and longitudinal analyses to be conducted utilizing the classical candidate gene approach and linkage analysis with emphasis both on known functional genes and unknown genes and associations with key physiological parameters.

The Caregene Study

The Caregene study aimed to explore the individual genetic variation in aerobic power and the response to physical training in patients with coronary artery disease (CAD) [45]. All patients ($n = 1,095$) are needed to fulfill the following inclusion criteria: biologically unrelated males or females, achieved evident exhaustion during graded exercise tests at baseline and after 3 months of cardiac rehabilitation comprising three exercise sessions per week. Exercise sessions included a wide range of activities such as running, cycling, rowing, and calisthenics. The advantage of this study design is that it provides a novel insight into understanding the role of health-related fitness genes in improving the overall condition of CAD patients.

The Gene-Exercise Research Study (GERS)

Two hundred and twenty-five sedentary, healthy men and women (50–75 years) were enrolled in the Gene-Exercise Research Study (GERS) and participated in a 24-week endurance exercise training program [46]. The aim of this study was to investigate the impact of common genetic variations on cardiovascular disease risk factors (i.e., plasma lipoprotein lipids, body composition and glucose tolerance, etc.) following a highly standardized exercise training program [46]. Numerous studies have been published to date [47–54].

Genathlete Study

In the Genathlete study, a classical case-control study, endurance athletes with high $\dot{V}O_2$ max were compared to control participants with a low to average $\dot{V}O_2$max [55–57]. Data were analyzed using the candidate gene approach, which allowed the distribution of particular genetic variants with respect to the phenotype $\dot{V}O_2$max in both groups to be assessed. As this type of assessment requires large subject numbers, this study was designed as a multicenter study. To exclude influences due to regionally different distribution of genetic variants, particular attention was paid to a comparable distribution of the regional origin of participants. Currently, this cohort involves more than 600 participants and therefore constitutes one of the largest matched case-control studies in this field [56, 57].

Elite Athlete Status Studies

The genotyping of athletes of the highest performance caliber such as world record holders, world champions, and Olympians is desirable and may circumvent the need for very large athlete cohorts in order to discover performance-associated polymorphisms (PAPs). There are a number of DNA biobanks from world-class athletes (including world record holders, world champions and Olympians) from a variety of countries and sports. The most significant elite endurance athlete cohorts based on current publication outcomes are:

Elite Russian athlete cohort: It has been suggested that the studies of truly elite athletes from a single sporting discipline should only be considered in order to discover PAPs [56, 58–63]. One of the largest studies of elite athletes amenable to such an investigation involves elite Russian athletes from mixed athletic disciplines [64–66]. In the most recent study, 998 male and 425 female Russian athletes of regional or national competitive standard were recruited from 24 different sports [66]. Athletes were stratified into five groups according to event duration (very long-, long- and middle-endurance), mixed anaerobic/aerobic activity group, and power group (predominantly anaerobic energy production).

Elite east African athlete cohorts: The phenomenal success of athletes from Ethiopia and Kenya in endurance running events is well recognized. Middle- and long-distance runners from Ethiopia and Kenya hold over 90% of both all-time world-records and current top-10 positions in world event rankings [67]. Moreover, these successful athletes come from localized ethnic subgroups within their respective countries [68, 69]. The Arsi region of Ethiopia contains roughly 5% of the Ethiopian population but accounted for 14 of the 23 distance runners selected for the country's 2008 Olympic team. Similarly, the Kalenjin tribe of Kenya has less than 0.1% of the world's population, yet members of this tribe have together won nearly 50 Olympic medals in middle- and long-distance events. This remarkable geographic clustering has provoked suggestions of a genetic basis for elite endurance running performance [70]. In order to investigate the east African running phenomenon, a first study [69, 71, 72] involved 114 endurance runners from the Ethiopian junior- and senior-level national athletics teams (32 female, 82 male), 315 controls from the general Ethiopian population (34 female, 281 male), 93 controls from the Arsi region of Ethiopia (13 female, 80 male), and 38 sprint and power event athletes from the Ethiopian national athletics team (20 female, 18 male). A similar approach was taken in a subsequent study [73] that involved recruiting 291 elite Kenyan endurance athletes (232 male, 59 female) and 85 control subjects (40 male, 45 female). 70 of the athletes (59 male, 11 female) had competed internationally representing Kenya ($n = 70$). Of the 70 athletes, 42 had won Olympic, World or Commonwealth medals, had a top three finish in an international marathon or equivalent road race, or have been ranked in the top 50 runners in the world at their event. Other athletes, classified as National, had competed at national level within Kenya ($n = 221$, 173 male, 48 female). All athletes had competed in distances from 3,000 m to the marathon, where the energy source is predominantly aerobic [74]. Control subjects were students from Kenyatta University and were representative of the Kenyan population in their geographical distribution throughout Kenya [68]. This running phenomenon provides a unique opportunity for discovery of performance genes.

Elite Australian athlete cohort: Two studies from Australia have provided valuable genetic information on elite sprinters and endurance performers. The cohort comprises of 429 elite Australian athletes from 14 different sports and 436 unrelated controls. A subgroup of 107 and 194 subjects were classified as elite sprinters and endurance runners, respectively [75].

Military Studies

The military provides a unique setting where large number of recruits can participate with relative ease in research studies involving precisely standardized training interventions and comparable assessment techniques. A further advantage of military cohorts relate to their prospective design and the possibility to analyze associations between particular genetic variations and various physiological measures. Nevertheless, despite clear advantages, there are only a limited number of military cohorts involving genetics of physical fitness within the published domain and all cohorts are limited by their respective low subject numbers.

British military recruits: The first significant study was conducted by Montgomery et al. using British military recruits [58]. Military recruits took part in a 10-week basic training program that involved intensive strength and endurance training sessions including an elbow flexion test ($n = 78$) [58] and/or 1.5 mile run at maximal exertion [76] ($n = 140$).

Turkish military recruits: A Turkish cohort of military recruits comprised of 186 Caucasian males involved in a 6-month training program including flexibility, circuit training, and 2,400–3,000 m runs with military equipment [77]. Like all other military studies, this cohort is limited by low subject numbers.

Chinese military recruits: This cohort comprised of 102 healthy but untrained military personnel from China who participated in an 18-week exercise training program, including running 5,000 m 3 times a week. A 2-week adaptive training program was also applied prior to the formal training. The intensity of training was increased based on heart rate corresponding to 95% (first 10-weeks) up to 105% (last 8-weeks) of the individual baseline ventilatory threshold. $\dot{V}O_2$max and running economy were also measured [78].

Specific Considerations Related to Race and Geographic Ancestry

The success of east African athletes in distance running has undoubtedly augmented the idea of "black" athletic supremacy. This idea is not new and has emerged from simplistic interpretations of performances at major athletic events such as the Olympic Games and World Championships combined with the belief that similar skin color indicates similar genetics. Despite the idea being perpetuated that "black" athletes are genetically adapted for athletic performance [79], until now, no studies had attempted to assess and quantify this genetic effect [71–73]. The concept of "black" athletic superiority is based on a preconception that each "race" constitutes a genetically homogeneous group, with "race" defined simply by skin color. This belief is contrary to the assertion that there is more genetic variation among Africans than between African and Eurasian populations [80]. The genetics of "race" is controversial and gives rise to a number of contrasting viewpoints with particular emphasis on the use of "race" as a tool in the diagnosis and treatment of disease. Some argue that there is a role for "race" in biomedical research and that the potential benefits to be gained in terms of diagnosis, treatment and research of disease outweigh the potential social costs of linking "race" or ethnicity with genetics [81]. Others, however, advocate that "race" should be abandoned as a tool for assessing the prevalence of disease genotypes and that "race" is not an acceptable surrogate for genetics in assessing the risk of disease and efficacy of treatment in human populations [82]. Arguments for the inclusion of "race" in biomedical research often focus on its use to identify single gene disorders and their medical outcomes. The genetic basis of complex phenotypes such as athletic performance is poorly understood and more difficult to study. It is estimated that most human genetic variation is shared by all humans and that a marginal proportion (normally less than 10%) is specific to major continental groups [83]. Estimates from the human genome project and analysis of haplotype frequencies show that most haplotypes (i.e., linked segments of genetic variation, rarely subject to reassortment by recombination) are shared between two of the three major geographic populations: Europe, Asia, and Africa [84]. It is currently estimated that the level of genetic diversity between human populations is not large enough to justify the use of the term "race" (see Jobling et al. [85] for a review). Consequently, any differences in physiology, biochemistry, and/or anatomy between groups defined solely by skin color (e.g., comparing "black" with "white") are not directly applicable to their source populations, even if the differences found are indeed genetically determined. This area of genetics is clearly confusing when studies comparing subjects of differing skin color can conclude on the one hand that the results can explain the success of this "racial" group (i.e., "blacks") in distance running [86], and on the other hand that results are compatible with "black" athletes being suited to events of short duration [87]. Such contradictions highlight the problem associated with grouping athletes based simply on skin color. Evidence that many of the world's best middle- and distance runners originate from distinct regions of Ethiopia and Kenya, rather than being evenly distributed throughout their respective countries [68, 69], appears to further sustain the idea that the success of east African runners is genetically mediated. In isolated populations, genetic drift can cause certain alleles to increase or decrease in frequency and if the variants are beneficial to sprint/power or endurance ability, may predispose the population to that type of performance. Alternatively, there may be selection for a particular phenotype such as endurance, if it offers a selective advantage in that environment. Indeed, some believe that certain east African tribes (e.g., the Nandi tribe in Kenya) have been genetically selected for endurance performance through cultural practices such as cattle raiding [88, 89]. It is unsurprising therefore that there are assertions in the literature that east Africans have the "proper genes" for distance running [90]. Despite these untested hypotheses having potential theoretical under-pinnings, it is unjustified to regard the phenomenal athletic success of east Africans as genetically mediated; to justify doing so one must identify the genes that are responsible. Many scientists advocating a biological/genetic explanation typically ignore the socio-economic and cultural factors that appear to better explain these phenomena [70, 91].

Genotyping and Aerobic Capacity and Endurance Performance

Genes and Polymorphisms of Interest

Despite numerous attempts to discover genes associated with aerobic capacity including endurance performance and elite athlete status, thus far there has been only limited progress due to few coordinated research efforts and lack of major funding. Much of the genetic data has been generated while exploring the etiology of lifestyle-related disorders such as obesity and metabolic syndrome. However, recent advances in molecular technologies especially methods involving high throughput is revolutionizing gene discovery. As of 2008, 214 autosomal gene entries and quantitative trait loci, 18 mitochondrial genes and 7 genes on the X chromosome have been reported to significantly associate with some component(s) of health-related fitness including endurance performance [1]. Most genes and polymorphisms discovered to date to associate with aerobic capacity and endurance performance are illustrated in Figs. 8.2 and 8.3, the number of recent publications with the studied endurance-related loci are summarized in Fig. 8.4 and the most significant genes are discussed below and listed in Table 8.2.

   ACE and the renin-angiotensin-system (RAS). The most widely-studied candi-date gene for endurance performance is the *ACE* gene. ACE is a peptidase known to regulate blood pressure by catalyzing the conversion of Angiotensin I to the vasoconstrictor Angiotensin II and also degrading the vasodilator bradykinin. Furthermore, interindividual variation in physiological ACE activity levels has been linked to polymorphisms in the *ACE* gene. For example, *ACE* Insertion-Deletion (I/D), in which I refers to the presence and D to the absence of a 287 bp sequence in an Alu sequence of intron 16 in the *ACE* gene at chromosome location 17q23 (see Fig. 8.3, Table 8.2), can account for up to 47% of ACE activity variance in subjects with an additive effect across the II, ID, and DD genotypes [92]. Regarding physical performance, *ACE* I/D genotypes have been associated with a wide range of phenotypes. *ACE* II subjects show significantly higher muscle effi-ciency gains from training than DD individuals [93], as well as greater improvements

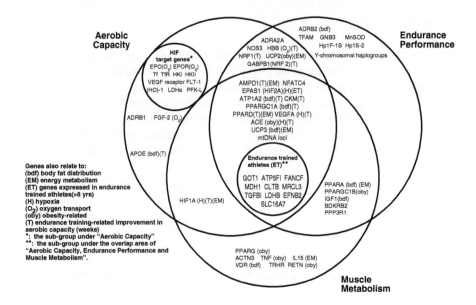

Fig. 8.2 Genes related to aerobic capacity, endurance performance and muscle metabolism

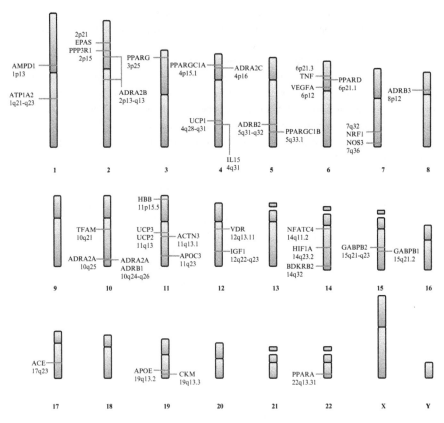

Fig. 8.3 Genes of interest at chromosomal locations. Only genes introduced in the chapter as well as some of the most extensively studied endurance-related genes are included (38 genes in total)

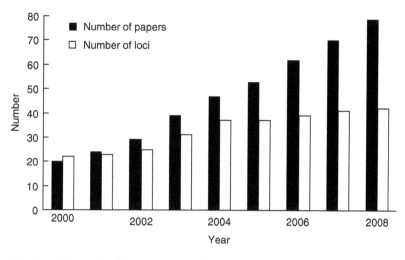

Fig. 8.4 Cumulative publications and number of loci for endurance-related genetic papers in the last decade (publications prior to 2000 were summarized)

in running economy, or ability to sustain submaximal pace with lower oxygen consumption [94]. Additionally, the I allele associates with muscular endurance gains from training [58], which may relate to higher Type 1 slow-twitch muscle fiber preponderance in *ACE* II subjects [95]. In terms of overall sporting ability, the I allele has been associated with superior performance in British mountaineers [58], South African triathletes [96], British distance runners [60], and Australian rowers [59]. In contrast, the D allele has been associated with success in power-oriented sports such as short-distance swimming [63] and sprinting [60]. The relationship between genotype and performance, however, remains ambiguous. For instance, the D allele has been found to be both positively [97] and negatively [98] associated with $\dot{V}O_2$max. Furthermore, a recent study of 230 elite Jamaican and American sprinters found no association of either allele with sprint athlete status [99]. Likewise a cohort of 192 athletes of mixed Caucasian nationalities and endurance sporting disciplines did not exhibit I allele frequencies that were significantly different from geographically-matched controls, nor did I allele frequency associate with $\dot{V}O_2$max in these athletes [56]. Several other studies involving Caucasian populations have also reported no association between the I allele and elite physical performance [63, 64, 100], although these studies have been criticized [101] for having small subject numbers [100], use of subjects from a mixture of sports [64], and variations in the definition of "elite athlete" and "control" subjects [63]. Despite inconsistencies in replication, the *ACE* gene remains a candidate to confer advantage to endurance performance. Notably and contrary to what was once believed "one gene one function," a significant association has also been reported between the *ACE* gene and development of myocardial infarction. Specifically, there is data implicating DD genotype as a potent risk factor in 610 patients with

Table 8.2 Endurance-related genes introduced in this chapter

Gene symbol	Name	Location	References
ACE	Angiotensin-converting-enzyme	17q23	[56, 58–60, 63, 64, 92–104]
ACTN3	α-Actinin-3	11q13-q14	[75, 105–117]
ADRA2A	Alpha2-adrenergic receptor	10q24-q26	[119, 121, 127, 128]
ADRA2B	Alpha2B-adrenergic receptor	2p13-q13	[129–133]
ADRA2C	Alpha2C-adrenergic receptor	4p16	[134, 135]
ADRB1	Beta1 adrenergic receptor	10q24-q26	[120, 136–146]
ADRB2	Beta2 adrenergic receptor	5q31-q32	[121, 139, 145, 147–155]
ADRB3	Beta3 adrenergic receptor	8p12	[122, 123, 156–162]
AMPD1	Adenosine monophosphate deaminase 1	1p13	[163–176]
APOC3	Apolipoprotein C-III	11q23	[177, 178]
CKM	Creatine kinase, muscle	19q13.2-q13.3	[45, 197–204]
HIF1A	Hypoxia-inducible factor 1	14q23.2	[205–211]
NOS3	Endothelial nitric oxide synthase	7q36	[57, 212–225]
PPARA	Peroxisome proliferative activated receptor, alpha	22q13.31	[65, 228, 229, 235–240]
PPARD	Peroxisome proliferative activated receptor, delta	6p21.1	[230–234, 241–248]
PPARG	Peroxisome proliferative activated receptor, gamma	3p25	[231, 249–254]
PPARGC1A	Peroxisome proliferative activated receptor, gamma, coactivator 1, alpha	4p15.1	[232–234, 248]
UCP1	Uncoupling protein 1	4q28-q31	[183–186]
UCP2	Uncoupling protein 2	11q13	[190–192]
UCP3	Uncoupling protein 3	11q13	[193–195]
VDR	Vitamin D receptor	12q13.11	[255–283]

myocardial infarction [102] and cardiovascular risk in general [103]. However, contrary to these reports, this association was not replicated in a larger study [104].

α-Actinin-3 (*ACTN3*). Actinin-3 is an actin-binding protein and a key component of the sarcomeric Z-line in skeletal muscle. Expression of *ACTN3* (at 11q13.1, Fig. 8.3, Table 8.2) is limited to fast glycolytic (type 2 fast-twitch) muscle fibers which can generate more force at high velocity. Homozygosity for the common nonsense polymorphism R577X in the *ACTN3* gene results in deficiency of actinin-3 in a large proportion of the global population [105]. Yang et al. [106] surveyed the XX genotype frequencies in three previously unexamined African populations (i.e., Kenya, Nigeria and Ethiopia) in comparison with non-African populations (i.e., Europe, Asia, Australia). Extremely low XX genotype frequencies were observed in Kenyan (1 vs. 1%) and Nigerian (0 vs. 0%) athletes vs. controls as well as much lower than in any other non-African populations (i.e., XX carriers in Australian Caucasians: 18%; Aboriginal Australian: 10%; Spanish: 18%; Japanese: 24%; Javanese: 25%). These results also implied that the *ACTN3* deficiency was not a major influence on performance in African athletes.

This polymorphism does not appear to result in pathology, although muscle function does appear to be influenced by this polymorphism [107–111]. Furthermore, a strong association has been reported between the *ACTN3* R577X polymorphism and elite athletic performance in Caucasian populations [75, 112–116]. The XX genotype was found at a lower frequency in elite Australian sprint/power athletes relative to controls [75], and this finding replicated in Finnish [114], Greek [115], and Russian athletes [112]. Particularly, in a study of 429 elite white athletes from 14 different sporting disciplines and 436 controls, the sprint athlete group showed a higher frequency of the RR genotype (50%) and a lower frequency of the RX genotype (45%), compared with controls (30 and 52%, respectively), while the elite endurance athletes displayed a higher frequency of the XX genotype (24%) than controls (18%) [75]. Interestingly, MacArthur et al. [117] established an exciting *ACTN3* knockout (KO) mouse model in order to investigate the mechanisms underlying *ACTN3* deficiency. These authors found the KO mice had similar muscle fiber proportions as the wild type but reduced muscle mass that appeared to be accounted for by the reduced fiber diameter of the fast-twitch muscle as observed in *ACTN3* deficient mice [117]. In addition to alterations in muscle fiber size, increased activity of aerobic enzymes, longer muscle contracting time and shorter recovery period from fatigue were attributed to the characteristics of the slow-twitch fibers. This KO mice model supported the idea of increased endurance but reduced muscle strength in XX carriers.

Adrenoreceptors (*ADRA2A, ADRA2B, ADRA2C, ADRB1, ADRB2, ADRB3*). The adrenergic receptors are a class of G protein-coupled receptors, which are located in cells of the sympathetic nervous system. Adrenoreceptor genes express in multiple cell types and play pivotal roles in cardiovascular, respiratory, metabolic, and immunological functions [118]. There are two main groups of adrenergic receptors, α and β, with several subtypes as distinguished by their respective pharmacological and molecular biological characteristics. The effects of alpha- and beta-receptors are mostly antagonistic. For example, the α2A-adrenergic receptor (*ADRA2A*) (at 10q24-q26, Fig. 8.3, Table 8.2) appears to have a critical role in regulating systemic sympathetic activity, and in doing so influences cardiovascular responses such as heart rate and blood pressure [119]. The human beta-1 adrenergic receptor (*ADRB1*; Fig. 8.3, Table 8.2) is encoded by an intronless gene on chromosome 10q24-26 and is a protein comprising 477 amino acids (1,434 bp intronless) encoded by a single exon [120]. The human beta 2-adrenergic receptor (*ADRB2*; Fig. 8.3, Table 8.2) is encoded by an intronless gene on chromosome 5q31-32 and is a protein comprising 413 amino acid (1,239 bp intronless) [121]. The beta 3-adrenergic receptor is another receptor type found in the heart (*ADRB3*; Fig. 8.3, Table 8.2), located on chromosome 8p12-p11.2 and is a protein comprising of 396 amino acids [122]. The specific function of ADRB3 is currently unknown [123]. All three beta-receptor types are involved in the control of the vascular system [124, 125] and distinguished by diverse affinity to ligands [126].

The exercise-related physiological impact of several polymorphisms of the different adrenergic receptor subtypes are presented below. However, most studies are small and lack replication.

Alpha-Adrenergic Receptors

The alpha2-adrenergic receptor gene (*ADRA2A*) is located on chromosome 10q24-26 [121] holding a restriction-fragment length polymorphism (RFLP) with the restriction enzyme Dra I [127]. Wolfarth et al. [128] found evidence that elite endurance status is weakly associated with this polymorphism (e.g., the difference in genotype distributions were found between elite endurance athletes and sedentary controls; higher frequency of 6.7-kb allele of Dra I in the athletes vs. controls), suggesting *ADRA2A* or a neighboring gene in LD may influence elite endurance performance; enhanced lipid mobilization of RFLP carriers was proposed as a likely mechanism [128].

For the alpha2B-adrenergic receptor (*ADRA2B*), located on chromosome 2p13-q13 (Fig. 8.3, Table 8.2), Rao et al. [129] reported an association with hypertension in the Hypertension Genetic Epidemiology Network (HyperGEN) study and this association was confirmed in a meta-analysis of genome-wide linkage scans [130]. In another study, Wilk et al. [131] reported an effect of a C/A polymorphism (C/A substitution at base-pair 6,579) in *ADRA2B* on resting heart rate with carriers of the A allele showing higher heart rate in white hypertensive subjects. Similar findings were reported for another polymorphic variant of *ADRA2B* (12Glu9) resulting in a insertion/deletion of three glutamic acids (amino acids 297–309) in the third intracellular loop of the receptor protein [132]. As such, heart rate was lower in homozygotes for the short allele (Glu9/Glu9) in a study of 166 obese Finnish men and women [132]. The impact of this polymorphism on the cardiac autonomic nervous system following exercise training (i.e., handgrip exercise) in 96 normotensive obese women has also been studied and the Glu9/Glu9 genotype found to associate with reduced responsiveness of the cardiac autonomic nervous system to exercise training [133].

A deletion polymorphism in the gene alpha2C-adrenergic receptor (*ADRA2C*; Fig. 8.3, Table 8.2) encodes the deletion of four consecutive amino acids at position 322–325 (α_{2C}-Del322–325). In subjects with this polymorphism, Small et al. [134] reported a notable increase in the risk of heart failure (odds ratio; OR: 5.65) in black patients compared to controls, suggesting this polymorphism may be a useful in identifying individuals at risk of heart failure. Notably, the clinical condition of heart failure patients heterozygous for the α_{2C}-Del polymorphism was impaired and left ventricular ejection fraction was reduced compared to healthy control subjects [135].

Beta-Adrenergic Receptors

Eighteen *ADRB1* variants have been described, although mainly the Ser49Gly and Arg389Gly polymorphisms appear to be of functional importance [136]. The polymorphism Arg389Gly is located at nucleotide 1,165 (where a neutral charged C is substituted for a positive charged G) and alters the encoded amino acid from Arg to Gly at amino acid 389 [137]. In vitro stimulation of the polymorphism with glycine (the "wild type"), results in an approximately threefold impaired increase of cAMP due to a reduced functional coupling of Gly-389-receptor to stimulatory G-protein (G_s), compared to the Arg389Arg genotype [137]. This change is attributed to a variation of the G-protein binding domain resulting in a changed tertiary structure of the receptor, due to a replacement of a neutral and small Gly residue by a basic and large Arg residue [137]. As a result, there is an impaired activation of protein kinase A with a consecutive decreased rate of the above-mentioned phosphorylation steps, leading to a possible negative inotropic and chronotropic response. The assumed difference between Gly389 and Arg389 homozygotes related to heart rate at rest and during exercise has not been replicated in vivo [138, 139]. The downregulation of beta-adrenergic receptors, resulting in an impaired adenyl cyclase activity (measured by intracellular cAMP concentration), is influenced by genotype. The activity of the downregulated enzyme (Arg389 polymorphism), caused by prolonged stimulation, is about as high as the activity of the desensitized wild type [140]. Among patients suffering from renal failure, the Gly389 homozygotes were observed to have higher left ventricular mass compared to the Arg389 homozygotes [141], while patients with severe heart failure homozygous for Arg389Arg had significantly enhanced exercise capacity compared to the Gly389Gly homozygotes [142].

Another polymorphism of interest is the Ser49Gly variant located in the extracellular amino-terminal region of the receptor, at nucleotide 145, where an A is substituted for a G, resulting in a nonsynonymous amino acid substitution from Ser to Gly at amino acid 49 in the receptor protein [143]. Desensitization studies indicated that, in the presence of a sustained stimulation by catecholamines, the signal promoted by the "myocardium-protective" Gly49 adrenergic receptor is turned off much faster and more completely than that promoted by the Ser49 variant. This effect could be explained by higher affinities of protein kinase A and/or G-protein receptor kinases. The existence of the Gly allele may result in myocardial protection and affect long-term prognosis in a favorable manner in patients with chronic heart failure [144]. This *ADRB1* polymorphism also seems to influence resting heart rate. Individuals heterozygous for the Ser49Gly polymorphism had average heart rate intermediate to those of either homozygote type, with Ser homozygote having the highest average heart rate and with Gly homozygote having the lowest [145]. Finally, Defoor et al. [146] showed that both Ser49Gly polymorphism and the combination of Ser49Gly and Gly389Arg influenced endurance capacity in patients with CAD, but not their trainability.

A review of the current literature on *ADRB2*, revealed a total of nine different polymorphisms [147], with the most extensively studied polymorphisms at amino acid 16 and 27 and the frequency of these polymorphisms influenced by ethnicity. The Glu27 allele is more common in Caucasian-Americans than in African-Americans, but less frequent in Chinese [139]. The Arg16Gly polymorphism is in LD with the Glu27Gln polymorphism, so that the allele Glu27 occurs almost always with Gly16 [148] and the allele Gln27 with Arg16 [149]. The agonist-promoted affinity to these receptors and the G_s-coupled mediated adenyl cyclase stimulation are not different between both variants, as distinguished by desensitization experiments. The substitution of Glu for Gln at position 27 (Glu27) is apparently associated with resistance to desensitization. These changes are most likely not due to differences in receptor synthesis, but in degradation [150]. Other *ADRB* polymorphisms do not appear to influence resting heart rate or systolic and diastolic blood pressure [145, 151]. Furthermore, Arg16Gly and Glu27Gln associate with body composition and influenced by physical activity [152–154]. For example, the changes in body mass, BMI, and waist-to-hip-ratio following exercise training differed significantly between carriers of the Glu allele and Gln homozygotes [153]. In sedentary male individuals, studies have found that homozygosity for Gln27 exhibited a greatest risk (OR: 3.45) of obesity [152]. Physical activity appeared to overcome this genetic predisposition as this effect was not seen in physically active men. Importantly, these findings suggest (in male subjects at least) that increasing physical activity is the best method to reduce body mass in individuals with the Gln27Gln genotype [152, 153]. Associations between genotype and body composition were also examined in women. Women with the Arg16 allele had significantly higher BMI and body mass than noncarriers and further evidence of an interaction between *ADRB2* and physical activity [154]. Notably, in the Genathlete Study, an excess of Gly carriers in sedentary controls were found compared to elite endurance athletes, suggesting a somewhat unfavorable effect of this allele on athletic performance [155]. This hypothesis requires further study.

ADRB3 (also a G_s-coupled receptor) is primarily expressed in adipose tissue and is thought to regulate energy balance through influencing both lipolysis in white adipocytes and thermogenesis in brown adipocytes [156, 157]. Stimulation of ADRB3 activates lipase resulting in an accumulation of fatty acids and subsequent activation of the uncoupling protein 1 (UCP1). As such, a *ADRB3* polymorphism with a missense mutation in codon 64 results in the replacement of Trp by Arg in the first intracellular loop of the receptor protein and early data seems to suggest an association with adiposity [158]. When the predictive capacity of this *ADRB3* variant on changes in metabolic markers following exercise training was assessed in healthy Japanese men ($n = 106$), no differences between genotypes were seen at baseline, but after 3 months of training, differences in *ADRB3* genotypes and exercise-mediated improvements in glucose tolerance and leptin resistance were found [159]. A number of meta-analyses have been conducted and produced somewhat different conclusions but have confirmed the association between the Trp64Arg polymorphism and body composition/blood lipids and the interaction with physical activity [160–162].

From a physiological point of view, the adrenergic system is of great importance for health-related fitness and performance hence there are a great number of relevant genetic studies (most outside the scope of the present review). These studies often produce significantly divergent results, and there is currently no consensus on the influence of polymorphisms of the adrenergic system on exercise-related phenotypes (and especially those with an effect on physical performance). Further studies are therefore urgently needed to elucidate the role of genetic variants in adrenergic receptor genes and their influence on exercise-related phenotypes.

Adenosine monophosphate deaminase 1 (AMPD1). In skeletal muscle, adenosine monophosphate deaminase (AMPD) is involved in catalyzing the hydrolysis of AMP to inosine monophosphate (IMP) and ammonia. The AMPD reaction, which is the first reaction of the purine nucleotide cycle, displaces the adenylate kinase reaction in the direction of ATP formation and prevents the increase in ADP during exercise; therefore more energy can be used to maintain prolonged muscle work [163]. A nonsense mutation (C34T) in exon 2 of the *AMPD1* gene on chromosome 1p13-p21 (see Fig. 8.3, Table 8.2) encoding for the skeletal muscle-specific isoform (M) of AMPD creates a nonsense codon resulting in premature termination of protein synthesis [164, 165]. This mutation is more common in Caucasian populations (i.e., approximately 2% of the general population) [166, 167]. Due to the important role of AMPD in muscle energy metabolism, *AMPD* deficiency may have a negative impact on human performance. Results to date have been conflicting with some [168–172] but not all studies [163, 173–176] presenting evidence in favor of this impairment in performance. In a recent study, the frequency of the T allele was significantly lower in elite Caucasian endurance athletes compared to controls (4.3 vs. 8.5%) but did not appear to diminish elite exercise performance. For example, $\dot{V}O_2$max did not differ significantly between the athlete carriers and noncarriers of this mutation (72.3±4.6 vs. 73.5±5.9 mL/kg/min), furthermore, none of the elite athletes were homozygous for this mutation [171]. Similarly, Lucia et al. [172] reported results from detailed assessments (including blood ammonia and lactate measurements) conducted in one elite runner considered by the authors as one of the best non-African runners in the world despite being heterozygous for the C34T mutation; the findings from this study support the idea that this partial deficiency does not impair elite endurance running performance which is in line with the previous study [171]. In contrast, *AMPD* deficiency has been associated with reduced sprint cycling performance when examined in 139 healthy subjects with different *AMPD1* genotypes, including 12 *AMPD*-deficient subjects, suggesting a functional role for AMPD during exercise [163]. Further research efforts are warranted to resolve the implications of *AMPD* deficiency.

Lipid metabolism (APOC3, UCP1, UCP2, UCP3). The *APOC3* gene (at 11q23.1-q23.2, Fig. 8.3, Table 8.2) encodes for the apolipoprotein C-III which retards triglyceride (TG) metabolism and therefore increased expression of *APOC3* may enhance the risk of cardiovascular disease. Pollin et al. [177] reported a null mutation (R19X) in *APOC3* gene relating to lower fasting and postprandial serum TG, higher levels of high density lipoprotein (HDL)-cholesterol (HDL-C), which is associated with a decreased risk of heart disease, and lower levels of low density lipoprotein (LDL)-cholesterol (LDL-C). These intriguing findings suggested a favorable and protective role of *APOC3* deficiency in plasma lipid metabolism and CAD. Interestingly, an earlier study by Woo and Kang [178] had investigated the association between the SstI polymorphism of *APOC3* gene and plasma lipids after 6 days of moderate aerobic exercise in 100 Korean men. These authors found significantly higher TG levels at baseline as well as a greater reduction in TG after the exercise intervention in individuals with the S2/S2 genotype in comparison with S1/S1 or S1/S2 genotypes. However, total cholesterol, HDL-C, LDL-C, glucose, and insulin were not influenced by genotype, either before or after the exercise intervention [178].

The inner mitochondrial membrane transporters (i.e., UCP1, 4q28-q31, Fig. 8.3, Table 8.2) dissipate the proton gradient and release energy as heat without the need for ATP [179–181]. Uncoupling proteins (UCPs) have received considerable research attention due to possible implications on weight loss [182]. UCP1 is mainly present in brown adipose tissue in rodents and shown to be necessary for cold-induced brown adipose tissue thermogenesis [183–186]. However, as brown adipose tissue is minimally expressed in humans [187], attention has now shifted to the UCP1 homologues UCP2 and UCP3 that also mediate and regulate proton leak and implicated in the pathogenesis of T2DM although their role in normal physiology remains unclear [188]. Given the capacity to oxidize fat is known to significantly influence endurance performance [189], numerous studies have attempted to identify polymorphisms in UCP2 and UCP3 that relate to human performance. The most studied polymorphism of the *UCP2* gene is Ala55Val located on chromosome 11q13 (Fig. 8.3, Table 8.2). In particular, the Val/Val genotype was associated with higher metabolic and exercise efficiency than Ala/Val or Ala/Ala genotypes [190, 191]. Notably, Ala55Val would appear to be in LD with a functional polymorphism in *UCP2* or neighboring genetic variants in *UCP3* gene owing to the location of the Ala55Val polymorphism (i.e., located in a domain of the protein without known function as well as the short distance between *UCP2* and *UCP3* genes) [191]. Furthermore, a recent study showed the 55Val allele frequency was over-represented in elite Russian endurance athletes ($n=351$) compared to 1,057 matched controls [192]. The −55C/T polymorphism in the promoter region of *UCP3* (at 11q13, Fig. 8.3, Table 8.2) has been negatively associated with BMI [193] and the T allele of this polymorphism with increased *UCP3* mRNA expression in skeletal muscle [194]. In contrast, Hudson et al. [195] did not find an association between the −55C/T polymorphism and ultraendurance performance in Caucasian male triathletes or controls.

In summary, further studies will be required to clarify the relationship between the *APOC3* gene and human athletic performance. Given the role of UCPs (especially UCP2 and UCP3) in energy balance are largely unknown, and in light of the importance attributed to the time course of sampling when assessing the effects of exercise on *UCP* gene expression [196], more stringent studies are needed in order to clarify the precise role of UCPs in the present context.

Creatine kinase – muscle associated variants (CKM). Creatine kinase (CK) is a dimeric enzyme comprising of either M(muscle)- or B(brain)-type subunits and forming three different isoenzymes: BB, MB, and MM, each encoded by separate genes. The muscle-specific isoform of creatine kinase (CKMM) is predominantly expressed in skeletal and heart muscle and encoded by the *CKM* gene located on chromosome 19q31.2-13.3 (Fig. 8.3, Table 8.2). CKMM is bound to the M line of the myofibril [197] and regulates the regeneration of ATP near the myosin heads [198]. CKMM activity has been shown to be lower in type 1 fibers than type 2 fibers and therefore low CKMM activity may be advantageous for endurance performance [199, 200]. Also of interest is the observation of reduced muscle power output and improved adaptability to endurance exercise in *CKMM* gene KO mice [201]. In the HERITAGE Family Study, a lower training responses (in terns of delta $\dot{V}O_2$max) was found in participants homozygous for the *CKMM*-NcoI polymorphism in 160 parents and 80 adult offsprings [202] and the linkage between the same *CKMM* marker and delta $\dot{V}O_2$ max reached significance after adjusting for the effects of age, sex, $\dot{V}O_2$ max, and body mass in 277 full sib pairs [203]. In contrast, no significant association was found between the *CKMM*-NcoI polymorphism and athlete status (50 top level Spanish professional cyclists, 27 elite Spanish runners and 119 sedentary controls) [203]. When 102 biologically unrelated male volunteers from northern China were assessed after an 18-week exercise training program (involving $3 \times 5,000$ m/week), a larger improvement in running economy was reported in *CKMM* AG heterozygotes than in AA and GG homozygous [204]. However, in 927 Caucasian CAD patients, no association between *CKMM*-NcoI genotypes and aerobic power was reported [45]. Further studies are urgently required to determine the significance of these contradictory findings.

   Hypoxia inducible factor 1 alpha (HIF1A). Hypoxia-inducible factor 1 (HIF1; Fig. 8.3 and Table 8.2) is a heterodimeric DNA transcription factor consisting of an α and β subunit. HIF1 induces the expression and regulates the response of a variety of genes to hypoxic stimuli [205–208]. Hence, under hypoxic conditions there is activation and upregulation of HIF-1α and consequently HIF-1 [208, 209]. The functional HIF-1 protein then activates transcription of several target genes involved in erythropoiesis, angiogenesis, and other metabolic pathways including those encoding for erythropoietin (*Epo*, see Fig. 8.2), vascular endothelial growth factor (*VEGF*, see Fig. 8.2), and the VEGF receptor *FLT-1* (Fms-like tyrosine kinase-1, see Fig. 8.2) [208]. Of the nine polymorphisms in the *HIF-1α* gene [210], three are most commonly studied (i.e., P582S, A-2500T, and T+140C). The A-2500T SNP has been found only in African-American subjects and appears to alter the binding site of the transcription factor CdxA [210]. Prior et al. [210] investigated the relationship between these three polymorphisms and $\dot{V}O_2$ max before and after a 24-week aerobic exercise training program and both P582S and the rare T-allele of the A-2500T genotype associated significantly with $\dot{V}O_2$ max. No associations with aerobic capacity were reported for the T+140C variants [210]. Recently, Döring et al. [211] investigated the *HIF-1α* gene in the previously described Genathlete cohort and found a difference between elite endurance athletes and controls for *HIF-1α* Pro582Ser (rs11549465) genotypes. Homozygote carriers of the major Pro-coding C allele were more frequent in athletes than in controls (84 vs. 75%). Compared to carriers of Ser-coding T allele, OR in the elite endurance athlete group for CC homozygotes was 1.76 (95% CI 1.18–2.64). A common *HIF-1α* haplotype (frequency: 15%) including the rs11549465 C allele and the minor A allele of rs17099207 in the 3′ flanking region of the gene showed a significant association with elite endurance athlete status (OR: 2.38, 95% CI: 1.21–4.66), whereas the most prevalent haplotype (frequency: 59%) comprising the rs11549465 C allele and the major G allele of rs1709920 showed no association with elite endurance athlete status (OR: 0.95, 95% CI: 0.59–1.52). These authors concluded that the *HIF-1α* Pro582Ser polymorphism was associated and therefore implicated in elite endurance performance status in Caucasian men [211]. Despite some encouraging results for HIF-1, particularly the association between the P582S polymorphism of *HIF-1α* and V̇O₂ max before and after training, more substantial evidence is required before a firm genetic link between *HIF-1α* polymorphisms and aerobic performance can be established.

Endothelial Nitric oxide synthase (NOS3). The vascular endothelium plays an important role in vascular homeostasis. Nitric oxide (NO) is produced by endothelial nitric oxide synthase (eNOS) in endothelial cells and is a key signaling molecule regulating vascular tone and affecting arterial blood pressure. NO is produced from the amino acid L-arginine by the enzymatic action of eNOS (a product of the *NOS3* gene; Fig. 8.3, Table 8.2). An inhibition of NO synthesis has been shown to increase blood pressure, both in humans and in animals [212, 213]. Endothelium-dependent vasodilation is one of the mechanisms considered responsible for the blood pressure-lowering effects of exercise therapy in subjects with hypertension. In particular, the shear stress-mediated effects of aerobic exercise training has been shown to enhance NOS3 activity and NO production [214, 215]. In addition to acute responses [216], long-term endurance training increases basal NO production [217, 218] resulting in an improvement in endothelial function [214, 219]. As the benefits of exercise training are highly variable between individuals, this would suggest that the level of adaptation to exercise training is to some significant degree under genetic control.

The human *eNOS* gene comprises 26 exons and 25 introns and is located on chromosome 7q35-36 [220]. In the promoter 5′-flanking region, a SNP with a T to C substitution occurring at nucleotide −786 (T-786C) has been identified. Studies have shown that individuals with the C allele had decreased promoter activity with a resulting impaired NO production compared with individuals without a C allele. Furthermore, a genetic polymorphism of a 27 base-pair tandem repeat in intron 4 (*ecNOS4a/b*) has been described [221]. A SNP, G894T within exon 7, has also been identified, resulting in a replacement of Glu by Asp at codon 298. In one of the first studies to examine the effects of exercise training on endothelial function in patients with CAD, no differences between the polymorphisms in exon 7 were found [222], although there was an impact of the polymorphism T-786C in response to exercise training. For individuals carrying the C allele, this training-induced improvement in endothelium-dependent vasodilatory capacity was significantly blunted compared with patients possessing the wild type [222]. In another study, Data et al. [223] examined the main effects of the *eNOS* T-786C gene polymorphism on forearm blood flow in endurance-trained and sedentary subjects and found significantly elevated vascular resistance in sedentary subjects possessing a C allele compared with carriers of non-C allele (i.e., TT homozygotes had the lowest vascular resistance). Among the endurance-trained group, carriers of the C allele showed elevated blood flow compared with carriers of non-C allele [223]. The influence of the *ecNOS4a/b* polymorphism on levels of blood pressure has also been evaluated [224]. In subjects who had the rare a-allele, systolic blood pressure was significantly elevated compared to noncarriers. However, in the modest and high physical activity groups, no differences between genotype were found. A significant inverse relationship was reported between systolic blood pressure and levels of physical activity in the a-allele group, in contrast to a positive relationship in the bb group. These findings, and the differing slopes of the regression lines between the two groups, demonstrate a notable interaction between the *NOS3* genotypes and levels of physical activity on systolic blood pressure [224].

When the association between the Glu298Asp polymorphism and endurance training-induced change in blood pressure were assessed in the HERITAGE Family Study, no significant differences between the genotypes were found in the sedentary state [225]. Notably, the change in diastolic blood pressure at 50 W training (i.e., constant-load cycle ergometer test at 50 W) showed a highly significant association with the *NOS3* genotype. Specifically, subjects homozygote for the Glu298 allele (Glu/Glu) showed a greater reduction in diastolic blood pressure at 50 W exercise after a 20-week endurance training program than the Asp298 homozygotes, whereas the heterozygotes showed an intermediate response. Furthermore, carriers of the Glu298 allele had a greater training-induced reduction in "rate-pressure product" (calculated by multiplying systolic blood pressure and heart rate) at 50 W exercise. These authors concluded that the Asp allele of the Glu298Asp polymorphism is associated with a training-induced decrease in submaximal diastolic blood pressure and rate-pressure product in sedentary subjects.

In the Genathlete study, Wolfarth et al. [57] examined the contribution of three *NOS3* polymorphisms and a microsatellite $(CA)_n$ repeat in intron 13 in elite endurance athletes ($n=316$) and sedentary controls ($n=299$). Comparing carriers and noncarriers for the most common $(CA)_n$ repeat alleles, significant differences between sedentary controls and elite endurance athletes were found, with more elite endurance athletes carrying the 164 bp allele. This association between the 164 bp allele of the $(CA)_n$ repeat in intron 13 and elite endurance athlete status is intriguing and may explain some of the differences in performance between elite endurance athletes and sedentary controls. In summary, the balance of evidence would favor *NOS3* as a gene worthy of further investigation with regard to effects on both health-related fitness and performance phenotypes.

Peroxisome proliferator-activated receptor associated genes (PPARA, PPARG, PPARD, PPARGC1A). This nuclear hormone receptor superfamily includes three types of transcription factors, namely peroxisome proliferator-activated receptor alpha, delta, and gamma (PPARα, PPARδ, PPARγ), which appear to play important roles in regulating lipid metabolism, particularly involved in peroxisomal oxidation [226]. The activity of PPARs shows tissue specificity. PPARα is widely expressed in liver, muscle, kidney, and intestine [227] and appears to control fatty acid beta-oxidation [228, 229]. PPARδ is mainly present in heart, skeletal muscle, and adipose tissues [230] and may activate PPARγ (more prevalent in adipose tissues) and other genes in mediating adipocyte differentiation [231]. A notable gene × gene interaction between PPARγ coactivator-1α (*PPARGC1α*) and *PPARδ* has been shown to influence muscle type transformation (i.e., a fast-twitch to a slow-twitch muscle fiber type conversion) [232–234]. The ligand-activated PPARα stimulates fatty acid oxidation mainly in liver, skeletal muscle, and heart, resulting in reduced fat storage in adipocytes and therefore may be an important genetic component of metabolic syndrome [235, 236]. Russel et al. [237] also reported higher expression of *PPARα* in type 1 muscle than in type 2 muscle. The intron 7 polymorphism of the *PPARα* gene (the intron 7G/C; 22q13.31, Fig. 8.3, Table 8.2) has been associated with left ventricular growth response to training in healthy young men [235]. The CC genotype showed greater left ventricular mass than GC/GG genotypes, suggesting a role of the C allele in cardiac hypertrophy which may result from reduced *PPARα* expression and reduced fat oxidation [238–240]. In the study of elite Russian athletes, Ahmetov et al. [65] found an excess of intron 7 G allele of the *PPARα* gene (80.3% in endurance athletes, 50.6% in power athletes and 70% in controls), confirming the potential influence of the G allele on endurance performance. The authors also examined the association between this gene variant and fiber type composition by examining muscle biopsies obtained from the vastus lateralis (in 40 young men) and found GG homozygotes ($n=25$) had a significantly higher percentage of slow-twitch muscle fibers (55.5 ± 2.0 vs. 38.5 ± 2.3%) than CC homozygotes ($n=4$). These authors concluded that *PPARα* intron 7 G/C polymorphism was associated with physical performance in Russian athletes, and this may be explained, in part, by the association between *PPARα* genotype and muscle fiber type composition.

PPARδ has been widely acknowledged as a key regulator of fatty acid oxidation and energy uncoupling in skeletal muscle [241–243]. Fatty acids and their metabolites have been shown to activate PPARδ [244]. Activation of *PPARδ* on (chromosome 6p21.2-p21.1, see Fig. 8.3, Table 8.2) and its ligands led to muscle fiber conversion and enhanced physical performance [232]. Furthermore, exercise-induced expression of *PPARGC1α*, which is involved in mitochondrial biogenesis and is a major factor that regulates muscle fiber type determination, may activate PPAR without the presence of ligands [241, 245]. In the study of elite Russian athletes, Ahmetov et al. [246] found a significant higher frequency of the *PPARδ*C allele in 898 endurance-oriented athletes (18.3%), compared with 610 controls (12.1%). In the HERITAGE Family Study, CC homozygotes showed a smaller increase in $\dot{V}O_2$ max in comparison with the CT and TT carriers in response to a 20-week endurance training in black subjects [247]. In elite Israeli elite athletes, no association was found between *PPARδ* +294C polymorphism and elite endurance performance [248]. However, the combined influence of *PPARGC1α* Gly482Ser (located at 4p15.1, Fig. 8.3, Table 8.2) and *PPARδ* T294C polymorphisms on endurance performance showed 20% of elite athletes having the Gly/Gly + CC profile. In contrast, the percentage was 2 and 3% in national-level endurance athletes and controls, respectively [248]. Some of these conflicting results may be due to the different populations studied.

The expression of *PPARγ* is confined mostly to adipose tissue, particularly *PPARγ2*, which has been shown to regulate adipocyte differentiation, glucose homeostasis, and lipid metabolism [249]. The Pro12Ala polymorphism of *PPARγ* gene (at 3p25, Fig. 8.3, Table 8.2) is a genetic variant related to obesity [250] and the rare allele Ala12 is the most prevalent in Caucasian populations (~12%) [249, 251, 252]. A strong gene×environment interaction has been reported between the Pro12Ala polymorphism and obesity and/or physical activity [253, 254].

Vänttinen et al. [253] have concluded that the effect of Pro12Ala on glucose uptake in skeletal muscle depended on levels of obesity with higher skeletal muscle glucose uptake found in nonobese carriers of the Ala12 allele comparing to carriers of the Pro12Pro genotype. The Pro12 allele was found to associate with T2DM in subjects with low levels of physical activity, indicating an interaction between *PPARγ2* and physical activity on the risk of T2DM in non-Hispanic whites [254].

In conclusion, there is good evidence that the *PPAR* genes can impact on endurance performance possibly by influencing muscle fiber type conversion. Further investigations are urgently required to replicate conflicting findings from different ethnic groups to reveal the effects of *PPAR* polymorphisms on exercise-related phenotypes.

Vitamin D-receptor (VDR). The extent to which sun exposure and vitamin D activity can influence muscle strength and muscle mass is subject to some considerable debate. Historically, exposure to ultraviolet radiation was popular amongst athletes and coaches and dates back to the beginning of the last century [255]. Two studies showed improvements in cardiovascular and skeletal muscular metabolism by use of UVB rays [256, 257]. Incidentally, vitamin D deficiency has been recognized to associated with muscle weakness [258–261]. The vitamin D receptor (*VDR*) gene is expressed in various tissues such as human skeletal muscle [262–264], heart muscle, liver, lung, and skin [265, 266]. The genetic polymorphisms of *VDR* gene include ApaI, BsmI, FokI, and TaqI, and defined by their specific restriction endonucleases, respectively. The influence of these polymorphisms on bone mass density (i.e., femoral neck, lumbar spine, and proximal forearm) [267] and muscle strength (i.e., quadriceps and grip strength) [267] have produced inconsistent findings. A strong association between VDR polymorphisms and bone mass density have been reported in several publications [268–273] but not all studies [274–278]. Interestingly, the most extensively studied polymorphism of *VDR* gene (at 12q13.11, Fig. 8.3, Table 8.2) is BsmI located in the intron between exon 8 and 9 (not near intron-exon borders) and is unlikely to have a functional role [279]. Nevertheless, the bb genotype of BsmI (but not BB and Bb) was found to strongly associate with quadriceps muscle strength in some [267, 280, 281], but not all studies [282, 283]. The F and f genotypes of the FokI polymorphism in exon 2 have shown what appears to be a functional influence on bone metabolism in response to a 1-month weight training program in 34 healthy males [284] and this is in line with several other studies [279, 283, 285]. For example, in 44 highly trained (>6 years) male athletes, increased spinal volume (based on determination of bone mass density) was only found in FF athletes, suggesting a gene × environment interaction [285]. In another study that compared strength training and aerobic training in 206 healthy men and women (age 50–81 years), the *VDR* FokI polymorphism was significantly influenced by strength training-induced changes in femoral neck bone mass density, while no aerobic training-induced changes were observed [279]. Furthermore, the FokI polymorphism has been shown to significantly associate with fat-free mass and sarcopenia in 302 older Caucasian men (age range 58–93 years) [283]. These findings will encourage further studies that focus on identifying the exact role of *VDR* FokI polymorphism and/or other covariants in bone mass density and muscle strength.

Clinical Implications of Genetic Findings in Association with Aerobic Capacity and Endurance Performance

There has been immense research interest in unraveling the factors that may influence athletic success and account for vastly different performances (e.g., sprint vs. endurance). Both genetic and environmental factors have been implicated and will undoubtedly play a role in the making of the elite athlete [286]. Molecular-based approaches are required to improve our understanding of the factors that limit physical performance in both health and disease and therefore deserving of much greater research emphasis. Important achievements in this area are summarized below.

Genes Related to Skeletal Muscle Metabolism

Skeletal muscle comprises a large percentage of body mass (approximately 30–40%) [287] and is insulin sensitive [288]. Skeletal muscle is responsible for insulin-mediated glucose uptake, and therefore it is vital that insulin sensitivity is maintained [288]. On the other hand, insulin acts to suppress fat oxidation in skeletal muscle [289, 290]. Therefore, skeletal muscle metabolism is important for maintaining and utilizing energy stores in the body. Impaired skeletal muscle metabolism can lead to the development of metabolic syndrome and increase cardiovascular risk [288]. In the light of already known genetic influences on skeletal muscle and athletic performance, it is intuitive that enhancing skeletal muscle function will lead to greater physical/sporting performance and equally to improved quality of life of patients with impaired muscle function (e.g., cachexia). A number of candidate genes have been implicated in skeletal muscle metabolism (e.g., *ACE*, *ACTN3*, *AMPD1*, *PPARδ* and *UCP3*, Fig. 8.2) although this area of research remains in its infancy. Some worthy highlights include previously described genes involved in skeletal muscle efficiency (i.e., *ACE* I allele – higher muscle efficiency), muscle energy metabolism (i.e., *AMPD1* – unfavorable XX genotype with reduced ATP production in skeletal muscle, *UCP3* – mainly expressed in skeletal muscle mitochondrial, *PPARδ*-regulator of fatty acid oxidation) and muscle fiber type conversion (i.e., *ACTN3*-deficiency of *ACTN3* cause reduced diameter of type 2 muscle fiber in mice, showing improved endurance capability). Two recent studies also draw attention to *HIF-1α* (see Fig. 8.2) and *ADRB2* and *BDKRB2* (out of eight muscle- or metabolism-related genes, see Fig. 8.2). The differential RNA expression of *HIF-1α* was observed in muscles in maintaining muscle homeostasis in normoxic conditions [291]. As for *ADRB2* and *BDKRB2*, a study was conducted in 438 endurance athletes who took part in two marathon running events. Two SNPs (*BDKRB2* rs1799722 and *ADRB2* rs1042713) were significantly related to endurance performance [292]. Despite the discovery of a significant number of interesting candidate genes (some replicated, others awaiting replication), this number is dwarfed by the number of genes likely to be implicated in skeletal muscle metabolism and have yet to be discovered.

   The clinical implications relating to muscle metabolism have been widely discussed in the context of gene-based therapy or gene doping [293–295]. Gene transfer technology has been successfully applied to life-threatening diseases such as tumors [296, 297], cardiomyopathies and muscular dystrophy [298, 299], adenosine deaminase deficiency [300], human severe combined immunodeficiency [301], and Parkinson's disease [302], and there are ever increasing signs that this knowhow is being applied to normal human traits, such as athletic performance. It has been suggested that the injection of insulin-like growth factor-1 (IGF-1) into skeletal muscle can result in muscle hypertrophy and improved muscle function with potential to aid recovery from injury [293]. However, the boundary between gene therapy and genetic enhancement is not clear. For example, the use of gene therapy to aid recovery from injury may also result in vastly superior muscle function (i.e., above normal). Such applications aimed at genetic enhancement are highly controversial albeit to date based on primarily theoretical arguments [293, 303, 304]. Undoubtedly, the development of molecular-based methods to enhance muscle function will be abused by those trying to obtain a competitive edge at all costs; nevertheless, this abuse should not hinder real efforts to improve our understanding of how genetic modifications can improve muscle function and in doing so dramatically improve the quality of life of patients suffering from a wide variety of clinical conditions (not to mention dealing with the consequences of an ever increasing aged population).

Genes Related to Oxygen Delivery

Energy provision is a major factor influencing exercise performance in both health and disease and influenced by oxygen availability. Although carbohydrates can be utilized without the need for oxygen (i.e., anaerobic metabolism), this metabolism can proceed only for a short duration and inevitably leads to a variable degree of metabolic acidosis with consequences on exercise tolerance. On the other hand, the metabolism of fat is exclusively under aerobic conditions. Prolonged exercise is reliant on fatty acid β-oxidation but requires a constant supply of carbohydrates and oxygen availability for exercise performance to be maintained. A number of clinical conditions are characterized by poor oxygen availability (e.g., peripheral vascular disease) even in the presence of adequate fuels. In such conditions, there are a number of avenues available for enhancing oxygen delivery and these generally involve improving oxygen carrying capacity and/or vascularization. Some of the most exciting and successful recent approaches aimed at enhancing oxygen delivery involve molecular approaches. In this context, genes such as *Epo*, *VEGF*, and fibroblast growth factor 2 (*FGF-2*, Fig. 8.2) can influence oxygen delivery through enhancing oxygen carrying capacity (*Epo*) and optimizing vascularization (*VEGF*, *FGF-2*). It is well known that the administration of recombinant human erythropoietin (rhEpo) profoundly enhances oxygen carrying capacity and therefore oxygen uptake, by increasing red blood cell count and hemoglobin concentration [305].

rhEpo is now the standard treatment for dialysis patients, an interesting therapeutic option for several forms of nonrenal anemia and the drug with the highest annual sales worldwide [306]. Oxygen delivery can also potentially be enhanced by novel applications of genomic information such as expressing the *Epo* gene introduced into somatic cells [307] or through Epo derivatives such as Novel erythropoiesis stimulating protein (NESP). Results to date have been encouraging as gene therapy-mediated expression of *Epo* enhanced hemoglobin concentration and hematocrit values in various animal models [308–310]. On the other hand, NESP results from mutations that have been introduced into the gene to exchange two out of the 165 amino acids and in doing so change function since it creates two additional recognition sites for the attachment of N-linked carbohydrates. Compared to rhEpo, NESP has five instead of 3 N-linked sugar side chains in addition to the one O-linked chain and this is important as the carbohydrate moiety of Epo critically determines the rate of metabolism and hence the plasma half-life time of NESP is prolonged [311]. There are important implications to the use of NESP as it results in less frequent dosing without compromising clinical effectiveness [312–314]. However, the use of such approaches is not without important limitations. High nonphysiological concentrations of Epo activate polycythemias [315] and an autoimmune reaction against transgenic and endogenous Epo [316, 317]. Further complications may also result from thrombosis due to very high hematocrit values.

The negative effects associated with novel attempts to improve oxygen delivery constitute a serious risk. These side effects will undoubtedly impact negatively on the use of Epo in the form of gene therapy in clinical practice [318]. It is essential to tailor the dose of Epo carefully according to the hematocrit level (different from patient to patient) to avoid complications related to polycythemia. Improving the regulation of *Epo* expression could also be of a great benefit, for example, to develop a homeostatic system of gene therapy to help sense and correct tissue hypoxia with normal regulation of the *Epo* gene, thus the level of red blood cells would stay stable once sufficient Epo is produced and hypoxia-response element would cease further transcription in the tissue [318]. The analysis of promoter elements and the cis-acting sequences may give an insight into the possible transacting factors that may regulate the oxygen-dependent expression of *Epo* [319] and so, to examine the possible early events of erythropoiesis, before and after *Epo* stimulation. This exquisite regulation may provide useful genetic strategies in controlled local delivery of polypeptides in various ischemic diseases. Meanwhile, more research is urgently needed to investigate normal *Epo* gene variation and how this variation may impact on physical performance. In addition to understanding the function of the *Epo* gene, other interesting candidate genes in this regard are *HIF-1α* gene (previously described) and the Epo receptor gene (*EPOR*, Fig. 8.2). The *EPOR* gene is located on chromosome 19p1.3 and contains several informative microsatellites [320]. A specific mutation, which is a G to A transition in nucleotide 6,002 of the *EPOR* gene (it converts a TGG codon for tryptophan into a TAG stop codon), truncated 70 amino acids in the C-terminal domain of the *EPOR* molecule, can cause a benign disease called autosomal dominant erythrocytosis that results in elevated hemoglobin values of about 22 g/dL [321, 322] due to an increased sensitivity of *EPOR* for *Epo* [323]. To date this is the only case in which a specific single variant in a distinct gene is directly linked to a physiological condition leading to superior physical performance as reflected by one of the family members winning several Olympic gold medals in cross-country skiing [324].

In addition to the putative roles of these genes in influencing oxygen delivery, there is an intriguing potential for genes such as *VEGF* and *FGF-2* to be involved in the regeneration of injured tissue [325, 326] although research into this question is only in its infancy. However, a cautious approach is required as gene therapy experiments involving *VEGF* transfer have revealed significant negative side effects. Despite these reservations, further studies are needed to determine the potential role and clinical impact of angiogenic factors.

Genes Related to Energy Delivery

Understanding and influencing energy balance is not only vital for athletic success in a wide range of sporting disciplines but also in treating a number of clinical conditions especially related to lifestyle disorders such as obesity and T2DM. It is for this reason that a significant amount of genetic research has been conducted to discover genes related to energy balance within the greater context of the impact of genes×behavior ×environment on the obesity epidemic [327]. Genetic-based approaches (e.g., genome-wide linkage, genome-wide association and candidate gene analysis) have the potential to identify the contributions of genetic variation to energy intake, energy expenditure, and fat accumulation and thereby lead to a better understanding of the etiology of obesity and the disruption of energy balance [328].

In this chapter several genes related to muscle energy metabolism have been introduced (i.e., *AMPD1, HIF1α, PPARα, PPARδ, UCP2, UCP3*, Fig. 8.2) clearly demonstrating the interconnections between multiple performance-related genes and energy delivery pathways. The balance of evidence now demonstrates that adipose tissue is not simply an energy storage site, but a key factor in fat and energy metabolism [329–332]. Adipose tissue TG can be released into the circulation in order to meet the demands of skeletal muscle for fatty acid oxidation during exercise [333]. In addition, skeletal muscle take up significant quantities of plasma fatty acids for storage (incorporation into intracellular lipids) [334]. Identifying the link between excess stores of body fat and altered substrate metabolism in muscle has been difficult. Several adipose-derived cytokines (adipokines), including leptin (LEP), resistin (RST), and tumor necrosis factor alpha (TNF-α) have been implicated in impairing insulin sensitivity in rodents [335, 336]. LEP and RST appear to have direct effects on the brain, skeletal muscle, and liver and play important roles in regulating energy balance, lipid metabolism and cardiovascular function [330, 331]. These cytokines have been implicated in increasing fatty acid oxidation and decreasing TG storage in muscle, and this may explain, in part at least, their insulin-sensitizing effect [337–340]. Since their discovery in the 1990s, several hundreds of papers involving LEP and RST have been published in the context of obesity and energy balance and some key findings relating to physical activity and muscle strength are summarized here. The Gln223Arg polymorphism in the leptin receptor *(LEPR)* gene was studied in 268 Pima Indians [329]. Carriers of the Arg223 allele had lower 24 h energy expenditure and levels of physical activity than Gln223Gln homozygotes. Similarly, lower physical activity levels were found in 222 prepubertal boys who were homozygous for Arg223Arg compared to Gln223Arg and Gln223Gln genotypes in the *LEPR* gene at the age of 7, although this difference disappeared 2 years later [332]. Three SNPs of *RST* (−420 C/G, 398 C/T, 540 G/A) were found to be associated with strength phenotypes in 482 subjects when strati-fied by gender and BMI [331]. G-420G had lower increases in one-repetition maximum (1RM) strength when compared with homozygous CC in men with a BMI≥25, likewise, homozygous 540 AA had lower increases in 1RM strength than homozygous GG. Furthermore, heterozygous C398T Caucasian women (BMI≥25) showed less strength improvement than other genotypes. In summary, adipose tissue is an important source of energy for skeletal muscle and together with adipose-derived cytokines (e.g., LEP, RST and TNF-α) play an important role in skeletal muscle metabolism in response to insulin sensitivity [288]. Therefore, discovery of genes related to energy balance and energy delivery, even in athletic/trained populations, have the immense power to aid the discovery of metabolic syndrome-related genes and develop new drugs for effective treatment.

The Future

Most of the knowledge in exercise genetics (including most of the information presented in this chapter) has been generated primarily using classical/"old fash-ioned" genetic methods such as SNPs and almost exclusively applied to cohorts with small sample sizes (the vast majority of studies $n \leq 1,000$) and rather unsophis-ticated multifactorial phenotypes (e.g., BMI, 1RM, aerobic capacity, athlete status, etc.). The data generated therefore from these studies and reviewed in this chapter need to be examined in light of the view held by most "hard core" geneticists that a study of any complex phenotype in humans is futile unless a cohort size of between 20,000 and 100,000 is used and therefore possessing sufficient statistical power for meaningful analysis and interpretation. If one accepts this view (not currently held by the authors of this chapter) then all studies reviewed in this chapter should be ignored. While somewhat extreme, an intermediate view (currently held by the authors of this chapter) is that the vast majority of the candidate genes for health-related fitness and sporting performance discovered to date and many reviewed here, are not the key candidates seriously implicated in the phenotypes of interest. Priority should therefore be given to recruiting sufficiently large study cohorts with adequately measured phenotypes to increase statistical power. This approach is also necessary for all future intervention and cross-sectional studies performed in this field.

As stated previously, it is accepted that there will be many interacting genes involved in exercise-related traits including sporting performance and hence it is timely that genetic research has moved to the genomics era, i.e., the simultaneous testing of multiple genes. The new approaches (some reviewed in this chapter) and technologies will no doubt be increasingly applied to searching the whole human genome instead of studying single genes or indeed SNPs as the cost of using such whole-genome methods becomes more affordable. Particularly, the cost of large-scale sequencing will become cheaper over the next years. Seemingly reputable claims have been made that it is only a matter of time before the entire human genome can be sequenced for $1,000 [341]. Recently, the newest Illumina sequencing machine HiSeq 2000 costs less than $10,000 in a single run (two human genomes and 30× coverage). This number has dramatically dropped from $60,000 in 2008 [342] . At present, no matter the success or failure of the GWAS approach, this approach is certainly providing, and will continue to provide, the insight into genetic architecture and the molecular basis underlying human diseases and complex traits. In the very near future, very large cohorts (i.e., 20,000–100,000 as recommended by "hard core" geneticists) will be routinely studied by GWAS and will provide good resources for all scientific fields including exercise genomics [343]. This development will require a move away from the traditional way of researching in exercise science/medicine (i.e., predominantly single laboratory studies) to large well-funded collaborations/consortia with leading industry partners and therefore substantial statistical/technological power and knowhow. Only with such resources can the most strongly-acting genes be identified with confidence, gene × environment interactions be studied accurately and gene × gene interactions revealed. A recent example in the area of exercise science/medicine is the IDEFICS (Identification and prevention of dietary- and lifestyle-induced health effects in children and infants) integrated project initiated with funding from the sixth Framework Programme of the European Commission [344]. With a cross-sectional cohort size of 16,224 young children (ages 2–10 years), IDEFICS is one of the largest single studies to investigate genetic and environmental factors in childhood obesity. The IDEFICS project has been highly successful in generating one of the largest DNA biobanks and multiple, high-quality phenotype datasets ever collected from a large cohort of young children (including objectively measured physical activity levels using accelerometry). The traditional method of collecting genetic material suitable for epidemiological studies and multiplex genotyping assays has been based on blood samples [345, 346]. This poses challenges, both financial and practical in large studies, particularly for young populations, such as children and young athletes. For this reason, the IDEFICS study adopted a saliva-based method for DNA collection [347]. Saliva is increasingly being collected in large studies because of its potential as diagnostic material [348] and has already been shown to be a viable source for human genomic DNA suitable for large genetic epidemiology studies [349]. Saliva samples are relatively inexpensive, convenient, and noninvasive compared to blood sampling [350]. Saliva sampling has therefore become more popular as the methods [346, 348, 351–358] for extraction of high-quality DNA has developed and as cost has reduced.

Based on these sampling techniques the new high scale sequencing tools are even more feasible. One first example in the area of sports performance has recently been successfully piloted [359]. The overall purpose was to identify new PAPs and/ or copy number variants (CNVs) that confer susceptibility to sprint and endurance performance by use of world-class athletes as subjects. GWAS was initially performed using Illumina HumanOmni1-Quad BeadChip (1,000,000 SNPs and 65,000 CNVs) or Human660W-Quad BeadChip (550,000 SNPs and 60,000 CNVs) in 47 sprinters and 47 controls from Jamaica, as well as 49 African-American sprinters and 47 controls from the USA. A total of 6,058 SNPs differed significantly between sprinters and controls in the Jamaican cohort. Two SNPs remained significantly associated with sprint performance after correcting for FDR, while one SNP showed a similar trend. In the African-American cohort, a total of 11,851 SNPs differed significantly between sprinters and controls. Two hundred and ninety-eight SNPs remained significantly associated with sprint performance after correcting for FDR. Differences in the numbers of PAPs discovered in the two cohorts may be due to using different chips: Illumina HumanOmni1-Quad BeadChip and Human660W-Quad BeadChip. Furthermore, in this first GWAS study applied to the world-class athlete, GWAS was restricted (due primarily to costs) to athletes of the highest sprint performance caliber such as world record holders, world champions and Olympians to identify SNPs that confer susceptibility to sprint performance. A similar approach is currently being applied to the two unique east African cohorts from Kenya and Ethiopia (previously described in this chapter) in order to discover genes involved in aerobic capacity/endurance performance. Further analysis using larger cohorts are required to replicate these GWAS results in order to discover sprint/endurance PAPs.

Some of the technological developments addressed in this chapter have intensified the debate surrounding the predictors of sporting success with the question of "nature" vs. "nurture" at the fore. The Finnish cross-country skier, Eero Maentyranta and the Californian body builder Flex Wheeler are often mentioned in this context. A special variant of the gene myostatin, which regulates muscle growth, is frequently associated with Wheeler. From animal experiments it is known that defective variants can lead to uninhibited muscle growth [360]. A detailed scientific investigation of Wheeler did not take place and a publication including biological parameters (e.g., Myostatin expression, in vitro cultures) does not exist. Therefore, in the case of Wheeler, the evidence remains anecdotal. With respect to the Finnish cross-country skiing athlete, an extensive scientific analysis was performed, the respective candidate gene was *EPOR* (as previously discussed in this chapter). This specific mutation was first described in the early 1990s by Juvonen et al. [321]. This disorder is benign and family members typically have a normal life expectancy. Eero Maentyranta was able to win several World Champion and Olympic titles most likely aided by this disorder and related hemoglobin values of about 22 g/dL. Based on these observations, the *EPOR* mutation has been described as being responsible for extraordinary aerobic capacity [324].

The search for PAPs is gaining momentum, but remains in its infancy. This has not deterred some who seek to exploit genetic-performance research. For example,

Genetic Technologies Limited has acquired the license for *ACTN3* and has already marketed a genetic test that they claim can provide an insight into the best event in which to compete in the sport of your choice, so that the individual can obtain the best results for their efforts. Although *ACTN3* is an interesting candidate gene of physical performance, the use of a genetic test for this one gene to assess potential for athletic success cannot be justified given the multifactorial nature of sporting performance. Although some genes do affect the interindividual variation in physical performance and trainability (as described earlier in this chapter), this knowledge cannot be used to predict sporting talent or to prepare a training schedule. Current genetic evidence does not warrant genotyping an individual to establish their ability to run fast when this trait can be measured far more effectively with a stopwatch.

A new approach to investigate the genetic basis of physical activity and performance is to examine genetic markers directly. This approach could potentially be applied in different ways in practice. Firstly, it may allow drawing conclusions about possible capabilities in the area of physical performance. Secondly, new perspectives may develop in the area of preventative and rehabilitative training therapy, such as a better and more efficient implementation of therapy plans, which are expected to provide important information on the indication and efficiency of specific programs at an early stage. In addition, it might be possible to establish therapies (including specialist training for sporting performance) based on new molecular techniques. Therapies are likely to offer currently unavailable possibilities to treat a large number of serious and life-threatening disorders. However, these exciting new developments are not without some risks. For instance, these techniques could be misused to manipulate genetic material in order to enhance sports performance. However, establishing a specific science on genetic manipulation to improve performance is rather unrealistic, as financial resources are clearly required and missing. It is more likely, however, that clinically relevant scientific approaches used to treat medical conditions such as anemia and muscle dystrophy will lead to similar adapted approaches being introduced to sport. With respect to current research efforts in the field of genetics, these expectations should not lead to prohibition or constraint of studies aiming to investigate genetic fundamentals of performance. Inevitably such findings would also be made in other areas of medical science and transferred to sport. Therefore, it is preferable to be proactive and to develop excellent expert knowhow in this field of research as this is the only possible way to prevent misuse of such knowledge.

Practical Applications

Molecular-based approaches are aimed to improve our understanding of the factors that limit physical performance in both health and disease. As described in the "Clinical implications of the genetic findings in association with aerobic capacity and endurance performance," these results can be used in improving the quality of life of patients with metabolic syndromes and other life-threatening diseases.

However, future success in identifying and understanding the clinical significance of exercise-related genes will rely exclusively on data generated by unique, state-of-the-art collaborations between academic institutions and leading industry partners and involving very well-phenotyped cohorts. When this approach is accepted and conditions favoring its adoption in the field of exercise science/medicine created, only then will new genes with major clinical significance be discovered (including replication of only a very small number of existing genes) and contribute meaningfully to disease prevention strategies in population worldwide.

References

1. Bray MS, Hagberg JM, PÉRusse L, Rankinen T, Roth SM, Wolfarth B, et al. The human gene map for performance and health-related fitness phenotypes: the 2006–2007 update. Med Sci Sports Exerc. 2009;41:35–73.
2. De Moor MH, Liu YJ, Boomsma DI, Li J, Hamilton JJ, Hottenga JJ, et al. Genome-wide association study of exercise behavior in Dutch and American adults. Med Sci Sports Exerc. 2009;41:1887–95.
3. Klissouras V. Heritability of adaptive variation. J Appl Physiol. 1971;31:338–44.
4. Klissouras V, Pirnay F, Petit J-M. Adaptation to maximal effort: genetics and age. J Appl Physiol. 1973;35:288–93.
5. Komi P, Viitasalo J, Havu M, Thorstensson A, Sjödin B, Karlsson J. Skeletal muscle fibres and muscle enzyme activities in monozygous and dizygous twins of both sexes. Acta Physiol Scand. 1977;100:385–92.
6. Weber G, Kartodihardjo W, Klissouras V. Growth and physical training with reference to heredity. J Appl Physiol. 1976;40:211–5.
7. Kovar R. Somatotypes of twins. Acta Univ Carol Gymn. 1977;13:49–59.
8. Sklad M. Skeletal maturation in monozygotic and dizygotic twins. J Hum Evol. 1977;6:145–9.
9. Williams LRT, Gross JB. Heritability of motor skill. Acta Genet Med. 1980;29:127–36.
10. Orvanova E. Body build, heredity and sport achievements. In: Wolanki N, Siniarska A, editors. Genetics of psychomotor traits in man. Warsaw: International Society of Sport Genetics and Somatology; 1984. p. 111–23.
11. Bouchard C, Lesage R, Lortie G, Simoneau JA, Hamel P, Boulay MR, et al. Aerobic performance in brothers, dizygotic and monozygotic twins. Med Sci Sports Exerc. 1986;18:639–46.
12. Fagard R, Bielen E, Amery A. Heritability of aerobic power and anaerobic energy generation during exercise. J Appl Physiol. 1991;70:357–62.
13. Missitzi J, Geladas N, Klissouras V. Heritability in neuromuscular coordination: implications for motor control strategies. Med Sci Sports Exerc. 2004;36:233–40.
14. Peeters M, Thomis M, Loos RJ, Derom CA, Fagard R, Claessens AL, et al. Heritability of somatotype components: a multivariate analysis. Int J Obes (Lond). 2007;31:1295–301.
15. Missitzi J, Geladas N, Klissouras V. Genetic variation of maximal velocity and EMG activity. Int J Sports Med. 2008;29:177–81.
16. Bouchard C, An P, Rice T, Skinner JS, Wilmore JH, Gagnon J, et al. Familial aggregation of VO2 max response to exercise training: results from the HERITAGE Family Study. J Appl Physiol. 1999;87:1003–8.
17. Bouchard C, Simoneau J, Lortie G, Boulay M, Marcotte M, Thibault M. Genetic effects in human skeletal muscle fiber type distribution and enzyme activities. Can J Physiol Pharmacol. 1986;64:1245–51.

18. Ahmetov I, Rogozkin V. Genes, athlete status and training – an overview. Med Sport Sci. 2009;54:43–71.
19. Bouchard C, Dionne FT, Simoneau JA, Boulay MR. Genetics of aerobic and anaerobic performances. Exerc Sport Sci Rev. 1992;20:27–58.
20. Huygens W, Thomis M, Peeters M, Aerssens J, Vlietinck R, Beunen GP. Quantitative trait loci for human muscle strength: linkage analysis of myostatin pathway genes. Physiol Genomics. 2005;22:390–7.
21. Mars GD, Windelinckx A, Huygens W, Peeters MW, Beunen GP, Aerssens J, et al. Genome-wide linkage scan for maximum and lengthdependent knee muscle strength in young men: significant evidence for linkage at chromosome 14q24.3. J Med Genet. 2008;45:275–83.
22. Mars GD, Windelinckx A, Huygens W, Peeters MW, Beunen GP, Aerssens J, et al. Genome-wide linkage scan for contraction velocity characteristics of knee musculature in the Leuven Genes for Muscular Strength Study. Physiol Genomics. 2008;35:36–44.
23. Stubbe JH, Boomsma DI, Vink JM, Cornes BK, Martin NG, Skytthe A et al. Genetic influences on exercise participation in 37, 051 twin pairs from seven countries. PLoS One. 2006;1:e22.
24. Amos C. Successful design and conduct of genome-wide association studies. Hum Mol Genet. 2007;16:R220–5.
25. Massey D, Parkes M. Genome-wide association scanning highlights two autophagy genes, ATG16L1 and IRGM, as being significantly associated with Crohn's disease. Autophagy. 2007;3:649–51.
26. Preece MA. The genetic contribution to stature. Horm Res. 1996;45 Suppl 2:56–8.
27. Silventoinen K, Kaprio J, Lahelma E, Koskenvuo M. Relative effect of genetic and environmental factors on body height: differences across birth cohorts among Finnish mean and women. Am J Public Health. 2000;90:627–30.
28. Silventoinen K, Sammalisto S, Perola M, Boomsma DI, Cornes BK, Davis C, et al. Heritability of adult body height: a comparative study of twin cohorts in eight countries. Twin Res. 2003;6:399–408.
29. Macgregor S, Cornes B, Martin N, Visscher P. Bias, precision and heritability of selfreported and clinically measured height in Australian twins. Hum Genet. 2006;120:571–80.
30. Perola M, Sammalisto S, Hiekkalinna T, Martin NG, Visscher PM, Montgomery GW, et al. Combined genome scans for body stature in 6, 602 European twins: evidence for common Caucasian loci. PLoS Genet. 2007;3:e97.
31. Gudbjartsson DF, Walters GB, Thorleifsson G, Stefansson H, Halldorsson BV, Zusmanovich P, et al. Many sequence variants affecting diversity of adult human height. Nat Genet. 2008;40:609–15.
32. Maher B. Personal genomes: the case of the missing heritability. Nature. 2008;456:18–21.
33. Lango Allen H, Estrada K, Guillaume L, Berndt SI, Weedon MN, Rivadeneira F, et al. Hundreds of variants clustered in genomic loci and biological pathways affect human height. Nature. 2010;467:832–8.
34. Heger M. Sequencing genes implicated in GWAS uncovers rare variants in disease cohort. http://www.genomeweb.com/sequencing/sequencing-genes-implicated-gwas-uncovers-rare-variants-disease-cohort. Accessed 27 July 2010.
35. Yang W, Kelly T, He J. Genetic epidemiology of obesity. Epidemiol Rev. 2007;29:49–61.
36. Dean M. Approaches to identify genes for complex human diseases: lessons from Mendelian disorders. Hum Mutat. 2003;22:261–74.
37. Rohde K. Genome-wide linkage analysis and association studies using SNP genotypes from the Affymetrix 10K and 100K chips. http://www.science.ngfn.de/10_238.htm. Accessed July 2010.
38. Hirschhorn JN, Lindgren CM, Daly MJ, Kirby A, Schaffner SF, Burtt NP, et al. Genomewide linkage analysis of stature in multiple populations reveals several regions wtih evidence of linkage to adult height. Am J Hum Genet. 2001;69:106–16.
39. Cowley Jr AW. The genetic dissection of essential hypertension. Genetics. 2006;7:829–40.

40. Lalouel JM. Large-scale search for genes predisposing to essential hypertension. Am J Hypertens. 2003;16:163–6.
41. Lee WK, Padmanabhan S, Dominiczak AF. Genetics of hypertension: from experimental models to clinical applications. J Hum Hypertens. 2000;14:631–47.
42. Lifton RP, Jeunemaitre X. Finding genes that cause human hypertension. J Hypertens. 1993;11:236–9.
43. Carlson CS, Eberle MA, Kruglyak L, Nickerson DA. Mapping complex disease loci in whole-genome association studies. Nature. 2004;429:446–52.
44. Bouchard C, Leon A, Rao D, Skinner J, Wilmore J, Gagnon J. The HERITAGE family study. Aims, design, and measurement protocol. Med Sci Sports Exerc. 1995;27:721–9.
45. Defoor J, Martens K, Matthijs G, Zielińska D, Schepers D, Philips T, et al. The caregene study: muscle-specific creatine kinase gene and aerobic power in coronary artery disease. Eur J Cardiovasc Pre Rehabil. 2005;12:415–7.
46. Gene – Exercise Research Study (GERS). http://clinicaltrials.gov/ct2/show/NCT00976742. Accessed 22 Oct 2010.
47. Wilund KR, Ferrell RE, Phares DA, Goldberg AP, Hagberg JM. Changes in high-density lipoprotein-cholesterol subfractions with exercise training may be dependent on cholesteryl ester transfer protein (CETP) genotype. Metabolism. 2002;6:774–8.
48. Phares DA, Halverstadt AA, Shuldiner AR, Ferrell RE, Douglass LW, Ryan AS, et al. Association between body fat response to exercise training and multilocus ADR genotypes. Obes Res. 2004;12:807–15.
49. Ghiu IA, Ferrell RE, Kulaputana O, Phares DA, Hagberg JM. Selected genetic polymorphisms and plasma coagulation factor VII changes with exercise training. J Appl Physiol. 2004;96:985–90.
50. McKenzie JA, Weiss EP, Ghiu IA, Kulaputana O, Phares DA, Ferrell RE, et al. Influence of the interleukin-6-174 G/C gene polymorphism on exercise training-induced changes in glucose tolerance indexes. J Appl Physiol. 2004;97:1338–42.
51. Weiss EP, Kulaputana O, Ghiu IA, Brandauer J, Wohn CR, Phares DA, et al. Endurance training-induced changes in the insulin response to oral glucose are associated with the peroxisome proliferator-activated receptor-gamma2 Pro12Ala genotype in men but not in women. Metabolism. 2005;54:97–102.
52. Halverstadt A, Phares DA, Wilund KR, Goldberg AP, Hagberg JM. Endurance exercise training raises high-density lipoprotein cholesterol and lowers small low-density lipoprotein and very low-density lipoprotein independent of body fat phenotypes in older men and women. Metabolism. 2007;56:444–50.
53. Obisesan TO, Ferrell RE, Goldberg AP, Phares DA, Ellis TJ, Hagberg JM. APOE genotype affects black-white responses of high-density lipoprotein cholesterol subspecies to aerobic exercise training. Metabolism. 2008;57:1669–76.
54. Jenkins NT, McKenzie JA, Damcott CM, Witkowski S, Hagberg JM. Endurance exercise training effects on body fatness, VO2max, HDL-C subfractions, and glucose tolerance are influenced by a PLIN haplotype in older Caucasians. J Appl Physiol. 2010;108:498–506.
55. Rivera MA, Dionne FT, Wolfarth B, Chagnon M, Simoneau JA, Pérusse L, et al. Muscle-specific creatine kinase gene polymorphisms in elite endurance athletes and sedentary controls. Med Sci Sports Exerc. 1997;29:1444–7.
56. Rankinen T, Wolfarth B, Simoneau JA, Maier-Lenz D, Rauramaa R, Rivera MA, et al. No association between the angiotensin-converting enzyme ID polymorphism and elite endurance athlete status. J Appl Physiol. 2000;88:1571–5.
57. Wolfarth B, Rankinen T, Mühlbauer S, Ducke M, Rauramaa R, Boulay MR, et al. Endothelial nitric oxide synthase gene polymorphism and elite endurance athlete status: the Genathlete study. Scand J Med Sci Sports. 2008;18:485–90.
58. Montgomery HE, Marshall R, Hemingway H, Myerson S, Clarkson P, Dollery C, et al. Human gene for physical performance. Nature. 1998;393:221–2.
59. Gayagay G, Yu B, Hambly B. Elite endurance athletes and the ACE I allele – the role of genes in athletic performance. Hum Genet. 1998;103:48–50.

60. Myerson S, Hemingway H, Budget R, Martin J, Humphries S, Montgomery H. Human angiotensin I-converting enzyme gene and endurance performance. J Appl Physiol. 1999;87: 1313–6.
61. Jelakovic B, Kuzmanic D, Milicic D. Influence of angiotensin converting enzyme (*ACE*) gene polymorphism and circadian blood pressure (BP) changes on left ventricle (LV) mass in competitive oarsmen. Am J Hypertens. 2000;13:182A.
62. Taylor R, CM CDS, Fallon K, Bockxmeer F. Elite athletes and the gene for angiotensin-converting enzyme. J Appl Physiol. 1999;87:1035–7.
63. Woods D, Hickman M, Jamshid Y, Brull D, Vassiliou V, Jones A, et al. Elite swimmers and the D allele of the ACE I/D polymorphism. Hum Genet. 2001;108:230–2.
64. Nazarov IB, Woods DR, Montgomery HE, Shneider OV, Kazakov VI, Tomilin NV, et al. The angiotensin converting enzyme I/D polymorphism in Russian athletes. Eur J Hum Genet. 2001;9:797–801.
65. Ahmetov II, Mozhayskaya IA, Flavell DM, Astratenkova IV, Komkova AI, Lyubaeva EV, et al. PPARa gene variation and physical performance in Russian athletes. Eur J Appl Physiol. 2006;97:103–8.
66. Ahmetov II, Williams AG, Popov DV, Lyubaeva EV, Hakimullina AM, Fedotovskaya ON, et al. The combined impact of metabolic gene polymorphisms on elite endurance athlete status and related phenotypes. Hum Genet. 2009;126:751–61.
67. Ash GI, Scott RA, Deason M, Dawson TA, Wolde B, Bekele Z, et al. No association between ACE gene variation and endurance athlete status in Ethiopians. Med Sci Sports Exerc. 2010 [Epub ahead of print], PMID: 20798657.
68. Onywera V, Scott R, Boit M, Pitsiladis Y. Demographic characteristics of elite Kenyan endurance runners. J Sports Sci. 2006;24:415–22.
69. Scott RA, Georgiades E, Wilson RH, Goodwin WH, Wolde B, Pitsiladis YP. Demographic characteristics of elite ethiopian endurance runners. Med Sci Sports Exerc. 2003;35:1727–32.
70. Scott RA, Pitsiladis YP. Genotypes and distance running: clues from Africa. Sports Med. 2007;37:1–4.
71. Moran CN, Scott RA, Adams SM. Y chromosome haplogroups of elite Ethiopian endurance runners. Hum Genet. 2004;115:492–7.
72. Scott RA, Wilson RH, Goodwin WH, Moran CN, Georgiades E, Wolde B, et al. Mitochondrial DNA lineages of Elite Ethiopian athletes. Comp Biochem Physiol B Biochem Mol Biol. 2005;140:497–503.
73. Scott RA, Moran CN, Wilson RH, Onywera V, Boit MK, Goodwin WH, et al. No association between angiotensin converting enzyme (ACE) gene variation and endurance athlete status in Kenyans. Comp Biochem Physiol A Mol Integr Physiol. 2005;141:169–75.
74. Gastin P. Energy system interaction and relative contribution during maximal exercise. Sports Med. 2001;31:725–41.
75. Yang N, MacArthur DG, Gulbin JP, Hahn AG, Beggs AH, Easteal S, et al. ACTN3 genotype is associated with human elite athletic performance. Am J Hum Genet. 2003;73:627–31.
76. Montgomery HE, Clarkson P, Dollery CM, Prasad K, Losi MA, Hemingway H, et al. Association of angiotensin-converting enzyme gene I/D polymorphism with change in left ventricular mass in response to physical training. Circulation. 1997;96:741–7.
77. Cerit M, Colakoglu M, Erdogan M, Berdeli A, Cam F. Relationship between ace genotype and short duration aerobic performance development. Eur J Appl Physiol. 2006;98:461–5.
78. He Z, Hu Y, Feng L, Lu Y, Liu G, Xi Y, et al. Polymorphisms in the HBB gene relate to individual cardiorespiratory adaptation in response to endurance training. Br J Sports Med. 2006;40:998–1002.
79. Hamilton B, Weston A. Perspectives on East African middle and long distance running. J Sci Med Sport. 2000;3:vi–viii.
80. Yu N, Chen FC, Ota S, Jorde LB, Pamilo P, Patthy L, et al. Larger genetic differences within Africans than between Africans and Eurasians. Genetics. 2002;161:269–74.

81. Burchard EG, Ziv E, Coyle N, Gomez SL, Tang H, Karter AJ, et al. The importance of race and Ethnic background in biomedical research and clinical practice. N Engl J Med. 2003;348:1170–5.
82. Cooper RS, Kaufman JS, Ward R. Race and genomics. N Engl J Med. 2003;348:1166–70.
83. Cavalli-Sforza LL, Feldman MW. The application of molecular genetic approaches to the study of human evolution. Nat Genet. 2003;33(Suppl):266–75.
84. International HapMap Consortium. A haplotype map of the human genome. Nature. 2005;437:1299–320.
85. Jobling MA, Hurles ME, Tyler-Smith C. Human evolutionary genetics: origins, peoples and disease. London: Garland Science Publishing; 2004. p. 523.
86. Weston AR, Mbambo Z, Myburgh KH. Running economy of African and Caucasian distance runners. Med Sci Sports Exerc. 2000;32:1130–40.
87. Ama PF, Simoneau JA, Boulay MR, Serresse O, Thériault G, Bouchard C. Skeletal muscle characteristics in sedentary black and Caucasian males. J Appl Physiol. 1986;61:1758–61.
88. Manners J. Kenya's running tribe. Sports Hist. 1997;17:14–27.
89. Entine J. Taboo: why black athletes dominate sports and why we're afraid to talk about it. New York: Public Affairs; 2001.
90. Larsen HB. Kenyan dominance in distance running. Comp Biochem Physiol A Mol Integr Physiol. 2003;136:161–70.
91. Scott RA, Pitsiladis YP. Genetics and the success of east African distance runners. Int Sports Med J. 2006;7:172–86.
92. Rigat B, Hubert C, Alhenc-Gelas F, Cambien F, Corvol P, Soubrier F. An insertion/deletion polymorphism in the angiotensin I-converting enzyme gene accounting for half the variance of serum enzyme levels. J Clin Invest. 1990;86:1343–6.
93. Williams AG, Rayson MP, Jubb M, World M, Woods DR, Hayward M, et al. The ACE gene and muscle performance. Nature. 2000;403:614.
94. Woods DR, World M, Rayson MP, Williams AG, Jubb M, Jamshidi Y, et al. Endurance enhancement related to the human angiotensin I-converting enzyme I-D polymorphism is not due to differences in the cardiorespiratory response to training. Eur J Appl Physiol. 2002;86:240–4.
95. Zhang B, Tanka H, Shono N, Miura S, Kiyonaga A, Shindo M, et al. The I allele of the angiotensin-converting enzyme gene is associated with an increased percentage of slow-twitch type I fibers in human skeletal muscle. Clin Genet. 2003;63:139–44.
96. Collins M, Xenophontos SL, Cariolou MA, Mokone GG, Hudson DE, Anastasiades L, et al. The ACE gene and endurance performance during the South African Ironman Triathlons. Med Sci Sports Exerc. 2004;36:1314–20.
97. Zhao B, Moochhala SM, Tham S, Lu J, Chia M, Byrne C, et al. Relationship between angiotensin-converting enzyme ID polymorphism and VO(2max) of Chinese males. Life Sci. 2003;73:2625–30.
98. Hagberg JM, Ferrell RE, McCole SD, Wilund KR, Moore GE. VO2 max is associated with ACE genotype in postmenopausal women. J Appl Physiol. 1998;85:1842–6.
99. Scott RA, Irving R, Irwin L, Morrison E, Charlton V, Austin K, et al. ACTN3 and ACE genotypes in elite Jamaican and US sprinters. Med Sci Sports Exerc. 2010;42:107–12.
100. Kalson NS, Thompson J, Davies AJ, Stokes S, Earl MD, Whitehead A, et al. The effect of angiotensin-converting enzyme genotype on acute mountain sickness and summit success in trekkers attempting the summit of Mt. Kilimanjaro (5,895 m). Eur J Appl Physiol. 2009;105:373–9.
101. Woods DR, Brull D, Montgomery HE. Endurance and the ACE I/D polymorphism. Sci Prog. 2000;83:317–36.
102. Cambien F, Poirier O, Lecerf L, Evans A, Cambou JP, Arveiler D, et al. Deletion polymorphism in the gene for angiotensin-converting enzyme is a potent risk factor for myocardial infarction. Nature. 1992;359:641–4.
103. Libby P. Atherosclerosis. In: BE FAS, Isselbacher KJ, Wilson JD, Martin JB, Kasper DL, Hauser SL, Longo DL, editors. Harrison's principles of internal medicine. New York: McGraw-Hill; 1998. p. 1345–52.

104. Agerholm-Larsen B, Nordestgaard BG, Tybjaerg-Hansen A. ACE gene polymorphism in cardiovascular disease meta-analyses of small and large studies in Whites. Arterioscler Thromb Vasc Biol. 2000;20:484–92.
105. North KN, Yang N, Wattanasirichaigoon D, Mills M, Easteal S, Beggs AH. A common nonsense mutation results in alphaactinin-3 deficiency in the general population. Nat Genet. 1999;21:353–4.
106. Yang N, MacArthur DG, Wolde B, Onywera VO, Boit MK, Lau SY, et al. The ACTN3 R577X polymorphism in East and West African athletes. Med Sci Sports Exerc. 2007;39:1985–8.
107. Clarkson PM, Devaney JM, Gordish-Dressman H, Thompson PD, Hubal MJ, Urso M, et al. ACTN3 genotype is associated with increases in muscle strength in response to resistance training in women. J Appl Physiol. 2005;99:154–63.
108. Clarkson PM, Hoffman EP, Zambraski E, Gordish-Dressman H, Kearns A, Hubal M, et al. ACTN3 and MLCK genotype associations with exertional muscle damage. J Appl Physiol. 2005;99:564–9.
109. Delmonico MJ, Kostek MC, Doldo NA, Hand BD, Walsh S, Conway JM, et al. Alpha-actinin-3 (ACTN3) R577X polymorphism influences knee extensor peak power response to strength training in older men and women. J Gerontol A Biol Sci Med Sci. 2007;62:206–12.
110. Moran CN, Yang N, Bailey ME, Tsiokanos A, Jamurtas A, MacArthur DG, et al. Association analysis of the ACTN3 R577X polymorphism and complex quantitative body composition and performance phenotypes in adolescent Greeks. Eur J Hum Genet. 2007;15:88–93.
111. Walsh S, Liu D, Metter EJ, Ferrucci L, Roth SM. ACTN3 genotype is associated with muscle phenotypes in women across the adult age span. J Appl Physiol. 2008;105:1486–91.
112. Ahmetov II, Druzhevskaya AM, Astratenkova IV, Popov DV, Vinogradova OL, Rogozkin VA. The ACTN3 R577X polymorphism in Russian endurance athletes. Br J Sports Med. 2010;44:649–52.
113. Druzhevskaya AM, Ahmetov II, Astratenkova IV, Rogozkin VA. Association of the ACTN3 R577X polymorphism with power athlete status in Russians. Eur J Appl Physiol. 2008;103:631–4.
114. Niemi AK, Majamaa K. Mitochondrial DNA and ACTN3 genotypes in Finnish elite endurance and sprint athletes. Eur J Hum Genet. 2005;13:965–9.
115. Papadimitriou ID, Papadopoulos C, Kouvatsi A, Triantaphyllidis C. The ACTN3 gene in elite Greek track and field athletes. Int J Sports Med. 2008;29:352–5.
116. Roth SM, Walsh S, Liu D, Metter EJ, Ferrucci L, Hurley BF. The ACTN3 R577X nonsense allele is under-represented in elite-level strength athletes. Eur J Hum Genet. 2008;16:391–4.
117. MacArthur DG, Seto JT, Chan S, Quinlan KG, Raftery JM, Turner N, et al. An Actn3 knockout mouse provides mechanistic insights into the association between α-actinin-3 deficiency and human athletic performance. Hum Mol Genet. 2008;17:1076–86.
118. Cagliani R, Fumagalli M, Pozzoli U, Riva S, Comi GP, Torri F, et al. Diverse evolutionary histories for beta-adrenoreceptor genes in humans. Am J Hum Genet. 2009;85:64–75.
119. Kurnik D, Muszkat M, Li C, Sofowora GG, Solus J, Xie HG, et al. Variations in the alpha2A-adrenergic receptor gene and their functional effects. Clin Pharmacol Ther. 2006;79:173–85.
120. Yang-Feng TL, Xue FY, Zhong WW, Cotecchia S, Frielle T, Caron, MG, et al. Chromosomal organization of adrenergic receptor genes. Proc Natl Acad Sci U S A. 1990;87:1516–20.
121. Kobilka BK, Matsui H, Kobilka T-F, Francke U, Caron MG, Lefkowitz RJ, et al. Cloning, sequencing, and expression of the gene coding for the human platelet alpha 2-adrenergic receptor. Science. 1987;238:650–6.
122. Eisenach JH, Wittwer ED. Beta-adrenoceptor gene variation and intermediate physiological traits: prediction of distand phenotype. Exp Physiol. 2010;95:757–64.
123. Gauthier C, Langin D, Balligand JL. Beta3-adrenoceptors in the cardiovascular system. Trends Pharmacol Sci. 2000;21:426–31.
124. Chruscinski A, Brede ME, Meinel L, Lohse MJ, Kobilka BK, Hein L. Differential distribution of beta-adrenergic receptor subtypes in blood vessels of knockout mice lacking beta(1)- or beta(2)-adrenergic receptors. Mol Pharmacol. 2001;60:955–62.

125. Rohrer DK, Chruscinski A, Schauble EH, Bernstein D, Kobilka BK. Cardiovascular and metabolic alterations in mice lacking both beta1- and beta2-adrenergic receptors. J Biol Chem. 1999;274:16701–8.

126. Hoffmann C, Leitz MR, Oberdorf-Maass S, Lohse MJ, Klotz KN. Comparative pharmacology of human beta-adrenergic receptor subtypes – characterization of stably transfected receptors in CHO cells. Naunyn Schmiedebergs Arch Pharmacol. 2004;369:151–9.

127. Hoehe MR, Berrettini WH, Lentes KU. Dra I identifies a two allele DNA polymorphism in the human alpha 2-adrenergic receptor gene (ADRAR), using a 5.5 kb probe (p ADRAR). Nucleic Acids Res. 1988;16:9070.

128. Wolfarth B, Rivera MA, Oppert JM, Boulay MR, Dionne FT, Chagnon M, et al. A polymorphism in the alpha2a-adrenoceptor gene and endurance athlete status. Med Sci Sports Exerc. 2000;32:1709–12.

129. Rao DC, Province MA, Leppert MF, Oberman A, Heiss G, Ellison RC, et al. A genome-wide affected sibpair linkage analysis of hypertension: the HyperGEN network. Am J Hypertens. 2003;16:148–50.

130. Province MA, Kardia SL, Ranade K, Rao DC, Thiel BA, Cooper RS, et al. A meta-analysis of genome-wide linkage scans for hypertension: the National Heart, Lung and Blood Institute Family Blood Pressure Program. Am J Hypertens. 2003;16:144–7.

131. Wilk JB, Myers RH, Pankow JS, Hunt SC, Leppert MF, Freedman BI, et al. Adrenergic receptor polymorphisms associated with resting heart rate: the HyperGEN Study. Ann Hum Genet. 2006;70:566–73.

132. Heinonen P, Koulu M, Pesonen U, Karvonen MK, Rissanen A, Laakso M, et al. Identification of a three-amino acid deletion in the alpha2B-adrenergic receptor that is associated with reduced basal metabolic rate in obese subjects. J Clin Endocrinol Metab. 1999;84:2429–33.

133. Ueno LM, Frazzatto ES, Batalha LT, Trombetta IC, do Socorro BM, Irigoyen C, et al. Alpha2B-adrenergic receptor deletion polymorphism and cardiac autonomic nervous system responses to exercise in obese women. Int J Obes (Lond). 2006;30:214–20.

134. Small KM, Wagoner LE, Levin AM, Kardia SL, Liggett SB. Synergistic polymorphisms of beta1- and alpha2C-adrenergic receptors and the risk of congestive heart failure. N Engl J Med. 2002;47:1135–42.

135. Brede M, Wiesmann F, Jahns R, Hadamek K, Arnolt C, Neubauer S, et al. Feedback inhibition of catecholamine release by two different alpha2-adrenoceptor subtypes prevents progression of heart failure. Circulation. 2002;106:2491–6.

136. Podlowski S, Wenzel K, Luther HP, Muller J, Bramlage P, Baumann G, et al. Beta1-adrenoceptor gene variations: a role in idiopathic dilated cardiomyopathy? J Mol Med. 2000;78:87–93.

137. Mason DA, Moore JD, Green SA, Liggett SB. A gain-of-function polymorphism in a G-protein coupling domain of the human beta1-adrenergic receptor. J Biol Chem. 1999;274:12670–4.

138. Buscher R, Belger H, Eilmes KJ, Tellkamp R, Radke J, Dhein S, et al. In-vivo studies do not support a major functional role for the Gly389Arg beta 1-adrenoceptor polymorphism in humans. Pharmacogenetics. 2001;11:199–205.

139. Xie HG, Dishy V, Sofowora G, Kim RB, Landau R, Smiley RM, et al. Arg389Gly beta 1-adrenoceptor polymorphism varies in frequency among different ethnic groups but does not alter response in vivo. Pharmacogenetics. 2001;11:191–7.

140. Rathz DA, Gregory KN, Fang Y, Brown KM, Liggett SB. Hierarchy of polymorphic variation and desensitization permutations relative to beta 1- and beta 2-adrenergic receptor signaling. J Biol Chem. 2003;278:10784–9.

141. Stanton T, Inglis GC, Padmanabhan S, Dominiczak AF, Jardine AG, Connell JM. Variation at the beta-1 adrenoceptor gene locus affects left ventricular mass in renal failure. J Nephrol. 2002;15:512–8.

142. Sandilands AJ, Parameshwar J, Large S, Brown MJ, O'Shaughnessy KM. Confirmation of a role for the 389R>G beta-1 adrenoceptor polymorphism on exercise capacity in heart failure. Heart. 2005;91:1613–4.

143. Moore JD, Mason DA, Green SA, Hsu J, Liggett SB. Racial differences in the frequencies of cardiac beta(1)-adrenergic receptor polymorphisms: analysis of c145A>G and c1165G>C. Hum Mutat. 1999;14:271.
144. Borjesson M, Magnusson Y, Hjalmarson A, Andersson B. A novel polymorphism in the gene coding for the beta(1)-adrenergic receptor associated with survival in patients with heart failure. Eur Heart J. 2000;21:1853–8.
145. Ranade K, Jorgenson E, Sheu WH, Pei D, Hsiung CA, Chiang FT, et al. A polymorphism in the beta1 adrenergic receptor is associated with resting heart rate. Am J Hum Genet. 2002;70:935–42.
146. Defoor J, Martens K, Zielinska D, Matthijs G, Van NH, Schepers D, et al. The CAREGENE study: polymorphisms of the beta1-adrenoceptor gene and aerobic power in coronary artery disease. Eur Heart J. 2006;27:808–16.
147. Reihsaus E, Innis M, MacIntyre N, Liggett SB. Mutations in the gene encoding for the beta 2-adrenergic receptor in normal and asthmatic subjects. Am J Respir Cell Mol Biol. 1993;8:334–9.
148. Heckbert SR, Hindorff LA, Edwards KL, Psaty BM, Lumley T, Siscovick DS, et al. Beta2-adrenergic receptor polymorphisms and risk of incident cardiovascular events in the elderly. Circulation. 2003;107:2021–4.
149. Dewar JC, Wheatley AP, Venn A, Morrison JF, Britton J, Hall IP. Beta2-adrenoceptor polymorphisms are in linkage disequilibrium, but are not associated with asthma in an adult population. Clin Exp Allergy. 1998;28:442–8.
150. Green SA, Turki J, Innis M, Liggett SB. Amino-terminal polymorphisms of the human beta 2-adrenergic receptor impart distinct agonist-promoted regulatory properties. Biochemistry. 1994;33:9414–9.
151. Bruck H, Leineweber K, Beilfuss A, Weber M, Heusch G, Philipp T, et al. Genotype-dependent time course of lymphocyte beta 2-adrenergic receptor down-regulation. Clin Pharmacol Ther. 2003;74:255–63.
152. Meirhaeghe A, Helbecque N, Cottel D, Amouyel P. Beta2-adrenoceptor gene polymorphism, body weight, and physical activity. Lancet. 1999;353:896.
153. Meirhaeghe A, Helbecque N, Cottel D, Amouyel P. Impact of polymorphisms of the human beta2-adrenoceptor gene on obesity in a French population. Int J Obes Relat Metab Disord. 2000;24:382–7.
154. Meirhaeghe A, Luan J, Selberg-Franks P, Hennings S, Mitchell J, Halsall D, et al. The effect of the Gly16Arg polymorphism of the beta(2)-adrenergic receptor gene on plasma free fatty acid levels is modulated by physical activity. J Clin Endocrinol Metab. 2001; 86:5881–7.
155. Wolfarth B, Rankinen T, Mühlbauer S, Scherr J, Boulay MR, Pérusse L, et al. Association between a beta2-adrenergic receptor polymorphism and elite endurance performance. Metabolism. 2007;56:1649–51.
156. Giacobino JP. Beta 3-adrenoceptor: an update. Eur J Endocrinol. 1995;132:377–85.
157. Katzmarzyk PT, Perusse L, Bouchard C. Genetics of abdominal visceral fat levels. Am J Hum Biol. 1999;11:225–35.
158. Widen E, Lehto M, Kanninen T, Walston J, Shuldiner AR, Groop LC. Association of a polymorphism in the beta 3-adrenergic-receptor gene with features of the insulin resistance syndrome in Finns. N Engl J Med. 1995;333:348–51.
159. Kahara T, Takamura T, Hayakawa T, Nagai Y, Yamaguchi H, Katsuki T, et al. Prediction of exercise-mediated changes in metabolic markers by gene polymorphism. Diabetes Res Clin Pract. 2002;57:105–10.
160. Allison DB, Heo M, Faith MS, Pietrobelli A. Meta-analysis of the association of the Trp64Arg polymorphism in the beta3 adrenergic receptor with body mass index. Int J Obes Relat Metab Disord. 1998;22:559–66.
161. Fujisawa T, Ikegami H, Kawaguchi Y, Ogihara T. Meta-analysis of the association of Trp64Arg polymorphism of beta 3-adrenergic receptor gene with body mass index. J Clin Endocrinol Metab. 1998;83:2441–4.

220 Y. Pitsiladis et al.

162. Kurokawa N, Nakai K, Kameo S, Liu ZM, Satoh H. Association of BMI with the beta3-adrenergic receptor gene polymorphism in Japanese: meta-analysis.9: 741–745, 2001. Obes Res. 2001;9:741–5.
163. Fischer H, Esbjornsson M, Sabina RL, Stromberg A, Peyrard-Janvid M, Norman B. AMP deaminase deficiency is associated with lower sprint cycling performance in healthy subjects. J Appl Physiol. 2007;103:315–22.
164. Morisaki T, Gross M, Morisaki H, Pongratz D, Zollner N, Holmes EW. Molecular basis of AMP deaminase deficiency in skeletal muscle. Proc Natl Acad Sci U S A. 1992;89:6457–61.
165. Sabina RL, Fishbein WN, Pezeshkpour G, Clarke PR, Holmes EW. Molecular analysis of the myoadenylate deaminase deficiencies. Neurology. 1992;42:170–9.
166. Norman B, Glenmark B, Jansson E. Muscle AMP deaminase deficiency in 2% of a healthy population. Muscle Nerve. 1995;18:239–41.
167. Verzijl HT, van Engelen BG, Luyten JA, Steenbergen GC, van den Heuvel LP, ter Laak HJ, et al. Genetic characteristics of myoadenylate deaminase deficiency. Ann Neurol. 1998;44:140–3.
168. Sabina RL, Swain JL, Olanow CW, Bradley WG, Fishbein WN, DiMauro S, et al. Myoadenylate deaminase deficiency. Functional and metabolic abnormalities associated with disruption of the purine nucleotide cycle. J Clin Invest. 1984;73:720–30.
169. De Ruiter CJ, May AM, van Engelen BG, Wevers RA, Steenbergen-Spanjers GC, de Haan A. Muscle function during repetitive moderateintensity muscle contractions in myoadenylate deaminase-deficient Dutch subjects. Clin Sci (Lond). 2002;102:531–9.
170. Rico-Sanz J, Rankinen T, Joanisse DR, Leon AS, Skinner JS, Wilmore JH, et al. Associations between cardiorespiratory responses to exercise and the C34T AMPD1 gene polymorphism in the HERITAGE Family Study. Physiol Genomics. 2003;14:161–6.
171. Rubio JC, Martin MA, Rabadan M. Frequency of the C34T mutation of the AMPD1 gene in world-class endurance athletes: does this mutation impair performance? J Appl Physiol. 2005;98:2108–12.
172. Lucia A, Martin MA, Esteve-Lanao J, San Juan AF, Rubio JC, Olivan J, et al. C34T mutation of the AMPD1 gene in an elite white runner. Br J Sports Med. 2006;40:e7.
173. Sinkeler SP, Binkhorst RA, Joosten EM, Wevers RA, Coerwinkei MM, Oei TL. AMP deaminase deficiency: study of the human skeletal muscle purine metabolism during ischaemic isometric exercise. Clin Sci (Colch). 1987;72:475–82.
174. De Ruiter CJ, Van EBG, Wevers RA, De Haan A. Muscle functionv during fatigue in myoadenylate deaminase-deficient Dutch subjects. Clin Sci (Colch). 2000;98:579–85.
175. Norman B, Sabina RL, Jansson E. Regulation of skeletal muscle ATP catabolism by AMPD1 genotype during sprint exercise in asymptomatic subjects. J Appl Physiol. 2001;91:258–64.
176. Tarnopolsky MA, Parise G, Gibala MJ, Graham TE, Rush JW. Myoadenylate deaminase deficiency does not affect muscle anaplerosis during exhaustive exercise in humans. J Physiol. 2001;553:881–9.
177. Pollin TI, Damcott CM, Shen HQ. A null mutation in human APOC3 confers a favorable plasma lipid profile and apparent cardioprotection. Science. 2008;322:1702–5.
178. Woo SK, Kang HS. Apolipoprotein C-III SstI genotypes modulate exercise-induced hypotriglyceridemia. Med Sci Sports Exerc. 2004;36:955–9.
179. Yoshitomi H, Yamashita K, Abe S, Tanak I. Differential regulation of mouse uncoupling proteins among brown adipose tissue, white adipose tissue, and skeletal muscle in chronic beta 3 adrenergic receptor agonist treatment. Biochem Biophys Res Commun. 1998;253:85–91.
180. Gleeson M, Blannin AK, Walsh NP, Field CN, Pritchard JC. Effect of exercise-induced muscle damage on the blood lactate response to incremental exercise in humans. Eur J Appl Physiol Occup Physiol. 1998;77:292–5.
181. Boss O, Hagen T, Lowell BB. Uncoupling proteins 2 and 3: potential regulators of mitochondrial energy metabolism. Diabetes. 2000;49:143–56.
182. Nedergaard J, Ricquier D, Kozak LP. Uncoupling proteins: current status and therapeutic prospects. EMBO Rep. 2005;6:917–21.

183. Klaus S, Casteilla L, Bouillaud F, Ricquier D. The uncouplingprotein UCP: a membraneous mitochondrial ion carrier exclusively expressed in brown adipose tissue. Int J Biochem. 1991;23:791–801.

184. Monemdjou S, Hofmann WE, Kozak LP, Harper ME. Increased mitochondrial proton leak in skeletal muscle mitochondria of UCP1-deficient mice. Am J Physiol Endocrinol Metab. 2000;279:E941–6.

185. Erlanson-Albertsson C. The role of uncoupling proteins in the regulation of metabolism. Acta Physiol Scand. 2003;178:405–12.

186. Klaus S, Rudolph B, Dohrmann C, Wehr R. Expression of uncoupling protein 1 in skeletal muscle decreases muscle energy efficiency and affects thermoregulation and substrate oxidation. Physiol Genomics. 2005;21:193–200.

187. Garruti G, Ricquier D. Analysis of uncoupling protein and its mRNA in adipose tissue deposits of adult humans. Int J Obes Relat Metab Disord. 1992;16:383–90.

188. Krauss S, Zhang CY, Lowell BB. The mitochondrial uncoupling-protein homologues. Nat Rev Mol Cell Biol. 2005;6:248–61.

189. Hawley JA, Brouns F, Jeukendrup A. Strategies to enhance fat utilisation during exercise. Sports Med. 1998;25:241–57.

190. Astrup A, Toubro S, Dalgaard LT, Urhammer SA, Sùrensen TIA, Pedersen O. Impact of the v/v 55 polymorphism of the uncoupling protein 2 gene on 24-h energy expenditure and substrate oxidation. Int J Obes Relat Metab Disord. 1999;23:1030–4.

191. Buemann B, Schierning B, Toubro S, Bibby BM, Sørensen T, Dalgaard L, et al. The association between the val/ala-55 polymorphism of the uncoupling protein 2 gene and exercise efficiency. Int J Obes Relat Metab Disord. 2001;25:467–71.

192. Ahmetov II, Hakimullina AM, Shikhova JV, Rogozkin VA. The ability to become an elite endurance athlete depends on the carriage of high number of endurance-related alleles. Eur J Hum Gene. 2008;16:341.

193. Halsall DJ, Luan J, Saker P. Uncoupling protein 3 genetic variants in human obesity: the c-55t promoter polymorphism is negatively correlated with body mass index in a UK Caucasian population. Int J Obes Relat Metab Disord. 2001;25:472–7.

194. Schrauwen P, Xia J, Walder K, Snitker S, Ravussin E. A novel polymorphism in the proximal UCP3 promoter region: effect on skeletal muscle UCP3 mRNA expression and obesity in male non-diabetic Pima Indians. Int J Obes Relat Metab Disord. 1999;23:1242–5.

195. Hudson DE, Mokone GG, Noakes TD, Collins M. The –55 C/T polymorphism within the UCP3 gene and performance during the South African Ironman Triathlon. Int J Sports Med. 2004;25:427–32.

196. Noland RC, Hickner RC, Jimenez-Linan M. Acute endurance exercise increases skeletal muscle uncoupling protein-3 gene expression in untrained but not trained humans. Metabolism. 2003;52:152–8.

197. Turner DC, Wallimann T, Eppenberger HM. A protein that binds specifically to the M-ine of skeletal muscle is identified as the muscle form of creatine kinase. Proc Natl Acad Sci U S A. 1972;70:702–5.

198. Wallimann T, Schlosser T, Eppenberger HM. Function of M-line-bound creatine kinase as intramyofibrillar ATP regenerator at the receiving end of the phosphorylcreatine shuttle in muscle. J Biol Chem. 1984;259:5238–46.

199. Holloszy JO, Coyle EF. Adaptations of skeletal muscle to endurance exercise and their metabolic consequences. J Appl Physiol. 1984;56:831–8.

200. Yamashita K, Yoshioka T. Profiles of creatine kinase isoenzyme compositions in single muscle fibers of different types. J Muscle Res Cell Motil. 1991;12:37–44.

201. van Deursen J, Heerschap A, Oeriemans F, Ruitenbeek W, Jap P, ter Laak H, et al. Skeletal muscles of mice deficient in muscle creatine kinase lack burst activity. Cell. 1993;74:621–31.

202. Rivera MA, Dionne FT, Simoneau JA, Pérusse L, Chagnon M, Chagnon Y, et al. Muscle-specific creatine kinase gene polymorphism and VO2max in the HERITAGE Family Study. Med Sci Sports Exerc. 1997;29:1311–7.

203. Rivera MA, Pérusse L, Simoneau JA, Gagnon J, Dionne FT, Leon AS, et al. Linkage between a muscle-specific CK gene marker and VO2max in the HERITAGE Family Study. Med Sci Sports Exerc. 1999;31:698–701.
204. Zhou DQ, Hu Y, Liu G, Gong L, Xi Y, Wen L. Muscle-specific creatine kinase gene polymorphism and running economy responses to an 18-week 5000-m training programme. Br J Sports Med. 2006;40:988–91.
205. Jiang BH, Rue E, Wang GL, Roe R, Semenza GL. Dimerization, DNA binding, and transactivation properties of hypoxia-inducible factor 1. J Biol Chem. 1996;271:17771–8.
206. Jiang C, Lu H, Vincent KA, Sankara S, Belanger AJ, Cheng SH, et al. Shankara S, Belanger AJ, Cheng SH, Gene expression profiles in human cardiac cells subjected to hypoxia or expressing a hybrid form of HIF-1 alpha. Physiol Genomics. 2002;8:23–32.
207. Semenza GL. HIF-1 and human disease: one highly involved factor. Genes Dev. 2000;14:1983–91.
208. Semenza GL. HIF-1: mediator of physiological and pathophysiological responses to hypoxia. J Appl Physiol. 2000;88:1474–80.
209. Jiang BH, Semenza GL, Bauer C, Marti HH. Hypoxia-inducible factor 1 levels vary exponentially over a physiologically relevant range of O2 tension. Am J Physiol. 1996;271:C1172–80.
210. Prior SJ, Hagberg JM, Phares DA, Brown MD, Fairfull L, Ferrell RE, et al. Sequence variation in hypoxia-inducible factor 1alpha (HIF1A): association with maximal oxygen consumption. Physiol Genomics. 2003;15:20–6.
211. Döring F, Onur S, Fischer A, Boulay MR, Pérusse L, Rankinen T, et al. A common haplotype and the Pro582Ser polymorphism of the hypoxia-inducible factor-1alpha (HIF1A) gene in elite endurance athletes. J Appl Physiol. 2010;108:1497–500.
212. Sander M, Chavoshan B, Victor RG. A large blood pressure-raising effect of nitric oxide synthase inhibition in humans. Hypertension. 1999;33:937–42.
213. Zatz R, Baylis C. Chronic nitric oxide inhibition model six years on. Hypertension. 1998;32:958–64.
214. Higashi Y, Sasaki S, Kurisu S, Yoshimizu A, Sasaki N, Matsuura H, et al. Regular aerobic exercise augments endothelium-dependent vascular relaxation in normotensive as well as hypertensive subjects: role of endothelium-derived nitric oxide. Circulation. 1999;100:1194–202.
215. Wang J, Wolin MS, Hintze TH. Chronic exercise enhances endothelium-mediated dilation of epicardial coronary artery in conscious dogs. Circ Res. 1993;73:829–38.
216. Kelley GA. Aerobic exercise and resting blood pressure among women: a meta-analysis. Prev Med. 1999;28:264–75.
217. Kingwell BA, Sherrard B, Jennings GL, Dart AM. Four weeks of cycle training increases basal production of nitric oxide from the forearm. Am J Physiol. 1997;272:H1070–7.
218. Woodman CR, Muller JM, Laughlin MH, Price EM. Induction of nitric oxide synthase mRNA in coronary resistance arteries isolated from exercise-trained pigs. Am J Physiol. 1997;273:H2575–9.
219. Testa M, Ennezat PV, Vikstrom KL, Demopoulos L, Gentilucci M, Loperfido F, et al. Modulation of vascular endothelial gene expression by physical training in patients with chronic heart failure. Ital Heart J. 2000;1:426–30.
220. Marsden PA, Heng HH, Scherer SW, Stewart RJ, Hall AV, Shi XM, et al. Structure and chromosomal localization of the human constitutive endothelial nitric oxide synthase gene. J Biol Chem. 1993;268:17478–88.
221. Yoshimura M, Yasue H, Nakayama M, Shimasaki Y, Ogawa H, Kugiyama K, et al. Genetic risk factors for coronary artery spasm: significance of endothelial nitric oxide synthase gene T-786->C and missense Glu298Asp variants. J Investig Med. 2000;48:367–74.
222. Erbs S, Baither Y, Linke A, Adams V, Shu Y, Lenk K, et al. Promoter but not exon 7 polymorphism of endothelial nitric oxide synthase affects training-induced correction of endothelial dysfunction. Arterioscler Thromb Vasc Biol. 2003;23:1814–9.
223. Data SA, Roltsch MH, Hand B, Ferrell RE, Park JJ, Brown MD. eNOS T-786C genotype, physical activity, and peak forearm blood flow in females. Med Sci Sports Exerc. 2003;35:1991–7.

224. Kimura T, Yokoyama T, Matsumura Y, Yoshiike N, Date C, Muramatsu M, et al. NOS3 genotype-dependent correlation between blood pressure and physical activity. Hypertension. 2003;41:355–60.
225. Rankinen T, Rice T, Perusse L, Chagnon YC, Gagnon J, Leon AS, et al. NOS3 Glu298Asp genotype and blood pressure response to endurance training: the HERITAGE family study. Hypertension. 2000;36:885–9.
226. Schoonjans K, Staels B, Auwerx J. Role of the peroxisome proliferator-activated receptor (PPAR) in mediating the effects of fibrates and fatty acids on gene expression. J Lipid Res. 1996;37:907–25.
227. Auboeuf D, Rieusset J, Fajas L, Vallier P, Frering V, Riou JP, et al. Tissue distribution and quantification of the expression of mRNAs of peroxisome proliferator-activated receptors and liver X receptor-a in humans: no alteration in adipose tissue of obese and NIDDM patients. Diabetes. 1997;46:1319–27.
228. Krey G, Braissant O, L'Horset F, Kalkhoven E, Perroud M, Parker MG, et al. Fatty acids, eicosanoids, and hypolipidemic agents identified as ligands of peroxisome proliferator-activated receptors by coactivator-dependent receptor ligand assay. Mol Endocrinol. 1997;11:779–91.
229. Kersten S, Desvergne B, Wahli W. Roles of PPARs in health and disease. Nature. 2000;405:421–4.
230. Holst D, Luquet S, Nogueira V, Kristiansen K, Leverve X, Grimaldi PA. Nutritional regulation and role of peroxisome proliferator-activated receptor δ in fatty acid catabolism in skeletal muscle. Biochim Biophys Acta. 2003;1633:43–50.
231. Berger J, Moller DE. The mechanisms of action of PPARs. Annu Rev Med. 2002;53: 409–35.
232. Wang YX, Zhang CL, Yu RT. Regulation of muscle fiber type and running endurance by PPARδ. PLoS Biol. 2004;2:e294.
233. Schuler M, Ali F, Chambon C. PGC1alpha expression is controlled in skeletal muscles by PPARbeta, whose ablation results in fiber-type switching, obesity, and type 2 diabetes. Cell Metab. 2006;4:407–14.
234. Pilegaard H, Richter EA. PGC-1α: important for exercise performance? J Appl Physiol. 2008;104:1264–5.
235. Jamshidi Y, Montgomery HE, Hense HW. Peroxisome proliferator – activated receptor alpha gene regulates left ventricular growth in response to exercise and hypertension. Circulation. 2002;105:950–5.
236. Uthurralt J, Gordish-Dressman H, Bradbury M. PPARalpha L162V underlies variation in serum triglycerides and subcutaneous fat volume in young males. BMC Med Genet. 2007;8:55.
237. Russell AP, Feilchenfeldt J, Schreiber S. Endurance training in humans leads to fiber type-specific increases in levels of peroxisome proliferator-activated receptor-gamma coactivator-1 and peroxisome proliferator-activated receptor-alpha in skeletal muscle. Diabetes. 2003;52:2874–81.
238. Kagaya Y, Kanno Y, Takeyama D, Ishide N, Maruyama Y, Takahashi T, et al. Effects of long-term pressure overload on regional myocardial glucose and free fatty acid uptake in rats. A quantitative autoradiographic study. Circulation. 1990;81:1353–61.
239. Allard MF, Schonekess BO, Henning SL, English DR, Lopaschuk GD. Contribution of oxidative metabolism and glycolysis to ATP production in hypertrophied hearts. Am J Physiol Heart Circ Physiol. 1994;267:742–50.
240. Barger PM, Brandt JM, Leone TC, Weinheimer CJ, Kelly DP. Deactivation of peroxisome proliferator-activated receptor a during cardiac hypertrophic frowth. J Clin Invest. 2000;105:1723–30.
241. Wang YX, Lee CH, Tiep S, Yu RT, Ham J, Kang H, et al. Peroxisomeproliferator-activated receptor d activates fat metabolism to prevent obesity. Cell. 2003;113:159–70.
242. Tanaka T, Yamamoto J, Iwasaki S, Asaba H, Hamura H, Ikeda Y, et al. Activation of peroxisome proliferator-activated receptor d induces fatty acid b-oxidation in skeletal muscle and attenuates metabolic syndrome. Proc Natl Acad Sci U S A. 2003;100:15924–9.

243. Dressel U, Allen TL, Pippal JB. The peroxisome proliferator-activated receptor beta/delta agonist, GW501516, regulates the expression of genes involved in lipid catabolism and energy uncoupling in skeletal muscle cells. Mol Endocrinol. 2003;17:2477–93.

244. Amri EZ, Bonino F, Ailhaud G, Abumrad NA, Grimaldi PA. Cloning of a protein that mediates transcriptional effects of fatty acids in preadipocytes. J Biol Chem. 1995;270:2367–71.

245. Goto M, Terada S, Kato M, Katoh M, Yokozeki T, Tabata I, et al. cDNA cloning and mRNA analysis of PGC-1 in epitrochlearis muscle in swimming-exercised rats. Biochem Biophys Res Commun. 2000;274:350–4.

246. Ahmetov II, Astranenkova IV, Rogozkin VA. Association of PPARD gene polymorphism with human physical performance. Mol Biol (Mosk). 2007;41:852–7.

247. Hautala AJ, Leon AS, Skinner JS, Rao DC, Bouchard C, Rankinen T. Peroxisome proliferator-activated receptor-delta polymorphisms are associated with physical performance and plasma lipids: the HERITAGE Family Study. Am J Physiol Heart Circ Physiol. 2007;292:H2498–505.

248. Eynon N, Meckel Y, Alves AJ, Yamin C, Sagiv M, Goldhammer E, et al. Is there an interaction between PPARD T294C and PPARGC1A Gly482Ser polymorphisms and human endurance performance? Exp Physiol. 2009;94:1147–52.

249. Auwerx J. PPARgamma, the ultimate thrifty gene. Diabetologia. 1999;42:1033–49.

250. Masud S, Ye S, SAS Group. Effect of the peroxisome proliferator activated receptor-gamma gene Pro12Ala variant on body mass index: a meta-analysis. J Med Genet. 2003;40:773–80.

251. Yen CJ, Beamer BA, Negri C, Silver K, Brown KA, Yarnall DP, et al. Molecular scanning of the human peroxisome proliferator activated receptor-g (hPPARg) gene in diabetic Caucasians: identification of a Pro12Ala missense mutation. Biochem Biophys Res Commun. 1997;241:270–4.

252. Altshuler D, Hirschhorn JN, Klannemark M, Lindgren CM, Vohl MC, Nemesh J, et al. The common PPAR Pro12Ala polymorphism is associated with decreased risk of type 2 diabetes. Nat Genet. 2000;26:76–80.

253. Vänttinen M, Nuutila P, Pihlajamäki J, Hällsten K, Virtanen KA, Lautamäki R, et al. The effect of the Ala12 allele of the peroxisome proliferator-activated receptor-gamma2 gene on skeletal muscle glucose uptake uepends on obesity: a positron emission tomography study. J Clin Endocrinol Metab. 2005;90:4249–54.

254. Nelson TL, Fingerlin TE, Moss LK, Barmada MM, Ferrell RE, Norris JM. Association of the peroxisome proliferator-activated receptor gamma gene with type 2 diabetes mellitus varies by physical activity among non-Hispanic whites from Colorado. Metabolism. 2007;56:388–93.

255. Hamilton B. Vitamin D and human skeletal muscle. Scand J Med Sci Sports. 2010;20:182–90.

256. Hoberman J. Faster, higher, stronger. A history of doping in sport. New York: The Free Press; 1992. p. 100–53.

257. Cannell J, Hollis B, Sorenson M, Taft T, Anderson J. Athletic performance and vitamin D. Med Sci Sports Exerc. 2009;41:1102–10.

258. Floyd F, Ayyar D, Barwick D, Hudgson P, Weightman D. Myopathy in chronic renal failure. Q J Med. 1974;XLIII:509–24.

259. Irani P. Electromyography in nutritional osteomalaic myopathy. J Neurol Neurosurg Psychiatry. 1976;39:686–93.

260. Russell J. Osteomalacic myopathy. Muscle Nerve. 1994;17:578–80.

261. Ceglia L. Vitamin D and skeletal muscle tissue and function. Mol Aspects Med. 2008;29:407–14.

262. Bischoff H, Borchers M, Gudat F, Duermueller U, Theiler R, Stahelin H, et al. In situ detection of 1, 25-dihydroxyvitamin D3 receptor in human skeletal muscle tissue. Histochem J. 2001;33:19–24.

263. Bischoff-Ferrari HA, Borchers M, Gudat F, Dürmüller U, Stähelin HB, Dick W. Vitamin D receptor expression in human muscle tissue decreases with age. J Bone Miner Res. 2004;19:265–9.

264. Bischoff-Ferrari HA, Dietrich T, Orav EJ, Hu FB, Zhang Y, Karlson EW, et al. Higher 25-hydroxyvitamin D concentrations are associated with better lower-extremity function in both active and inactive persons aged > or =60 y. Am J Clin Nutr. 2004;80:752–8.

265. Pfeifer M, Begerow B, Minne H. Vitamin D and muscle function. Osteoporos Int. 2002;13:187–94.

266. Nibbelink KA, Tishkoff DX, Hershey SD, Rahman A, Simpson RU. 1, 25(OH)2-vitamin D3 actions on cell proliferation, size, gene expression, and receptor localization, in the HL-1 cardiac myocyte. J Steroid Biochem Mol Biol. 2007;103:533–7.
267. Geusens P, Vandevyver C, Vanhoof J, Cassiman J, Boonen S, Raus J. Quadriceps and grip strength are related to vitamin D receptor genotype in elderly nonobese women. J Bone Miner Res. 1997;12:2082–8.
268. Morrison NA, Yeoman R, Kelly PJ, Eisman JA. Contribution of trans-acting factor alleles to normal physiological variability: vitamin D receptor gene polymorphisms and circulating osteocalcin. Proc Natl Acad Sci U S A. 1992;89:6665–9.
269. Morrison NA, Qi JC, Tokita A, Kelly PJ, Crofts L, Nguyen TV, et al. Prediction of bone density from vitamin D receptor alleles. Nature. 1994;367:284–7.
270. Kikuchi R, Uemura T, Gorai I, Ohno S, Minaguchi H. Early and late postmenopausal bone loss is associated with BsmI vitamin D receptor gene polymorphism in Japanese women. Calcif Tissue Int. 1999;64:102–6.
271. Van Pottelbergh I, Goemaere S, De Bacquer D, De Paepe A, Kaufman M. Vitamin D receptor gene allelic variants, bone density, and bone turnover in community-dwelling men. Bone. 2002;31:631–7.
272. Duman BS, Tanakol R, Erensoy N, Oztürk M, Yilmazer S. Vitamin D receptor alleles, bone mineral density and turnover in postmenopausal osteoporotic and healthy women. Med Princ Pract. 2004;13:260–6.
273. Remes T, Väisänen SB, Mahonen A, Huuskonen J, Kröger H, Jurvelin JS, et al. Bone mineral density, body height, and vitamin D receptor gene polymorphism in middle-aged men. Ann Med. 2005;37:383–92.
274. Uitterlinden AG, Pols HA, Burger H, Huang Q, Van Daele PL, Van Duijn CM, et al. A large-scale population-based study of the association of vitamin D receptor gene polymorphisms with bone mineral density. J Bone Miner Res. 1996;11:1241–8.
275. Aerssens J, Dequeker J, Peeters J, Breemans S, Broos P, Boonen S. Polymorphisms of the VDR, ER and COLIA1 genes and osteoporotic hip fracture in elderly postmenopausal women. Osteoporos Int. 2000;11:583–91.
276. van der Sluis IM, de Muinck Keizer-Schrama SM, Krenning EP, Pols HA, Uitterlinden AG. Vitamin D receptor gene polymorphism predicts height and bone size, rather than bone density in children and young adults. Calcif Tissue Int. 2003;73:332–8.
277. Dvornyk V, Liu PY, Long JR, Zhang YY, Lei SF, Recker RR, et al. Contribution of genotype and ethnicity to bone mineral density variation in Caucasians and Chinese: a test for five candidate genes for bone mass. Chin Med J (Engl). 2005;118:1235–44.
278. Macdonald HM, McGuigan FE, Stewart A, Black AJ, Fraser WD, Ralston S, et al. Largescale population-based study shows no evidence of association between common polymorphism of the VDR gene and BMD in British women. J Bone Miner Res. 2006;21:151–62.
279. Rabon-Stith KM, Hagberg JM, Phares DA. Vitamin D receptor FokI genotype influences bone mineral density response to strength training, but not aerobic training. Exp Physiol. 2005;90:653–61.
280. Hopkinson NS, Li KW, Kehoe A, Humphries SE, Roughton M, Moxham J, et al. Vitamin D receptor genotypes influence quadriceps strength in chronic obstructive pulmonary disease. Am J Clin Nutr. 2008;87:385–90.
281. Guo SW, Magnuson VL, Schiller JJ, Wang X, Wu Y, Ghosh S. Meta-analysis of vitamin D receptor polymorphisms and type 1 diabetes: a HuGE review of genetic association studies. Am J Epidemiol. 2006;164:711–24.
282. Grundberg E, Brändström H, Ribom EL, Ljunggren O, Mallmin H, Kindmark A. Genetic variation in the human vitamin D receptor is associated with muscle strength, fat mass and body weight in Swedish women. Eur J Endocrinol. 2004;150:323–8.
283. Roth SM, Zmuda JM, Cauley JA, Shea PR, Ferrell RE. Vitamin D receptor genotype is associated with fat-free mass and sarcopenia in elderly men. J Gerontol A Biol Sci Med Sci. 2004;59:10–5.
284. Tajima O, Ashizawa N, Ishii T. Interaction of the effects between vitamin D receptor polymorphism and exercise training on bone metabolism. J Appl Physiol. 2000;88:1271–6.

285. Nakamura O, Ishii T, Ando Y. Potential role of vitamin D receptor gene polymorphism in determining bone phenotype in young male athletes. J Appl Physiol. 2002;283:1973–9.
286. Pitsiladis YP, Scott R. The makings of the perfect athlete. Lancet. 2005;366:S16–7.
287. Clarke IJ, Henry BA. Targeting energy expenditure in muscle as a means of combating obesity. Clin Exp Pharmacol Physiol. 2010;37:121–4.
288. Stump CS, Henriksen EJ, Wei Y, Sowers JR. The metabolic syndrome: role of skeletal muscle metabolism. Ann Med. 2006;38:389–402.
289. Kelley DE. Skeletal muscle fat oxidation: timing and flexibility are everything. J Clin Invest. 2005;115:1699–702.
290. Kiens B. Skeletal muscle lipid metabolism in exercise and insulin resistance. Physiol Rev. 2006;85:205–43.
291. Mounier R, Pedersen BK, Plomgaard P. Muscle-specific expression of hypoxia-inducible factor in human skeletal muscle. Exp Physiol. 2010;95:899–907.
292. Tsianos GI, Evangelou E, Boot A, Zillikens MC, van Meurs JB, Uitterlinden AG, et al. Associations of polymorphisms of eight muscle- or metabolism-related genes with performance in Mount Olympus marathon runners. J Appl Physiol. 2010;108:567–74.
293. Schneider AJ, Friedmann T. Gene transfer in sports: an opening scenario for genetic enhancement of normal "human traits". Adv Genet. 2006;51:37–49.
294. Dartmouth scientists genetically engineer muscular mice. http://www.futurepundit.com/archives/003886.html. Accessed 16 Nov 2006.
295. Keim B. Athletes beware, scientists hot on gene doping trail. http://www.wired.com/wiredscience/2010/02/gene-doping-detection/. Accessed 4 Feb 2010.
296. Hernandez J, Cooper J, Babel N, Morton C, Rosemurgy AS. TNFalpha gene delivery therapy for solid tumors. Expert Opin Biol Ther. 2010;10:993–9.
297. López-Lázaro M. A new view of carcinogenesis and an alternative approach to cancer therapy. Mol Med. 2010;16:144–53.
298. Muntoni F, Wells D. Genetic treatments in muscular dystrophies. Curr Opin Neurol. 2007;20:590–4.
299. Bushby K, Lochmüller H, Lynn S, Straub V. Interventions for muscular dystrophy: molecular medicines entering the clinic. Lancet. 2009;374:1849–56.
300. Gene therapy for cancer. http://www.medic8.com/cancer/gene-therapy.htm. Accessed Oct 2010.
301. Kulkarni M. Gene therapy for human severe combined immunodeficiency disease. http://www.buzzle.com/articles/gene-therapy-for-human-severe-combined-immunodeficiency-scid-disease.html. Accessed Oct 2010.
302. Gene therapy for Parkinson's disease is safe and some patients benefit, according to study. http://www.sciencedaily.com/releases/2007/06/070622101037.htm. Accessed 25 June 2007.
303. Lagay F. Gene therapy or genetic enhancement: does it make a difference? Virtual Mentor. 2001;3:2.
304. Hanna KE. Genetic enhancement. http://www.genome.gov/10004767. Accessed April 2006.
305. Jelkmann W. Erythropoietin: structure, control of production, and function. Physiol Rev. 1992;72:449–89.
306. Eckardt KU. After 15 years of success – perspectives of erythropoietin therapy. Nephrol Dial Transplant. 2001;16:1745–9.
307. Gaffney GR, Parisotto R. Gene doping: a review of performance-enhancing genetics. Pediatr Clin North Am. 2007;54:807–22.
308. Osborne WR, Ramesh N, Lau S, Clowes MM, Dale DC, Clowes AW. Gene therapy for long-term expression of erythropoietin in rats. Proc Natl Acad Sci U S A. 1995;92:8055–8.
309. Seppen J, Barry SC, Harder B, Osborne WR. Lentivirus administration to rat muscle provides efficient sustained expression of erythropoietin. Blood. 2001;98:594–6.
310. Tripathy SK, Goldwasser E, Lu MM, Barr E, Leiden JM. Stable delivery of physiologic levels of recombinant erythropoietin to the systemic circulation by intramuscular injection of replication-defective adenovirus. Proc Natl Acad Sci U S A. 1994;91:11557–61.

311. Macdougall IC, Gray SJ, Elston O, Breen C, Jenkins B, Browne J, et al. Pharmacokinetics of novel erythropoiesis stimulating protein compared with epoetin alfa in dialysis patients. J Am Soc Nephrol. 1999; 10:2392–5.
312. Vanrenterghem Y, Barany P, Mann J. Novel erythropoiesis stimulating protein (NESP) maintains hemoglobin (Hb) in ESRD patients when administered once weekly or once every other week. J Am Soc Nephrol. 1999;10:A1365.
313. Graf H, Lacombe JL, Braun J, Gomes da Costa AA. Novel erythropoiesis stimulating protein (NESP) effectively maintains hemoglobin (Hb) when administered at a reduced dose frequency compared with recombinant human erythropoietin (rHuEpo) in ESRD patients. J Am Soc Nephrol. 2000;11:A1317.
314. Weiss LG, Clyne N, Divino Filho J, Frisenette-Fich C, Kurkus J, Svensson B. The efficacy of once weekly compared with two or three times weekly subcutaneous Epoetin beta: results from a randomized controlled multicentre trial. Swedish Study Group. Nephrol Dial Transplant. 2000;15:2014–9.
315. Regulier E, Schneider BL, Deglon N, Beuzard Y, Aebischer P. Continuous delivery of human and mouse erythropoietin in mice by genetically engineered polymer encapsulated myoblasts. Gene Ther. 1998;5:1014–22.
316. Chenuaud P, Larcher T, Rabinowitz JE, Provost N, Cherel Y, Casadevall N, et al. Autoimmune anemia in macaques following erythropoietin gene therapy. Blood. 2004;103:3303–4.
317. Gao G, Lebherz C, Weiner DJ, Grant R, Calcedo R, McCullough B, et al. Erythropoietin gene therapy leads to autoimmune anemia in macaques. Blood. 2004;103:3300–2.
318. Binley K, Askham Z, Iqball S, Spearman H, Martin L, de AM, et al. Long-term reversal of chronic anemia using a hypoxia-regulated erythropoietin gene therapy. Blood. 2002;100:2406–13.
319. Fandrey J. Oxygen-dependent and tissue-specific regulation of erythropoietin gene expression. Am J Physiol Regul Integr Comp Physiol. 2004;286:R977–88.
320. Noguchi CT, Bae KS, Chin K, Wada Y, Schechter AN, Hankins WD. Cloning of the human erythropoietin receptor gene. Blood. 1991;78:2548–56.
321. Juvonen E, Ikkala E, Fyhrquist F, Ruutu T. Autosomal dominant erythrocytosis caused by increased sensitivity to erythropoietin. Blood. 1991;78:3066–9.
322. de la Chapelle A, Träskelin AL, Juvonen E. Truncated erythropoietin receptor causes dominantly inherited benign human erythrocytosis. Proc Natl Acad Sci U S A. 1993;90:4495–9.
323. de la Chapelle A, Sistonen P, Lehvaslaiho H, Ikkala E, Juvonen E. Familial erythrocytosis genetically linked to erythropoietin receptor gene. Lancet. 1993;341:82–4.
324. Longmore GD. Erythropoietin receptor mutations and Olympic glory [news]. Nat Genet. 1993;4:108–10.
325. Lee RJ, Springer ML, Blanco-Bose WE, Shaw R, Ursell PC, Blau HM. VEGF gene delivery to myocardium: deleterious effects of unregulated expression. Circulation. 2000;102:898–901.
326. Walgenbach KJ, Gratas C, Shestak KC, Becker D. Ischaemia-induced expression of bFGF in normal skeletal muscle: a potential paracrine mechanism for mediating angiogenesis in ischaemic skeletal muscle. Nat Med. 1995;1:453–9.
327. Bray MS. Implications of gene-behavior interactions: prevention and intervention for obesity. Obesity (Silver Spring). 2008;16:S72–8.
328. Fernández JR, Casazza K, Divers J, López-Alarcón M. Disruptions in energy balance: does nature overcome nurture? Physiol Behav. 2008;22:105–12.
329. Stefan N, Vozarova B, Del Parigi A. The Gln223Arg polymorphism of the leptin receptor in Pima Indians: influence on energy expenditure, physical activity and lipid metabolism. Int J Obes Relat Metab Disord. 2002;26:1629–32.
330. Meier U, Gressner AM. Endocrine regulation of energy metabolism: review of pathobiochemical and clinical chemical aspects of leptin, ghrelin, adiponectin, and resistin. Clin Chem. 2004;50:1511–25.
331. Pistilli EE, Gordish-Dressman H, Seip RL, Devaney JM, Thompson PD, Price TB, et al. Resistin polymorphisms are associated with muscle, bone, and fat phenotypes in White men and women. Obesity (Silver Spring). 2007;15:392–402.

332. Richert L, Chevalley T, Manen D, Bonjour JP, Rizzoli R, Ferrari S. Substitution in the leptin receptor bone mass in prepubertal boys is associated with a Gln223Arg amino acid. J Clin Endocrinol Metab. 2007;92:4380–6.
333. Frayn KN, Arner P, Yki-Järvinen H. Fatty acid metabolism in adipose tissue, muscle and liver in health and disease. Essays Biochem. 2006;42:89–103.
334. Dyck DJ, Heigenhauser GJ, Bruce CR. The role of adipokines as regulators of skeletal muscle fatty acid metabolism and insulin sensitivity. Acta Physiol (Oxf). 2006;186:5–16.
335. Bruce CR, Dyck DJ. Cytokine regulation of skeletal muscle fatty acid metabolism: effect of interleukin-6 and tumor necrosis factor alpha. Am J Physiol Endocrinol Metab. 2004;287:E616–21.
336. Junkin KA, Dyck DJ, Mullen KL, Chabowski A, Thrush AB. Resistin acutely impairs insulin-stimulated glucose transport in rodent muscle in the presence, but not absence, of palmitate. Am J Physiol Regul Integr Comp Physiol. 2009;296:R944–51.
337. Yamauchi T, Kamon J, Waki H, Terauchi Y, Kubota N, Hara K, et al. The fat-derived hormone adiponectin reverses insulin resistance associated with both lipoatrophy and obesity. Nat Med. 2001;7:941–6.
338. Singh MK, Krisan AD, Crain AM, Collins DE, Yaspelkis III BB. High-fat diet and leptin treatment alter skeletal muscle insulin-stimulated phosphatidylinositol 3-kinase activity and glucose transport. Metabolism. 2003;52:1196–205.
339. Yaspelkis BB 3rd, Singh MK, Krisan AD, Krisan AD, Collins DE, Kwong CC, et al. Chronic leptin treatment enhances insulin-stimulated glucose disposal in skeletal muscle of high-fat fed rodents. Life Sci. 2004;74:1801–16.
340. Dyck DJ. Adipokines as regulators of muscle metabolism and insulin sensitivity. Appl Physiol Nutr Metab. 2009;34:396–402.
341. Question of the Year. NG: what would you do if it became possible to sequence the equivalent of a full human genome for only $1,000? http://www.nature.com/ng/qoty/index.html. Accessed Jan 2007.
342. Applied Biosystems: Applied Biosystems Surpasses Industry Milestone in Lowering the Cost of Sequencing Human Genome; Data made available to worldwide scientific community; Project completed for less than $60,000. http://it.tmcnet.com/news/2008/03/12/3323298.htm. Accessed 23 Jan 2011.
343. Telegraph completely mangles debate over value of genetic research. http://scienceblogs.com/geneticfuture/2009/04/telegraph_completely_mangles_d.php. Accessed 21 April 2009.
344. Bammann K, Peplies J, Sjöström M, Lissner L, De Henauw S, Galli C, et al. Assessment of diet, physical activity and biological, social and environmental factors in a multi-centre European project on diet- and lifestyle-related disorders in children (IDEFICS). J Public Health. 2006;14:279–89.
345. Philibert RA, Zadorozhnyaya O, Beach SR, Brody GH. Comparison of the genotyping results using DNA obtained from blood and saliva. Psychiatr Genet. 2008;18:275–81.
346. Matheson LA, Duong TT, Rosenberg AM, Yeung RS. Assessment of sample collection and storage methods for multicenter immunologic research in children. J Immunol Methods. 2008;339:82–9.
347. Koni AC, Scott RA, Wang G, Bailey MES, Peplies J, Bammann K, et al. DNA yield and quality of saliva samples and suitability for large scale epidemiological studies in children. Int J Obes (Lond). 2010, in press. ISSN 0307–0565
348. Streckfus CF, Bigler LR. Saliva as a diagnostic fluid. Oral Dis. 2002;8:69–76.
349. Ng DP, Koh D, Choo S, Chia KS. Saliva as a viable alternative source of human genomic DNA in genetic epidemiology. Clin Chim Acta. 2006;367:81–5.
350. McMichael GL, Gibson CS, O'Callaghan ME, Goldwater PN, Dekker GA, Haan EA, et al. DNA from buccal swabs suitable for high-throughput SNP multiplex analysis. J Biomol Tech. 2009;20:232–5.
351. Nishita DM, Jack LM, McElroy M, McClure JB, Richards J, Swan GE, et al. Clinical trial participant characteristics and saliva and DNA metrics. BMC Med Res Methodol. 2009;9:71.

352. Rylander-Rudqvist T, Hakansson N, Tybring G, Wolk A. Quality and quantity of saliva DNA obtained from the self-administrated oragene method – a pilot study on the cohort of Swedish men. Cancer Epidemiol Biomarkers Prev. 2006;15:1742–5.
353. Garcia-Closas M, Egan KM, Abruzzo J, Newcomb PA, Titus-Ernstoff L, Franklin T, et al. Collection of genomic DNA from adults in epidemiological studies by buccal cytobrush and mouthwash. Cancer Epidemiol Biomarkers Prev. 2001;10:687–96.
354. Feigelson HS, Rodriguez C, Robertson AS, Jacobs EJ, Calle EE, Reid YA, et al. Determinants of DNA yield and quality from buccal cell samples collected with mouthwash. Cancer Epidemiol Biomarkers Prev. 2001;10:1005–8.
355. King IB, Satia-Abouta J, Thornquist MD, Bigler J, Patterson RE, Kristal AR, et al. Buccal cell DNA yield, quality, and collection costs: comparison of methods for large-scale studies. Cancer Epidemiol Biomarkers Prev. 2002;11:1130–3.
356. Quinque D, Kittler R, Kayser M, Stoneking M, Nasidze I. Evaluation of saliva as a source of human DNA for population and association studies. Anal Biochem. 2006;353:272–7.
357. Hansen TV, Simonsen MK, Nielsen FC, Hundrup YA. Collection of blood, saliva, and buccal cell samples in a pilot study on the Danish nurse cohort: comparison of the response rate and quality of genomic DNA. Cancer Epidemiol Biomarkers Prev. 2007;16:2072–6.
358. Rogers NL, Cole SA, Lan HC, Crossa A, Demerath EW. New saliva DNA collection method compared to buccal cell collection techniques for epidemiological studies. Am J Hum Biol. 2007;19:319–26.
359. Fuku N, Scott RA, Mikami E, Wang G, Deason M, Irwin L, et al. Analysis of multiple performance-associated genetic polymorphisms in sprint and endurance running world record holders. Med Sci Sports Exerc. 2010;42:795.
360. Grobet L, Martin LJ, Poncelet D, Pirottin D, Brouwers B, Riquet J, et al. A deletion in the bovine myostatin gene causes the double-muscled phenotype in cattle. Nat Genet. 1997;17:71–4.

Chapter 9
A Synopsis of Exercise Genomics Research and a Vision for its Future Translation into Practice

Linda S. Pescatello and Stephen M. Roth

Keywords Adenosine monophosphate deaminase 1 • Adrenoreceptors • Angiotensin-converting enzyme • Alpha actinin 3 • Allele • Apolipoprotein E • Blood pressure • Body composition • Copy number variation • Dopamine receptor one • Epigenetic • Epistasis • Exercise prescription (Ex R$_x$) • Gene (or Genotype)×environment interaction • Genome-wide association study • Hardy-Weinberg equilibrium • *HE*ealth *RI*sk factors exercise *Tr*Aining and *GE*netics Family Study • Hypoxia-inducible factor 1 alpha • Linkage disequilibrium • Lipid • Lipoprotein • Maximal oxygen consumption • Minor allele frequency • Nescient helix-hoop-helix 2 • Nitric oxide synthase (*NOS1, NOS2, NOS3*) • Obesity • Overweight • Peroxisome proliferative-activated receptor-associated genes • Physical activity • Potassium inwardly rectifying channel, subfamily J, member 11 (*KCNJ11*) • Proteomics • Quantitative trait loci • Single nucleotide polymorphism • RNA interference • Transcription factor 7-like 2 • Type 2 diabetes mellitus • Uncoupling protein-associated genes

Introduction

The purpose of this volume, *Exercise Genomics* of the *Molecular and Translational Medicine Series*, is to present an overview of the rapidly expanding research examining the role of genomics in modifying the impact of exercise and physical activity on performance and health and fitness-related traits. We have brought together leading scientists from key exercise genomics research groups from around the world to provide updates and analysis of the key scientific developments and discoveries that have occurred in this young field. In addition, these scientists lend insights and expert opinion about the future of exercise genomics, especially the translation of these developments and discoveries into practice for academicians, clinicians, health/

L.S. Pescatello (✉)
Human Performance Laboratory, Department of Kinesiology, Neag School of Education, University of Connecticut, Gampel Pavilion Room 206, 2095 Hillside Road, U-1110, Storrs, CT 06269-1110, USA
e-mail: Linda.Pescatello@uconn.edu

L.S. Pescatello and S.M. Roth (eds.), *Exercise Genomics*,
Molecular and Translational Medicine, DOI 10.1007/978-1-60761-355-8_9,
© Springer Science+Business Media, LLC 2011

fitness and clinical exercise professionals, and researchers alike. The topics addressed by these scientific experts include chapters on fundamental concepts (Chap. 1) and statistical and methodological considerations (Chap. 2) in exercise genomics, and the exercise genomics of physical activity (Chap. 3), type 2 diabetes mellitus (T2D) (Chap. 4), body composition and obesity (Chap. 5), plasma lipoprotein-lipids and blood pressure (Chap. 6), muscle strength and size (Chap. 7), and aerobic capacity and endurance performance (Chap. 8). These topics were chosen because they represent leading content areas of investigation in exercise genomics [1, 2].

The overall tone of the various commentaries on the future role of exercise genomics in the practice of medicine and human performance by these experts is one of guarded optimism. The optimism surrounding the vision for the future is based on the anticipated development of personalized genomic medicine and the significant impact it will have on the future position of exercise in public health; primary, secondary, and tertiary preventive medicine; and rehabilitation. In addition, in the field of human performance, it is envisioned that exercise genomics will generate scientific advances in our understanding of the mechanisms driving the adaptations to training and the nature of the limiting factors in sports performance. Despite the promise of genomics advancing basic and applied exercise science, work translating this knowledge into practice has proceeded more slowly than originally envisioned for many reasons that are detailed in the preface and chapters of this book. Consequently, the optimism that initially surrounded the use of exercise genomics in personalized medicine has become somewhat guarded because personalized exercise prescriptions (Ex R_x) based upon genetic information remain a vision of the future rather than a reality of the present.

The contributors to this volume are leading international researchers in their respective areas of exercise genomics. Thus, we have decided to write the concluding chapter as a synopsis of the take home messages contained within each of the chapters. This last chapter highlights two to three key developments and discoveries as well as challenges discussed by the author(s) of each chapter followed by the authors' vision for the future of exercise genomics and the translation of exercise genomics into practice. This chapter-by-chapter synopsis concludes with a discussion of common themes that have emerged from this book intertwined with our vision for the future position of exercise genomics in personalized medicine and human performance.

Chapter 1 Fundamental Concepts in Exercise Genomics

Stephen M. Roth, and Martine A. Thomis

Key Development/Discoveries

- The success of association analysis depends largely on the choice of the candidate gene(s) under study. Figure 1.2 presents several possible "guiding" sources of information to select strong candidate genes.
- A shift has been seen from "single candidate gene studies" to multiple gene studies, or studies exploring gene variants within certain (signaling) pathways. Given the

reduction in genotyping cost and the development of high-throughput single nucleotide polymorphism (SNP) array techniques, it has become possible to genotype >1,000,000 SNPs per individual and associate these genotypes with the phenotype of interest. This approach is known as genome-wide association study (GWAS).

Key Challenges

- In general, complex traits are governed by genetic and environmental factors, but determining the fraction of variability attributed to each is very challenging [3]. Both genetic and environmental factors can contribute to complex traits in various ways, making such distinctions challenging due to the large sample sizes that are required to isolate these effects.
- GWAS are quickly becoming the standard approach in genetic association analysis, and advances in systems biology and functional genomics are making detailed functional analysis of candidate genes and polymorphisms easier to tackle. While the introduction of GWAS has proved fruitful for a number of fields and may shed light on the gene variants important to exercise-related adaptations, GWAS have significant limitations, especially when contributing variants have rare alleles. A growing literature is indicating at least a fraction of the genetic contribution in complex common disease traits is determined by relatively rare alleles [4]. Combinations of these rare alleles would then contribute, perhaps in concert with more common alleles, to the phenotypic outcome. Despite the progress made by GWAS, a surprising finding is how little these studies have contributed to the identification of genetic factors for some traits, providing support for the rare allele hypothesis.

The Future?

- While the bulk of this book is focused on the role of DNA sequence variation in interindividual variation in exercise responses and adaptations, the last decade has revealed a considerable role for nonprotein-coding genes, specifically those genes that produce regulatory RNA sequences that are never translated into protein. These regulatory RNAs have significant roles in the regulation of gene expression, posttranscriptional modification, and protein interactions [5].
- The developments and discoveries discussed in this book are pointing more and more to a future of whole genome sequencing, which would allow identification and analysis of all gene variants in an individual. The future clinical usefulness of genetic information will ultimately hinge not only on population attributable risk, but also on individual disease prediction and treatment outcomes that will necessarily be derived from an individual's DNA sequence. As costs drop over the next decade, larger scale studies will be designed that will exploit both common and rare alleles (and their combinations) to more accurately determine

genetic contributions for complex disease traits. Indeed, large-scale consortia
have been organized for a number of health-related traits to better perform
well-powered GWAS and genetic epidemiology investigations [6–9].

- More and more investigations will be able to address multiple levels of
analysis within a single study, such as genetic association, epigenetics, pro-
teomics, metabolomics, and functional genomics. Such studies will help
solidify those candidate genes and polymorphisms emerging from GWAS
findings and help establish the clinical and translational relevance of those
loci for public health.

Practical Applications

- As we learn more about the genes and polymorphisms that conclusively contribute
to exercise and health and fitness-related traits, we will learn more about the
significant interindividual variability that has plagued our interpretation of
exercise and other interventions for many years. Thus, we will be able to return
to those intervention studies with the knowledge gained from years of reduc-
tionist methods and better understand the physiological variability that underlies
individual responses and move towards personalized medicine that has been the
very promise of genomics and genomic medicine.

Chapter 2 Statistical and Methodological Considerations in Exercise Genomics

Heather Gordish-Dressman, and Joseph M. Devaney

Key Developments/Discoveries

- Analysis of nonfamilial populations falls into two major types, candidate gene
association studies and their extension to GWAS. The candidate gene approach
examines a limited number of associations with gene loci with known related
functions that could be relevant to the phenotype of interest. GWAS, on the other
hand, explore nearly all loci known to have a polymorphism to determine if any
are associated with the phenotype of interest. The candidate gene approach is
useful if there is prior knowledge of a gene, its function, and relationship to the
phenotype of study. In contrast, GWAS are used when there is no or minimal
prior knowledge and there is general interest in testing up to one million loci to
see if any are associated with the phenotype. Over 100 loci for more than 40
common diseases have been identified though GWAS in just the last few years
and that number is growing [10]. GWAS is an especially important development
in the study of complex diseases, which most likely involve many loci, each of

which contributes minimally to the effect size [11]. A recent GWAS development is the multistage design where a smaller number of individuals are subjected to genotyping the entire genome; only those SNPs found to be significant or promising are then genotyped in successively larger samples. Gene expression is used to discover pathways that drive diseases such as muscular dystrophy [12], the response of skeletal muscle to resistance training [13], and predictors of the maximal oxygen consumption (VO_2 max) in response to aerobic exercise training [14]. This development can be coupled to GWAS to identify individual differences in the quantitative levels of gene expression (i.e., expression quantitative loci [eQTLs]).

- Two SNPs in high linkage disequilibrium (LD) are essentially giving the same information and are expected to show the same associations with the phenotype. There is no reason to test both SNPs against the phenotype. The total number of SNPs tested can be decreased by excluding redundant SNPs that are in high LD with each other. Testing for LD leads to a decrease in the overall error rate and an increased confidence in drawing the correct conclusions from the data.

- Epistasis is the effect of one locus modified by the presence or absence of an allele at another locus. There are several methods to deal with testing for epistasis. The most common way uses standard methods to incorporate several SNPs into the same statistical model, often with terms defining the interactions between loci. A recent method of combining SNPs into a single model is the genetic risk score described by Horne et al. [15].

Key Challenges

- Many of the issues arising from GWAS stem from the data analysis. The problem of multiple testing becomes a critical issue when testing upwards of 1,000,000 SNPs in a single experiment [16]. An important consideration for GWAS is thus replication; any SNP association initially found to be significant should ideally be replicated in another independent sample [17, 18].

- Allele frequencies can vary widely between ethnic groups which can be problematic in association studies leading to population stratification [19]. If an allele is more frequent in one ethnic group and the sample has many individuals of that group, the strength of the association could be positively biased. Alternatively, if a true relationship between an allele and an outcome exists only in one ethnic group, but the sample has few individuals of that group, the association, if present, may not be detected.

- Quality control of genotyping is essential to any association study including GWAS. Genotyping errors can cause spurious results, especially if the errors occur differentially between the cases and controls in a case control study [10]. Therefore, several quality control features should be present including the SNP genotyping call rate, the SNP minor allele frequencies (MAF), the results of

Hardy-Weinberg equilibrium (HWE), and concordance rates in duplicate samples. Chanock et al. [17] also recommend those SNPs shown to have significant associations be genotyped on a different platform to confirm results and known associations be verified in the sample under study.

The Future?

- The statistical challenges of a GWAS are many, but it will be an important method that will be used for the foreseeable future in the study of exercise genomics. However, with the identification of new regions of the genome obtained by GWAS, new biological insights will be obtained leading to clinical advances. This will lead to the development of new biomarkers of exercise performance and health and fitness-related phenotypes which can be used to track the positive effects of exercise.
- Matching gene expression data with GWAS data will lead to the development of an arsenal of new genes for further study. The discovery of new genetic variants and the genes that they exert control over may solidify pathways present in the literature.

Practical Applications

- One of the most important steps when analyzing SNP data is adequately defining the phenotype or outcome of interest whose form determines the statistical methods that will be used (please see Table 2.1). The website titled a New View of Statistics (http://www.sportsci.org/resource/stats/) put together by Hopkins [20] details all of the methods discussed here with examples taken from exercise and sports science and is a valuable resource for analysis (see Appendix).
- There are several different measures of LD, each having its own characteristics. Those most commonly encountered are the r^2 (correlation coefficient) and D' (Lewontin's D'). For an excellent definition and comparison of LD measurements, see Devlin and Risch [21]. There are several resources available to calculate LD and a helpful list is given at http://www.genes.org.uk/software/ LD-software.shtml (see Appendix).
- There are several issues to be considered when performing a GWAS and when interpreting the results of a published GWAS report. These considerations include, among other things, the study design, selection of study subjects, sample size, quality control, analysis of the data, and replication. An excellent review describes in detail those factors to consider when reading or performing a GWAS [17].

Chapter 3 Can You Be Born a Couch Potato?
The Genomic Regulation of Physical Activity

J. Timothy Lightfoot

Key Developments/Discoveries

- All available data in human and animal models show conclusively that the physical activity level of an organism is significantly affected by heritage. The use of animal models, in particular inbred mice strains where the mice within each strain are virtual clones of each other due to the homozygosity of their genome [22], allows the use of positional cloning approaches with smaller cohorts of animals ($n=300$–600) than in human studies ($n=1{,}000$–20,000). Furthermore, studies involving inbred mice strains are sensitive to QTL that explain less than 2% of the phenotypic variation compared to 6% that is typically seen in human studies.
- Several authors [23, 24] and at least one scientific group (Members of the Complex Trait Consortium) have recommended additional criteria to identify potential candidate genes to guard against false positive classification of genes as candidate genes linked to a phenotype. In particular, DiPetrillo et al. [23] recommend having at least three independent lines of evidence available before declaring a gene a candidate gene. These independent lines of evidence may arise from several experimental strategies including functional relevance, positional cloning (QTL) studies, combined genotype studies (using several different intercrosses or cohorts of subjects), regional or genome-wide haplotype studies, gene expression differences, or gene manipulation studies. Currently, only two genes meet the criteria of having at least three independent lines of evidence to suggest candidacy as a regulatory gene for physical activity. They are dopamine receptor one (*Drd1*) and nescient helix-loop-helix 2 (*Nhlh2*).

Key Challenges

- Because of the heterozygosity of the human genome, GWAS require multiple thousands of subjects to offset statistical power difficulties. The lack of power in human GWAS can lead to the nonidentification (i.e., false negatives) of QTL that may be associated with physical activity, but do not play a large role in the determination of the phenotype (i.e., areas that explain a small amount of variance). Most QTL thus far associated with physical activity have explained less than 6% of the variability in the phenotype.
- Positional cloning applied to human subjects is often called GWAS. Positional cloning approaches have identified QTL associated with physical activity. However, the width of the QTL can and often includes many genes leading to

false positive classification of some genes as candidates for involvement in the phenotype and a lack of power which leads to nonidentification of QTL that may play smaller but no less important roles in physical activity. These difficulties have led to less than stellar results when determining the genes underlying QTL, with some authors claiming less than 20 candidate genes have been identified from existing QTL studies [24]. Thus, the concern regarding the power of a design to identify QTL is a valid concern.

The Future?

• From the available literature, it is clear that physical activity levels are heritable. However, understanding the genetic and biological mechanisms that control physical activity is at a very early stage. To this point, the available mapping studies have indicated few significant QTL involved in physical activity regulation that are shown in Table 3.3. The small number of significant QTL make it possible there are only a few genes involved, but the more probable scenario is there are a large number of genes that play small roles in the ultimate determination of the complex trait we classify as physical activity as well as many "sets of genes" that through their interactions (i.e., epistasis) affect activity.
• Future deliberations of the genetic control of physical activity may have to not only consider possible genes that alter protein structure and function, but also potential regulatory mechanism arising from noncoding genomic regions. The evolving understanding of RNA interference (RNAi) mechanisms [25, 26], how RNAi effectively regulates gene expression, and how RNAi arise from both "coding" and "noncoding" portions of the genome [27] require the consideration of how these novel RNAi mechanisms may affect the physiological processes that govern physical activity. Incorporation of potential regulation of physical activity arising from "noncoding" areas of the genome may be an important avenue for further consideration. It is interesting that two of the three identified QTL associated with activity in humans [7] localize within intergenic areas of the genome.

Practical Applications

• As progress is made with identifying genes and genetic mechanisms regulating physical activity, any data that aid in understanding why individuals are not physically active will contribute to the understanding and possible prevention of the large number of conditions and diseases caused by physical inactivity [28] as well as decreasing the significant cost to health care from physical inactivity [29, 30].
• Whether there exists a general disposition toward a low level of activity being inherited – our so-called "couch potato" – or whether a high level of activity is passed from the parents is unknown. In the end, however, it may be unimportant to determine whether high or low levels of activity are passed from parents to their

children. For it is clear that magnitude of the genetic influence on activity exhibited by all of the described studies makes activity levels a "predisposition" rather than a "predestination," even though it may be a strong predisposition. Therefore, the critical question may not be whether you are "born a couch potato." Rather, the critical question may be what are the genetic/biological mechanisms that predispose to a higher or lower level of activity and whether they can be altered?

Chapter 4 Interaction Between Exercise and Genetics in Type 2 Diabetes Mellitus: An Epidemiological Perspective

Paul W. Franks, and Ema C. Brito

Key Developments/Discoveries

- Notwithstanding the important role lifestyle factors play in the etiology of T2D, persons living similar lifestyles can vary considerably in their susceptibility to the disease, with the variance being least among biologically related individuals suggesting a genetic basis to the disease. In the past 4 years, major advances have been made in unraveling the genetic architecture of T2D. This search has cumulated in the discovery and confirmation of around 40 common predisposing loci [31], but the variance in disease risk explained by these variants is much lower than predicted from heritability studies [32]. Thus, the genetic associations discovered to date are likely to represent no more than the tip of the iceberg with respect to the genetic landscape of T2D.
- Around 25 T2D loci have been discovered and replicated to date, most of which localize to genes that appear to influence beta-cell function (M. McCarthy, personal communication). These findings highlight the role of inherited defects in beta-cell function rather than defects in genes causing insulin resistance in the etiology of T2D.
- GWAS have confirmed the three previously identified signals for T2D which localize to transcription factor 7-like 2 (*TCF7L2*), peroxisome proliferative-activated receptor, gamma (*PPARG*), and potassium inwardly rectifying channel, subfamily J, member 11 (*KCNJ11*), and identified many new susceptibility loci [33–38]. Genes examined in studies of gene×physical activity interactions that include adrenergic beta-2 receptor (*ADRB2*), *PPARG*, encoding uncoupling proteins (*UCP2* and *UCP3*), nitric oxide synthase (*NOS1*, *NOS2*, *NOS3*), and hepatic lipase gene (*LIPC*), often have inconsistent results.

Key Challenges

- It is important to bear in mind that even though genetic association studies are resilient to confounding, studies of gene×environment interactions are not, as they inherit the limitations and susceptibilities that beset both genetic and nongenetic association studies. Moreover, confounding by parallel interaction effects can also occur. Therefore, it may be necessary to include a range of potential confounders in interaction models, in addition to product terms comprised of the genotype of interest and putative environmental confounding variables.

- As with observational studies, few reports of interactions from clinical trials have been adequately replicated and most, if not all, are underpowered for the detection of realistic interaction effects. However, it is impossible to blind the allocation of a lifestyle intervention; thus, results from lifestyle intervention trials may still be prone to the confounding effects of factors that correlate with the intervention. For example, in exercise intervention studies, participants may change their dietary behaviors even though this is not an explicit feature of the intervention. Such changes could confound the interpretation of the main effects of the intervention and gene×treatment interactions.

- Most epidemiological studies of gene×physical activity interactions on T2D or its antecedents have used questionnaires to characterize lifestyle behaviors. Although most of the commonly used physical activity questionnaires appropriately classify the behavior when compared with gold standard methods, the correlation between methods is usually low $r < 0.25$ and reporting biases and heteroscadicity associated with disease outcomes can complicate the interpretation of results [39, 40]. Studies of gene×physical activity interaction may benefit from the availability of objective physical activity assessment methods.

The Future?

- Although many studies have investigated gene×physical activity interactions during the past decade, rarely have the results from these studies been adequately replicated. This emphasizes the need for future interaction studies to utilize large sample collections, well-measured exposures and phenotypes, appropriate analytic methods, and a conservative approach to the interpretation and reporting of results.

- The availability of detailed information on gene×environment interactions may enhance our understanding of the molecular basis of T2D, elucidate the mechanisms through which lifestyle exposures influence diabetes risk, and possibly help to refine strategies for diabetes prevention or treatment. The ultimate hope is genetics might one day be used in primary care to inform the targeting of interventions that comprise exercise regimes and other lifestyle therapies to individuals are most likely to respond well to them.

Practical Applications

- The studies conducted to date have laid important and necessary groundwork, but in and of themselves they are insufficient to guide the implementation of exercise genomics into clinical practice. For this to be a realistic possibility requires a new era of studies that are specifically designed and powered for the detection of gene×lifestyle interactions and others which show how the implementation of such knowledge can be used to improve treatment outcomes, possibly by using personal genomics to guide the application of treatments in intervention studies.

• It may be more feasible to identify individuals at high risk of diabetes who, because of their genetic characteristics, are likely to respond well to exercise interventions, as an example, and target these persons. This does not of course mean that healthy lifestyle behaviors would be discouraged in the remainder of the population, but one might prioritize other, more effective, preventive strategies in these individuals while continuing to promote the virtues of active lifestyles.

Chapter 5 The Interaction Between Genetic Variation and Exercise in Determining Body Composition and Obesity Status

Mary H. Sailors, and Molly S. Bray

Key Developments/Discoveries

• The latest published version of the Human Obesity Map has reported in 426 studies 127 candidate genes that are potentially associated with an obesity phenotype [41]. This report has identified 22 genes shown in at least five published studies to have associations with obesity-related phenotypes (see Table 5.1). According to Bouchard, these genes fall into five major categories: (1) thriftiness; (2) hyperphagia; (3) low lipid oxidation; (4) adipogenesis; and (5) low physical activity [42]. Since physical activity and exercise are critical components of energy balance, it is not surprising that many of the genes identified to date for obesity and body composition have also been shown to interact with or be modified by exercise and/or physical activity.

• The literature provides considerable evidence that the effects of genetic variants on body mass and composition can be substantially modified by physical activity. For complex traits such as obesity and body size, most genetic variants account for only a small portion of the total variance in the trait, and although genetic variation has been estimated to account for up to half of the population variance in body size, environmental and behavioral factors explain the rest of the variance. Thus, an important concept to glean from studies of gene×environment interaction is that most genetic variation is not deterministic, i.e., the effects attributed to any given variant are often modifiable, depending on both the physiologic and physical environments associated with the gene action.

Key Challenges

- One of the difficulties in definitively determining the effects of any genetic variant on the exercise response in terms of body composition is the wide variety of "replication" studies reported. Differences in populations (e.g., men vs. women, diabetics vs. healthy individuals, premenopausal vs. postmenopausal women, etc.) and study design (e.g., exercise alone vs. combinations of exercise, diet, and behavior interventions, case/control vs. cohort studies, etc.) may account for the discrepancies reported for a given genetic variant.
- While the average physiological response to an exercise training protocol is decreased body weight, decreased fat mass, and favorable changes in adipose distribution, some individuals do not respond in a similar manner to a given amount of exercise. By setting physical activity guidelines based solely on the mean response across subjects, one may fail to recognize that these guidelines may be highly efficacious for some individuals and ineffective for others. Identifying genetic variation that moderates or mediates the effect of exercise and physical activity may be the first step in formulating more efficacious Ex R$_x$ recommendations for exercise and physical activity for those with overweight and obesity.
- Although exercise has predictable effects on metabolism, it has long been recognized that such effects can be highly variable among individuals. Understanding how genetic variation in genes related to energy metabolism influences overall adiposity or body composition following exercise training or physical activity is a critical component in our ability to design effective programs focused on healthy energy balance.

The Future?

- Most studies do not test for gene×exercise interactions and few studies to date have examined the body composition response to exercise in the context of genetic variation. Further research in this area is certainly warranted in order to formulate more efficacious Ex R$_x$ recommendations for those who are overweight and obese.
- Prospective studies in which individuals are selected on the basis of genotype and undergo an exercise intervention are needed to establish and verify genetic markers that can predict body composition change from exercise.

Practical Applications

- Recommendations for the utilization of genetic information to improve intervention strategies that include physical activity or exercise are [43]:

- First, genetic markers that are highly replicable and strongly predict the body composition to exercise must be identified. This will require prospective exercise intervention by genotype studies that focus primarily on body composition change to identify potential genetic markers.
- Second, the ability to quantify the genetic markers must be accurate, affordable, and practical. Technology for assessing genomic information is quickly becoming faster and less expensive; therefore, it will be plausible in the future to rapidly assess an individual for their particular genetic information.
- Third, the assessment of genetic markers needs to be acceptable to a population. Individuals should view the assessment of genetic markers as another form of health screening.
- Finally, assurance against misuse of genetic information must be of utmost importance. Currently, concerns over the misuse of genetic information plague many individuals, therefore safeguards to ensure the integrity of this information need to be in place.

Chapter 6 Interactive Effects of Genetics and Acute Exercise and Exercise Training on Plasma Lipoprotein-Lipid and Blood Pressure Phenotypes

James M. Hagberg

Key Developments/Discoveries

- Limited data consistently demonstrate plasma lipoprotein-lipid and blood pressure responses to exercise training are moderately heritable (i.e., 0.14–0.59). A substantial evidence base clearly indicates apolipoprotein E (*APOE*) genotype is probably one of the strongest predictors of plasma lipoprotein-lipid levels, though studies examining exercise training responses remain equivocal.
- The most frequently studied genes with respect to blood pressure responses to acute exercise are the angiotensin-converting enzyme (*ACE*), angiotensinogen (*AGT*), adrenergic receptor (*ADR*), and nitric oxide synthase (*NOS3*) genes. Common variants in these genes appear to affect the blood pressure responses to acute exercise. However, it is not possible at this time to generate a more precise conclusion because of the very small number of studies that have addressed this issue that included small sample sizes and small numbers of polymorphisms. In addition, these studies have measured different blood pressure phenotypes in response to different types and amounts of exercise.

Key Challenges

- Very little is known about the heritability of the plasma lipoprotein-lipid and blood pressure responses to endurance training. Clearly, substantially more studies are required to provide the data necessary to verify that all of these responses to training are heritable.
- The inability to generate strong conclusions from lipoprotein-lipid and blood pressure candidate gene association studies is the result of: (1) a generally small set of previously published data, (2) the huge number of potential candidate genes most of which have not been examined, (3) the substantial number of SNPs that have been studied already in the few candidate genes that have been investigated, (4) the generally small sample sizes used in most studies, and (5) the inconsistency of the results to date.

The Future?

- Only four studies have assessed genome-wide linkage for plasma lipoprotein-lipid and BP responses to exercise training [44–47] and only one of these four studies [46] found *any* significant linkages for these important cardiovascular disease risk factor responses to exercise training. Also, no GWAS utilizing large SNP chips have yet been done for these phenotypes. Clearly, substantially more studies are required to potentially identify novel chromosomal loci that are robustly linked with the plasma lipid-lipoprotein and blood pressure responses to exercise training.
- It should be acknowledged that the inclusion of precisely measured phenotypes in exercise genomics studies (e.g., heart rate, blood pressure, and VO_2 max at baseline and their changes with acute exercise and exercise training) and the repeated measures aspect of assessing a phenotype before and after training in the same individual markedly enhance the statistical power for detecting SNPs related to these exercise-related phenotypes as compared to disease gene discovery and disease susceptibility genetic studies. However, unless another large trial like the *HE*ealth, *RI*sk factors, exercise *TrA*ining and *GE*netics Family Study or HERITAGE is initiated, it is hard to see how replicated, definitive evidence will be generated to validly quantify the effect of genetic variations on plasma lipoprotein-lipid and BP responses, especially regarding their responses to exercise training.

Practical Applications

- Our initial hope of finding a small number of genetic variations that have substantial independent effects on any phenotype was clearly overly simplistic. The evidence summarized in this chapter should indicate that we have taken only very small steps towards deriving robust conclusions relative to the genetic factors that underlie the interindividual differences in the responses of plasma lipoprotein-lipid and blood pressure to acute exercise and exercise training. Some evidence is available concerning highly plausible candidate genes that might influence these responses. However, at the present time these results are simply proof-of-principle in terms of identifying specific genetic screening panels that would robustly predict optimal responders to acute exercise or exercise training in terms of plasma lipoprotein-lipid or blood pressure.

Chapter 7 Genetic Aspects of Muscular Strength and Size

Monica J. Hubal, Maria L. Urso, and Priscilla M. Clarkson

Key Developments/Discoveries

- Baseline muscle strength and size are highly variable as are the muscle size and strength responses to resistance training. Observed variations in the amount of strength and muscle size gains from resistance training were found to be 5–150 and 5–40%, respectively, over the course of a standardized strength training intervention [48], with an estimated 35–85% of strength gains attributed to inheritance [49–51].
- The three main categories of genes found to be associated with muscle strength and size traits are: structural genes, growth factors, and inflammatory factors. While most strength- and size-related loci studied to date fit into one of these three categories, a few gene associations with muscle traits have been found in genes outside of the normal hypertrophy pathways.
- While the field of exercise genomics is young, the studies reviewed in this chapter demonstrate that various genes can harbor genetic polymorphisms explaining some of the large variability in muscle strength and size traits. However, in most cases, single variants and single genes do not account for high percentages of trait variability on their own and few interactions between multiple genetic variations have been investigated to date.

Key Challenges

- The vast majority of published genomics studies have used a candidate gene approach, where investigators select genes and variants of interest for study. A key problem with this approach is the current lack of knowledge about underlying mechanisms driving each trait, making candidate gene selection difficult.
- A key limitation of GWAS studies is that multiple testing corrections necessitate very stringent filters for significance (typically $p < 10^{-7}$ or 10^{-8}). Given the stringency

of these filters, GWAS studies often require thousands to tens of thousands of subjects to find significant loci in cross-sectional designs. Although GWAS is touted as an "agnostic" approach to gene discovery, where variant selection for study is random and not informed by a priori hypotheses, there also is the potential for bias in the selection of the million loci represented on the GWAS arrays [52].

The Future?

- The future will bring full sequencing of the genome via highly parallel ("next generation") sequencing techniques [53]. The predicted cost of sequencing all three billion base pairs will drop from millions of dollars towards $1,000 per subject over the next decade, which is nearly the current cost per sample for GWAS studies examining 500K to 1M SNPs.
- It is clear from the genetic variation literature summarized in this chapter that not only are the mechanisms driving strength and size variability not fully understood, but studies done to date have also varied widely in many confounding factors such as different exercise regimens, muscle groups, or populations tested. To address these issues, it is important that future studies utilize muscle samples to elucidate molecular consequences of candidate SNPs in determining if chosen variations affect mRNA levels, splicing of transcripts, and/or protein levels.
- It is also possible that variations in one gene can control expression of other genes and related proteins, which can be explored using software that indexes known gene and protein relationships, commonly referred to as network or pathway analysis. Future studies will incorporate sequence information, transcriptional and translational data, protein localization, tissue characteristics (muscle composition and size), and environmental data like training status. Methods of systems biology modeling of gene networks are just being developed and applied to different diseases, and in the future, could be applied to muscle traits like strength and size.

Practical Applications

- Better understanding of the genetics underlying muscle strength and size could have several practical applications, including the advancement of personal genomics that can be used to predict who will respond positively and negatively to different interventions like exercise and drug therapy.
- In addition to the use of exercise genomics to predict athletic performance, knowledge of muscle trait-related loci could have more direct impact on current athletes if scientists determine how to exploit "good genes." How to prevent or regulate genetic manipulations or gene "doping" is an emerging field, tied to the advancement of knowledge of muscle-related genes.
- Musculoskeletal health across the population will be enhanced in the future with greater knowledge of genomic contributors to these health-related traits. For

example, individuals who have genetic backgrounds that are associated with lower strength may want to adopt strength training regimens, especially as they age, to maintain healthy muscle function. Another example would be the tailoring of rehabilitation programs after injury, based on genetic associations with strength development.

Chapter 8 Genomics of Aerobic Capacity and Endurance Performance: Clinical Implications

Yannis Pitsiladis, Guan Wang, and Bernd Wolfarth

Key Developments/Discoveries

- The first exercise genomic studies in the 1970s assessed indirectly the genetic basis of human performance using twin models and compared the intrapair variation between monozygotic and dizygotic twins, a concept referred to as the heritability estimate. Despite some interesting findings of high heritability for exercise-related traits, the limitations and criticisms of the early indirect methods required the focus to be shifted to the continuously developing molecular-based laboratory methods to test directly the interaction between genetic and environmental factors, not only in family or twin studies, but also in studies involving populations of interest. A more contemporary view based on results from molecular studies is that genetics can explain 40–50% of $\dot{V}O_2$ max when adjusted for age, body mass, and body composition [54]; substantially lower than suggested using heritability estimates from these earlier studies of about 90% [55].The broad range of gene discovery methods for polygenic traits such as aerobic capacity and endurance performance is displayed in Fig. 8.1.
- The number of large genetic cohorts with extensive health/fitness and physical performance phenotypes is limited due to the high costs involved in creating and maintaining such cohorts, but development of such cohorts (potentially through collaborative consortia) will be critical to the identification of influence genetic variants relevant to exercise genomics and personalized Ex R_x.
- Most genes and polymorphisms discovered to date are related to aerobic capacity, endurance performance, and muscle metabolism (see Figs. 8.2 and 8.3). The most significant genes include *ACE*; α Actinin 3 (*ACTN3*); alpha-(2A, 2B, 2C) and beta-(B2, B3) adrenoreceptors; adenosine monophosphate deaminase 1 (*AMPD1*), apolipoprotein C-III (*APOC3*), uncoupling protein genes (*UCP1, UCP2, UCP3*); creatine kinase-muscle associated variants (*CKM*); hypoxia-inducible factor 1 alpha (*HIF1A*); endothelial nitric oxide synthase (*NOS3*); peroxisome proliferator-activated receptor-associated genes (*PPARA, PPARG, PPARD, PPARGCIA*); and vitamin D receptor (*VDR*) (see Table 8.2).

Key Challenges

- The concept of "black" athletic superiority is based on a preconception that each "race" constitutes a genetically homogeneous group, with "race" defined simply by skin color. This belief is contrary to the assertion that there is more genetic variation among Africans than between African and Eurasian populations [56]. Estimates from the human genome project and analysis of haplotype frequencies show that most haplotypes are shared between two of the three major geographic populations: Europe, Asia, and Africa [57]. It is currently estimated that the level of genetic diversity between human populations is not large enough to justify the use of the term "race" as a reason for athletic superiority.
- When gene therapy is introduced into practice, e.g., preventive and rehabilitative training therapy, it is likely that, comparable to conventional doping, unethical athletes, coaches, practitioners, or officials will examine these techniques and introduce them into sports. Similar to the time point at which this may happen, it is difficult to estimate the extent of this manipulation. Considering current investigations on doping mentality and particularly the readiness to assume risks in sports, leisure sport may be more affected than elite sports.

The Future?

- GWAS will provide insight into the genetic architecture and molecular basis underlying human diseases and complex traits such as aerobic capacity and endurance performance. In the future, massive cohorts will be studied by GWAS and will provide valuable information for all scientific fields including exercise genomics, though large exercise-based cohorts or consortia will be needed to exploit these technological advances.
- With respect to parameters of physical performance, genome science is currently at an early stage. On the one hand, this is because physical performance is a very complex phenotype that requires high standards regarding study populations. On the other hand, this is a subarea of science in which financial resources are sparse. Compared to the efforts done in the past 10 years to investigate the genetic basis of other clinically relevant phenotypes, e.g., obesity, type 2 diabetes, and hypertension, the scientific knowledge on the genetic basis of physical performance may come to be seen as rather rudimentary.

Practical Applications

- To have a clear understanding of the effects of these genes on human performance would be of great help to develop gene-based exercise training programs for athletes in their particular fields and prevent further injuries caused by training and competition. However, it will be a long way to go to achieve this goal.

- Understanding the roles of genes in regulating energy intake and expenditure could also help to develop an adequate training diet to maintain muscle mass, prevent injury or illness, and reduce recovery time.
- Current evidence indicates that it is possible to relate genetic findings with physical performance only in few cases, and at present, gene research does not provide practical benefits to find athletic talents. As physical performance is a complex phenotype, talent finding purely based on genetic evidence will be unlikely even in the future. In this context, it needs to be borne in mind that only about 30–40% of the variability of separate components of performance (e.g., VO_2 max) is determined by genetic parameters. The other 60–70% of the variability is due to influences of the environment. The degree to which a specific prediction of maximum performance can be made using genetic markers is currently unclear.

Common Themes and Our Vision for the Future

The purpose of the concluding section of this chapter is to present common exercise genomics themes that have emerged from the preceding chapters relating to key developments, discoveries, and challenges that are intertwined with our vision for the future position of exercise genomics in personalized medicine and human performance. As is clear from several of this book's chapters, many of the key developments and discoveries in exercise genomics have evolved from the HERITAGE study [58]. One of the underlying assumptions of HERITAGE is that it would be easier to identify and dissect the genetic component of the health and fitness-related phenotype responses to a standardized exercise training program than to undertake the same effort with these traits measured in a cross-sectional cohort. The use of a standardized intervention provides a way to identify genes related to response phenotypes, which provides more successful gene identification due to the minimization of extraneous environmental factors and generally higher gene effect sizes. This assumption now appears to be correct because the quality of the exercise program or physical activity exposure is an important consideration in determining the importance of findings from exercise genomics studies [2]. Additional criteria that have evolved to assess the quality of an exercise genomics study include: sample size, quality of phenotype measurements, study design, adjustment for multiple testing, quality of genotyping, and replication [2, 17, 18].

Replication of findings in subsequent exercise genomic studies is a significant challenge. This major challenge in exercise genomics research has led to another key development – a candidate gene is only as good as the criteria by which it was selected. These criteria should include: (1) QTL or genes under the highest linkage peaks from GWAS or designed linkage analysis, and CNV regions or SNP from GWAS; (2) animal models related to the specific characteristics of the phenotype of interest; (3) knowledge of genes involved in the pathophysiology of diseases related to the phenotype under study; (4) knowledge of genes involved in typical physiology; and (5) differences in mRNA levels based on gene expression microarray scans. DiPetrillo et al. [23] have recommended a minimum of three out of five criteria be met before declaring a gene a candidate gene.

The small number of significant QTL identified to date as being involved in the regulation of exercise, physical activity, and health- and fitness-related traits makes it possible that there are only a few genes involved. However, what has become evident is that there are a large number of genes each explaining small portions of the variance in these complex traits, and many "sets of genes" via their interactions (i.e., epistasis) are also influencing them. In total, genetic variation accounts for a significant portion of variance in many exercise performance and health- and fitness-related phenotypes with environmental and behavioral factors explaining the rest of the variance. For these many reasons, the genetic component of exercise performance and health- and fitness-related traits in most cases remain largely unknown.

Due to the realization that genetic variants account for only a small portion of the total variance in a trait as well as the rapid advancements in technology, GWAS have become the standard approach in genetic association analysis. Reason for the increasing popularity of the GWAS design is the ability to detect smaller gene effects by narrowing down the genomic target region more precisely, maximizing the amount of variation captured by a SNP with a fixed set of markers, and reducing genotyping costs. However, as with other types of genetic association analysis, GWAS have limitations that include: the small contributions made by common genes and the larger contributions that may be made by rare alleles that presently are not included in the sequencing panel, lack of large sample sizes needed to perform GWAS, the stringent level of statistical power required to establish statistical significance, and the lack of a priori hypotheses. A growing literature is indicating that at least a fraction (and perhaps more) of the genetic contribution in complex common disease traits is determined by rare alleles [4]. Despite the progress made by GWAS, a surprising finding is how little GWAS contribute to the identification of genetic factors that account for some traits, providing support for the rare allele hypothesis or the importance of epigenetic factors in trait variability.

Matching gene expression data (mRNA) with SNP data will lead to the development of an arsenal of new genes for further study, as evidenced in Bouchard's preface to this book and his discussion of the intriguing work of Timmons et al. [14]. The importance of regulatory RNAs in exercise-related adaptations has also emerged recently. Thus, future investigations of the genetic control of exercise, physical activity, and health- and fitness-related traits will consider candidate genes that not only alter protein structure and function, but also potential regulatory mechanisms arising from noncoding genomic regions. More and more investigations will need to address multiple levels of analysis within a single study, such as genetic association, epigenetics, proteomics, metabolomics, and functional genomics to better identify causal variants and establish "cause and effect." In addition to the scientific challenges of exercise genomics research, nonscientific concerns exist. These concerns include the privacy of genetic information, the marketing of genetic information directly to the consumer, and the misuse of gene therapy [59].

Baldwin and Haddad [60] recently conducted a PubMed search with the word *exercise* and retrieved 82,826 peer reviewed articles published in the past 10 years. Of these articles, over 5% linked to genetics and related areas of investigation such as proteomics, genomics, epigenetics, and signaling pathways. Baldwin and Haddad [60] also surveyed experts in the field of exercise science to solicit their opinion on keys areas of investigation that will drive the field in the future. Exercise genomics, discovering biomarkers for predicting exercise responders and nonresponders, and exercise and disease prevention were key areas of investigation identified by these experts. A frequently stated objective for exploring genetic associations and health- and fitness-related phenotypes is to improve health and quality of life in healthy and diseased individuals through personalized medicine [59]. The hope is that efforts from genomic studies will lead to the use of genetic information to develop novel risk assessment profiles. Such profiles could then be used to improve or create individually tailored treatment plans or Ex R$_x$ and/or modify living environments to favorably impact the health outcomes of interest. The ultimate goal of exercise genomics research is to establish mechanisms for the response of exercise performance, physical activity, and health- and fitness-related traits to exercise and translate findings into personalized medicine approaches to better prevent, treat, and control disease processes and fine-tune training regimens. The expert contributors to this volume all acknowledge there exists a great deal of challenging work ahead to realize this goal [61, 62].

References

1. Bray MS, Hagberg JM, Perusse L, Rankinen T, Roth SM, Wolfarth B, Bouchard C. The human gene map for performance and health-related fitness phenotypes: the 2006–2007 update. Med Sci Sports Exerc. 2009;41(1):35–73.
2. Rankinen T, Roth SM, Bray MS, Loos R, Perusse L, Wolfarth B, et al. Advances in exercise, fitness, and performance genomics. Med Sci Sports Exerc. 2010;42(5):835–46.
3. Hemminki K, Lorenzo Bermejo J, Forsti A. The balance between heritable and environmental aetiology of human disease. Nat Rev Genet. 2006;7(12):958–65.
4. Bodmer W, Bonilla C. Common and rare variants in multifactorial susceptibility to common diseases. Nat Genet. 2008;40(6):695–701.
5. Safdar A, Abadi A, Akhtar M, Hettinga BP, Tarnopolsky MA. miRNA in the regulation of skeletal muscle adaptation to acute endurance exercise in C57Bl/6J male mice. PLoS One. 2009;4(5):e5610.
6. Barrett JC, Hansoul S, Nicolae DL, Cho JH, Duerr RH, Rioux JD, et al. Genome-wide association defines more than 30 distinct susceptibility loci for Crohn's disease. Nat Genet. 2008;40(8):955–62.
7. DE Moor MH, Liu YJ, Boomsma DI, Li J, Hamilton JJ, Hottenga JJ, et al. Genome-wide association study of exercise behavior in Dutch and American adults. Med Sci Sports Exerc. 2009;41:1887–95.
8. Frayling TM. Genome-wide association studies provide new insights into type 2 diabetes aetiology. Nat Rev Genet. 2007;8(9):657–62.
9. Loos RJ, Lindgren CM, Li S, Wheeler E, Zhao JH, Prokopenko I, et al. Common variants near MC4R are associated with fat mass, weight and risk of obesity. Nat Genet. 2008; 40(6):768–75.

10. Pearson TA, Manolio TA. How to interpret a genome-wide association study. JAMA. 2008;299(11):1335–44.
11. Hirschhorn JN, Daly MJ. Genome-wide association studies for common diseases and complex traits. Nat Rev Genet. 2005;6(2):95–108.
12. Hoffman EP, DuBois DC, Hoffman RI, Almon RR. Expression profiling and pharmacogenomics of muscle and muscle disease. Curr Opin Pharmacol. 2003;3(3):309–16.
13. Chen YW, Nader GA, Baar KR, Fedele MJ, Hoffman EP, Esser KA. Response of rat muscle to acute resistance exercise defined by transcriptional and translational profiling. J Physiol. 2002;545(Pt 1):27–41.
14. Timmons JA, Knudsen S, Rankinen T, Koch LG, Sarzynski M, Jensen T, et al. Using molecular classification to predict gains in maximal aerobic capacity following endurance exercise training in humans. J Appl Physiol. 2010;108(6):1487–96.
15. Horne BD, Anderson JL, Carlquist JF, Muhlestein JB, Renlund DG, Bair TL, et al. Generating genetic risk scores from intermediate phenotypes for use in association studies of clinically significant endpoints. Ann Hum Genet. 2005;69(Pt 2):176–86.
16. Hunter DJ, Kraft P. Drinking from the fire hose – statistical issues in genomewide association studies. N Engl J Med. 2007;357(5):436–9.
17. NCI-NHGRI Working Group on Replication in Association Studies, Chanock SJ, Manolio T, Boehnke M, Boerwinkle E, Hunter DJ, et al. Replicating genotype-phenotype associations. Nature. 2007;447(7145):655–60.
18. Little J, Higgins JP, Ioannidis JP, Moher D, Gagnon F, von Elm E, et al. STrengthening the REporting of genetic association studies (STREGA) – an extension of the STROBE statement. Eur J Clin Invest. 2009;39(4):247–66.
19. Thomas DC. Statistical methods in genetic epidemiology. Oxford: Oxford University Press; 2004.
20. Hopkins WG. A new view of statistics. http://www.sportsci.org/resource/stats/index.html. Accessed 20 Jan 2011.
21. Devlin B, Risch N. A comparison of linkage disequilibrium measures for fine-scale mapping. Genomics. 1995;29(2):311–22.
22. Silver LM. Mouse genetics: concepts and applications. New York: Oxford University Press; 1995.
23. DiPetrillo K, Wang X, Stylianou IM, Paigen B. Bioinformatics toolbox for narrowing rodent quantitative trait loci. Trends Genet. 2005;21(12):683–92.
24. Flint J, Valdar W, Shifman S, Mott R. Strategies for mapping and cloning quantitative trait genes in rodents. Nat Rev Genet. 2005;6(4):271–86.
25. Axtell MJ, Snyder JA, Bartel DP. Common functions for diverse small RNAs of land plants. Plant Cell. 2007;19(6):1750–69.
26. Siepel A. Darwinian alchemy: human genes from noncoding DNA. Genome Res. 2009; 19(10):1693–5.
27. Forrest AR, Abdelhamid RF, Carninci P. Annotating non-coding transcription using functional genomics strategies. Brief Funct Genomic Proteomic. 2009;8(6):437–43.
28. Booth FW, Gordon SE, Carlson CJ, Hamilton MT. Waging war on modern chronic diseases: primary prevention through exercise biology. J Appl Physiol. 2000;88(2):774–87.
29. Chenoweth D, Leutzinger J. The economic cost of physical inactivity and excess weight in american adults. J Phys Act Health. 2006;3(2):148–63.
30. Centers for Disease Control and Prevention (U.S.). Chronic diseases and their risk factors: the Nation's leading causes of death. Atlanta: Department of Health and Human Services, Centers for Disease Control and Prevention; 1999.
31. Lyssenko V, Groop L. Genome-wide association study for type 2 diabetes: clinical applications. Curr Opin Lipidol. 2009;20(2):87–91.
32. Maher B. Personal genomes: the case of the missing heritability. Nature. 2008;456(7218): 18–21.
33. Grarup N, Rose CS, Andersson EA, Andersen G, Nielsen AL, Albrechtsen A, et al. Studies of association of variants near the HHEX, CDKN2A/B, and IGF2BP2 genes with type 2 diabetes and impaired insulin release in 10, 705 Danish subjects: validation and extension of genome-wide association studies. Diabetes. 2007;56(12):3105–11.

34. Zeggini E, Weedon MN, Lindgren CM, Frayling TM, Elliott KS, Lango H, et al. Replication of genome-wide association signals in UK samples reveals risk loci for type 2 diabetes. Science. 2007;316(5829):1336–41.
35. Steinthorsdottir V, Thorleifsson G, Reynisdottir I, Benediktsson R, Jonsdottir T, Walters GB, et al. A variant in CDKAL1 influences insulin response and risk of type 2 diabetes. Nat Genet. 2007;39(6):770–5.
36. Sladek R, Rocheleau G, Rung J, Dina C, Shen L, Serre D, et al. A genome-wide association study identifies novel risk loci for type 2 diabetes. Nature. 2007;445(7130):881–5.
37. Diabetes Genetics Initiative of Broad Institute of Harvard and MIT, Lund University, and Novartis Institutes of BioMedical Research, Saxena R, Voight BF, Lyssenko V, Burtt NP, de Bakker PI, et al. Genome-wide association analysis identifies loci for type 2 diabetes and triglyceride levels. Science. 2007;316(5829):1331–6.
38. Scott LJ, Mohlke KL, Bonnycastle LL, Willer CJ, Li Y, Duren WL, et al. A genome-wide association study of type 2 diabetes in Finns detects multiple susceptibility variants. Science. 2007;316(5829):1341–5.
39. Wareham NJ, Jakes RW, Rennie KL, Mitchell J, Hennings S, Day NE. Validity and repeatability of the EPIC-norfolk physical activity questionnaire. Int J Epidemiol. 2002;31(1):168–74.
40. Friedenreich CM, Courneya KS, Neilson HK, Matthews CE, Willis G, Irwin M, et al. Reliability and validity of the past year total physical activity questionnaire. Am J Epidemiol. 2006;163(10):959–70.
41. Rankinen T, Zuberi A, Chagnon YC, Weisnagel SJ, Argyropoulos G, Walts B, et al. The human obesity gene map: the 2005 update. Obesity (Silver Spring). 2006;14(4):529–644.
42. Bouchard C. The biological predisposition to obesity: beyond the thrifty genotype scenario. Int J Obes (Lond). 2007;31(9):1337–9.
43. Bray MS. Implications of gene-behavior interactions: prevention and intervention for obesity. Obesity (Silver Spring). 2008;16 Suppl 3:S72–8.
44. Feitosa MF, Rice T, North KE, Kraja A, Rankinen T, Leon AS, et al. Pleiotropic QTL on chromosome 19q13 for triglycerides and adiposity: the HERITAGE family study. Atherosclerosis. 2006;185(2):426–32.
45. Feitosa MF, Borecki IB, Rankinen T, Rice T, Despres JP, Chagnon YC, et al. Evidence of QTLs on chromosomes 1q42 and 8q24 for LDL-cholesterol and apoB levels in the HERITAGE family study. J Lipid Res. 2005;46(2):281–6.
46. Rankinen T, An P, Rice T, Sun G, Chagnon YC, Gagnon J, et al. Genomic scan for exercise blood pressure in the health, risk factors, exercise training and genetics (HERITAGE) family study. Hypertension. 2001;38(1):30–7.
47. Rice T, Rankinen T, Chagnon YC, Province MA, Perusse L, Leon AS, et al. Genomewide linkage scan of resting blood pressure: HERITAGE family study. health, risk factors, exercise training, and genetics. Hypertension. 2002;39(6):1037–43.
48. Hubal MJ, Gordish-Dressman H, Thompson PD, Price TB, Hoffman EP, Angelopoulos TJ, et al. Variability in muscle size and strength gain after unilateral resistance training. Med Sci Sports Exerc. 2005;37(6):964–72.
49. Thomis MA, Beunen GP, Van Leemputte M, Maes HH, Blimkie CJ, Claessens AL, et al. Inheritance of static and dynamic arm strength and some of its determinants. Acta Physiol Scand. 1998;163(1):59–71.
50. Thomis MA, Beunen GP, Maes HH, Blimkie CJ, Van Leemputte M, Claessens AL, et al. Strength training: importance of genetic factors. Med Sci Sports Exerc. 1998;30(5):724–31.
51. Perusse L, Lortie G, Leblanc C, Tremblay A, Theriault G, Bouchard C. Genetic and environmental sources of variation in physical fitness. Ann Hum Biol. 1987;14(5):425–34.
52. Tucker T, Marra M, Friedman JM. Massively parallel sequencing: the next big thing in genetic medicine. Am J Hum Genet. 2009;85(2):142–54.
53. Schadt EE. Molecular networks as sensors and drivers of common human diseases. Nature. 2009;461(7261):218–23.
54. Bouchard C, An P, Rice T, Skinner JS, Wilmore JH, Gagnon J, et al. Familial aggregation of VO2 max response to exercise training: results from the HERITAGE family study. J Appl Physiol. 1999;87(3):1003–8.

55. Klissouras V. Heritability of adaptive variation. J Appl Physiol. 1971;31(3):338–44.
56. Yu N, Chen FC, Ota S, Jorde LB, Pamilo P, Patthy L, et al. Larger genetic differences within Africans than between Africans and Eurasians. Genetics. 2002;161(1):269–74.
57. International HapMap Consortium. A haplotype map of the human genome. Nature. 2005;437(7063):1299–320.
58. Bouchard C, Leon AS, Rao DC, Skinner JS, Wilmore JH, Gagnon J. The HERITAGE family study. Aims, design, and measurement protocol. Med Sci Sports Exerc. 1995;27(5):721–9.
59. Kostek MA, Hubal MJ, Pescatello LS. The role of genetics in developing muscle strength. Am J Lifestyle Med. in press.
60. Baldwin KM, Haddad F. Research in the exercise sciences: where we are and where do we go from here – part II. Exerc Sport Sci Rev. 2010;38(2):42–50.
61. Pescatello LS. The promises and challenges of the use of genomics in the prescription of exercise for hypertension. Cur Hypertens Rev. 2010;1(6):32–4.
62. Roth SM. Perspective on the future use of genomics in exercise prescription. J Appl Physiol. 2008;104(4):1243–5.

Appendix: Web-Based Resources

Commonly accessed web-based resources that include useful information about genes, genetic variation, and other genomics applications are listed below. Many such resources are available and only the most widely used are shown here. Readers with interests in more specific databases are encouraged to review the regularly published "database issue" of *Nucleic Acids Research*, most recently described by Cochrane and Galperin [1].

Additionally, two websites cited in Chap. 2 are listed at the bottom of the Appendix. These sites provide links to numerous statistical resources relevant to both exercise- and genetics-related research methods.

Commonly Used Genomic Databases and Related Resources

Database of genomic variants: A catalog of structural variation in the human genome (e.g., copy number variants or CNVs). The content of the database is only representing structural variation identified in healthy control samples. Additional information can be found in Zhang et al. [2]: http://projects.tcag.ca/variation/.

Ensembl: The Ensembl database contains genome sequence information for a variety of species and includes comparative genomics, variation, and gene regulatory information. Ensembl is maintained by the European Bioinformatics Institute and the Wellcome Trust Sanger Institute. Additional information can be found in Flicek et al. [3]: http://www.ensembl.org.

FastSNP database: The FastSNP database allows users to select functional polymorphisms for genomic association studies. Additional information can be found in Yuan et al. [4]: http://fastsnp.ibms.sinica.edu.tw.

GeneCards: The GeneCards database integrates genomic information for genes from a variety of sources. It is maintained by the Crown Human Genome Center at the Weizmann Institute of Science in Israel. Additional information can be found in Safran et al. [5]: http://www.genecards.org.

L.S. Pescatello and S.M. Roth (eds.), *Exercise Genomics*,
Molecular and Translational Medicine, DOI 10.1007/978-1-60761-355-8,
© Springer Science+Business Media, LLC 2011

Genome-wide association studies (GWAS): A catalog of all published GWAS with at least 100,000 SNPs studied in the initial phase. Additional information can be found in Hindorff et al. [6]: http://www.genome.gov/GWAStudies/.

HapMap: The International Haplotype Map (HapMap) Consortium releases accurate and complete SNP genotypes generated in 269 individuals from four geographically diverse populations: The Yoruba in Ibadan, Nigeria; Japanese in Tokyo, Japan; Han Chinese in Beijing, China; and the CEPH (U.S. Utah residents with ancestry from northern and western Europe). Genotypes on all of these SNPs (1.5–4.05 milj per reference group) can be downloaded for analyses. Additional information can be found in Frazer et al. [7]: http://hapmap.ncbi.nlm.nih.gov/.

Human genome epidemiology (HuGE) network and database: The National Office of Public Health Genomics established the Human Genome Epidemiology Network (HuGENet) to help translate genetic research findings into opportunities for preventive medicine and public health by advancing the synthesis, interpretation, and dissemination of population-based data on human genetic variation in health and disease. They have established an integrated, searchable knowledge base of genetic associations and *HuGE*. Additional information can be found in Lin et al. [8]: http://www.cdc.gov/genomics/hugenet/default.htm, http://hugenavigator.net/.

National Center for Biotechnology Information (NCBI). NCBI has a variety of biomedical and genomic information resources, including the PubMed and Entrez Gene and Entrez SNP databases (links listed separately below). The Entrez Gene database contains gene-specific information across a variety of species along with multiple content areas linked to a variety of sub-databases within the NCBI program. The Entrez SNP database provides access to gene polymorphisms searching by both genes and reference SNP (rs number) labels. Additional information can be found in Maglott et al. [9] and Sayers et al. [10]: http://www.ncbi.gov, http://www.ncbi.nlm.nih.gov/sites/entrez?db=pubmed, http://www.ncbi.nlm.nih.gov/sites/entrez?db=gene, http://www.ncbi.nlm.nih.gov/sites/entrez?db=snp.

Online Mendelian Inheritance in Man (OMIM®): The OMIM database is a comprehensive, authoritative, and timely compendium of human genes and genetic phenotypes. The full-text, referenced overviews in OMIM contain information on all known mendelian disorders and over 12,000 genes. OMIM focuses on the relationship between phenotype and genotype. It is updated daily, and the entries contain copious links to other genetics resources. NCBI and the Johns Hopkins University maintain the database. Additional information about the history and use of the OMIM database can be found at the OMIM website: http://www.ncbi.nlm.nih.gov/omim.

PupaSuite: PupaSuite is an interactive web-based SNP analysis tool that allows for the selection of relevant SNPs within a gene, based on different characteristics of the SNP itself, such as validation status, type, frequency/population data, and putative functional properties. Additional information can be found in Conde et al. [11]: http://pupasuite.bioinfo.cipf.es/.

UCSC Genome Browser: The UCSC Genome Browser contains the reference sequence and working draft assemblies for a large collection of genomes. The site is maintained by the Genome Bioinformatics Group, a cross-departmental team within the Center for Biomolecular Science and Engineering at the University of California Santa Cruz. Additional information can be found in Rhead et al. [12]: http://genome.ucsc.edu.

Vertebrate genome annotation (*VEGA*) *database*: The VEGA database is a central repository for high quality manual annotation of vertebrate finished genome sequence. Additional information can be found in Loveland [13]: http://vega.sanger.ac.uk/index.html.

Additional Statistics Resources

A new view of statistics: Assembled and maintained by Will G. Hopkins, this site details all of the methods discussed in Chap. 2, with examples taken from exercise and sports science: http://www.sportsci.org/resource/stats/.

Listings of freely available software for the analysis of GWAS: http://www.genes.org.uk/software/LD-software.shtml, http://pngu.mgh.harvard.edu/~purcell/plink/.

Listing of freely available software for calculating linkage disequilibrium measurements: http://www.genes.org.uk/software/LD-software.shtml.

Online encyclopedia for genetic epidemiology studies: This website aims to collate information and links about and for genetic research studies relevant to population genetics and health. It is designed to help professionals working in genetic epidemiology or associated fields: http://www.dorak.info/epi/genetepi.html.

References

1. Cochrane GR, Galperin MY. The 2010 nucleic acids research database issue and online database collection: a community of data resources. Nucleic Acids Res. 2010;38(database issue):D1–4.
2. Zhang J, Feuk L, Duggan GE, Khaja R, Scherer SW. Development of bioinformatics resources for display and analysis of copy number and other structural variants in the human genome. Cytogenet Genome Res. 2006;115(3–4):205–14.
3. Flicek P, Aken BL, Ballester B, Beal K, Bragin E, Brent S, et al. Ensembl's 10th year. Nucleic Acids Res. 2010;38(database issue):D557–62.
4. Yuan HY, Chiou JJ, Tseng WH, Liu CH, Liu CK, Lin YJ, et al. FASTSNP: An always up-to-date and extendable service for SNP function analysis and prioritization. Nucleic Acids Res. 2006;34(Web server issue):W635–41.
5. Safran M, Solomon I, Shmueli O, Lapidot M, Shen-Orr S, Adato A, et al. GeneCards 2002: towards a complete, object-oriented, human gene compendium. Bioinformatics. 2002;18(11):1542–3.
6. Hindorff LA, Sethupathy P, Junkins HA, Ramos EM, Mehta JP, Collins FS, Manolio TA. Potential etiologic and functional implications of genome-wide association loci for human diseases and traits. Proc Natl Acad Sci U S A. 2009;106(23):9362–7.

7. International HapMap Consortium, Frazer KA, Ballinger DG, Cox DR, Hinds DA, Stuve LL, et al. A second generation human haplotype map of over 3.1 million SNPs. Nature. 2007;449(7164):851–61.

8. Lin BK, Clyne M, Walsh M, Gomez O, Yu W, Gwinn M, Khoury MJ. Tracking the epidemiology of human genes in the literature: the HuGE published literature database. Am J Epidemiol. 2006;164(1):1–4.

9. Maglott D, Ostell J, Pruitt KD, Tatusova T. Entrez gene: gene-centered information at NCBI. Nucleic Acids Res. 2007;35(database issue):D26–31.

10. Sayers EW, Barrett T, Benson DA, Bolton E, Bryant SH, Canese K, et al. Database resources of the national center for biotechnology information. Nucleic Acids Res. 2010;38(database issue):D5–16.

11. Conde L, Vaquerizas JM, Dopazo H, Arbiza L, Reumers J, Rousseau F, et al. PupaSuite: Finding functional single nucleotide polymorphisms for large-scale genotyping purposes. Nucleic Acids Res. 2006;34(Web server issue):W621–5.

12. Rhead B, Karolchik D, Kuhn RM, Hinrichs AS, Zweig AS, Fujita PA, et al. The UCSC genome browser database: update 2010. Nucleic Acids Res. 2010;38(database issue):D613–9.

13. Loveland J. VEGA, the genome browser with a difference. Brief Bioinform. 2005;6(2): 189–93.

Index

9 781617 797309